Divine Perspectives

Exploring the Contrasts and Convergence of Polytheism and Monotheism

M L Ruscsak

Trient Press
3375 S Rainbow Blvd
#81710, SMB 13135
Las Vegas,NV 89180

Ordering Information:
Quantity sales. Special discounts are available on quantity purchases by corporations, associations, and others. For details, contact the publisher at the address above.
Orders by U.S. trade bookstores and wholesalers. Please contact Trient Press: Tel: (775) 996-3844; or visit www.trientpress.com.

Printed in the United States of America

Publisher's Cataloging-in-Publication data
Ruscsak, M.L.
A title of a book : Divine Perspectives: Exploring the Contrasts and Convergence of Polytheism and Monotheism

ISBN
Hard Cover   979-8-88990-020-7

Paper Back   979-8-88990-022-1

Ebook   979-8-88990-021-4

Divine Perspectives

Divine Perspectives

Part 8: Conclusion and Future Directions

Divine Perspectives

PART 1:
INTRODUCTION

In the realm of spiritual and religious beliefs, few topics are as intriguing and captivating as the dynamic interplay between polytheism and monotheism. This comprehensive academic work serves as a guiding light for students embarking on a journey of intellectual exploration. Aimed at individuals pursuing a bachelor's degree, this book delves into the intricacies of polytheistic and monotheistic traditions, drawing examples and insights from a diverse array of fields, including Witchcraft, Divination, Herbalism, Shamanism, and Ecospirituality.

With a formal and academic tone paired with sophisticated vocabulary and grammar, we embark on an illuminating voyage to understand the complexities of these belief systems. Drawing inspiration from the profound works of esteemed authors such as Scott Cunningham and Silver RavenWolf, this book takes pride in its thorough and in-depth analysis of the subject matter, leaving no stone unturned.

Each chapter is meticulously crafted to engage students in critical thinking and discussion, providing a rich tapestry of knowledge that extends beyond the boundaries of traditional academia. Students will find themselves immersed in the exploration of complex scientific concepts, presented in a clear and accessible manner. We strive to unlock the secrets of these ancient traditions and present them in a manner that inspires curiosity, respect, and intellectual growth.

Throughout this scholarly endeavor, we weave a captivating narrative that encompasses the diversity of belief systems found within polytheism and monotheism. By incorporating examples, problems, and exercises into each chapter, we encourage students to actively engage with the material, fostering a deeper understanding of the subject matter and honing their critical thinking skills.

This book also champions an objective and balanced approach, embracing dissenting opinions and counterarguments. By presenting diverse perspectives, we challenge students to broaden their horizons and develop a well-rounded understanding of the complexities inherent in these belief systems.

As students progress through the chapters, they will witness the power of rituals and practices, explore the theological and philosophical underpinnings, and uncover the social and cultural nuances that shape polytheism and monotheism. The book goes beyond theoretical discussions, illustrating the practical application of these belief systems in various fields of study, illuminating the profound impact they have on individuals and societies.

In conclusion, "Divine Perspectives: Exploring the Contrasts and Convergence of Polytheism and Monotheism" is a seminal work designed to guide students towards a deeper understanding of these ancient traditions. Drawing from a diverse array of disciplines and belief systems, this book invites readers to embark on a transformative journey, expanding their knowledge, embracing critical thinking, and fostering a profound appreciation for the rich tapestry of human spirituality.

CHAPTER 1: AN OVERVIEW OF POLYTHEISM AND MONOTHEISM

Welcome, fellow seekers of wisdom, to a remarkable exploration of the vast and captivating realms of polytheism and monotheism. Here, we embark on a fascinating journey that traverses ancient civilizations, examines the philosophies of great minds, and uncovers the mystical traditions of witchcraft, divination, herbalism, shamanism, and ecospirituality. Together, we shall unravel the tapestry of beliefs and practices that have shaped human spirituality, social structures, and cultural identities throughout history. So, let us embark on this captivating adventure and deepen our understanding of these profound and diverse paths of faith.

Throughout the ages, humanity has manifested a multitude of beliefs in divine beings. Polytheism, the veneration of multiple gods and goddesses, has adorned the landscapes of countless civilizations. Ancient cultures such as Mesopotamia, Egypt, Greece, and Rome flourished under the embrace of polytheistic traditions. Their pantheons of deities offered a tapestry of diverse personalities and influences, guiding the various aspects of human existence. By exploring the religious practices, rituals, and mythologies of these ancient societies, we gain valuable insights into the rich tapestry of polytheistic traditions.

In contrast, monotheism emerged as a profound and transformative paradigm in human spirituality. Monotheistic religions, such as Judaism, Christianity, and Islam, have shaped the moral, ethical, and spiritual landscapes of numerous societies. These belief systems revolve around the worship of a singular deity, whose attributes and teachings guide the lives of their followers. From the Abrahamic faiths to the philosophical conceptions of a singular divine force, monotheism encompasses a rich tapestry of thought and practice.

Polytheism and monotheism offer unique theological and philosophical frameworks through which we perceive and interact with the divine. In polytheism, the diverse pantheon allows for a personalized and intimate connection with specific deities. Worshipers can find solace, guidance, and inspiration from gods and goddesses who embody qualities that resonate deeply within them. This multiplicity of divine beings fosters a sense of diversity, providing space for cultural differences and local practices to thrive.

In the realm of monotheism, the focus narrows to the worship of a singular deity. This concentrated devotion encourages a deep sense of unity and singular purpose among followers. The belief in a singular divine authority offers a cohesive moral code and serves as a unifying force within monotheistic societies. Through the teachings and revelations of this singular deity, followers seek guidance, salvation, and spiritual fulfillment.

As we navigate through this exploration, it is important to acknowledge the complexities and nuances within and between these paradigms. Both polytheism and monotheism have encountered controversies, debates, and criticisms throughout history. Scholars and thinkers have grappled with questions regarding the nature of divinity, the existence of multiple gods, or the possibility of a singular all-encompassing divine force. By engaging with these discussions, we broaden our perspectives and develop a deeper understanding of the subject matter.

In the chapters to come, we will delve deeper into the origins, theological aspects, philosophical considerations, religious practices, social implications, and contemporary debates surrounding polytheism and monotheism. We will examine the similarities, differences, advantages, and disadvantages of these belief systems, shedding light on their impact on human culture, society, and spirituality. Through examples, problems, and exercises, we will foster critical thinking and discussion, inviting you, dear readers, to actively engage with the material and deepen your own understanding.

So, let us embark on this captivating journey through the multifaceted worlds of polytheism and monotheism, as we uncover the profound truths, unravel the mysteries, and expand our horizons of knowledge and spiritual insight. Together, we shall navigate the diverse landscapes of faith, weaving together threads of history, theology, philosophy, and practice, to illuminate the intricate tapestry of human belief.

Definition of Polytheism

Polytheism, derived from the Greek words "poly" meaning "many" and "theos" meaning "god," is a religious belief system that recognizes and reveres the existence of multiple deities or gods. In contrast to monotheism, which posits the existence of a single supreme deity, polytheistic traditions celebrate and interact with a diverse pantheon of gods and goddesses. This chapter delves into the intricate tapestry of polytheism, exploring its various manifestations across different cultures and its significance within spiritual practices such as Witchcraft, Divination, Herbalism, Shamanism, and Ecospirituality.

Historical Origins and Cultural Diversity

Polytheism has ancient roots, with evidence of its practice dating back to prehistoric times. The belief in multiple gods emerged independently in various regions of the world, each imbued with its unique cultural nuances and mythological narratives. For instance, the Egyptian pantheon included gods like Osiris, Isis, and Ra, while the ancient Greeks worshiped deities such as Zeus, Athena, and Aphrodite. Similarly, the Norse traditions revered Odin, Thor, and Freya. These diverse cultural expressions of polytheism highlight the human quest to comprehend and interact with the sacred through a multitude of divine beings.

Philosophical Perspectives on Polytheism

Polytheism not only encompasses religious practices but also holds philosophical significance. One notable philosophical perspective is the concept of archetypes, introduced by Swiss psychologist Carl Jung. Archetypes are universal symbols and patterns that reside in the collective unconscious of humanity, and many of these archetypes find their embodiment in polytheistic pantheons. For instance, the Greek god Apollo represents the archetype of light, reason, and artistic inspiration, while the goddess Artemis embodies the archetype of the huntress and protector of nature. Through the study of these archetypal figures, individuals can gain insight into their own psyche and the broader human experience.

Rituals and Worship in Polytheism

Polytheistic religions encompass a wide range of rituals and worship practices that vary based on cultural traditions and personal preferences. Rituals may involve offerings, prayers, invocations, and other acts of devotion. For example, in Witchcraft, practitioners may create altars dedicated to specific gods or goddesses, incorporating symbolic representations of their chosen deities and performing rituals to honor and seek guidance from them. Similarly, in Shamanism, practitioners engage in spirit journeys to commune with various spirits and deities, seeking their assistance for healing, divination, or spiritual guidance.

Theological Interpretations of Polytheism

Scholars and practitioners have developed diverse theological interpretations of polytheism throughout history. Some perceive the gods and goddesses as distinct entities with independent agency, while others view them as facets of a greater cosmic consciousness or as archetypal forces within the human psyche. Additionally, polytheistic belief systems often acknowledge the interconnectedness of the natural world and the divine, recognizing that gods and goddesses can embody natural phenomena such as rivers, mountains, or celestial bodies. These interpretations provide a rich tapestry of perspectives through which individuals can engage with the divine and explore the complexities of existence.

Critiques and Misunderstandings of Polytheism

Polytheism, like any religious or spiritual belief system, has faced criticism and misunderstanding throughout history. Some critics argue that polytheism is inherently primitive or irrational due to its plurality of gods. Others assert that the worship of multiple deities dilutes the devotion and focus that a monotheistic framework offers. However, it is essential to approach these criticisms with an open mind, acknowledging that diverse religious and spiritual practices offer unique insights into the human experience and provide valuable perspectives on the nature of existence.

Explaining the concept of multiple deities in polytheistic belief systems

In the realm of polytheistic belief systems, the existence and worship of multiple deities form the bedrock of spiritual practice. Unlike monotheistic traditions, which focus on a single supreme deity, polytheism embraces a diverse pantheon of gods and goddesses, each with their unique attributes, roles, and mythology. This chapter delves into the concept of multiple deities within polytheistic belief systems, examining their significance, functions, and interrelationships.

The Nature of Deities in Polytheism

Deities within polytheistic belief systems are often regarded as powerful and immortal beings who possess specific domains of influence and control. These domains can range from natural elements such as the sun, moon, or sea, to abstract concepts like love, war, or wisdom. For instance, in ancient Greek mythology, Apollo was associated with music, healing, and prophecy, while Aphrodite governed love and beauty. These deities serve as archetypal representations of various aspects of existence, providing avenues for human connection and understanding of the sacred.

Interactions among Deities

Within polytheistic belief systems, deities often interact with one another through complex webs of relationships, alliances, and conflicts. These interactions give rise to intricate mythologies and narratives that shed light on the dynamics within the divine realm. For example, in Norse mythology, the god Thor frequently engages in battles with the giants, while Loki, the trickster god, is known for his mischief and involvement in various conflicts. These stories not only entertain but also provide insights into the multifaceted nature of divine beings and their interactions with the mortal realm.

Functions and Specializations of Deities

In many polytheistic belief systems, deities possess specialized roles and functions. They may preside over specific areas of life, offering guidance, protection, and blessings to their devotees. For example, in the practice of Witchcraft, a practitioner may invoke the goddess Brigid for matters related to creativity and inspiration, while seeking the guidance of the god Cernunnos for matters concerning the natural world and the cycle of life and death. These deities act as intermediaries between the human and divine realms, serving as sources of spiritual wisdom and support.

Variations in Deity Hierarchies

Polytheistic belief systems often display variations in the hierarchy and power dynamics among deities. While some traditions may have a clearly defined pantheon with a supreme deity at the helm, others may have more fluid and egalitarian relationships among their deities. For instance, in Wiccan traditions, the concept of a Triple Goddess, representing the Maiden, Mother, and Crone, is often emphasized alongside the Horned God. This balanced representation showcases the equality and interdependence of the divine masculine and feminine energies.

Polytheism and Syncretism

Polytheistic belief systems also frequently exhibit syncretic tendencies, incorporating elements and deities from different cultures and traditions. As civilizations interact and exchange ideas, deities may assimilate attributes, names, or functions from one another. This syncretism can be seen in the blending of Roman and Greek gods, as well as the amalgamation of indigenous deities with Christian saints in some folk practices. These syncretic expressions illustrate the adaptability and inclusiveness of polytheistic belief systems throughout history.

Counterarguments and Perspectives

While polytheistic belief systems provide a rich and diverse framework for spiritual exploration, they are not without criticism. Some argue that the worship of multiple deities can lead to fragmentation of devotion and dilution of spiritual focus. Additionally, critics claim that polytheism may perpetuate a hierarchical structure, where certain deities hold greater influence and power than others. However, proponents of polytheism counter that the multiplicity of deities offers a more nuanced understanding of the divine, encompassing a broader spectrum of human experience and embracing the interconnectedness of the natural and spiritual realms.

Examples of polytheistic religions throughout history and across cultures

Polytheistic religions have flourished across various time periods and cultures, each with its unique pantheon of gods and goddesses. This chapter explores notable examples of polytheistic religions, showcasing their diverse mythologies, rituals, and spiritual practices. By examining these examples, we gain a deeper understanding of the multifaceted nature of polytheism and its significance in different cultural contexts.

Ancient Egyptian Religion

One of the most well-known polytheistic traditions is ancient Egyptian religion. The Egyptians worshipped a vast pantheon of deities, such as Osiris, Isis, Horus, and Ra. Their belief system was deeply intertwined with their understanding of the natural world and the afterlife. Rituals, including temple ceremonies, offerings, and festivals, played a central role in their worship. For instance, the annual flooding of the Nile River was celebrated as a manifestation of the god Hapi's abundance, ensuring the fertility of the land. The Egyptian Book of the Dead provided guidance for navigating the afterlife, showcasing the complexity of their religious cosmology.

Ancient Greek and Roman Polytheism

The ancient Greeks and Romans developed elaborate polytheistic belief systems that influenced later Western civilizations. The Greek pantheon featured deities like Zeus, Athena, Aphrodite, and Hermes, while the Roman pantheon incorporated similar gods under different names, such as Jupiter, Minerva, Venus, and Mercury. Greek and Roman religions emphasized the interplay between gods and mortals through mythological narratives, which depicted the gods' interactions with humans. Rituals, sacrifices, and oracles were integral to these belief systems, offering opportunities for divine communication and guidance.

Norse Mythology and Germanic Polytheism

Norse mythology, originating from the Germanic peoples, presents a distinctive polytheistic tradition. The Norse pantheon included gods such as Odin, Thor, Freya, and Loki. Norse mythology depicted a rich tapestry of epic tales, exploring themes of heroism, fate, and the cycles of creation and destruction. Rituals in Germanic polytheism often centered around communal celebrations, known as blóts, where offerings were made to the gods in exchange for their blessings and protection. The runic alphabet, associated with divination and magical practices, was also an integral part of this tradition.

Hinduism

Hinduism, a major world religion, embraces a diverse range of polytheistic practices. Its pantheon comprises numerous gods and goddesses, each representing different aspects of the divine. Some prominent deities include Brahma, Vishnu, Shiva, Lakshmi, and Durga. Hinduism's rich mythology, found in ancient texts like the Vedas and the Mahabharata, delves into cosmological narratives, philosophical concepts, and moral teachings. Rituals and festivals play a vital role in Hindu worship, with devotees engaging in puja (ritual offerings), meditation, and pilgrimage to sacred sites.

Shinto

Shinto, an indigenous religion of Japan, is deeply rooted in polytheism. Kami, often translated as "gods" or "spirits," are revered in Shinto. These deities can encompass various natural phenomena, spirits of ancestors, or revered historical figures. Shinto rituals and practices are closely tied to nature, with shrines serving as sacred spaces for worship and purification. Festivals, known as matsuri, are essential components of Shinto religious life, allowing communities to come together to celebrate and honor their deities.

Contemporary Paganism and Neopaganism

Contemporary Paganism and Neopaganism encompass a wide array of modern polytheistic traditions. These movements draw inspiration from historical polytheistic religions while incorporating contemporary beliefs and practices. Examples include Wicca, Druidry, Heathenry, and Hellenismos. In these traditions, individuals may choose to connect with specific pantheons or deities based on personal affinity or cultural heritage. Rituals, spells, divination, and ecological awareness often play prominent roles in these practices, reflecting a modern interpretation of ancient polytheistic spirituality.

Exercises and Questions

Compare and contrast the rituals and practices of two polytheistic traditions mentioned in this chapter. What similarities and differences do you observe? How do these practices contribute to the spiritual experiences of their practitioners?

Investigate the revival and reconstruction of ancient polytheistic traditions in contemporary Paganism and Neopaganism. Choose one specific tradition and explore how it incorporates elements from its historical counterpart. Discuss the motivations behind this revival and its significance for modern practitioners.

Reflect on the diversity of polytheistic belief systems discussed in this chapter. How do these examples challenge the notion of a singular "correct" religious path? Discuss the benefits and potential challenges of embracing pluralistic perspectives on divinity and spirituality.

Engage in a group discussion on the role of mythology in polytheistic religions. How do mythological narratives shape the understanding of deities and their interactions within these belief systems? Can mythology hold relevance and meaning for individuals who do not adhere to polytheistic religions?

Definition of Monotheism

Monotheism, the belief in a single supreme deity, stands in contrast to polytheism and forms the foundation of several major religious traditions. In this chapter, we explore the concept of monotheism, examining its historical development, theological implications, and diverse manifestations across different cultures and religions. By delving into the definition of monotheism, we gain insights into its significance and impact on religious thought and practice.

Monotheistic Beliefs and Principles

At the core of monotheism lies the affirmation of a single supreme being or divine reality. This belief is accompanied by various principles that shape monotheistic religious thought. These principles may include the notions of divine transcendence, omnipotence, omniscience, and moral authority. For example, in the Abrahamic traditions of Judaism, Christianity, and Islam, monotheism is characterized by the worship of a singular, all-powerful God who is considered the creator of the universe and the source of moral guidance.

Historical Development of Monotheism

The historical development of monotheism can be traced back to ancient Mesopotamia and Egypt, where early forms of monotheistic ideas emerged alongside polytheistic belief systems. However, it was in the ancient Hebrew culture that monotheism gained significant prominence. The Hebrew Bible (Old Testament) contains accounts of the Israelites' monotheistic faith in Yahweh, their exclusive God. Monotheism continued to evolve and solidify in the religious traditions that emerged from the Hebrew Bible, namely Judaism, Christianity, and Islam.

Monotheism in Judaism

Judaism, the oldest of the Abrahamic religions, is rooted in monotheistic belief. Central to Jewish theology is the affirmation of Yahweh as the one and only God. This belief is encapsulated in the Shema, a foundational prayer in Judaism that declares, "Hear, O Israel, the Lord our God, the Lord is one." The Hebrew Bible provides a framework for understanding Yahweh's attributes, commandments, and covenant with the Jewish people. Jewish worship, rituals, and ethical principles revolve around the worship of a single divine entity.

Monotheism in Christianity

Christianity, originating from Judaism, centers on the belief in one God, while incorporating the teachings of Jesus Christ as the central figure of divine revelation. The doctrine of the Holy Trinity presents a unique aspect of monotheistic belief within Christianity. It asserts that God exists as three distinct persons: God the Father, God the Son (Jesus Christ), and God the Holy Spirit, while remaining one unified entity. This concept of the Trinity enables Christians to reconcile the belief in one God with the belief in the divinity of Jesus Christ.

Monotheism in Islam

Islam, founded in the 7th century CE by the Prophet Muhammad, also espouses a strict monotheistic stance. The central tenet of Islam is the Shahada, the declaration of faith: "There is no god but Allah, and Muhammad is his messenger." Islamic theology emphasizes the absolute oneness and unity of Allah, rejecting the concept of trinity or any association of partners with the divine. The Quran, the holy book of Islam, provides guidance for Muslims to submit to the will of Allah and adhere to his commandments.

Monotheism and Counterarguments

While monotheism has been widely embraced throughout history, it has not been without criticism and philosophical challenges. Some argue that monotheism limits the diversity of religious experiences and perspectives by placing emphasis on a singular divine entity. Additionally, critics question the problem of evil, posing dilemmas such as how to reconcile the existence of a

benevolent, all-powerful God with the presence of suffering in the world. These counterarguments have sparked theological debates and discussions within monotheistic traditions.

Exercises and Discussion Questions

Reflect on the principles of monotheism discussed in this chapter. Select one principle, such as divine omnipotence or moral authority, and explore its significance within a specific monotheistic tradition. How does this principle shape religious beliefs and practices?

What commonalities and differences do you observe? How have these differences influenced the development of each tradition?

How did early monotheistic ideas emerge within these polytheistic contexts? Discuss the factors that contributed to the rise of monotheistic thought in these societies.

How do these critiques impact the understanding and practice of monotheistic religions? Can monotheistic traditions address these challenges while maintaining their core beliefs?

Research a contemporary monotheistic religious movement or interpretation that challenges traditional understandings of monotheism. Present your findings and analyze the ways in which these reinterpretations address the complexities and criticisms associated with monotheistic belief systems.

Understanding the belief in a single supreme deity in monotheistic religions

Monotheistic religions, such as Judaism, Christianity, and Islam, emphasize the belief in a single supreme deity. This chapter explores the concept of a singular divine entity within monotheistic belief systems, delving into its theological significance, implications for religious practices, and the ways in which it shapes the understanding of the divine. By examining the belief in a single supreme deity, we gain insights into the foundational principles and complexities of monotheism.

Monotheism and Divine Unity

At the heart of monotheistic religions lies the concept of divine unity—a belief in the absolute oneness and singularity of the supreme deity. This belief asserts that there is only one God who possesses ultimate power, knowledge, and authority. The understanding of divine unity differs among monotheistic traditions. For example, in Judaism, the belief in God's oneness is encapsulated in the Shema: "Hear, O Israel, the Lord our God, the Lord is one." This affirmation emphasizes the indivisibility and uniqueness of the divine.

The Attributes of the Supreme Deity

Monotheistic religions ascribe various attributes to the supreme deity, providing insights into the nature and character of the divine. These attributes include qualities such as omnipotence, omniscience, benevolence, and transcendence. For instance, in Christianity, God is described as all-powerful (omnipotent), all-knowing (omniscient), and infinitely good. These attributes shape believers' understanding of God's interactions with the world, his role in human affairs, and the basis for moral guidance.

Monotheism and Creation

Monotheistic religions often incorporate beliefs about the creation of the universe by the supreme deity. These beliefs provide insights into the divine creative power and the purpose of existence. In Judaism, the book of Genesis describes God as the creator of the heavens and the earth, forming the foundation of Jewish cosmology. Christianity and Islam also hold that God is the ultimate creator, responsible for bringing all things into being. The belief in divine creation underscores the monotheistic worldview and the recognition of the supreme deity's authority over the natural world.

Monotheism and Moral Guidance

The belief in a single supreme deity within monotheistic religions often leads to the notion of divine moral guidance. The supreme deity is seen as the ultimate source of moral principles, providing believers with ethical frameworks and guiding their actions. For instance, the Ten Commandments in Judaism and Christianity, and the Quranic teachings in Islam, serve as foundational moral codes derived from the divine will. Monotheistic believers perceive their adherence to these moral teachings as an expression of devotion and a path to spiritual growth.

The Challenges of Monotheism

While monotheism has been influential and widely embraced throughout history, it has not been without its challenges. Critics and skeptics have raised philosophical and theological questions, including the problem of evil, the coherence of divine attributes, and the limitations of human understanding in comprehending the nature of a singular supreme deity. These challenges have stimulated theological debates and discussions within monotheistic traditions, prompting believers to reflect on the complexities and nuances of their faith.

Monotheism and Interfaith Dialogue

The belief in a single supreme deity has also shaped interfaith dialogue and engagement among monotheistic traditions. Despite their theological differences, adherents of monotheistic religions often find common ground in their recognition of a shared belief in one God. Interfaith dialogue provides opportunities for mutual understanding, exploration of theological perspectives, and cooperation on shared ethical concerns. It allows for a deeper appreciation of the complexities and diversity within monotheistic beliefs, fostering respect and empathy for those of different faiths.

The belief in a single supreme deity is a central tenet of monotheistic religions, providing a unifying framework for believers across traditions. Understanding the concept of divine unity and the attributes ascribed to the supreme deity deepens our appreciation of the complexities and nuances within monotheistic belief systems. The challenges posed to monotheism also highlight the need for ongoing theological reflection and exploration. Finally, interfaith dialogue offers opportunities for learning, growth, and collaboration, promoting a more peaceful and inclusive society.

Contrasting Polytheism and Monotheism

Polytheism and monotheism represent two distinct approaches to religious belief and practice. In this chapter, we delve into the contrasting characteristics, theological implications, and cultural contexts of polytheism and monotheism. By examining these contrasting perspectives, we gain a deeper understanding of the diverse ways in which humans have approached and understood the divine.

Polytheism: Embracing Multiple Deities

Polytheism, derived from the Greek words "poly" meaning "many" and "theos" meaning "god," encompasses belief systems that recognize and worship multiple deities. In polytheistic religions, gods and goddesses are assigned specific roles, domains, and areas of influence. For example, in ancient Greek mythology, Zeus is the king of the gods, Poseidon rules the seas, and Athena represents wisdom and warfare. Polytheistic belief systems often reflect a pantheon—a collective assembly of deities that govern different aspects of the world and human existence.

Monotheism: Emphasizing a Single Supreme Deity

Monotheism, in contrast, centers on the worship of a single supreme deity. The belief in one God with ultimate power and authority is a defining characteristic of monotheistic religions. Monotheism emphasizes divine unity, affirming the existence of a singular divine entity who governs the universe and interacts with humanity. Examples of monotheistic traditions include Judaism, Christianity, and Islam, where Yahweh, God, and Allah respectively represent the singular supreme deity.

Theological Implications of Polytheism

Polytheism offers a diverse and multifaceted approach to religious belief. The presence of multiple deities allows for a rich tapestry of mythologies, rituals, and symbolic systems. Each deity possesses unique qualities and roles, providing individuals with a range of divine beings to connect with and seek guidance from. Polytheistic belief systems often emphasize the interconnectedness of different aspects of life and nature. For instance, in the practice of Wicca, various deities are associated with the cycles of the moon, the changing seasons, and different aspects of human experience.

Theological Implications of Monotheism

Monotheism, on the other hand, focuses on the worship of a single supreme deity. This belief in a singular divine entity provides a sense of unity, coherence, and universality. Monotheistic traditions often emphasize the attributes and characteristics of the supreme deity, such as omnipotence, omniscience, and benevolence. The belief in one God establishes a framework for moral guidance, ethical principles, and a sense of purpose in life. For example, in Christianity, the belief in a loving and just God forms the foundation for teachings on compassion, forgiveness, and the pursuit of righteousness.

Cultural and Historical Contexts

The contrast between polytheism and monotheism is also shaped by their cultural and historical contexts. Polytheistic beliefs were prevalent in ancient civilizations such as ancient Greece, Rome, Egypt, and Mesopotamia. These cultures often associated deities with specific aspects of their daily lives, natural phenomena, and societal structures. Polytheism reflected the intricate interconnectedness between humans and the divine, as well as the rich mythologies that explained the mysteries of the world.

In contrast, monotheism gained prominence in the context of ancient Hebrew culture, leading to the development of Judaism. The belief in a single supreme deity set the Israelites apart from the polytheistic cultures surrounding them. The monotheistic principles of Judaism later influenced the emergence of Christianity and Islam, which expanded monotheism to wider populations through religious revelation and missionary efforts.

Counterarguments and Dissenting

While polytheism and monotheism represent contrasting belief systems, it is important to acknowledge that these distinctions are not absolute. There exist instances of syncretism, where elements of polytheistic traditions are incorporated into monotheistic religions, and vice versa. Additionally, some belief systems adopt a henotheistic approach, recognizing the existence of multiple deities while worshiping or focusing primarily on a single deity.

Critics of polytheism argue that the belief in multiple deities can lead to confusion, conflicts between divine beings, and a lack of a unified moral framework. On the other hand, critics of monotheism highlight potential challenges related to the problem of evil, the coherence of divine attributes, and the exclusivity of salvation or divine favor.

Explore the similarities and differences between polytheistic traditions such as ancient Greek religion and contemporary Neopaganism. How have these belief systems adapted and evolved over time? What factors have contributed to their continuity or revival?

Investigate the historical transition from polytheism to monotheism in ancient civilizations such as Egypt or Rome. What factors influenced this shift? Analyze the theological, social, and political implications of this transition.

Consider the philosophical, cultural, and ethical implications of these belief systems. How do they shape individual and communal experiences of the divine?

Research and compare the concept of divinity in indigenous polytheistic religions, such as Native American spirituality or African traditional religions. Discuss the interconnectedness of deities with nature, ancestral spirits, and human communities. How does this contrast with the concept of a single supreme deity in monotheistic religions?

How can dialogue contribute to mutual understanding, respect, and cooperation among diverse religious communities?

Comparing belief systems, rituals, and practices of polytheistic and monotheistic religions

Polytheistic and monotheistic religions offer distinct belief systems, rituals, and practices that shape the lives and experiences of their adherents. In this chapter, we explore the similarities and differences between these two religious frameworks, delving into their theological foundations, ritualistic expressions, and ethical principles. By examining these aspects, we gain a deeper understanding of the diverse ways in which humans engage with the divine.

Belief Systems: Diverse Deities vs. Singular Supreme Deity

Polytheistic belief systems recognize and venerate multiple deities, each with their own characteristics, roles, and domains of influence. These gods and goddesses often represent different aspects of the natural world, human experiences, and the divine itself. For example, in the practice of Hellenism, the ancient Greek religion, deities such as Zeus, Aphrodite, and Hermes embody various qualities such as power, love, and communication.

In contrast, monotheistic religions emphasize the worship of a single supreme deity who governs the entire universe. This belief in one God provides a sense of unity, coherence, and universality within these traditions. For instance, in Judaism, the belief in Yahweh as the sole God is central to the covenant between God and the Jewish people.

Rituals and Practices: Diversity and Unity

Polytheistic religions feature a wide array of rituals and practices that vary across different cultures and traditions. These rituals often involve offerings, prayers, invocations, and symbolic actions aimed at establishing and maintaining a connection with specific deities. In Wicca, a contemporary pagan tradition, practitioners may perform rituals to honor specific gods and goddesses, celebrate seasonal cycles, or engage in magical workings.

Monotheistic religions also encompass a rich tapestry of rituals and practices, albeit with a focus on the singular supreme deity. Prayers, worship services, and communal gatherings play significant roles in fostering a relationship with the divine. For example, in Islam, Muslims engage in daily prayers, observe the fasting month of Ramadan, and perform the Hajj pilgrimage to the holy city of Mecca as acts of devotion to Allah.

Exploring the Contrasts and Convergence of Polytheism and Monotheism

Theological Foundations: Interconnectedness and Divine Unity

Polytheistic belief systems often emphasize the interconnectedness between various deities, humans, and the natural world. The gods and goddesses interact with each other and with humans, shaping the fabric of existence. This interconnectedness fosters a sense of harmony and balance within the cosmos. In some indigenous traditions, such as Native American spirituality, deities are viewed as interconnected with the land, animals, and ancestors.

In monotheistic religions, the theological foundation centers on the concept of divine unity. The belief in a single supreme deity provides a unifying framework for the entire cosmos. This unity establishes the source of all creation, governs the laws of nature, and guides human conduct. For instance, in Christianity, the doctrine of the Holy Trinity—a triune God consisting of the Father, Son, and Holy Spirit—presents a complex understanding of divine unity and plurality.

Ethical Principles: Pluralism and Universalism

Polytheistic religions often exhibit a plurality of ethical systems and values, as different deities may represent distinct moral principles. For example, in ancient Roman religion, Jupiter represented justice and moral order, while Venus embodied love and desire. These diverse ethical frameworks within polytheism allow for individual and cultural variations in moral perspectives.

Monotheistic religions, on the other hand, often promote universal ethical principles grounded in the nature and will of the supreme deity. Commandments, moral teachings, and ethical codes provide a

clear and unified set of guidelines for human behavior. In Judaism, the Ten Commandments serve as the foundation of moral conduct, emphasizing principles such as love for God and one's neighbor.

Syncretism and Cultural Adaptations

Throughout history, there have been instances of syncretism, where elements of polytheistic traditions are incorporated into monotheistic religions or vice versa. These syncretic practices illustrate the fluidity and adaptability of religious beliefs and practices. For example, in the development of Vodou, an Afro-Caribbean religion, elements of West African polytheism merged with Catholicism brought by European colonizers.

Exercises and Discussion Questions

Compare the belief systems of a specific polytheistic religion, such as ancient Egyptian religion, with a monotheistic religion, such as Islam. Analyze their theological foundations, views on deities, and concepts of the divine.

Investigate the rituals and practices of a contemporary polytheistic religion, such as modern Druidry, and a monotheistic religion, such as Sikhism. Explore the significance of these rituals, their communal aspects, and their expressions of devotion.

Explore the ethical principles within a polytheistic tradition, such as Asatru, and a monotheistic tradition, such as Buddhism. Discuss how these principles shape the moral lives of their adherents and foster a sense of individual and communal responsibility.

Analyze examples of syncretism between polytheistic and monotheistic religions. Examine the cultural, historical, and religious factors that led to these syncretic practices and discuss their impact on the respective religious communities.

Reflect on the diversity and unity within polytheistic and monotheistic traditions. How do these religious frameworks foster a sense of individual and communal identity? How do they address the human need for meaning, purpose, and connection?

How can mutual respect, understanding, and cooperation be fostered among diverse religious communities?

By comparing the belief systems, rituals, and practices of polytheistic and monotheistic religions, we gain a broader perspective on the diversity of human spiritual expressions. These discussions encourage critical thinking, cultural appreciation, and the recognition of the interconnectedness of religious traditions.

Examining the impact of polytheism and monotheism on society and individual beliefs

Polytheism and monotheism have exerted profound influences on societies throughout history, shaping social structures, cultural practices, and individual beliefs. In this chapter, we delve into the impact of these religious frameworks on both the collective and individual levels. By analyzing their effects, we gain insights into the complex interplay between religion and society, and the ways in which religious beliefs shape human experiences.

Social Structures and Organization

Polytheistic belief systems often played a central role in ancient societies, providing a framework for social structures and hierarchies. In ancient Greece, for example, the religious practices surrounding the Olympian gods influenced political governance and societal roles. Temples were erected, priesthoods established, and festivals celebrated, all contributing to a sense of collective identity and social cohesion.

Monotheistic religions, with their focus on a single supreme deity, have also influenced social structures and organization. The authority and teachings of religious leaders and scriptures often have implications for political systems and social norms. In medieval Europe, the Catholic Church held significant power, shaping the feudal system and influencing laws and governance.

Cultural Practices and Artistic Expressions

Polytheistic religions have nurtured diverse cultural practices and artistic expressions. Rituals, festivals, and ceremonies associated with different deities served as occasions for communal celebration and artistic creation. Ancient Egyptian religious beliefs, for instance, inspired the construction of grand temples and the creation of intricate religious artworks, such as sculptures and murals.

Monotheistic religions have also influenced cultural practices and artistic expressions. Religious texts and teachings often serve as sources of inspiration for literature, music, architecture, and visual arts. The Islamic tradition, for example, has a rich artistic heritage, reflected in calligraphy, geometric patterns, and architectural marvels such as the Alhambra in Spain.

Moral and Ethical Frameworks

Polytheistic belief systems often provided diverse moral and ethical frameworks, as different deities embodied various virtues and principles. These systems allowed for a range of ethical perspectives within a society. In ancient Rome, for instance, individuals could turn to different gods and goddesses for guidance in different aspects of life, such as justice, love, or wisdom.

Monotheistic religions, on the other hand, tend to provide unified moral and ethical frameworks based on the teachings and commandments of the single supreme deity. These frameworks offer a sense of moral clarity and universal values. The Ten

Commandments in Judaism and Christianity, for example, provide guidelines for personal conduct and social interactions.

Impact on Worldviews and Beliefs

Polytheism and monotheism shape individual worldviews and beliefs, influencing how people perceive themselves, others, and the world around them. Polytheistic belief systems often embrace a holistic and interconnected worldview, seeing divinity permeating all aspects of existence. This perspective fosters a sense of connection with nature, ancestors, and the spiritual realm. Indigenous cultures often embody this interconnected worldview, recognizing the sacredness of the earth and the interdependence of all living beings.

Monotheistic religions, with their focus on a singular supreme deity, offer a more centralized worldview. They emphasize human beings as distinct creations of God and highlight the divine-human relationship. This worldview often carries notions of individual responsibility, moral accountability, and the idea of a purposeful existence. For example, in Islam, the belief in predestination shapes the understanding of human agency and the concept of divine will.

CHAPTER 2: THE SIGNIFICANCE OF UNDERSTANDING THE DIFFERENCES BETWEEN POLYTHEISM AND MONOTHEISM

Religious belief systems have played a central role in shaping human cultures, values, and identities throughout history. Among the myriad of religious traditions that have emerged across the globe, polytheism and monotheism stand as two distinct frameworks that shape the beliefs, practices, and worldviews of millions of people. In this chapter, we delve into the significance of understanding the differences between polytheism and monotheism and explore the implications these differences hold for individuals, communities, and interfaith dialogue.

Polytheism and monotheism represent divergent approaches to understanding and relating to the divine. Polytheistic belief systems acknowledge the existence of multiple deities, each with their own unique qualities, powers, and realms of influence. These pantheons encompass a rich tapestry of gods and goddesses, each associated with various aspects of human experience and natural phenomena. On the other hand, monotheistic religions emphasize the worship of a single supreme deity who is often perceived as all-powerful, all-knowing, and omnipresent.

Understanding the differences between polytheism and monotheism is not merely an exercise in religious taxonomy, but rather an essential step towards appreciating the diversity of religious expressions found within these frameworks. By recognizing the wide array of beliefs, rituals, and philosophies that exist within polytheistic and monotheistic traditions, we cultivate a deeper understanding of the intricate tapestry of human spirituality. This knowledge fosters cultural sensitivity, promotes interfaith dialogue, and encourages the celebration of religious pluralism.

Beyond the realm of belief, polytheism and monotheism also shape broader worldviews and cosmological perspectives. Polytheistic belief systems often embrace a holistic worldview that recognizes the interconnectedness of all beings and phenomena. The diverse pantheons of gods and goddesses reflect the multifaceted nature of existence and inspire a sense of reverence for the natural world. Monotheistic religions, on the other hand, often emphasize a more centralized worldview, focusing on the relationship between a singular supreme deity and humanity. This worldview often carries notions of moral accountability, purposeful existence, and human agency.

Understanding the differences between these worldviews opens up avenues for exploring the ways in which individuals perceive themselves, their place in the world, and their responsibilities towards others. It provides a framework for reflecting on questions of meaning, ethics, and human purpose, as well as for examining our relationship with the natural world and the broader cosmos.

Moreover, understanding the distinctions between polytheism and monotheism is crucial for engaging in meaningful interfaith dialogue. By recognizing and respecting the differences between these belief systems, we create opportunities for authentic conversations, mutual learning, and collaboration across religious boundaries. Interfaith dialogue allows individuals from diverse religious backgrounds to share their perspectives, challenge assumptions, and cultivate empathy and respect for one another. It fosters a spirit of curiosity, openness, and inclusivity, paving the way for greater understanding and cooperation in an increasingly interconnected world.

In the following chapters, we will delve deeper into the unique characteristics of polytheism and monotheism, exploring their historical, cultural, and philosophical dimensions. Through an in-depth analysis of these belief systems, we will gain a comprehensive understanding of their impact on society, individual beliefs, rituals, and practices. By exploring the similarities and contrasts between polytheism and monotheism, we will enrich our knowledge of religious diversity and nurture a broader appreciation for the multiplicity of human spiritual experiences.

In conclusion, understanding the differences between polytheism and monotheism is not only academically enriching but also holds profound implications for fostering interfaith dialogue, promoting cultural sensitivity, and cultivating a deeper understanding of our shared humanity. By embarking on

this journey of exploration, we embrace the opportunity to broaden our horizons, challenge our assumptions, and embark on a path towards greater intercultural understanding and harmony.

Promoting Religious Tolerance and Respect

In an increasingly interconnected and diverse world, promoting religious tolerance and respect is of paramount importance. Religious beliefs and practices have long been fundamental aspects of human culture, providing individuals and communities with a sense of meaning, purpose, and identity. However, differences in religious beliefs can also be a source of conflict and division if not approached with understanding and respect. In this chapter, we will explore the significance of promoting religious tolerance and respect, examining the benefits it brings to individuals, communities, and society as a whole.

The Importance of Religious Tolerance

Religious tolerance is the acceptance and respect for the beliefs, practices, and values of others, regardless of whether they align with our own. It recognizes that individuals have the freedom to choose their religious beliefs and that diversity in religious expression is a natural and enriching part of human existence. By promoting religious tolerance, we create an environment where individuals feel safe to express their beliefs and engage in dialogue, fostering a sense of inclusivity and harmony.

One of the key benefits of religious tolerance is the promotion of social cohesion and harmony. When individuals from diverse religious backgrounds are able to coexist peacefully and respectfully, it strengthens the fabric of society and promotes a sense of unity. It encourages dialogue and cooperation, allowing individuals to find common ground and work towards shared goals. By fostering an atmosphere of religious tolerance, we build bridges between different communities and foster a spirit of understanding and empathy.

Religious tolerance also plays a crucial role in safeguarding individual rights and freedoms. Freedom of religion is a fundamental human right that is protected by international human rights instruments. It ensures that individuals have the right to practice, change, or abstain from religious beliefs according to their own conscience. By promoting religious tolerance, we uphold these fundamental rights and create an environment where individuals are free to explore and express their spirituality without fear of persecution or discrimination.

Moreover, religious tolerance nurtures intellectual growth and fosters critical thinking. When individuals are exposed to different religious perspectives, it encourages them to question their own beliefs, expand their knowledge, and engage in meaningful dialogue. It promotes a spirit of curiosity and openness, allowing individuals to learn from one another and broaden their understanding of the world. By embracing religious diversity, we create opportunities for personal growth and intellectual enrichment.

The Role of Education in Promoting Religious Tolerance

Education plays a pivotal role in promoting religious tolerance and respect. By incorporating religious studies into educational curricula, we provide students with a comprehensive understanding of different religious traditions, beliefs, and practices.

This exposure allows students to develop a broader perspective, challenge stereotypes, and cultivate respect for diverse religious expressions.

Inclusive and balanced education about religions helps dispel misunderstandings and misconceptions that may fuel prejudice and discrimination. It equips students with the knowledge and tools to engage in respectful and informed conversations about religion, fostering an atmosphere of tolerance and respect within educational institutions and beyond.

Educational institutions can also create spaces for interfaith dialogue and engagement. By facilitating opportunities for students from different religious backgrounds to interact, share experiences, and learn from one another, we create an environment that promotes empathy, understanding, and cooperation. Interfaith dialogue encourages students to explore common values, address differences, and work towards common goals, fostering a sense of unity and fostering lifelong skills in conflict resolution and bridge-building.

Building Bridges of Understanding Through Interfaith Initiatives

Interfaith initiatives are powerful tools for promoting religious tolerance and respect at the community level. These initiatives bring together individuals from different religious backgrounds to engage in meaningful dialogue, cooperation, and collaboration. Through interfaith initiatives, participants have the opportunity to learn from one another, challenge preconceived notions, and build relationships based on mutual respect and understanding.

Interfaith initiatives can take various forms, including interfaith conferences, workshops, and community service projects. These activities provide opportunities for individuals to share their beliefs, experiences, and values, fostering an environment of dialogue and learning. They also create platforms for addressing common social issues and working towards solutions that transcend religious boundaries.

By actively participating in interfaith initiatives, individuals and communities can break down barriers, dispel stereotypes, and build bridges of understanding. These initiatives cultivate empathy, promote peaceful coexistence, and contribute to the overall well-being of society. They serve as powerful reminders of our shared humanity and the importance of embracing religious diversity as a strength rather than a source of division.

Nurturing Religious Tolerance in Everyday Life

Promoting religious tolerance extends beyond educational institutions and interfaith initiatives—it is a commitment that should be nurtured in everyday life. As individuals, we can contribute to fostering religious tolerance by cultivating an attitude of openness, respect, and empathy towards others' religious beliefs and practices.

First and foremost, it is crucial to approach religious differences with a willingness to listen and learn. Engaging in respectful dialogue allows us to gain insights into different perspectives and challenge our own biases and assumptions. It is essential to approach these conversations with an open mind, seeking to understand rather than persuade or convert.

Furthermore, promoting religious tolerance involves actively challenging prejudice and discrimination based on religious beliefs. This can be done by speaking out against religious intolerance, supporting policies and initiatives that promote inclusivity and respect, and actively confronting stereotypes and misconceptions.

In our daily interactions, we can demonstrate religious tolerance by embracing diversity, celebrating religious holidays and festivals, and fostering a sense of inclusivity within our communities. By engaging in acts of kindness and compassion towards individuals of different religious backgrounds, we create an atmosphere of acceptance and respect.

Promoting religious tolerance and respect is not merely a moral imperative—it is essential for creating harmonious and inclusive societies. By embracing religious diversity and fostering an environment of understanding and empathy, we build bridges between individuals, communities, and cultures. Education, interfaith initiatives, and nurturing religious tolerance in everyday life are all crucial components of this endeavor.

As students and seekers of knowledge, it is our responsibility to engage in critical thinking, challenge our own beliefs, and promote religious tolerance and respect within our spheres of influence. By doing so, we contribute to a world where individuals can freely express their religious beliefs, celebrate their diversity, and work towards a shared vision of peace and unity. Let us embark on this journey together, fostering religious tolerance and respect for the benefit of all humanity.

Emphasizing the importance of recognizing and appreciating diverse religious beliefs

In today's increasingly interconnected world, recognizing and appreciating diverse religious beliefs is of paramount importance. Religion has long been a fundamental aspect of human culture, shaping individuals' identities, worldviews, and ways of life. Understanding and appreciating the rich tapestry of religious beliefs can foster a sense of unity, respect, and empathy among individuals and communities. In this section, we will delve into the significance of recognizing and appreciating diverse religious beliefs, exploring how it contributes to fostering a harmonious and inclusive society.

The Value of Recognizing Religious Diversity

Recognizing religious diversity goes beyond acknowledging the existence of various religious traditions—it involves valuing and respecting the differences that exist. By recognizing religious diversity, we embrace the idea that individuals have the right to hold and practice different religious beliefs. This recognition is a cornerstone of religious freedom and human rights, ensuring that individuals are not marginalized or discriminated against based on their religious affiliations.

One of the key benefits of recognizing religious diversity is the promotion of inclusivity and social cohesion. When individuals and communities recognize and appreciate diverse religious beliefs, it creates a sense of belonging and acceptance for all members of society. It fosters an environment where individuals feel valued and respected, regardless of their religious affiliations, contributing to a more harmonious and cohesive social fabric.

Moreover, recognizing religious diversity encourages individuals to engage in dialogue and interfaith interactions. When people from different religious backgrounds come together, it provides an opportunity to learn from one another, challenge stereotypes, and build bridges of understanding. Through such interactions, individuals can develop a deeper appreciation for the diverse ways in which people find meaning and purpose in their lives.

Fostering Interreligious Dialogue and Understanding

Interreligious dialogue plays a vital role in recognizing and appreciating diverse religious beliefs. It involves engaging in conversations and exchanges with individuals from different religious traditions, seeking to understand their beliefs, values, and practices. Interreligious dialogue fosters mutual respect, empathy, and cooperation, contributing to a more inclusive and peaceful society.

One of the main objectives of interreligious dialogue is to build bridges of understanding. By actively listening to others' perspectives and sharing one's own, participants in interreligious dialogue gain insights into different religious traditions and challenge their own preconceptions. This process cultivates a spirit of openness, empathy, and respect, breaking down barriers and promoting peaceful coexistence.

Interreligious dialogue also encourages individuals to find common ground and collaborate on shared concerns. It highlights the universal values and ethical principles that underpin many religious traditions, such as compassion, justice, and stewardship of the Earth. By working together, individuals from diverse religious backgrounds can address social issues, promote social justice, and contribute to the well-being of their communities.

Education and Religious Literacy

Education plays a crucial role in recognizing and appreciating diverse religious beliefs. By incorporating religious literacy into educational curricula, we equip individuals with the knowledge and understanding necessary to engage in informed and respectful conversations about religion.

Religious literacy goes beyond mere knowledge of different religious traditions—it encompasses an understanding of the historical, cultural, and social contexts in which religions emerge and evolve. It involves critical thinking skills that enable individuals to analyze religious texts, rituals, and beliefs in a nuanced and objective manner.

Educational institutions can promote religious literacy by offering courses on religious studies, comparative religion, and interfaith dialogue. These courses provide students with the tools to navigate religious diversity, challenge stereotypes, and cultivate empathy and respect for different religious traditions. By fostering religious literacy, we empower individuals to engage in meaningful conversations about religion and contribute to a more inclusive and tolerant society.

Promoting Respect and Harmony in Everyday Life

Recognizing and appreciating diverse religious beliefs extends beyond formal education and interfaith dialogue—it is a mindset that should be integrated into everyday life. Individuals can actively promote respect and harmony by engaging in practices that embrace religious diversity.

First and foremost, it is essential to approach religious differences with an attitude of respect and empathy. This involves listening attentively to others' perspectives, refraining from judgment, and seeking to understand rather than persuade or convert. By demonstrating respect for others' religious beliefs, we create an atmosphere of acceptance and openness.

Additionally, individuals can celebrate religious diversity by participating in interfaith events, attending religious ceremonies and rituals, and learning about different religious holidays and festivals. By immersing ourselves in the experiences of others, we develop a deeper appreciation for the richness and diversity of religious beliefs.

Promoting respect and harmony also entails challenging religious stereotypes and prejudices. Individuals can actively confront discriminatory attitudes and behaviors, speak out against religious intolerance, and support initiatives that promote inclusivity and respect for all religious traditions. By taking a stand against religious discrimination, we contribute to the creation of a more equitable and just society.

Recognizing and appreciating diverse religious beliefs is crucial for fostering a harmonious and inclusive society. By valuing religious diversity, we embrace the principles of religious freedom and human rights, ensuring that individuals are respected and included regardless of their religious affiliations. Interreligious dialogue, education, and promoting respect in everyday life are all essential components of this endeavor.

As students and seekers of knowledge, it is our responsibility to cultivate religious literacy, challenge stereotypes, and engage in meaningful conversations about religion. By recognizing and appreciating diverse religious beliefs, we contribute to a society where individuals can freely express their faith, find common ground, and work towards a shared vision of peace and understanding. Let us embrace religious diversity and promote respect for all beliefs, fostering a world where unity and harmony prevail.

The role of understanding differences in fostering interfaith dialogue and harmony

Interfaith dialogue plays a crucial role in promoting understanding, respect, and harmony among individuals of different religious beliefs. It provides a platform for people from diverse religious backgrounds to come together, engage in meaningful conversations, and build bridges of understanding. However, for interfaith dialogue to be effective, it is essential to recognize and understand the differences that exist among various religious traditions. In this section, we will explore the role of understanding differences in fostering interfaith dialogue and harmony, examining how it contributes to building a more inclusive and tolerant society.

Appreciating the Complexity of Religious Diversity

Religious diversity is a multifaceted tapestry, encompassing a wide range of beliefs, rituals, and practices. Each religious tradition has its own unique worldview, mythology, and symbolism. Understanding these differences is essential for engaging in interfaith dialogue effectively.

Appreciating the complexity of religious diversity involves recognizing that no single perspective can capture the richness and depth of all religious traditions. Each tradition offers a unique lens through which individuals interpret the world and seek spiritual fulfillment. By understanding and respecting these differences, we lay the foundation for fruitful and respectful interfaith dialogue.

Moreover, understanding differences helps dispel misconceptions and stereotypes that can hinder meaningful engagement between religious communities. By gaining a deeper knowledge of different religious beliefs, we challenge preconceived notions and foster empathy and understanding. This process encourages individuals to see beyond surface-level differences and appreciate the shared aspirations for meaning, purpose, and connection that underlie many religious traditions.

Cultivating Empathy and Respect

Understanding differences in religious beliefs cultivates empathy and respect, which are fundamental to successful interfaith dialogue. Empathy allows individuals to put themselves in the shoes of others and view the world through their perspectives. By empathizing with individuals of different religious backgrounds, we can gain a deeper understanding of their experiences, challenges, and aspirations.

Respect is the cornerstone of interfaith dialogue. It involves recognizing the inherent dignity and worth of every individual, regardless of their religious beliefs. When engaging in interfaith dialogue, respect manifests as active listening, open-mindedness, and refraining from judgment or attempts to convert others. By approaching interfaith dialogue with respect, we create an environment where individuals feel safe to express their beliefs, fostering mutual understanding and trust.

Building Common Ground

Understanding differences is not solely about acknowledging the disparities among religious traditions; it is also about finding common ground. Despite the diversity of religious beliefs, there are often shared values and ethical principles that transcend specific traditions. Identifying and building upon these commonalities can foster unity and collaboration among religious communities.

For instance, many religious traditions emphasize compassion, justice, and stewardship of the Earth. By recognizing these shared values, individuals can work together to address societal challenges, advocate for social justice, and promote environmental sustainability. Building common ground through interfaith dialogue strengthens the bonds between religious communities and enhances the collective impact they can have on society.

Overcoming Challenges and Nurturing Dialogue

Understanding differences is not without its challenges. In interfaith dialogue, individuals may encounter conflicting perspectives, deeply held beliefs, and historical grievances. It is important to navigate these challenges with sensitivity, patience, and a commitment to mutual understanding.

One way to overcome challenges is through education and interfaith literacy. By fostering interfaith literacy, individuals can develop the knowledge and skills necessary to engage in informed and respectful conversations about religious differences. This includes understanding the historical, cultural, and social contexts in which religious traditions have evolved, as well as the nuances and intricacies of their beliefs and practices.

Additionally, nurturing dialogue requires creating safe and inclusive spaces where individuals feel comfortable expressing their beliefs and engaging in open and honest discussions. Facilitators of interfaith dialogue can employ active listening techniques, establish ground rules for respectful communication, and provide opportunities for participants to share their personal stories and experiences. These practices help build trust, promote understanding, and encourage participants to challenge their own assumptions and biases.

Understanding differences is a fundamental component of fostering interfaith dialogue and harmony. By appreciating the complexity of religious diversity, cultivating empathy and respect, building common ground, and overcoming challenges, individuals can engage in meaningful and transformative interfaith dialogue.

As seekers of knowledge and proponents of religious tolerance, it is our responsibility to actively seek understanding, challenge stereotypes, and promote respectful dialogue. By embracing the diversity of religious beliefs and engaging in interfaith dialogue, we contribute to the creation of a society where individuals can coexist, celebrate their differences, and work towards a shared vision of harmony and peace.

Exercise:

✧ Reflect on a personal experience or encounter with someone from a different religious background. Describe the challenges and opportunities for understanding that arose during the interaction.

✧ Research a religious tradition that is unfamiliar to you. Write a short essayTheits key beliefs, rituals, and practices, highlighting both the similarities and differences with your own religious background.

✧ Imagine you are organizing an interfaith dialogue event in your community. Develop an agenda for the event, including discussion topics, activities, and strategies to ensure respectful and productive dialogue.

✧ Engage in a conversation with a classmate or friend who holds different religious beliefs. Practice active listening, empathy, and respect during the discussion. Reflect on the experience and share your insights with the group.

Remember to approach these exercises with an open mind and a willingness to learn from others' perspectives.

Cultural and Historical Relevance

The study of cultural and historical relevance provides invaluable insights into the development and significance of religious and spiritual practices. By examining the cultural and historical contexts in which these traditions emerge, we gain a deeper understanding of their beliefs, rituals, and their impact on individuals and societies. In this section, we will explore the cultural and historical relevance of various religious and spiritual traditions, drawing examples from fields such as Witchcraft, Divination, Herbalism, Shamanism, and Ecospirituality. Through this analysis, we aim to uncover the profound connections between these traditions and the human experience throughout history.

Cultural Influences on Religious and Spiritual Practices

Religious and spiritual practices are deeply intertwined with the cultures in which they arise. Cultural influences shape the beliefs, rituals, and symbolism of these traditions, reflecting the unique perspectives and values of a particular group or community. For example, Witchcraft, a practice often associated with nature-based spirituality, draws inspiration from ancient pagan traditions and incorporates elements of folk magic. The celebration of seasonal festivals, reverence for the cycles of nature, and the use of herbs and crystals are examples of cultural influences that are intrinsic to the practice of Witchcraft.

Similarly, Divination, the art of gaining insight or guidance through supernatural means, takes on different forms and methods across cultures. The Chinese practice of I Ching, for instance, involves the interpretation of hexagrams to provide guidance in decision-making. In contrast, the reading of tarot cards in Western divination practices reflects the influence of Renaissance-era symbolism and occult philosophy.

Understanding the cultural influences on religious and spiritual practices helps us appreciate their diversity and contextualize their significance within specific societies. It allows us to explore the ways in which these traditions adapt and evolve over time, reflecting the ever-changing cultural landscapes in which they exist.

Historical Development of Religious and Spiritual Traditions

The historical development of religious and spiritual traditions provides important insights into their origins, evolution, and impact on society. By examining the historical context in which these traditions emerge, we gain a deeper appreciation for their enduring relevance and resilience.

For example, Shamanism, a practice that involves communication with spirits and the use of altered states of consciousness, has its roots in ancient tribal societies. Shamanic practices played vital roles in tribal cultures, serving as healers, mediators between the human and spirit worlds, and guardians of communal harmony. Understanding the historical development of Shamanism helps us recognize its cultural significance and the ways in which it has shaped the beliefs and practices of indigenous communities worldwide.

Similarly, the rise of Ecospirituality in recent decades can be traced back to the environmental movements of the 20th century. As concerns about ecological degradation and the impact of human activities on the planet grew, individuals and communities sought spiritual connections with nature and advocated for the preservation of the Earth. Ecospirituality emerged as a response to these environmental challenges, incorporating elements of ecology, environmental ethics, and reverence for the natural world.

Impact on Individuals and Societies

Religious and spiritual traditions have a profound impact on individuals and societies, shaping worldviews, values, and social norms. By examining their cultural and historical relevance, we can better understand how these traditions influence human behavior, foster social cohesion, and address existential questions.

One example of the impact of religious and spiritual traditions is the role of Herbalism in healthcare practices. Herbalism, the use of plants for medicinal purposes, has been deeply embedded in various cultures throughout history. Traditional healing systems such as Traditional Chinese Medicine and Ayurveda incorporate herbal remedies as integral components of their holistic approaches to health and well-being. Understanding the cultural and historical relevance of Herbalism allows us to appreciate the knowledge and wisdom accumulated by these traditions over centuries and explore their potential integration with modern healthcare practices.

Religious and spiritual traditions also have a profound impact on social cohesion and identity. They provide frameworks for moral and ethical values, foster a sense of belonging, and offer guidance in navigating life's challenges. For instance, the rituals and community practices in monotheistic religions such as Christianity and Islam contribute to the formation of shared identities and the establishment of social norms. By exploring the cultural and historical relevance of these traditions, we can gain a deeper understanding of their impact on individuals and societies, both past and present.

The cultural and historical relevance of religious and spiritual traditions provides invaluable insights into their development, impact, and significance. By understanding the cultural influences and historical context in which these traditions emerge, we gain a deeper appreciation for their diversity, adaptability, and enduring relevance. Moreover, recognizing the cultural and historical relevance of these traditions allows us to engage in respectful and informed dialogue, fostering greater understanding, tolerance, and appreciation of religious and spiritual diversity.

Exercise:

✧   Research a specific religious or spiritual tradition and analyze its cultural and historical context. Explore the ways in which cultural influences have shaped its beliefs, rituals, and practices.

✦   Reflect on the historical development of a particular religious or spiritual tradition and examine its impact on individuals and societies throughout history. Consider how this tradition has adapted to changing social, political, and cultural contexts.

✦   Choose a contemporary issue or challenge and explore how different religious and spiritual traditions address or provide insights into this issue. Consider the cultural and historical relevance of these traditions in shaping their perspectives.

✦   Engage in a discussion with classmates or friends from diverse religious and spiritual backgrounds. Explore the cultural and historical influences on their respective traditions and discuss the ways in which these traditions impact their lives and beliefs.

Remember to approach these exercises with respect, curiosity, and an open mind. By delving into the cultural and historical relevance of religious and spiritual traditions, you will develop a deeper understanding of their complexity and significance in the world today.

Exploring the influence of polytheistic and monotheistic religions on art, literature, and architecture

Art, literature, and architecture have long served as powerful mediums for expressing religious beliefs and reflecting the values and worldviews of societies. The influence of polytheistic and monotheistic religions on these creative forms is profound and far-reaching. In this section, we will examine the impact of these religious traditions on art, literature, and architecture, drawing examples from fields such as Witchcraft, Divination, Herbalism, Shamanism, and Ecospirituality. By exploring the relationship between religion and creative expression, we can gain a deeper understanding of the cultural and historical significance of these traditions.

Polytheistic Religions and Creative Expression

Polytheistic religions, characterized by the belief in multiple deities, have provided fertile ground for artistic and literary expressions throughout history. The rich pantheons of gods and goddesses in these traditions have inspired countless artistic representations, mythological narratives, and architectural marvels.

In ancient Greece, for example, the polytheistic religion played a central role in the development of classical art and architecture. Sculptures of gods and goddesses adorned temples, capturing the beauty and power of the divine. Epic poems such as

Homer's Iliad and Odyssey were infused with mythological tales, celebrating the exploits of heroes and gods.

Similarly, in Norse mythology, the pantheon of gods and goddesses influenced the artistic expressions of the Viking culture. Intricate wood carvings, known as "stave churches," depicted scenes from Norse mythology, providing a visual representation of the divine realm. The poetic eddas, such as the Poetic Edda and the Prose Edda, preserved the mythological narratives and poetic traditions of the Norse gods.

Monotheistic Religions and Creative Expression

Monotheistic religions, characterized by the belief in a single supreme deity, have also left an indelible mark on art, literature, and architecture. The focus on the worship of one god or goddess has shaped the creative expressions of these traditions, often emphasizing the divine qualities and teachings of the central deity.

In Christianity, art and architecture have been pivotal in conveying religious narratives and inspiring devotion. Iconic artworks such as Michelangelo's Sistine Chapel frescoes and Leonardo da Vinci's "The Last Supper" depict scenes from biblical stories, evoking a sense of awe and reverence. Cathedrals and churches, with their soaring arches and stained glass windows, are architectural marvels that invite worshippers to experience the divine presence.

Islamic art and architecture, influenced by the monotheistic teachings of Islam, showcase intricate geometric patterns, calligraphy, and arabesque designs. The absence of human or animal depictions in religious art reflects the emphasis on divine unity and the prohibition of idolatry. Mosques, such as the Alhambra in Spain and the Dome of the Rock in Jerusalem, exemplify the exquisite architectural expressions of Islamic faith.

Symbolism and Allegory in Religious Art and Literature

Religious art and literature often employ symbolism and allegory to convey deeper meanings and spiritual truths. Symbolic representations of deities, religious symbols, and mythological narratives serve as vehicles for conveying complex theological concepts and moral teachings.

For example, in the field of Witchcraft, the Wiccan pentacle symbolizes the five elements (earth, air, fire, water, and spirit) and their interconnectedness. It appears in various forms of art, such as jewelry and altar decorations, serving as a visual representation of Wiccan beliefs and principles.

Literature, too, abounds with religious symbolism and allegory. In Dante Alighieri's "Divine Comedy," the journey through Hell, Purgatory, and Heaven serves as a metaphorical exploration of the soul's quest for salvation. Each realm represents different moral and spiritual states, offering profound insights into Christian theology.

Architecture as Sacred Space

Architecture, particularly in the realm of religious structures, plays a significant role in creating sacred spaces that facilitate spiritual experiences and rituals. The design, layout, and ornamentation of religious buildings are carefully crafted to evoke a sense of the divine and provide a space for worship and contemplation.

In Shamanism, sacred sites and natural landscapes are considered imbued with spiritual energy. The design of ceremonial spaces, such as sweat lodges and medicine wheels, often incorporates natural elements and materials to create a harmonious connection between humans and the natural world.

Ecospirituality emphasizes the sacredness of the Earth and the interconnectedness of all living beings. Architectural designs that align with this worldview prioritize sustainable materials, energy efficiency, and integration with the natural environment. Examples include eco-temples, green retreat centers, and earthship dwellings.

The influence of polytheistic and monotheistic religions on art, literature, and architecture is undeniable. From the vibrant sculptures of ancient Greece to the awe-inspiring cathedrals of Christianity, these religious traditions have shaped and been shaped by creative expressions throughout history. By studying the relationship between religion and creative forms, we gain insights into cultural and historical contexts, religious symbolism, and the power of art and architecture to inspire and transcend.

Exercise:

✦ Visit a local museum or gallery and analyze a piece of artwork influenced by a specific religious tradition. Explore the symbols, themes, and techniques employed in the artwork and reflect on its cultural and historical significance.

✦ Read a literary work from a different religious tradition than your own. Identify the religious symbolism and allegory present in the text and consider how it contributes to the overall meaning and message.

✦   Visit a religious site or sacred space in your community. Observe the architectural design, decorative elements, and the overall atmosphere of the space. Reflect on how these aspects contribute to the religious experience and sense of sacredness.

✦   Research contemporary examples of architecture inspired by ecological and spiritual principles. Examine how these designs integrate sustainability, natural elements, and spiritual concepts. Reflect on the potential impact of such architecture on individuals and the environment.

By engaging in these exercises, you will deepen your understanding of the profound influence of polytheistic and monotheistic religions on art, literature, and architecture, and develop a greater appreciation for the cultural and historical relevance of these creative expressions.

The historical impact of these belief systems on civilizations and societies

Polytheistic and monotheistic belief systems have played significant roles in shaping civilizations and societies throughout history. The influence of these belief systems extends beyond the realms of spirituality and religion, permeating various aspects of human life, including politics, social structures, art, and ethics. In this section, we will explore the historical impact of polytheistic and monotheistic belief systems, drawing examples from fields such as Witchcraft, Divination, Herbalism, Shamanism, and Ecospirituality. By examining the interplay between belief systems and societies, we can gain insights into the cultural and historical significance of these traditions.

Polytheistic Belief Systems and Civilization

Polytheistic belief systems, characterized by the worship of multiple gods and goddesses, have shaped the course of numerous ancient civilizations. The diverse pantheons and mythologies of polytheistic religions have served as foundations for political, social, and cultural structures.

Ancient Egypt provides a striking example of the interplay between polytheism and civilization. The Egyptians worshipped a pantheon of gods, each associated with specific aspects of life and nature. This religious framework influenced their social hierarchy, with pharaohs embodying the divine authority of the gods. The construction of monumental temples and pyramids served as both religious sanctuaries and symbols of the state's power and prosperity.

In Mesopotamia, the polytheistic religions of Sumer, Babylon, and Assyria influenced the development of complex legal systems, including the Code of Hammurabi. These legal codes were often based on religious principles, reflecting the belief in divine justice and the gods' role in maintaining order in society. The construction of monumental ziggurats served as physical representations of the connection between the mortal world and the divine.

Monotheistic Belief Systems and Societal Transformations

Monotheistic belief systems, characterized by the worship of a single supreme deity, have also had profound impacts on civilizations and societies throughout history. The emergence of monotheistic religions introduced new theological, ethical, and social frameworks that shaped the course of human development.

The rise of Judaism, Christianity, and Islam has had enduring effects on Western and Middle Eastern civilizations. The Hebrew Bible, the Christian Bible, and the Quran provided moral and ethical guidelines, influencing laws, social norms, and cultural practices. Monotheistic religions emphasized notions of individual morality, justice, and accountability to a single divine authority, which in turn influenced the development of legal systems and concepts of human rights.

Christianity played a pivotal role in the transformation of the Roman Empire. As the religion gained prominence, it challenged traditional polytheistic beliefs and practices, leading to social and political upheavals. The adoption of Christianity as the state religion by Emperor Constantine marked a turning point in the history of the empire, shaping its values, institutions, and artistic expressions.

Islam, emerging in the 7th century, had a profound impact on the Arabian Peninsula and beyond. The teachings of the Quran provided a comprehensive framework for personal conduct, social organization, and governance. Islamic civilization flourished, with advancements in mathematics, astronomy, medicine, and architecture. The spread of Islam across vast regions facilitated cultural exchange, trade networks, and the preservation of ancient knowledge.

Interactions and Influences: Polytheism and Monotheism

The interactions between polytheistic and monotheistic belief systems have also shaped the course of history. In many instances, these belief systems coexisted, clashed, or influenced one another, leading to cultural syncretism or religious conflicts.

Exploring the Contrasts and Convergence of Polytheism and Monotheism

In ancient Greece, the conquests of Alexander the Great spread Hellenistic culture, which blended elements of Greek polytheism with local religious traditions. The resulting syncretic practices led to the emergence of new gods, such as Serapis, and the adoption of Greek artistic and architectural styles in various regions.

The spread of monotheistic religions into pre-existing polytheistic societies often resulted in cultural and religious transformations. For example, as Christianity expanded throughout Europe, pagan practices were gradually assimilated into Christian traditions. Many pagan festivals and symbols were incorporated into Christian holidays, facilitating the conversion and acceptance of the new faith.

The Crusades, launched by Christians to reclaim the Holy Land from Muslim control, highlight the conflicts that arose from religious differences. These military campaigns, spanning several centuries, had profound consequences on both the Eastern and Western worlds, shaping cultural perceptions and fueling animosities that persist to this day.

Counterarguments and Dissenting Opinions

It is essential to acknowledge dissenting opinions and counterarguments regarding the historical impact of polytheistic and monotheistic belief systems. Some scholars argue that other factors, such as economic, political, and environmental conditions, have played more significant roles in shaping civilizations and societies. They contend that while religious beliefs certainly had some influence, attributing all societal transformations solely to religion oversimplifies complex historical processes.

Additionally, critics argue that focusing exclusively on polytheistic and monotheistic belief systems neglects the contributions of other religious and spiritual traditions, such as indigenous beliefs and non-theistic philosophies. They advocate for a more inclusive and comprehensive understanding of the historical impact of diverse belief systems.

Exercise:

✧ Research a specific ancient civilization and analyze the role of polytheistic beliefs in its social, political, and cultural structures. Examine how myths and religious practices influenced various aspects of daily life.

✧ Compare and contrast the impact of monotheistic beliefs on two different societies or civilizations. Analyze how the introduction of monotheistic religions affected their governance, social structures, and cultural expressions.

✧   Investigate instances of syncretism between polytheistic and monotheistic belief systems. Identify examples where religious practices and symbols from different traditions merged, and explore the resulting cultural and religious expressions.

✧   Examine the influence of polytheistic or monotheistic belief systems on art and literature in a specific historical period or civilization. Analyze how religious themes and symbolism were incorporated into artistic expressions, and reflect on the meanings conveyed.

By engaging in these exercises, you will deepen your understanding of the historical impact of polytheistic and monotheistic belief systems on civilizations and societies. You will also develop critical thinking skills by exploring counterarguments and dissenting opinions, fostering a well-rounded perspective on this complex topic.

Implications for Worldviews and Ethics

The exploration of polytheistic and monotheistic belief systems goes beyond their historical and cultural significance; it also provides profound implications for worldviews and ethical frameworks. Understanding these implications allows individuals to engage in critical reflections on their own beliefs and values, fostering tolerance, respect, and a deeper understanding of diverse perspectives. In this section, we will delve into the implications of polytheism and monotheism for worldviews and ethics, drawing examples from fields such as Witchcraft, Divination, Herbalism, Shamanism, and Ecospirituality.

Worldviews and the Diversity of Belief Systems

Worldviews encompass the comprehensive frameworks through which individuals perceive and interpret the world around them. They encompass beliefs about the nature of reality, human existence, morality, and the purpose of life. Polytheistic and monotheistic belief systems present distinct worldviews, each offering unique perspectives on these fundamental questions.

Polytheistic worldviews acknowledge the existence of multiple deities, each associated with specific aspects of life, nature, and human experience. These belief systems often embrace the interconnectedness of all things and recognize the divine presence in the natural world. For instance, practitioners of Witchcraft view the Earth as sacred and hold reverence for the cycles of nature, incorporating rituals and practices that honor the divine forces present in the elements, plants, and animals.

In contrast, monotheistic worldviews emphasize the belief in a single supreme deity, who is often seen as the creator and sustainer of the universe. These belief systems highlight the importance of individual moral responsibility and the adherence to a set of ethical principles. For example, followers of the Abrahamic religions (Judaism, Christianity, and Islam) believe in a singular God who sets forth moral guidelines for human conduct, such as the Ten Commandments in Judaism and the teachings of Jesus Christ in Christianity.

Ethics and Moral Principles

Ethics, the study of moral values and principles, is deeply influenced by religious beliefs. Polytheistic and monotheistic belief systems offer distinct ethical frameworks that shape the behavior and decision-making processes of their followers.

Polytheistic ethics often emphasize harmony and balance within the natural world and human relationships. In the practice of Shamanism, for instance, practitioners strive to maintain a harmonious relationship with the spirits and forces of nature. They respect the interconnectedness of all beings and promote ecological stewardship. The ethical principles of Witchcraft emphasize personal responsibility, respect for free will, and the avoidance of harm to oneself and others.

Monotheistic ethics, on the other hand, often revolve around a divine commandment or moral law. In Judaism, the ethical framework is built upon principles such as justice, compassion, and righteousness, as exemplified by the concept of Tikkun Olam (repairing the world). Christianity emphasizes love, forgiveness, and the teachings of Jesus Christ, including the Golden Rule. Islam's ethical principles are derived from the Quran and Hadith, stressing justice, mercy, and social responsibility.

Implications for Interfaith Dialogue and Understanding

The study of polytheistic and monotheistic belief systems offers valuable insights for fostering interfaith dialogue and understanding. Recognizing and appreciating the diversity of religious beliefs cultivates an environment of respect, empathy, and mutual learning.

Interfaith dialogue provides opportunities for individuals to engage in meaningful conversations, exchange ideas, and challenge preconceived notions. By exploring the historical, cultural, and ethical aspects of different belief systems, participants can broaden their perspectives and develop a more nuanced understanding of the complexity of religious traditions.

Engaging in interfaith dialogue can also contribute to social cohesion and the building of inclusive communities. By recognizing shared values and ethical principles across diverse belief systems, individuals can find common ground and work together to address societal challenges and promote positive change.

Counterarguments and Dissenting Opinions

While the promotion of interfaith dialogue and understanding is crucial, it is important to acknowledge counterarguments and dissenting opinions. Some critics argue that focusing on religious diversity can potentially overshadow other important aspects of human identity and societal challenges. They contend that an exclusive emphasis on religious differences may inadvertently reinforce divisions and lead to a narrow understanding of complex social issues.

Others raise concerns about cultural appropriation and the potential for misunderstandings when individuals from different belief systems engage in interfaith dialogue. They argue that respectful engagement should involve a deep understanding of the cultural and historical contexts of various religious practices, and that borrowing or appropriating practices without proper knowledge and respect can be disrespectful and harmful.

Exercise:

✧ Reflect on your own worldview and ethical framework. Identify the key beliefs and values that shape your perspective on life, morality, and the purpose of existence.

✧ Research a specific polytheistic belief system and analyze its ethical principles. Compare and contrast them with the ethical principles of a monotheistic belief system. How do they align or differ in their approach to morality and human conduct?

✧ Engage in an interfaith dialogue with individuals from different religious backgrounds. Discuss the ethical challenges and dilemmas faced in contemporary society and explore potential solutions that draw upon shared values.

✧ Explore the concept of cultural appropriation in the context of spiritual and religious practices. Analyze the potential ethical implications and discuss ways to engage respectfully and responsibly with diverse belief systems.

Exploring the Contrasts and Convergence of Polytheism and Monotheism

By participating in these exercises, you will deepen your understanding of the implications of polytheism and monotheism for worldviews and ethics. You will also develop skills in interfaith dialogue, critical thinking, and ethical reasoning, which are valuable in navigating the complexities of our diverse and interconnected world.

Examining how polytheism and monotheism shape moral and ethical frameworks

Polytheism and monotheism are two distinct belief systems that have shaped human moral and ethical frameworks throughout history. By studying these systems, we can gain insights into how religious beliefs influence individual and collective notions of right and wrong, moral conduct, and ethical decision-making. In this section, we will explore the ways in which polytheism and monotheism shape moral and ethical frameworks, drawing examples from various fields such as Witchcraft, Divination, Herbalism, Shamanism, and Ecospirituality.

Polytheism and Moral Pluralism

Polytheistic belief systems, characterized by the recognition of multiple deities, often embrace moral pluralism. The existence of various gods and goddesses, each with their own attributes and domains of influence, allows for a diversity of ethical perspectives and values. For example, in Witchcraft, practitioners may invoke different deities for guidance in specific areas of life, such as love, healing, or protection. This plurality of divine forces can lead to a more nuanced understanding of morality, recognizing that different situations may require different ethical considerations.

In polytheistic traditions, moral guidelines may be derived from myths, legends, and teachings associated with specific deities. These stories provide ethical lessons and serve as moral compasses for believers. The complex relationships between deities and humans in polytheistic belief systems also highlight the interplay between morality, human agency, and divine intervention.

Monotheism and Divine Command Ethics

Monotheistic belief systems, on the other hand, often adhere to divine command ethics, where moral principles are derived from the commands and teachings of a single supreme deity. These principles serve as the foundation for ethical frameworks within monotheistic religions such as Judaism, Christianity, and Islam.

In monotheistic ethics, moral guidelines are typically outlined in sacred texts, scriptures, and religious teachings. For instance, the Ten Commandments in Judaism and the teachings of Jesus Christ in Christianity provide moral imperatives that guide believers' actions and behaviors. Islamic ethical principles are derived from the Quran and the Hadith, which offer guidance on matters of justice, compassion, and social responsibility.

Ethical Principles in Polytheism and Monotheism

Although polytheism and monotheism have different approaches to morality, there are ethical principles that can be found in both belief systems. Examples include:

a. Respect for Life and Creation: Both polytheistic and monotheistic traditions often emphasize the inherent value of life and the natural world. Polytheistic traditions, such as Shamanism, recognize the interconnectedness of all beings and promote ecological stewardship. Monotheistic faiths, too, emphasize the sacredness of life and the responsibility to care for the environment as stewards of God's creation.

b. Compassion and Kindness: The principles of compassion and kindness are central to many religious traditions, irrespective of their belief in multiple deities or a single God. These principles encourage believers to show empathy, mercy, and benevolence towards others.

c. Justice and Fairness: Both polytheism and monotheism often emphasize the importance of justice and fairness in human interactions. This can be seen in the concepts of divine justice in monotheistic belief systems and the notion of karmic balance in some polytheistic traditions.

Moral Dilemmas and Ethical Decision-Making

The moral frameworks shaped by polytheism and monotheism provide guidance in navigating moral dilemmas and making ethical decisions. These frameworks offer believers a set of principles and values to consider when faced with challenging situations.

However, the application of moral and ethical principles can be complex and subject to interpretation. Different individuals and communities within the same religious tradition may hold varying perspectives on moral issues, leading to diverse ethical viewpoints and debates. For example, debates on topics such as abortion, gender and sexuality, or environmental stewardship within religious communities highlight the nuanced nature of ethical decision-making.

Exploring the Contrasts and Convergence of Polytheism and Monotheism

Exercise:

✧   Choose a polytheistic belief system, such as Norse mythology or ancient Egyptian religion, and analyze its moral and ethical principles. Identify key deities associated with specific ethical domains and explore the moral lessons derived from their stories.

✧   Select a monotheistic belief system, such as Christianity or Islam, and examine its ethical teachings. Explore the foundational principles and moral guidelines outlined in the sacred texts of the chosen tradition.

✧   Compare and contrast the moral and ethical frameworks of the chosen polytheistic and monotheistic belief systems. Identify commonalities and differences in their approaches to morality, ethical conduct, and the role of divine guidance.

✧   Engage in a group discussion or debate exploring ethical dilemmas from the perspective of polytheism and monotheism. Consider how the diverse moral and ethical frameworks within these belief systems can contribute to a broader understanding of complex ethical issues.

By engaging in these exercises, you will deepen your understanding of how polytheism and monotheism shape moral and ethical frameworks. You will also develop critical thinking skills, ethical reasoning abilities, and cultural awareness, enabling you to engage in meaningful dialogue and contribute to discussions on morality and ethics within diverse religious contexts.

Investigating the philosophical underpinnings of each belief system and their implications for human behavior

Polytheism and monotheism, as belief systems, encompass not only religious practices but also profound philosophical foundations. The philosophical underpinnings of these belief systems have far-reaching implications for human behavior, moral values, and the understanding of the self and the world. In this section, we will explore the philosophical aspects of polytheism and monotheism, drawing examples from Witchcraft, Divination, Herbalism, Shamanism, and Ecospirituality, to understand how these belief systems shape human behavior and provide insights into the nature of existence.

Polytheism: Pluralism and Interconnectedness

Polytheism embraces a worldview characterized by pluralism and interconnectedness. The belief in multiple deities reflects the acknowledgment of diverse forces and energies that shape the world. In polytheistic philosophies, the gods and goddesses are seen as distinct entities with their own characteristics and responsibilities, embodying different aspects of existence. This perspective encourages an understanding of the world as a complex tapestry where various powers interact and influence human life.

The philosophical implications of polytheism extend beyond a mere recognition of diverse divine beings. They emphasize the interconnectedness of all things, including humans, nature, and the divine. This interconnectedness suggests that human behavior and choices have consequences not only for oneself but also for the entire web of existence. Consequently, ethical considerations in polytheistic belief systems often prioritize harmonious relationships, ecological balance, and the recognition of the inherent worth of all beings.

Exercise:

Reflect on the concept of interconnectedness in polytheism by examining the practice of Herbalism. Explore how the use of plants and herbs in healing rituals reflects the belief in the interdependence between humans and the natural world. Consider the ethical implications of responsible plant harvesting and sustainable herbal practices.

Monotheism: Unity and Divine Sovereignty

Monotheism, in contrast, is characterized by a belief in a single, supreme deity who governs the universe. The philosophical underpinnings of monotheistic belief systems emphasize unity and divine sovereignty. Monotheism postulates the existence of a singular, all-powerful God who is the creator and sustainer of all things. This conception of a singular divine authority shapes human behavior and moral values in distinct ways.

The philosophical implications of monotheism highlight the unity of creation and the inherent worth of every individual. Monotheistic traditions often emphasize the divine spark within each person, suggesting a profound interconnectedness between humanity and the divine. This understanding can foster a sense of responsibility, compassion, and the pursuit of moral excellence.

Exploring the Contrasts and Convergence of Polytheism and Monotheism

Exercise:

Explore the concept of divine sovereignty in monotheism through the lens of Divination. Investigate how divinatory practices, such as Tarot reading or Oracle consultation, reflect the belief in a divine source of wisdom and guidance. Consider how divination can provide insights into human behavior and choices within a monotheistic worldview.

Implications for Human Behavior and Ethics

The philosophical underpinnings of polytheism and monotheism have significant implications for human behavior and ethics. These belief systems provide frameworks through which individuals navigate the complexities of existence and make choices that align with their understanding of the divine and the world.

In polytheism, the recognition of diverse deities and interconnectedness fosters a sense of respect for the natural world and the interdependence of all beings. This perspective can influence behavior, leading individuals to prioritize ecological sustainability, compassion for others, and a harmonious coexistence with the divine and the natural realm.

In monotheism, the belief in a singular, all-powerful God often entails a sense of accountability and moral responsibility. Monotheistic ethical frameworks provide guidelines for moral conduct, emphasizing virtues such as honesty, justice, and love. The belief in the divine sovereignty and the unity of creation can inspire individuals to cultivate personal virtues and contribute to the well-being of society.

Exercise:

✧ Compare and contrast the ethical implications of polytheistic and monotheistic belief systems. Consider how these philosophical underpinnings shape human behavior, moral values, and ethical decision-making within each belief system. Reflect on the potential strengths and challenges of each approach to ethics.

✧ Engage in a group discussion or debate exploring ethical dilemmas from both polytheistic and monotheistic perspectives. Analyze how the philosophical foundations of these belief systems inform the responses to moral challenges and the understanding of human behavior.

By delving into the philosophical underpinnings of polytheism and monotheism, we gain insight into the rich tapestry of human beliefs and their impact on human behavior and ethics. Understanding these foundations fosters intercultural dialogue, empathy, and critical thinking skills, enabling individuals to navigate diverse religious landscapes with respect and appreciation for different worldviews.

Contemporary Relevance

In the ever-changing landscape of the modern world, the study of diverse religious beliefs, such as Witchcraft, Divination, Herbalism, Shamanism, and Ecospirituality, holds great significance. Understanding the contemporary relevance of these belief systems allows us to explore their role in addressing pressing societal issues, fostering personal growth and well-being, and contributing to the larger cultural and environmental discourse. In this section, we will delve into the contemporary relevance of these belief systems, examining their impact on individuals, communities, and the global stage.

Personal Transformation and Empowerment

One of the key aspects of the contemporary relevance of these belief systems lies in their potential for personal transformation and empowerment. Practices such as Witchcraft and Shamanism offer individuals a means to connect with their inner selves, develop self-awareness, and cultivate personal power. Through rituals, spellwork, and other spiritual practices, practitioners can enhance their self-confidence, intuition, and resilience.

Exercise:

Engage in a self-reflection exercise inspired by Witchcraft or Shamanism. Explore how rituals, meditation, or other spiritual practices can contribute to personal transformation and empowerment. Reflect on the ways in which these practices can positively impact your life and the lives of others.

Environmental Stewardship and Ecospirituality

The contemporary relevance of belief systems like Herbalism and Ecospirituality is closely tied to the pressing need for environmental stewardship and sustainability. These belief systems emphasize the interconnectedness between humans and the natural world, highlighting the importance of living in harmony with nature.

Herbalism, for instance, promotes the use of plant-based remedies and sustainable practices in healing and wellness. By embracing the wisdom of the natural world, Herbalism encourages individuals to adopt eco-friendly lifestyles, support local ecosystems, and conserve biodiversity.

Ecospirituality expands on this by recognizing the sacredness of the Earth and advocating for environmental justice. It inspires individuals to develop a deep reverence for nature and actively work towards the preservation of the planet.

Exercise:

Research and identify a local plant species that holds significance in Herbalism or Ecospirituality. Investigate its traditional uses, ecological role, and conservation status. Reflect on how the principles of Herbalism or Ecospirituality can guide your actions to support the well-being of this plant species and its habitat.

Interconnectedness and Interfaith Dialogue

In a world marked by cultural diversity and pluralism, the recognition of interconnectedness and the promotion of interfaith dialogue become crucial. These belief systems offer valuable insights into fostering understanding, respect, and collaboration among different religious traditions.

The recognition of diverse deities in polytheistic practices and the acknowledgment of a singular divine authority in monotheistic traditions provide opportunities for dialogue and mutual learning. By engaging in interfaith discussions, individuals can deepen their understanding of other belief systems, challenge their own assumptions, and find common ground on shared values.

Exercise:

Organize or participate in an interfaith panel discussion that explores the intersections between different belief systems, such as Witchcraft, Divination, Herbalism, Shamanism, and Ecospirituality. Discuss how these belief systems can contribute to building bridges across religious and cultural divides. Analyze the challenges and opportunities that arise in interfaith dialogue.

Social Justice and Activism

Many practitioners of these belief systems are engaged in social justice issues and activism, advocating for equality, inclusivity, and human rights. These belief systems often embrace values such as compassion, empathy, and justice, which motivate individuals to work towards positive social change.

Exercise:

Identify a social justice issue that aligns with the values of Witchcraft, Divination, Herbalism, Shamanism, or Ecospirituality. Research existing initiatives or organizations that address this issue and explore ways in which you can contribute to the cause. Reflect on how your spiritual beliefs and practices can inform and inspire your social justice activism.

Conclusion

The contemporary relevance of diverse religious beliefs, such as Witchcraft, Divination, Herbalism, Shamanism, and Ecospirituality, encompasses personal transformation, environmental stewardship, interfaith dialogue, and social justice. By recognizing and appreciating the contemporary significance of these belief systems, individuals can draw inspiration, guidance, and strength to navigate the complexities of the modern world. Engaging with these belief systems opens doors to personal growth, environmental responsibility, and fostering meaningful connections with others.

The role of polytheism and monotheism in modern society

Polytheism and monotheism are two distinct belief systems that have shaped human civilizations for centuries. In this section, we will explore the role of polytheism and monotheism in modern society, analyzing their influence on various aspects of individual and collective life. By examining their philosophical underpinnings, ethical implications, and cultural significance, we can gain a deeper understanding of how these belief systems continue to impact contemporary society.

Philosophical Underpinnings

Polytheism and monotheism have different philosophical foundations that shape their respective worldviews and perspectives on divinity. Polytheism, as the belief in multiple deities, recognizes and venerates a pantheon of gods and goddesses. This pluralistic perspective acknowledges the diversity of divine forces and allows for a multiplicity of interpretations and approaches to spirituality. In contrast, monotheism asserts the existence of a single supreme deity, emphasizing unity, transcendence, and the notion of a divine plan.

Exploring the Contrasts and Convergence of Polytheism and Monotheism

Exercise:

Engage in a comparative analysis of the philosophical underpinnings of polytheism and monotheism. Reflect on the implications of these different perspectives on human understanding of the divine, the nature of reality, and the purpose of life.

Cultural Significance

Polytheism and monotheism have played significant roles in shaping the cultural landscapes of various societies throughout history. From ancient civilizations to modern nations, religious beliefs have influenced art, literature, architecture, and societal norms. Polytheistic traditions often celebrate a rich mythology, with gods and goddesses representing different aspects of nature, human experience, and cosmic forces. Monotheistic religions, on the other hand, have produced sacred texts, moral codes, and architectural wonders that reflect their singular focus on the divine.

Exercise:

Choose a specific artwork, literary work, or architectural structure influenced by either polytheistic or monotheistic beliefs. Analyze its cultural significance, symbolic representations, and the impact of its religious context on its creation and interpretation.

Ethical Implications

Polytheism and monotheism also shape ethical frameworks and moral guidelines for their followers. While the ethical systems within each belief system can vary, they often provide a moral compass for individuals and communities. Polytheistic traditions may emphasize a more relativistic approach, with each deity embodying distinct virtues and values. This allows for diverse ethical perspectives within the belief system. In monotheistic religions, ethical principles are typically rooted in the teachings of a single divine authority, providing a more unified and absolute moral framework.

Exercise:

Compare and contrast the ethical implications of polytheism and monotheism. Explore how these belief systems address topics such as justice, compassion, honesty, and social responsibility. Consider the potential benefits and challenges of a relativistic versus an absolute ethical framework.

Individual and Community Identity

Polytheism and monotheism play significant roles in shaping individual and community identities. Beliefs and practices associated with these traditions provide individuals with a sense of purpose, belonging, and personal identity. Polytheistic traditions often allow individuals to connect with specific deities who resonate with their personal inclinations or aspirations. This individualized approach allows for a diverse range of spiritual paths within the overall framework of the belief system. Monotheistic religions, on the other hand, emphasize a collective identity centered around the worship of a single divine being, fostering a sense of unity and shared purpose among their followers.

Exercise:

Reflect on your own religious or spiritual identity. Consider how your beliefs and practices contribute to your sense of self and community. Explore the ways in which polytheistic or monotheistic principles align or differ from your own understanding of identity.

Contemporary Challenges and Opportunities

Polytheism and monotheism face various challenges and opportunities in the modern world. Globalization, secularization, and the rise of scientific knowledge have led to increased religious diversity and the emergence of new spiritual movements. Polytheistic and monotheistic belief systems must navigate these changes, engaging with contemporary issues such as religious pluralism, environmental sustainability, social justice, and interfaith dialogue. By adapting to these challenges and embracing opportunities for growth and collaboration, polytheistic and monotheistic traditions can continue to provide spiritual guidance and inspiration in the modern age.

Exercise:

Choose a contemporary issue or challenge facing polytheistic or monotheistic traditions. Discuss potential approaches or strategies that these belief systems can adopt to address the issue effectively and remain relevant in the modern world.

Conclusion

Polytheism and monotheism hold significant roles in modern society, shaping individual beliefs, cultural expressions, ethical frameworks, and collective identities. By understanding the philosophical underpinnings, cultural significance, ethical implications, and contemporary challenges of these belief systems, individuals can engage in critical reflection and dialogue, fostering mutual understanding and respect among diverse religious perspectives. As we navigate the complexities of the modern world, the exploration of polytheistic and monotheistic beliefs allows for a deeper appreciation of the human quest for meaning, spirituality, and connection with the divine.

Exercise:

Engage in a group discussion or debate on the role of polytheism and monotheism in modern society. Present different viewpoints and consider alternative perspectives, encouraging critical thinking and respectful dialogue.

Exploring the impact of these belief systems on political, social, and cultural contexts

Polytheistic and monotheistic belief systems have had profound impacts on political, social, and cultural contexts throughout history. In this section, we will delve into the intricate relationship between these belief systems and their influence on various aspects of human society. By examining historical examples and analyzing their implications, we can gain a deeper understanding of how polytheism and monotheism shape political structures, social hierarchies, and cultural expressions.

Political Impact

Polytheistic and monotheistic belief systems have significantly influenced political structures and governance models in different societies. In polytheistic traditions, deities often held positions of power and were regarded as patrons or protectors of specific cities or states. Ancient civilizations such as Mesopotamia and Egypt had complex religious hierarchies intertwined with their political systems. Monotheistic religions, on the other hand, introduced the concept of a supreme deity whose authority transcended earthly rulers. This notion of divine sovereignty has influenced the development of theocratic states and the idea of the divine right of kings.

Exercise:

Examine the political systems of two ancient civilizations, one polytheistic and one monotheistic. Compare their structures, power dynamics, and the role of religious beliefs in shaping political authority.

Social Impact

Polytheism and monotheism have shaped social hierarchies, norms, and values in different ways. Polytheistic belief systems often assigned specific roles and responsibilities to different deities, reflecting the various aspects of human life and society. This pluralistic approach allowed for a diverse range of social interactions and hierarchies. In contrast, monotheistic religions have advocated for moral codes and ethical principles that promote notions of equality, justice, and compassion. These values have influenced social movements, the treatment of marginalized groups, and the development of social welfare systems.

Exercise:

Discuss the social impact of polytheism and monotheism on gender roles, social justice, and community cohesion. Reflect on how these belief systems have influenced social norms, relationships, and the distribution of power within societies.

Cultural Impact

Polytheism and monotheism have left indelible marks on cultural expressions, artistic traditions, and rituals. Polytheistic belief systems often celebrated a diverse pantheon of gods and goddesses, each associated with specific domains such as fertility, war, or wisdom. These divine figures inspired religious ceremonies, artistic representations, and mythologies that reflected the cultural values and aspirations of ancient civilizations. In monotheistic traditions, the focus on a single divine entity has produced sacred texts, religious iconography, and architectural marvels that have become emblematic of cultural identities.

Exercise:

Choose a specific cultural artifact or practice influenced by either polytheistic or monotheistic beliefs. Analyze its symbolism, cultural significance, and the ways in which it reflects the spiritual worldview and values of the associated belief system.

Counterarguments and Dissenting Opinions

It is important to acknowledge that not all historical interactions between polytheistic or monotheistic belief systems and political, social, and cultural contexts have been positive or harmonious. There have been instances of religious intolerance, conflicts, and the imposition of beliefs on indigenous cultures. It is crucial to recognize and critically evaluate these counterarguments and dissenting opinions to gain a comprehensive understanding of the impact of these belief systems.

Exercise:

Engage in a debate or discussion on the positive and negative impacts of polytheistic and monotheistic belief systems on political, social, and cultural contexts. Present and evaluate different perspectives, considering the historical, social, and cultural factors that contribute to these viewpoints.

Conclusion

Polytheistic and monotheistic belief systems have exerted significant influence on political, social, and cultural contexts throughout history. By examining their impact, we can appreciate the intricate interplay between religious beliefs and human societies. Understanding the historical and contemporary implications of these belief systems allows us to foster dialogue, respect, and appreciation for diverse religious perspectives, promoting a more inclusive and harmonious world.

Exercise:

Reflect on how the exploration of the impact of polytheistic and monotheistic belief systems on political, social, and cultural contexts has shaped your understanding of the complex relationship between religion and society. Discuss any new insights or questions that have emerged through this exploration.

CHAPTER 3: HISTORICAL CONTEXT OF POLYTHEISM AND MONOTHEISM

In this chapter, we will embark on a journey through history to explore the rich and diverse historical contexts in which polytheism and monotheism emerged and flourished. By understanding the historical foundations of these belief systems, we can gain valuable insights into their development, evolution, and societal significance. Through the lens of Witchcraft, Divination, Herbalism, Shamanism, and Ecospirituality, we will delve into the ancient civilizations that laid the groundwork for the polytheistic and monotheistic traditions we encounter today.

Prehistoric Origins

The roots of polytheism and monotheism can be traced back to prehistoric times when early human societies sought to make sense of the world and the forces that shaped their existence. These ancient cultures developed complex mythologies, rituals, and practices that revolved around the worship of multiple deities or a singular divine being. Archaeological evidence, cave paintings, and ancient artifacts offer glimpses into the cosmologies and spiritual beliefs of our early ancestors.

Ancient Mesopotamia and Egypt

The civilizations of Mesopotamia and Egypt played significant roles in the development of polytheistic belief systems. Mesopotamia, known as the "Cradle of Civilization," gave rise to the Sumerians, Babylonians, and Assyrians, who worshipped a pantheon of gods and goddesses associated with natural phenomena, agriculture, and societal functions. The ancient Egyptians, with their complex religious practices, revered numerous deities, including Osiris, Isis, and Ra, each holding specific roles and responsibilities.

Exercise:

Compare and contrast the polytheistic beliefs and practices of Mesopotamia and Egypt, examining their pantheons, religious rituals, and societal impact.

Ancient Greece and Rome

Ancient Greece and Rome are renowned for their contributions to Western civilization and their influential polytheistic religions. Greek mythology introduced a rich cast of gods and goddesses, such as Zeus, Athena, and Aphrodite, who embodied various aspects of human life and nature. The Romans, heavily influenced by Greek culture, developed their own pantheon, merging deities from various conquered civilizations into their religious framework.

Exercise:

Explore the similarities and differences between Greek and Roman polytheism, focusing on the roles of mythology, religious practices, and the impact on societal structures.

Monotheism: Judaism and the Abrahamic Traditions

The emergence of monotheism marked a significant shift in religious thought, with Judaism playing a central role in its development. The Hebrew Bible, or Tanakh, laid the foundation for the monotheistic beliefs upheld by Judaism, Christianity, and Islam. The concept of a single, all-powerful God, Yahweh, brought forth a new understanding of divinity and shaped the moral and ethical principles of these Abrahamic traditions.

Exercise:

Examine the core tenets and theological principles of Judaism and its influence on the subsequent development of monotheistic belief systems, such as Christianity and Islam.

Counterarguments and Dissenting Opinions

As with any academic exploration, it is essential to consider counterarguments and dissenting opinions to develop a well-rounded understanding of the historical context of polytheism and monotheism. Some scholars propose alternative theories, challenge traditional narratives, or offer nuanced interpretations of historical evidence. By engaging with these divergent perspectives, we can expand our knowledge and foster critical thinking.

In this chapter's exploration of the historical context of polytheism and monotheism, we have journeyed through time, unraveling the intricate tapestry of ancient civilizations and their religious beliefs. From prehistoric cultures to the mighty empires of Mesopotamia, Egypt, Greece, and Rome, and the emergence of monotheistic traditions, we have witnessed the transformative power of these belief systems on human societies.

Ancient Polytheistic Religions

In this section, we will delve into the fascinating world of ancient polytheistic religions, exploring their beliefs, practices, and cultural significance. Polytheism, the worship of multiple deities, was prevalent in various ancient civilizations, leaving indelible imprints on human history. By examining the polytheistic traditions of Witchcraft, Divination, Herbalism, Shamanism, and Ecospirituality, we will unravel the intricate tapestry of these ancient belief systems and gain insights into their impact on society and individual spiritual experiences.

Mesopotamian Polytheism: The Gods of Sumer and Babylon

Our journey begins in Mesopotamia, the cradle of civilization, where the Sumerians and Babylonians flourished. These ancient cultures held a rich pantheon of gods and goddesses, each representing different aspects of nature, human life, and societal functions. For instance, the Sumerians revered Inanna, the goddess of love and fertility, while Enki was regarded as the god of wisdom and water. The Babylonians, influenced by their Sumerian predecessors, worshipped Marduk, the chief deity associated with kingship and power.

Egyptian Polytheism: The Mythology of the Pharaohs

In ancient Egypt, polytheism was at the heart of religious practices and played a significant role in shaping the Egyptian civilization. The Egyptians worshipped a multitude of gods and goddesses, attributing divine qualities to natural forces, celestial bodies, and animal forms. Ra, the sun god, was believed to traverse the sky each day, providing life-giving light and warmth. Osiris, the god of the afterlife and resurrection, played a pivotal role in Egyptian funerary rituals and beliefs.

Exercise:

Select a specific Egyptian god or goddess and explore their symbolism, associations, and importance within Egyptian polytheistic religion. Discuss their role in mythology and cultural practices.

Greek Polytheism: The Pantheon of Gods and Heroes

The ancient Greeks embraced a complex polytheistic system that intertwined with their daily lives, cultural expressions, and worldview. Greek mythology introduced a diverse pantheon of gods and goddesses, with Zeus as the supreme deity ruling over Mount Olympus. Each god or goddess possessed unique powers, dominions, and personalities, with Athena representing wisdom and warfare, Apollo embodying music and prophecy, and Aphrodite symbolizing love and beauty.

Exercise:

Compare and contrast the Greek pantheon with other polytheistic traditions, highlighting the distinctive attributes and roles of key deities. Analyze the influence of Greek mythology on various aspects of Greek society, such as art, literature, and religious practices.

Roman Polytheism: Adaptation and Syncretism

The Romans, heavily influenced by Greek culture, adopted and adapted much of the Greek pantheon, merging it with their own deities and religious practices. This process of syncretism resulted in a distinctive Roman polytheistic system. Jupiter, the Roman equivalent of Zeus, became the chief deity, embodying power and divine authority. The Romans also revered goddesses such as Minerva, associated with wisdom and strategic warfare, and Venus, the goddess of love and fertility.

Exercise:

Investigate the process of syncretism in Roman polytheism, examining the incorporation of Greek deities into the Roman religious framework. Discuss the cultural, political, and religious implications of this syncretic approach.

Celtic Polytheism: Nature Spirits and Ancestor Worship

Moving beyond the Mediterranean region, we encounter the rich tapestry of Celtic polytheism. The Celts revered nature spirits and held deep reverence for their ancestors. They believed in a multitude of deities associated with natural phenomena, such as Danu, the mother goddess, and Lugh, the god of light and skill. Celtic religious practices often involved rituals, sacrifices, and divination to communicate with the divine and seek guidance.

Exercise:

Explore the role of nature spirits and ancestor worship in Celtic polytheism, analyzing their significance within Celtic culture and spiritual practices. Discuss the ways in which the Celts interacted with and revered the natural world.

Ancient polytheistic religions formed the spiritual backbone of numerous civilizations, providing a framework for understanding the cosmos, human existence, and societal structures. Through the exploration of Mesopotamian, Egyptian, Greek, Roman, and Celtic polytheism, we have witnessed the diversity and complexity of these ancient belief systems. The gods and goddesses worshipped in these religions represented various facets of the human experience, from the natural elements to human virtues and vices.

Examining polytheistic belief systems in Mesopotamia, Egypt, and Greece

Polytheistic belief systems have played a significant role in shaping the religious and cultural landscapes of various civilizations throughout history. This section focuses on three major ancient civilizations: Mesopotamia, Egypt, and Greece. By exploring the polytheistic traditions within these societies, we gain insight into their cosmologies, religious practices, and the roles of gods and goddesses within their respective pantheons. Through a comparative analysis, we can identify both shared characteristics and distinct features that highlight the diversity and complexity of polytheistic belief systems.

Mesopotamian Polytheism: Ancestor of Ancient Religions

Mesopotamia, known as the "land between the rivers," encompassed the region of present-day Iraq and parts of Syria and Iran. It was home to several ancient civilizations, including the Sumerians, Babylonians, and Assyrians, who each developed their own polytheistic religious systems. The Mesopotamian pantheon consisted of numerous deities, with each city-state often elevating its patron deity to a prominent position.

The Sumerians, the earliest known civilization in Mesopotamia, worshipped a pantheon that included deities such as An, the god of the heavens, and Enlil, the god of wind and storms. The Babylonians, under the influence of their Sumerian predecessors, worshipped gods like Marduk, the chief deity associated with kingship and power. The Assyrians, known for their military prowess, revered deities like Ashur, the god of war and empire.

Exploring the Contrasts and Convergence of Polytheism and Monotheism

Exercise:

Research and analyze the role of a specific deity from Mesopotamian polytheism, examining their mythology, attributes, and significance within the religious and cultural contexts of Mesopotamia.

Egyptian Polytheism: A Tapestry of Gods and Myths

Ancient Egypt is renowned for its elaborate polytheistic belief system, centered around a vast pantheon of gods and goddesses. Egyptian religious beliefs were deeply intertwined with the natural world and the cycles of life and death. At the center of the Egyptian pantheon stood Ra, the sun god, who represented the creative and life-giving power of the sun. Other prominent deities included Osiris, the god of the afterlife and resurrection, and Isis, the goddess of magic and motherhood.

The Egyptians believed in the concept of ma'at, which encompassed order, balance, and justice. The gods and goddesses played vital roles in maintaining ma'at, and religious rituals and offerings were essential to ensure their continued favor. The construction of monumental temples and the practice of mummification were also significant aspects of Egyptian religious life.

The polytheistic belief system of ancient Egypt was a complex tapestry of gods and myths that shaped every aspect of Egyptian society. The Egyptians viewed their gods and goddesses as both divine beings and cosmic forces that influenced the world around them. Each deity had their own distinct attributes, roles, and mythology, contributing to the multifaceted nature of Egyptian polytheism.

At the heart of the Egyptian pantheon stood Ra, the sun god and the creator of the universe. Ra represented the life-giving power of the sun and was associated with concepts such as light, warmth, and growth. As the supreme deity, Ra held a prominent position in Egyptian religious beliefs and was often depicted as a falcon-headed man or as a sun disk.

Another significant deity in Egyptian polytheism was Osiris, the god of the afterlife and resurrection. Osiris played a pivotal role in Egyptian mythology, being the husband of Isis and the father of Horus. He symbolized the cycle of life, death, and rebirth and was particularly venerated during funeral rites and ceremonies related to the afterlife. The story of Osiris's death and resurrection served as a powerful narrative that conveyed the Egyptians' beliefs in the possibility of an eternal existence beyond death.

Isis, the goddess of magic and motherhood, was another prominent figure in the Egyptian pantheon. She was revered as a protector of the pharaoh, a healer, and a nurturing mother. Isis played a crucial role in the Osiris myth, where she used her magical abilities to revive her husband and conceive their son Horus. Her worship extended beyond Egypt's borders, and she became known as a goddess of wisdom and feminine power.

The concept of ma'at was fundamental to Egyptian religious beliefs. Ma'at encompassed the notions of order, balance, and justice in both the natural and human realms. It represented the harmonious functioning of the universe, and the gods and goddesses were responsible for maintaining ma'at. Egyptians believed that if ma'at was disrupted, chaos would ensue. Therefore, religious rituals, offerings, and moral conduct were crucial to ensure the preservation of ma'at and the continued favor of the deities.

The construction of grand temples was a significant aspect of Egyptian religious life. These temples served as sacred spaces where the gods and goddesses were worshipped and where rituals and ceremonies took place. The temples were architectural marvels adorned with intricate carvings, statues, and paintings, reflecting the Egyptians' dedication to their gods.

The practice of mummification also played a crucial role in Egyptian religious beliefs. Egyptians believed in an afterlife where the soul would continue its existence. Mummification, the preservation of the body, was performed to ensure the continuity of life after death. This process involved carefully removing organs, treating the body with preservatives, and wrapping it in bandages. The belief in the afterlife and the necessity of preserving the physical form emphasized the Egyptians' reverence for the cycle of life and the quest for immortality.

Exercise:

✧ Explore the mythology and symbolism of a specific Egyptian deity, discussing their role within the pantheon and their significance in Egyptian religious and cultural contexts. Analyze their representations in art and architecture, as well as their associations with specific rituals and ceremonies.

✧ Investigate the rituals and practices associated with mummification in ancient Egypt, discussing their religious and cultural significance. Compare the different techniques and beliefs surrounding mummification in different periods of Egyptian history.

✧ Select a specific Egyptian deity and explore their symbolism, roles, and associations within Egyptian polytheism. Discuss their mythological narratives and their relationship with other deities in the Egyptian pantheon.

In conclusion, Egyptian polytheism was a rich and intricate belief system that permeated every aspect of ancient Egyptian life. The gods and goddesses, such as Ra, Osiris, and Isis, played vital roles in maintaining order, balance, and justice within the cosmos. The concepts of ma'at, the construction of temples, and the practice of mummification were all integral parts of Egyptian religious practices. Exploring Egyptian polytheism allows us to gain insights into the worldview, values, and cultural expressions of this fascinating ancient civilization.

Greek Polytheism: The Birthplace of Mythology

Greek polytheism, often referred to as Hellenism, has had a profound influence on Western civilization. The Greeks worshipped a pantheon of gods and goddesses who reflected various aspects of human nature and the world around them. Zeus, the king of the gods, held supreme authority over Mount Olympus. Athena, the goddess of wisdom and warfare, embodied strategic thinking and courage. Apollo, the god of music and prophecy, represented the arts and the pursuit of knowledge.

Greek mythology, with its epic tales of heroes, gods, and monsters, served as a framework for understanding the human condition. The Greeks engaged in religious practices such as offering sacrifices, participating in festivals, and consulting oracles for guidance. The Olympic Games, held every four years, were also rooted in Greek religious traditions, dedicated to the gods and accompanied by rituals.

Conclusion

Polytheistic belief systems in Mesopotamia, Egypt, and Greece provided their respective civilizations with a rich spiritual framework. The gods and goddesses embodied various aspects of the natural world, human attributes, and societal ideals. Rituals, offerings, and myths formed integral parts of religious practice, guiding individuals and communities in their relationship with the divine.

Highlighting the pantheon of gods and goddesses in each civilization and their significance

In ancient civilizations, the belief in multiple gods and goddesses, known as polytheism, was a central aspect of religious and cultural practices. These pantheons of divine beings played significant roles in shaping the worldview, values, and rituals of these societies. This section will delve into three prominent civilizations—Mesopotamia, Egypt, and Greece—and explore their pantheons of gods and goddesses, examining their individual significance and their collective impact on the respective civilizations.

I. Mesopotamian Pantheon:

Enuma Elish: Creation Myth and the Divine Hierarchy

Analysis of the Enuma Elish, the Mesopotamian creation myth, and its portrayal of the divine order

Overview of key gods and goddesses in the Mesopotamian pantheon, such as Anu, Enlil, and Inanna

Exploration of their roles, attributes, and interactions within the pantheon and with humans

Examination of the influence of the divine hierarchy on social and political structures in Mesopotamian society

Babylonian and Assyrian Deities:

In-depth analysis of prominent deities like Marduk, Ishtar, and Ea

Examination of their associations, domains, and religious significance

Discussion of religious rituals, festivals, and cult practices dedicated to specific deities

Exploration of the divine aspects reflected in architectural structures, art, and inscriptions

II. Egyptian Pantheon:

Divine Family Dynamics: Osiris, Isis, and Horus

Investigation of the myth of Osiris, Isis, and Horus and its influence on Egyptian religious beliefs

Exploring the Contrasts and Convergence of Polytheism and Monotheism

Analysis of the roles and symbolism of Osiris as the god of the afterlife, Isis as the mother goddess, and Horus as the divine heir

Discussion of the cultural and societal implications of the divine family dynamics

Ra and the Solar Deities:

Examination of the significance of Ra, the sun god, and his association with creation and rulership

Analysis of other solar deities like Amun-Ra and Atum and their respective roles within the pantheon

Exploration of the connections between solar symbolism, pharaonic authority, and the religious worldview

III. Greek Pantheon:

Olympian Gods and Goddesses:

Overview of the twelve Olympians, including Zeus, Hera, Athena, Apollo, and Aphrodite

Analysis of their domains, characteristics, and interactions with humans and each other

Discussion of the role of the Greek pantheon in mythological narratives and epic literature

Regional Deities and Cults:

Exploration of regional gods and goddesses, such as Demeter, Dionysus, and Artemis

Analysis of their associations with specific regions, cities, or natural phenomena

Examination of cult practices, rituals, and festivals dedicated to regional deities

Conclusion:

The pantheons of gods and goddesses in ancient civilizations like Mesopotamia, Egypt, and Greece played vital roles in shaping the religious, cultural, and social landscapes of these societies. These divine beings were not only worshipped and revered but also served as archetypes and symbols that reflected various aspects of human existence. By understanding the significance of these pantheons, we gain valuable insights into the beliefs, values, and aspirations of these ancient civilizations.

Exercises:

Choose one god or goddess from each of the three civilizations discussed and analyze their attributes, symbols, and associations. Compare and contrast their roles and significance within their respective pantheons.

Explore the impact of the pantheons on artistic expressions, such as sculpture, paintings, or temple architecture, in each civilization. Discuss how the representation of gods and goddesses in art reflects their cultural importance.

Investigate the influence of the pantheons on societal roles and hierarchies. Analyze how certain gods or goddesses were associated with specific social groups or professions and how this impacted the power dynamics within these civilizations.

Transition to Monotheism

Throughout history, the development and transition of religious belief systems have played a significant role in shaping human societies and cultures. One crucial shift in religious paradigms occurred with the emergence and spread of monotheism, the belief in a single supreme deity. This section will explore the transition from polytheism to monotheism in different civilizations and examine the factors, historical contexts, and implications of this transformative process.

I. The Emergence of Monotheistic Concepts:

The emergence of monotheistic concepts marks a significant turning point in the history of religious belief systems. Monotheism, the belief in a single supreme deity, presents a contrasting worldview to polytheism, which recognizes multiple gods and goddesses. This section will delve into the definition and characteristics of monotheism as a religious belief system, compare it with polytheism, and explore the philosophical and theological foundations that underpin this concept.

Monotheism, at its core, asserts the existence of one supreme being who possesses ultimate power and authority. Unlike polytheism, which acknowledges the presence of multiple deities with varying domains of influence, monotheism emphasizes the unity and singularity of the divine. This monotheistic belief system offers a cohesive and centralized framework for understanding the divine, attributing all aspects of creation and existence to a single entity.

In contrast to the multifaceted pantheons of polytheistic religions, monotheism presents a more streamlined and coherent theological perspective. The monotheistic deity embodies characteristics such as omnipotence, omniscience, and omnipresence, reflecting a divine nature that encompasses all-encompassing power, complete knowledge, and ubiquitous presence. These attributes contribute to a sense of divine sovereignty and the belief that the monotheistic deity governs and guides all aspects of existence.

The emergence of monotheistic concepts can be traced back to ancient civilizations, where early religious ideas laid the groundwork for monotheistic thought. For instance, in ancient Egypt, Akhenaten's Atenism emerged as an early form of monotheism. Akhenaten worshiped the sun disc, Aten, as the supreme deity, emphasizing the singular divine power and rejecting the traditional polytheistic beliefs of the time. This early example showcases the inclination of human societies to explore and experiment with monotheistic ideas.

In the Hebrew tradition, monotheism played a pivotal role in shaping their religious beliefs. The Hebrews' concept of Yahweh, their primary deity, evolved over time, transitioning from a tribal god to a national and universal deity. The Hebrew Bible, or the Old Testament, elucidates the unique and exclusive nature of Yahweh, emphasizing the belief in one true God and condemning the worship of other deities. The Hebrew prophets played a significant role in promoting monotheistic beliefs and denouncing idolatry, further solidifying the transition to monotheism within Hebrew society.

Furthermore, Zoroastrianism, a dualistic religion originating in ancient Persia, contributed to the development and spread of monotheistic beliefs. Zoroastrianism revolves around the concept of Ahura Mazda, the supreme deity, who represents the forces of good in opposition to the forces of evil. This dualistic worldview and the focus on a singular supreme deity influenced later monotheistic religions, including Judaism and Christianity. The Persian conquests and the subsequent influence of Persian culture and religion on the Hebrews further contributed to the assimilation of monotheistic elements within their religious framework.

Hellenistic philosophy also played a crucial role in the synthesis of monotheistic thought. During the Hellenistic period, Greek philosophical ideas merged with monotheistic beliefs, resulting in the development of philosophical schools such as Neoplatonism and Stoicism. Philosophers like Philo of Alexandria sought to reconcile

Greek philosophy with monotheistic concepts, highlighting the compatibility and interconnectedness of these intellectual traditions.

The emergence and development of Christianity, as a monotheistic religion, further propelled the spread of monotheistic belief systems. Rooted in the teachings of Jesus Christ, Christianity emerged within the Roman Empire and gradually gained prominence as a distinct monotheistic faith. The theological foundations of Christianity, including the concept of the Trinity, solidified the monotheistic nature of the religion and influenced subsequent theological developments.

The transition to monotheism has had profound implications for religious diversity and pluralism. The exclusive claims of monotheistic religions have given rise to challenges and tensions, as they can clash with the belief systems and practices of polytheistic or other monotheistic traditions. However, monotheistic religions have also fostered interfaith dialogue and efforts towards religious tolerance, seeking to promote understanding and peaceful coexistence among diverse religious communities.

Furthermore, monotheism has influenced social structures, authority, and power dynamics within societies. Religious institutions and clergy often play a central role in monotheistic belief systems, serving as intermediaries between the divine and the human. Monotheistic religions have shaped moral and ethical frameworks, influencing societal values, laws, and social norms.

In conclusion, the emergence of monotheistic concepts has represented a significant shift in human religious thought and practice. Through an exploration of various civilizations and religious traditions, we have witnessed the evolution of monotheistic belief systems. From early proto-monotheistic elements to the influence of Zoroastrianism, Hellenistic philosophy, and the rise of Christianity, the journey to monotheism has shaped the religious, cultural, and social landscapes of human civilization. Understanding the historical contexts, philosophical underpinnings, and implications of this transition deepens our appreciation of the diverse religious beliefs and practices that have shaped our world.

II. The Hebrews and the Transition to Monotheism:

The Hebrews, an ancient Semitic people, played a significant role in the transition to monotheism. Their religious beliefs and practices underwent a transformation that ultimately led to the establishment of a monotheistic framework centered around their primary deity, Yahweh. This section will explore the Hebrew pantheon, the evolution of Yahweh's position, the role of Hebrew prophets, and the social, political, and cultural factors that contributed to the acceptance of monotheistic ideas among the Hebrews.

The Hebrew pantheon consisted of a collection of gods and goddesses, with Yahweh gradually emerging as the most prominent and central deity. Initially, Yahweh was worshipped as a tribal god, associated with a specific group of people. However, over time, the Hebrews' perception of Yahweh expanded beyond a local deity, and he came to be recognized as the national and universal God. This shift in perspective represented a crucial step in the Hebrews' journey towards monotheism.

The Hebrew Bible, also known as the Old Testament, provides insights into the unique and exclusive nature of Yahweh. It emphasizes Yahweh's supreme power, sovereignty, and distinctiveness. The Hebrews believed that Yahweh was the creator of the universe, the one true God who demanded exclusive worship and fidelity. This elevated status of Yahweh set the stage for the eventual transition to monotheism.

The Hebrew prophets played a pivotal role in promoting monotheistic beliefs and condemning polytheistic practices among the Hebrews. These prophetic figures, including Moses, Isaiah, and Jeremiah, acted as intermediaries between Yahweh and the Hebrew community, conveying divine messages and advocating for monotheistic worship. The prophets delivered teachings and revelations that emphasized Yahweh's oneness and the rejection of idolatry.

The Hebrew prophetic literature highlights the call for monotheism and the rejection of polytheistic worship. The prophetic texts often contain fierce denunciations of the worship of other gods, stressing the exclusive devotion owed to Yahweh. Through their prophecies, the Hebrew prophets aimed to redirect the religious focus of the Hebrews towards Yahweh alone, thereby solidifying the transition to monotheism.

Several factors contributed to the acceptance of monotheistic ideas among the Hebrews. First, the historical and cultural context in which the Hebrews lived played a crucial role. The Hebrews experienced various social, political, and religious changes, including interactions with neighboring cultures and the Babylonian exile. These circumstances exposed the Hebrews to diverse religious beliefs and practices, which likely influenced their own religious evolution.

Additionally, the Hebrews' perception of Yahweh was shaped by their collective experiences as a community. Their historical narratives, such as the exodus from Egypt and the establishment of the Israelite kingdom, reinforced the belief in Yahweh as the deliverer, protector, and covenant-making deity. These foundational stories solidified the Hebrews' attachment to Yahweh and fostered a sense of loyalty and commitment to monotheistic worship.

Furthermore, the Hebrews' monotheistic beliefs provided them with a sense of identity and unity as a distinct people. Monotheism served as a unifying force, distinguishing them from neighboring cultures and religious practices. By adhering to a singular deity, the Hebrews forged a cohesive religious and cultural identity that fostered a strong communal bond.

In conclusion, the Hebrews played a pivotal role in the transition to monotheism. The evolution of Yahweh's position from a tribal god to a national and universal deity, the influence of the Hebrew prophets, and the historical and cultural factors that shaped their religious development all contributed to the acceptance of monotheistic ideas among the Hebrews. The Hebrews' journey towards monotheism highlights the dynamic nature of religious belief systems and the complex interplay between historical, social, and cultural factors in shaping religious paradigms.

III. The Influence of Zoroastrianism and its Impact on Monotheistic Beliefs:

Zoroastrianism, an ancient Iranian religion founded by Zoroaster (also known as Zarathustra), exerted a significant influence on the development of monotheistic beliefs. With its dualistic worldview and emphasis on the struggle between good and evil forces, Zoroastrianism laid the groundwork for monotheistic concepts that later influenced religions such as Judaism, Christianity, and Islam. This section will explore the key elements of Zoroastrianism, its concept of Ahura Mazda as the supreme deity, and the Persian influence on monotheistic beliefs.

Zoroastrianism embraced a dualistic perspective that perceived the universe as a battleground between the forces of good and evil. Zoroaster's teachings emphasized the existence of Ahura Mazda as the supreme deity representing truth, righteousness, and order. Ahura Mazda was believed to be the creator of the universe and the source of all good. Opposing Ahura Mazda was Angra Mainyu, the embodiment of falsehood, evil, and chaos. The struggle between these two opposing forces, known as the cosmic battle, formed the central theme of Zoroastrianism.

Ahura Mazda's portrayal as the supreme deity in Zoroastrianism provided a foundation for monotheistic beliefs. The concept of a single, all-powerful God who stood above other deities resonated with later monotheistic traditions. Ahura Mazda's attributes aligned with the characteristics typically associated with a supreme deity, such as omniscience, omnipotence, and benevolence. Zoroastrianism's emphasis on monotheistic principles paved the way for the development of similar concepts in subsequent monotheistic religions.

The Persian influence on monotheistic beliefs can be observed in the historical context of the Hebrews and the emergence of monotheism within Judaism. The Hebrews came into contact with Persian culture and religion during the period of Persian domination, particularly after the Babylonian exile. This exposure to Persian ideas had a profound impact on Hebrew religious thought.

Persian concepts such as judgment, resurrection, and the eventual emergence of Satan found their way into Jewish and Christian literature. The Persian belief in a final judgment, where individuals would be held accountable for their actions, influenced the Hebrew concept of divine judgment and the establishment of a moral order. Similarly, the idea of resurrection and an afterlife gained prominence within Jewish and Christian eschatology, likely influenced by Persian beliefs.

Furthermore, the Persian influence is evident in the development of the figure of Satan in Jewish and Christian literature. The Zoroastrian concept of Angra Mainyu, the embodiment of evil, may have contributed to the emergence of Satan as a malevolent force opposing God. The dualistic framework provided by Zoroastrianism laid the groundwork for the development of Satan as a distinct character in monotheistic narratives.

The impact of Zoroastrianism on monotheistic beliefs extended beyond the Hebrews and influenced Christianity as well. Early Christians, particularly those living in regions with a strong Zoroastrian presence, encountered Zoroastrian ideas and motifs. This exposure likely shaped certain aspects of Christian theology, including the concepts of cosmic battle, dualism, and the struggle between good and evil.

In conclusion, Zoroastrianism played a crucial role in shaping monotheistic beliefs through its dualistic worldview, the concept of Ahura Mazda as the supreme deity, and the Persian influence on monotheistic religions. The emphasis on a cosmic battle between good and evil, the development of monotheistic principles, and the introduction of theological concepts like judgment and resurrection all find resonance in later monotheistic traditions. The rich tapestry of Zoroastrianism's influence continues to be woven into the fabric of monotheistic religions, adding depth and complexity to their theological landscapes.

IV. The Rise of Monotheism in Late Antiquity:

The rise of monotheism in late antiquity marked a significant shift in religious beliefs and practices across various regions. During this period, monotheistic traditions such as Christianity and Islam gained prominence and transformed the religious landscape of the ancient world. This section will explore the historical context, key figures, and factors contributing to the rise of monotheism in late antiquity.

Historical Context:

Late antiquity refers to the period between the 3rd and 7th centuries CE, characterized by significant political, social, and cultural changes. It was a time of transition, marked by the decline of classical empires and the emergence of new religious movements. The spread of Christianity and the subsequent rise of Islam played a central role in shaping the monotheistic landscape of late antiquity.

The Rise of Christianity:

Christianity, rooted in the teachings of Jesus Christ, experienced remarkable growth and influence during late antiquity. Despite early persecution, the religion gained traction through the efforts of influential figures such as Saint Paul, who spread its teachings across the Mediterranean world. The conversion of Emperor Constantine to Christianity in the 4th century CE marked a significant turning point, leading to the religion's acceptance and establishment as the state religion of the Roman Empire.

Christianity offered a monotheistic framework that appealed to individuals seeking spiritual fulfillment and salvation. Its emphasis on a personal relationship with God, the redemptive power of Jesus Christ, and the promise of eternal life resonated with people's aspirations for meaning and transcendence. The spread of Christianity was also facilitated by the organizational structure of the early Church, its missionary activities, and the translation of religious texts into local languages.

The Emergence of Islam:

In the 7th century CE, the Arabian Peninsula witnessed the rise of Islam, a monotheistic religion founded by the Prophet Muhammad. Islam presented a distinct monotheistic belief system centered around the worship of Allah, the one true God. Muhammad's revelations, recorded in the Quran, served as the foundation for Islamic teachings and practices.

The rapid expansion of Islam across the Arabian Peninsula and beyond was driven by several factors. The message of monotheism, social justice, and equality appealed to diverse communities, challenging prevailing social hierarchies. Additionally, the military successes of early Islamic armies, combined with a relatively tolerant approach toward conquered peoples, facilitated the spread of the faith.

Factors Contributing to the Rise of Monotheism:

Political Context: The political climate of late antiquity played a crucial role in the rise of monotheism. The adoption of Christianity as the state religion by the Roman Empire and later the establishment of Islam as a dominant political and religious force in the Arabian Peninsula created favorable conditions for the growth and consolidation of monotheistic beliefs.

Cultural and Intellectual Exchange: Late antiquity was characterized by significant cultural and intellectual exchange between different regions and civilizations. This exchange facilitated the spread of ideas, including monotheistic concepts, as scholars, traders, and travelers disseminated religious teachings and engaged in philosophical debates.

Social and Religious Dynamics: Monotheistic religions offered a sense of community, moral guidance, and a distinct religious identity. They provided individuals with a framework for understanding the world, navigating social relationships, and seeking personal salvation. The rise of monotheism coincided with a period of social and religious transformation, as people sought new ways to make sense of their existence.

In conclusion, the rise of monotheism in late antiquity was a multifaceted phenomenon shaped by historical, cultural, and religious factors. The growth of Christianity and the emergence of Islam as major monotheistic traditions transformed the religious landscape of the ancient world. These monotheistic belief systems offered individuals a sense of purpose, community, and spiritual fulfillment during a period of profound societal change. The influence of monotheism in late antiquity continues to resonate in contemporary religious practices and beliefs, reflecting its enduring significance in human history.

Conclusion:

The transition from polytheism to monotheism marked a significant shift in religious beliefs and practices across different civilizations. The emergence of monotheistic concepts challenged traditional polytheistic systems and presented new theological, philosophical, and social frameworks. Through the examination of various civilizations and religious traditions, we can gain a deeper understanding of the historical, cultural, and intellectual contexts that facilitated this transition. Exploring the transition to monotheism provides valuable insights into the dynamic nature of human religious expression and its profound impact on societies throughout history.

Investigating the emergence and development of monotheistic belief systems

The study of religious belief systems reveals a fascinating tapestry of human spirituality and the diverse ways in which individuals and societies have sought to understand and connect with the divine. One prominent trajectory in this exploration is the emergence and development of monotheistic belief systems, which center around the worship of a single supreme deity. This section will delve into the historical, cultural, and theological factors that contributed to the rise of monotheism, exploring its roots in ancient civilizations and tracing its evolution through time.

I. Proto-Monotheistic Tendencies in Ancient Civilizations:

While monotheism as a distinct religious belief system emerged later in history, there were notable proto-monotheistic tendencies in several ancient civilizations. These early religious concepts and practices laid the groundwork for monotheistic ideas and provide valuable insights into the evolution of human spirituality. This section will explore examples of proto-monotheistic tendencies in ancient civilizations, including Egypt, Akhenaten's Atenism, and the Hebrews.

Egypt: The Precedence of Aten

In ancient Egypt, a civilization renowned for its polytheistic traditions, there was an exceptional development during the reign of Pharaoh Akhenaten (1353-1336 BCE). Akhenaten introduced a radical monotheistic experiment known as Atenism, which focused on the worship of a single deity, Aten, represented by the sun disc.

Atenism departed from the conventional Egyptian pantheon by emphasizing the supremacy of Aten as the ultimate creator and sustainer of life. Akhenaten sought to shift religious practices, redirecting worship from the multitude of gods and goddesses to the singular deity, Aten. This marked a significant departure from traditional polytheism, reflecting a proto-monotheistic inclination.

The Hymn to the Aten, a poetic composition composed during Akhenaten's reign, provides insights into the monotheistic character of Atenism. The hymn expresses the uniqueness and omnipotence of Aten, portraying the deity as the sole source of life, light, and sustenance. While Atenism was short-lived and faced opposition after Akhenaten's death, it represents a notable instance of proto-monotheistic thought within ancient Egypt.

Akhenaten's Atenism: Monotheism in Ancient Egypt

Akhenaten's Atenism, as mentioned above, deserves further examination due to its distinctive monotheistic features. During his reign, Akhenaten made significant religious and artistic reforms, emphasizing the singular worship of Aten. Temples dedicated to other deities were closed, and images of Aten were prominently displayed, symbolizing the Pharaoh's connection with the divine.

Atenism's monotheistic tendencies extended beyond religious practice. The artistic representations of Akhenaten and his family depict them in a naturalistic style, emphasizing their physical features and familial relationships. This marked a departure from the traditional idealized and formalized artistic conventions of Egyptian art, reflecting a more personal and intimate connection with the divine.

Akhenaten's Atenism faced opposition from the religious establishment, and after his death, Egypt reverted to its polytheistic traditions. However, the Atenist experiment remains a crucial precursor to later monotheistic developments, highlighting the potential for proto-monotheistic ideas to emerge even within highly polytheistic cultures.

Hebrews: Monotheistic Seeds in Ancient Israel

The ancient Hebrews, an influential Semitic people, played a vital role in the development of monotheism. The Hebrew Bible, particularly the Torah, presents a progressive revelation of monotheistic ideas within ancient Israelite society.

The Hebrews' religious beliefs evolved over time, with early indications of henotheism, the worship of one god while recognizing the existence of others. Yahweh, the personal name of God, became increasingly central in Hebrew theology. The Exodus narrative and the revelation of the Ten Commandments reinforced Yahweh's unique status as the deliverer and lawgiver of the Hebrew people.

The Hebrew prophets played a significant role in promoting monotheistic beliefs and challenging polytheistic practices. Prophetic texts, such as those of Isaiah, Jeremiah, and Ezekiel, contain powerful declarations of Yahweh's singular divinity, condemning idolatry and calling for exclusive devotion to the one true God.

The Hebrews' encounter with other cultures, such as the Babylonians and Persians, also influenced their religious worldview. During the Babylonian exile, the Hebrews grappled with questions of national identity and the relationship between Yahweh and foreign deities. This period saw a growing emphasis on monotheistic principles, with Yahweh portrayed as the supreme and universal God.

The Hebrews' transition to monotheism was a complex process influenced by historical, cultural, and religious factors. It set the stage for the emergence of the monotheistic traditions of Judaism, Christianity, and Islam, which would shape the religious landscape of the world.

Conclusion

The presence of proto-monotheistic tendencies in ancient civilizations, such as Egypt and the Hebrews, demonstrates the human inclination toward a singular supreme deity. These early religious expressions laid the foundation for the development of monotheistic beliefs that would later shape the course of history. The exploration of these proto-monotheistic ideas provides valuable insights into the evolution of human spirituality and the enduring quest for understanding the nature of the divine.

II. Monotheism in Ancient Israel:

Ancient Israel holds a significant place in the history of monotheism. The development of monotheistic beliefs and practices among the Israelites shaped not only their own religious identity but also had a profound influence on later monotheistic traditions. This section will explore the emergence and evolution of monotheism in ancient Israel, focusing on the unique religious worldview of the Israelites and the role of key figures and texts in promoting monotheistic beliefs.

The Unique Religious Worldview of the Israelites

The religious worldview of the ancient Israelites was distinct in its emphasis on monotheism. The Israelites believed in the existence of a single, supreme deity known as Yahweh. This belief set them apart from the polytheistic practices of their neighboring cultures.

Yahweh was understood as the creator and sustainer of the universe, the God who entered into a covenant relationship with the Israelites. This covenant, established with the patriarchs and reaffirmed through Moses, formed the basis of Israel's religious identity and provided a framework for their monotheistic beliefs.

The Evolution of Monotheism in Ancient Israel

The Hebrew Bible, particularly the Torah, provides valuable insights into the development of monotheism among the Israelites. It traces the evolution of their religious beliefs and the challenges they faced in maintaining monotheism amidst the influences of surrounding polytheistic cultures.

✧   **Early Indications of Monotheistic Tendencies**

Early in Israel's history, there were indications of henotheistic tendencies, where Yahweh was recognized as the primary God while acknowledging the existence of other gods. However, as Israel's understanding of Yahweh deepened, monotheistic principles began to emerge.

✧   **The Exodus and the Revelation of Yahweh**

The Exodus narrative played a crucial role in solidifying the monotheistic beliefs of the Israelites. The deliverance of the Israelites from slavery in Egypt and the revelation of the divine law at Mount Sinai established Yahweh's unique position as their God and the source of their moral and religious obligations.

✧   **The Role of the Prophets**

The Hebrew prophets played a central role in promoting and defending monotheism. They challenged the worship of other gods, denounced idolatry, and proclaimed the exclusive sovereignty of Yahweh. The prophetic texts, found in books such as Isaiah, Jeremiah, and Ezekiel, contain powerful declarations of Yahweh's oneness and supremacy.

The Monotheistic Identity of Ancient Israel

Monotheism became a defining aspect of Israel's religious identity. It influenced their worship practices, ethical teachings, and social structures. The monotheistic worldview provided a foundation for monotheistic beliefs and practices in subsequent religious traditions, including Judaism, Christianity, and Islam.

The Israelites' commitment to monotheism was tested throughout their history. They faced the temptation to adopt the gods of their neighbors and encountered periods of idolatry and syncretism. However, monotheism remained a core tenet of their faith, and monotheistic principles continued to shape their religious and cultural development.

Conclusion

The emergence and evolution of monotheism among the ancient Israelites marked a significant milestone in the history of religious thought. Their unique religious worldview, centered on the worship of Yahweh as the sole God, set the stage for the development of monotheistic traditions that would profoundly impact human civilization. The monotheistic identity of ancient Israel continues to resonate through the religious beliefs and practices of millions of people worldwide.

III. Zoroastrianism and the Dualistic Monotheism:

Zoroastrianism, originating in ancient Persia, represents a notable example of a dualistic monotheistic belief system. This section will delve into the key aspects of Zoroastrianism, including its dualistic worldview, the concept of Ahura Mazda as the supreme deity, and the eternal struggle between good and evil forces.

The Origins and Teachings of Zoroastrianism

Zoroastrianism, founded by the prophet Zoroaster (or Zarathustra) around the 6th century BCE, emerged in the region of ancient Persia, present-day Iran. Zoroaster's teachings were compiled in the holy scriptures known as the Avesta.

Dualistic Worldview and Cosmic Struggle

Central to Zoroastrianism is its dualistic worldview, which posits the existence of two opposing cosmic forces: Ahura Mazda (the Wise Lord) and Angra Mainyu (the Destructive Spirit). This duality forms the basis of Zoroastrian theology and ethics.

Ahura Mazda: Supreme Deity of Light and Wisdom

In Zoroastrianism, Ahura Mazda represents the supreme deity associated with goodness, light, wisdom, and truth. Ahura Mazda is regarded as the creator of the universe, embodying qualities such as justice and order. The followers of Zoroastrianism strive to align themselves with the divine attributes of Ahura Mazda.

Angra Mainyu: The Destructive Spirit

Angra Mainyu, also known as Ahriman, is the opposing force to Ahura Mazda in Zoroastrianism. Angra Mainyu embodies evil, chaos, and falsehood. The struggle between Ahura Mazda and Angra Mainyu forms the cosmic battle between good and evil, light and darkness.

Ethical Dualism and Human Agency

Zoroastrianism places significant emphasis on human agency and ethical responsibility. Individuals are seen as active participants in the ongoing struggle between good and evil. They are encouraged to choose the path of righteousness and align themselves with the divine will of Ahura Mazda.

Eschatology and the Final Triumph of Good

Zoroastrian eschatology envisions a future apocalyptic event in which Ahura Mazda will ultimately triumph over evil. This belief in a final judgment, resurrection, and the eventual defeat of Angra Mainyu influenced later monotheistic traditions such as Judaism, Christianity, and Islam.

Influence on Later Monotheistic Beliefs

Zoroastrianism exerted a considerable influence on later monotheistic religions, particularly during the Achaemenid Persian Empire. Persian cultural and religious ideas, including concepts of judgment, resurrection, and the battle between good and evil, found their way into Jewish, Christian, and Islamic thought.

Conclusion

Zoroastrianism's dualistic monotheism with its focus on the cosmic struggle between Ahura Mazda and Angra Mainyu provides a distinctive perspective on monotheistic beliefs. The concepts of good and evil, light and darkness, and the ethical responsibility of human beings resonate throughout Zoroastrian teachings. The impact of Zoroastrianism extends beyond its historical context, influencing the development of monotheistic traditions and contributing to the diversity of religious thought in human history.

IV. Monotheism in the Hellenistic World and Beyond:

The Hellenistic period, which followed the conquests of Alexander the Great, witnessed the spread of Greek culture and the fusion of various civilizations. During this time, monotheistic ideas and belief systems emerged, challenging the prevailing polytheistic traditions. This section will explore the development of monotheism in the Hellenistic world and its subsequent impact on religious thought.

The Influence of Greek Philosophy

Greek philosophy, particularly the works of Plato and Aristotle, played a significant role in shaping monotheistic thought in the Hellenistic world. Philosophers like Plato posited the existence of a supreme, transcendent being, often referred to as the "First Cause" or the "Prime Mover," who was responsible for the order and harmony observed in the universe.

The Jewish Influence

The Jewish community, known for its monotheistic beliefs, encountered the Hellenistic culture and underwent a complex process of acculturation. The conquests of Alexander the Great and the subsequent rule of the Seleucid Empire in Judea brought Greek influence to the region, leading to a clash between Hellenistic culture and Jewish traditions.

Hellenistic Judaism and the Development of Jewish Monotheism

Hellenistic Judaism emerged as a unique blend of Jewish monotheism and Hellenistic thought. It sought to reconcile Jewish religious beliefs with Greek philosophy, resulting in the development of concepts such as the Logos (the divine Word) and the notion of a transcendent, all-powerful God.

Philo of Alexandria and Syncretism

Philo of Alexandria, a prominent Jewish philosopher of the Hellenistic period, sought to bridge the gap between Greek philosophy and Jewish monotheism. He proposed a synthesis of Greek philosophy, particularly Platonic ideas, with Jewish theological concepts. Philo's writings became influential in shaping Hellenistic Jewish thought and contributed to the philosophical underpinnings of early Christian theology.

The Rise of Mystery Cults and Syncretism

The Hellenistic period witnessed the proliferation of mystery cults, which offered initiation rituals and promised individual salvation. These cults often combined elements of Greek, Egyptian, and Eastern religious traditions, blurring the boundaries between different belief systems. Syncretism, the merging of different religious practices and ideas, led to the emergence of hybrid religious systems that incorporated monotheistic elements.

Neoplatonism and the One

Neoplatonism, a philosophical and mystical movement that flourished during the late Hellenistic and early Christian eras, emphasized the existence of a transcendent, ineffable "One" as the ultimate source of all reality. Influenced by Plato and other ancient Greek philosophers, Neoplatonism sought to reconcile philosophical inquiry with mystical experiences and the longing for union with the divine.

Impact on Christianity and Beyond

The rise of monotheistic ideas in the Hellenistic world, along with the spread of Hellenistic culture and the conquests of Alexander the Great, laid the groundwork for the subsequent emergence of Christianity. Early Christian theologians, influenced by Hellenistic philosophy and Jewish monotheism, developed a distinct monotheistic framework that shaped the foundations of the Christian faith.

Conclusion

The Hellenistic period marked a significant shift in religious thought, as monotheistic ideas began to challenge the dominance of polytheism. Greek philosophy, Jewish monotheism, and syncretistic practices in the Hellenistic world contributed to the development of monotheistic belief systems. These ideas continued to evolve and have a lasting impact on subsequent religious traditions, particularly Christianity. The interplay between Greek philosophical concepts, Jewish monotheism, and the cultural exchanges of the Hellenistic era enriched the religious landscape of the time and set the stage for the development of diverse monotheistic traditions in the centuries that followed.

Tracing the transition from polytheism to monotheism in ancient civilizations (e.g., Akhenaten's Atenism)

The transition from polytheism to monotheism represents a significant shift in religious belief systems, reshaping the spiritual landscapes of ancient civilizations. One notable example of this transition can be found in the religious reforms initiated by the pharaoh Akhenaten during the Amarna Period in ancient Egypt. Examining Akhenaten's Atenism provides valuable insights into the process of transitioning from a polytheistic worldview to the worship of a single deity.

The Context of Ancient Egyptian Polytheism

Ancient Egypt, renowned for its rich polytheistic belief system, worshipped a pantheon of gods and goddesses, each associated with different aspects of nature, society, and the afterlife. The religious practices and rituals of the Egyptians were deeply intertwined with their daily lives, with offerings and ceremonies designed to ensure the favor of the gods and maintain cosmic order.

The Rise of Atenism

During the reign of Pharaoh Akhenaten (1353-1336 BCE), significant religious reforms were enacted, ultimately leading to the emergence of Atenism. Akhenaten, previously known as Amenhotep IV, sought to consolidate religious power and emphasize the worship of the solar deity, Aten. This marked a departure from the traditional pantheon, where deities like Amun-Ra and Osiris held central roles.

The Key Tenets of Atenism

Atenism centered on the belief in a single god, the Aten, represented by the sun's disc with rays extending downward, ending in human hands. The Aten was perceived as the sole creator of the universe and the source of life, providing light, warmth, and sustenance to all living beings. Akhenaten emphasized the Aten's unique and exclusive status as the supreme deity.

Religious and Cultural Impact

The introduction of Atenism had significant implications for Egyptian society. Akhenaten shifted the focus of worship to the Aten and established a new capital, Amarna, dedicated to the Aten's cult. The pharaoh and his family were depicted in unique artistic styles, emphasizing naturalistic portrayals and the intimacy between the royal family and the Aten.

Resistance and Aftermath

Although Akhenaten implemented his religious reforms with determination, Atenism faced resistance from traditional priests, nobles, and the populace. The abrupt and radical nature of the changes, including the closure of temples dedicated to other gods, sparked social and political unrest. After Akhenaten's death, his son Tutankhamun restored the traditional pantheon and reversed the religious policies of his father.

Legacy and Influence

Despite its relatively short-lived prominence, Atenism left a lasting impact on Egyptian religious and artistic expressions. The concept of monotheism introduced by Akhenaten challenged the established order of polytheistic worship and offered an alternative understanding of divine power. The Aten's association with cosmic harmony, light, and creation resonated with subsequent religious and philosophical traditions.

Comparative Analysis

Akhenaten's Atenism provides an intriguing case study for examining the broader transition from polytheism to monotheism in ancient civilizations.

Comparative analysis with other monotheistic developments, such as the emergence of Yahweh worship among the Hebrews or the later rise of monotheistic belief systems in the Hellenistic world, helps to identify commonalities and differences in the process and motivations behind these transitions.

Conclusion

The transition from polytheism to monotheism, exemplified by Akhenaten's Atenism, represents a profound shift in religious thought and practice. By tracing the historical, cultural, and theological aspects of this transition, we gain valuable insights into the dynamics of religious change and the complexities of monotheistic belief systems. Akhenaten's experimentation with monotheism in ancient Egypt sets a precedent for future developments in monotheistic traditions and their enduring impact on human history.

Abrahamic Religions

The Abrahamic religions—Judaism, Christianity, and Islam—are a group of monotheistic faiths that trace their origins back to the figure of Abraham. These religions share certain core beliefs, texts, and ethical principles while also having distinct theological and historical developments. This section will explore the key characteristics and historical trajectories of Judaism, Christianity, and Islam.

✧ Judaism

Judaism is the oldest of the Abrahamic religions, with roots dating back more than 3,000 years. It is centered around the Hebrew Bible (Tanakh) and the teachings and traditions contained therein. Key elements of Judaism include:

1. Covenant with God: Judaism emphasizes the covenant between God and the Jewish people, as established with Abraham. This covenant outlines the expectations, commandments, and promises between God and the Jewish community.

2. Torah and Law: The Torah, comprising the first five books of the Hebrew Bible, serves as the foundational religious text for Judaism. It includes legal codes, moral teachings, narratives, and wisdom literature.

3. Synagogue Worship: Synagogues are central places of worship and community gatherings for Jews. Services often involve prayer, Torah reading, and communal rituals.

4.   Ethical Monotheism: Judaism places a strong emphasis on ethical behavior and the worship of a single, transcendent God. Jews are called to follow moral principles and live a righteous life in accordance with God's commandments.

✧   Christianity

Christianity emerged in the 1st century CE as a distinct religious movement within Judaism, eventually evolving into a separate faith. It centers on the life, teachings, death, and resurrection of Jesus Christ. Key elements of Christianity include:

1.   Jesus Christ: Christians believe that Jesus is the Messiah, the Son of God who came to Earth to redeem humanity. His teachings, miracles, crucifixion, and resurrection form the cornerstone of Christian faith.

2.   New Testament: The New Testament, which includes the Gospels, Acts, Epistles, and Revelation, complements and expands upon the Hebrew Bible. It narrates the life of Jesus, provides theological teachings, and documents the early Christian community.

3.   Sacraments and Worship: Christians engage in sacramental practices such as baptism and the Eucharist (also known as Communion or the Lord's Supper). Worship is conducted in churches, with sermons, hymns, and rituals.

Salvation and Grace: Christianity teaches that salvation comes through faith in Jesus Christ and God's grace, rather than solely through adherence to religious laws. The concept of salvation and the afterlife play central roles in Christian theology.

✧   Islam

Islam emerged in the 7th century CE in the Arabian Peninsula through the revelations received by the Prophet Muhammad. It is based on the Quran, which Muslims believe to be the direct word of God. Key elements of Islam include:

1.   Five Pillars of Islam: The Five Pillars form the framework for Muslim religious practice and include the declaration of faith (Shahada), daily prayers (Salat), giving of alms (Zakat), fasting during Ramadan (Sawm), and pilgrimage to Mecca (Hajj).

2.   Quran and Sunnah: The Quran is the central religious text in Islam, believed to be a revelation from God. The Sunnah, based on the practices and sayings of Muhammad, provides additional guidance on how to live a faithful life.

3.   Mosque and Friday Prayer: Muslims gather for congregational worship in mosques, which serve as community centers and educational institutions. Friday Prayer (Jummah) is an important weekly communal worship gathering.

4.   Tawhid and Submission to God: Islam emphasizes the oneness of God (Tawhid) and the complete submission of believers to God's will. Muslims strive to live a righteous life and follow Islamic principles in all aspects of life.

The Abrahamic religions have shaped the course of human history and continue to be influential today. While sharing commonalities in their monotheistic foundations and Abrahamic heritage, each religion has its unique doctrines, practices, and interpretations. Understanding the complexities and contributions of these religions is vital for comprehending the religious landscape of the world and fostering interfaith dialogue and understanding.

Exploring the historical context of Judaism as the precursor to Christianity and Islam

Judaism, as one of the oldest monotheistic religions, serves as a significant precursor to both Christianity and Islam. Understanding the historical context in which Judaism emerged is crucial for comprehending the development of these later Abrahamic religions. This section will delve into the historical context of Judaism and its influence on the subsequent rise of Christianity and Islam.

Ancient Israel and the Hebrew Bible

The origins of Judaism can be traced back to ancient Israel, a region situated in the eastern Mediterranean. Around the 2nd millennium BCE, the Israelites, a Semitic people, established their presence in the land. The Hebrew Bible, also known as the Tanakh, serves as a primary historical and religious text for understanding this period.

A. Covenant and Monotheism

Central to the development of Judaism was the concept of the covenant, a sacred agreement between God and the Israelites. According to biblical accounts, God entered into a covenant with Abraham, promising him numerous descendants and the land of Canaan. This covenant established a special relationship between God and the

Israelite people, emphasizing their chosen status and the ethical obligations they had to fulfill.

Another significant aspect of ancient Israelite religion was its monotheistic inclination. While neighboring civilizations often practiced polytheism, the Israelites emphasized the worship of a single, all-powerful God. This monotheistic belief set them apart from other societies of the time and laid the foundation for the subsequent development of monotheistic faiths.

B. Exile and Return

The history of ancient Israel is marked by various periods of political turmoil, including foreign conquests and the subsequent exile of the Israelite population. In the 6th century BCE, the Babylonians conquered the kingdom of Judah, leading to the exile of many Israelites in Babylon. This period, known as the Babylonian Captivity, had a profound impact on Jewish identity and religious practices.

However, the Babylonian Captivity was not the end of the story for the Israelites. After the Persian conquest of Babylon, King Cyrus issued a decree allowing the exiled Israelites to return to their homeland. This marked the beginning of the restoration of Jewish life in the region and set the stage for the subsequent developments that would shape the history of Judaism.

Judaism's Influence on Christianity

Christianity emerged in the 1st century CE as a distinct religious movement within Judaism. Jesus of Nazareth, considered by Christians to be the Messiah and the Son of God, preached a message that resonated with many Jews of the time. The historical context of Judaism played a crucial role in shaping the early Christian movement.

A. Messianic Expectations

In the 1st century CE, many Jews held Messianic expectations, anticipating the arrival of a Messiah who would liberate them from Roman rule and establish a new era of peace and justice. Jesus' teachings and actions were seen by some as fulfilling these Messianic hopes, leading to his growing popularity among certain Jewish circles.

B. Jesus' Crucifixion and Resurrection

Jesus' crucifixion and subsequent resurrection became central events in Christian theology. According to Christian belief, Jesus' sacrificial death and resurrection provided salvation and reconciliation between God and humanity. These events, deeply rooted in Jewish religious concepts and symbols, took on new significance within the emerging Christian framework.

C. The Expansion of Christianity

Following Jesus' death and resurrection, his followers, known as the apostles, spread his teachings, eventually reaching beyond Jewish communities. The inclusion of non-Jewish converts, known as Gentiles, into the early Christian movement significantly transformed its character and led to the separation of Christianity from its Jewish roots.

Judaism's Influence on Islam

Islam, founded by the Prophet Muhammad in the 7th century CE, also emerged in a predominantly Jewish and Christian context. The historical context of Judaism played a significant role in shaping the development of Islamic beliefs and practices.

A. Islamic View of Judaism

Islam recognizes Judaism as one of the earlier Abrahamic religions and holds a deep respect for Jewish prophets, such as Moses and Abraham, considering them as important figures in the history of divine revelation. Islamic teachings acknowledge the Hebrew Bible and share many narratives and moral principles with Judaism.

B. Connection to Abraham and Monotheism

Similar to Judaism, Islam emphasizes the connection to the figure of Abraham, who is considered a patriarch and a prophet. Islamic teachings uphold monotheism as a core principle, declaring the oneness of God (Allah) and rejecting polytheistic beliefs.

C. The Qur'an and Jewish Influences

The Qur'an, the central religious text of Islam, contains references to numerous Jewish figures and stories, including Adam, Noah, Moses, and David. These shared narratives demonstrate the historical and theological links between Judaism and Islam and underscore their common Abrahamic heritage.

Conclusion

The historical context of Judaism as the precursor to Christianity and Islam is essential for comprehending the development and interplay of these Abrahamic religions. The roots of Judaism in ancient Israel, the covenant with God, the exile and return, and the influence of Judaism on the emergence and expansion of Christianity and Islam all contribute to a deeper understanding of the interconnectedness and historical evolution of these religious traditions.

The impact of monotheistic beliefs on the development of Western civilization

Monotheistic beliefs, particularly those associated with Judaism, Christianity, and Islam, have had a profound and lasting impact on the development of Western civilization. The ethical principles, social structures, intellectual traditions, and cultural values derived from monotheistic religions have shaped various aspects of Western society. This section will explore the significant impact of monotheistic beliefs on the development of Western civilization.

Ethical and Moral Foundations

Monotheistic religions have provided a moral and ethical framework that has influenced Western societies for centuries. The Ten Commandments in Judaism, the teachings of Jesus in Christianity, and the moral codes outlined in the Qur'an in Islam have played a central role in shaping ethical values and guiding individual and communal behavior.

A. Concepts of Righteousness and Justice

Monotheistic beliefs emphasize the concepts of righteousness, justice, and the pursuit of the common good. The notion that individuals are accountable to a single divine being encourages personal responsibility and the promotion of fairness and equality. These principles have laid the foundation for Western legal systems, human rights movements, and the development of democratic ideals.

B. Emphasis on Compassion and Social Responsibility

Monotheistic teachings emphasize compassion, empathy, and the importance of caring for others, particularly the marginalized and vulnerable members of society. The value placed on acts of charity and social responsibility has influenced Western charitable institutions, welfare systems, and initiatives aimed at addressing social injustices.

Intellectual and Philosophical Contributions

Monotheistic beliefs have also made significant contributions to Western intellectual and philosophical traditions, fostering critical thinking, theological debates, and the pursuit of knowledge. The philosophical inquiries and theological discourses within monotheistic frameworks have stimulated intellectual curiosity and shaped Western philosophical, scientific, and artistic endeavors.

A. Development of Rationality and Reasoning

Monotheistic religions have encouraged the use of reason and critical thinking in the interpretation of sacred texts and the exploration of theological concepts. This emphasis on rationality has contributed to the development of Western philosophy, scientific inquiry, and the tradition of logical reasoning.

B. Influence on Education and Higher Learning

The establishment of universities and educational institutions in Western civilizations owes much to the influence of monotheistic religions. Early Christian monastic schools, Islamic madrasas, and Jewish centers of learning provided a foundation for the pursuit of knowledge, scholarly research, and the preservation of ancient texts. These institutions played a vital role in the development of Western education systems and the advancement of various academic disciplines.

Cultural and Artistic Expressions

Monotheistic beliefs have profoundly influenced Western artistic expressions, architecture, literature, and music. The grand cathedrals, mosques, and synagogues, adorned with intricate artwork and sacred symbols, stand as testaments to the cultural impact of monotheistic religions.

A. Art and Architecture

Religious themes and narratives have been central to Western art, with depictions of biblical stories, saints, and religious icons serving as inspiration for artists throughout history. The artistic expressions found in religious manuscripts, paintings, sculptures, and stained glass windows reflect the religious devotion and the quest for spiritual transcendence.

B. Literary Traditions

Monotheistic religions have also contributed to Western literary traditions, producing sacred texts, theological treatises, and philosophical works. The Bible, the Qur'an, and religious commentaries have shaped the literary landscape, inspiring countless writers, poets, and playwrights.

C. Music and Devotional Practices

Music has played a vital role in religious worship and spiritual practices within monotheistic traditions. Choral music, hymns, and chants have been integral to religious ceremonies and have influenced the development of Western music, including classical, choral, and sacred compositions.

Conclusion

The impact of monotheistic beliefs on the development of Western civilization is far-reaching and multifaceted. The ethical foundations, intellectual contributions, and cultural expressions derived from monotheistic religions have shaped Western societies, influencing moral values, philosophical inquiries, educational systems, artistic traditions, and cultural identities. Recognizing and understanding the influence of monotheistic beliefs is essential for comprehending the historical and cultural development of Western civilization.

Polytheism and Monotheism in Eastern Religions

Monotheistic beliefs, particularly those associated with Judaism, Christianity, and Islam, have had a profound and lasting impact on the development of Western civilization. The ethical principles, social structures, intellectual traditions, and cultural values derived from monotheistic religions have shaped various aspects of Western society. This section will explore the significant impact of monotheistic beliefs on the development of Western civilization.

Ethical and Moral Foundations

Monotheistic religions have provided a moral and ethical framework that has influenced Western societies for centuries. The Ten Commandments in Judaism, the teachings of Jesus in Christianity, and the moral codes outlined in the Qur'an in Islam have played a central role in shaping ethical values and guiding individual and communal behavior.

A. Concepts of Righteousness and Justice

Monotheistic beliefs emphasize the concepts of righteousness, justice, and the pursuit of the common good. The notion that individuals are accountable to a single divine being encourages personal responsibility and the promotion of fairness and equality. These principles have laid the foundation for Western legal systems, human rights movements, and the development of democratic ideals.

B. Emphasis on Compassion and Social Responsibility

Monotheistic teachings emphasize compassion, empathy, and the importance of caring for others, particularly the marginalized and vulnerable members of society. The value placed on acts of charity and social responsibility has influenced Western charitable institutions, welfare systems, and initiatives aimed at addressing social injustices.

Intellectual and Philosophical Contributions

Monotheistic beliefs have also made significant contributions to Western intellectual and philosophical traditions, fostering critical thinking, theological debates, and the pursuit of knowledge. The philosophical inquiries and theological discourses within monotheistic frameworks have stimulated intellectual curiosity and shaped Western philosophical, scientific, and artistic endeavors.

A. Development of Rationality and Reasoning

Monotheistic religions have encouraged the use of reason and critical thinking in the interpretation of sacred texts and the exploration of theological concepts. This emphasis on rationality has contributed to the development of Western philosophy, scientific inquiry, and the tradition of logical reasoning.

B. Influence on Education and Higher Learning

The establishment of universities and educational institutions in Western civilizations owes much to the influence of monotheistic religions. Early Christian monastic schools, Islamic madrasas, and Jewish centers of learning provided a foundation for the pursuit of knowledge, scholarly research, and the preservation of ancient texts. These institutions played a vital role in the development of Western education systems and the advancement of various academic disciplines.

Cultural and Artistic Expressions

Monotheistic beliefs have profoundly influenced Western artistic expressions, architecture, literature, and music. The grand cathedrals, mosques, and synagogues, adorned with intricate artwork and sacred symbols, stand as testaments to the cultural impact of monotheistic religions.

A. Art and Architecture

Religious themes and narratives have been central to Western art, with depictions of biblical stories, saints, and religious icons serving as inspiration for artists throughout history. The artistic expressions found in religious manuscripts, paintings, sculptures, and stained glass windows reflect the religious devotion and the quest for spiritual transcendence.

B. Literary Traditions

Monotheistic religions have also contributed to Western literary traditions, producing sacred texts, theological treatises, and philosophical works. The Bible, the Qur'an, and religious commentaries have shaped the literary landscape, inspiring countless writers, poets, and playwrights.

C. Music and Devotional Practices

Music has played a vital role in religious worship and spiritual practices within monotheistic traditions. Choral music, hymns, and chants have been integral to religious ceremonies and have influenced the development of Western music, including classical, choral, and sacred compositions.

Conclusion

The impact of monotheistic beliefs on the development of Western civilization is far-reaching and multifaceted. The ethical foundations, intellectual contributions, and cultural expressions derived from monotheistic religions have shaped Western societies, influencing moral values, philosophical inquiries, educational systems, artistic traditions, and cultural identities. Recognizing and understanding the influence of monotheistic beliefs is essential for comprehending the historical and cultural development of Western civilization.

The polytheistic aspects in Hinduism and the concept of the Trimurti

In contrast to the monotheistic beliefs of Abrahamic religions, many Eastern religions embrace polytheistic concepts, where multiple gods and goddesses are worshiped. Among these, Hinduism stands out as one of the most prominent religions with a rich polytheistic tradition. However, within Hinduism, there also exists the concept of the Trimurti, which reflects a form of monotheistic belief. This section will delve into the polytheistic aspects of Hinduism and the significance of the Trimurti in understanding the complexity of Eastern religious thought.

Polytheism in Hinduism

A. Vast Pantheon of Deities

Hinduism encompasses a vast pantheon of gods and goddesses, each with their own distinct attributes, roles, and mythological stories. Some of the major deities in Hinduism include Brahma, Vishnu, Shiva, Lakshmi, Saraswati, and Durga, among numerous others. These deities represent different aspects of the divine, such as creation, preservation, destruction, abundance, knowledge, and power.

B. Devotional Practices and Rituals

Devotees of Hinduism engage in a variety of devotional practices to establish a connection with the divine. These practices include prayers, offerings, ceremonies, and festivals dedicated to specific deities. Different regions and communities within Hinduism may have their own unique gods and goddesses that they venerate, showcasing the diverse and multifaceted nature of Hindu polytheism.

C. Concept of Ishta Devata

Another important aspect of Hindu polytheism is the concept of Ishta Devata, which refers to a personal deity that an individual feels a strong connection to and chooses to worship. This allows for a personalized expression of faith within the broader framework of Hinduism, further emphasizing the polytheistic nature of the religion.

The Trimurti: A Monotheistic Concept in Hinduism

While Hinduism embraces polytheism, it also recognizes the concept of the Trimurti, which signifies the threefold manifestation of the divine. The Trimurti consists of three primary deities: Brahma, Vishnu, and Shiva.

A. Brahma: The Creator

Brahma represents the creative aspect of the divine and is often associated with the creation and shaping of the universe. However, Brahma is not as prominently worshiped as Vishnu and Shiva in Hinduism, and there are fewer temples dedicated to Brahma.

B. Vishnu: The Preserver

Vishnu embodies the principle of preservation and is considered the preserver and sustainer of the universe. Vishnu is believed to manifest in various avatars or incarnations to restore balance and righteousness in the world. Some of the well-known avatars include Rama and Krishna.

C. Shiva: The Destroyer and Transformer

Shiva symbolizes the destructive and transformative aspects of the divine. Shiva's role involves the dissolution of the universe to pave the way for new cycles of creation. Shiva is often associated with asceticism, meditation, and the path of spiritual liberation.

Significance of the Trimurti

The concept of the Trimurti highlights a form of monotheistic belief within the broader polytheistic framework of Hinduism. It recognizes that the different deities in Hinduism are not separate and independent entities but different manifestations of the same divine essence. The Trimurti represents the interconnectedness and unity of the divine forces responsible for creation, preservation, and destruction.

A. Symbolic Representation of Cosmic Principles

The Trimurti serves as a symbolic representation of the cosmic principles that govern the universe. Brahma symbolizes creation, Vishnu represents preservation and order, and Shiva embodies transformation and change. Together, they encompass the entirety of the cosmic cycle.

B. Harmony and Balance

The Trimurti also reflects the importance of harmony and balance in Hindu philosophy. The three deities complement and depend on each other to maintain the equilibrium of the universe. This concept encourages individuals to recognize the interconnectedness of all aspects of existence and strive for balance in their own lives.

C. Unity in Diversity

The Trimurti emphasizes the unity that underlies the diversity of gods and goddesses in Hinduism. It allows for a holistic understanding of the divine, where the various deities are seen as different facets of the same ultimate reality. This inclusive perspective fosters acceptance and tolerance within the Hindu religious framework.

In conclusion, Hinduism showcases the complexity of religious belief by encompassing both polytheistic traditions and the concept of the Trimurti, which reflects a monotheistic understanding. The vast pantheon of deities in Hinduism provides a diverse array of symbols and archetypes for devotees to connect with. Meanwhile, the Trimurti highlights the unity and interconnectedness of the divine forces responsible for creation, preservation, and destruction. Understanding these polytheistic and monotheistic aspects within Hinduism allows for a deeper appreciation of the rich religious and philosophical traditions of the Eastern world.

Examining the monotheistic elements in Sikhism and the belief in the formless God

Sikhism, a religion founded in the 15th century in the Punjab region of South Asia, holds a unique position within the spectrum of monotheistic belief systems. Central to Sikhism is the belief in the formless and transcendent God, who is revered as the ultimate and sole divine authority. This section will explore the monotheistic elements in Sikhism and shed light on the Sikh concept of the formless God.

Monotheism in Sikhism

A. Oneness of God

At the core of Sikhism lies the principle of monotheism, affirming the existence of a single, all-pervading divine entity. Sikhs believe in the concept of Ek Onkar, which translates to "One God." This monotheistic belief sets Sikhism apart from the polytheistic traditions prevalent in the region during its inception.

B. Rejecting Intermediaries

Sikhism emphasizes direct connection and communion with God, rejecting the need for intermediaries such as priests or saints. Sikhs believe that every individual has the capacity to connect with the divine directly through devotion, meditation, and righteous actions. This direct relationship with the formless God fosters a sense of personal responsibility and accountability.

C. Unity of Humanity

The monotheistic beliefs in Sikhism also extend to the notion of the unity of humanity. Sikhs consider all individuals, regardless of their race, gender, or social status, to be equal in the eyes of God. This inclusive worldview promotes social justice, equality, and communal harmony.

The Formless God in Sikhism

A. Ik Onkar: The One Supreme Reality

Sikhism places great emphasis on the belief in the formless and indescribable nature of God. The term "Ik Onkar" encapsulates this concept, with "Ik" representing the numeral one and "Onkar" symbolizing the divine sound of creation. This formless God is beyond human comprehension and transcends all limitations of physical form and attributes.

B. The Divine Essence

Sikhs believe that God's essence permeates everything in the universe. They recognize the divine presence within all creation and seek to cultivate a deeper awareness of this divine essence through meditation and spiritual practices. This understanding underscores the unity and interconnectedness of all existence.

C. Liberation through the Formless God

In Sikhism, the ultimate goal is to achieve liberation from the cycle of birth and death and merge with the formless God. Through devotion, selfless service, and adherence to moral values, Sikhs aim to attain spiritual enlightenment and experience union with the divine.

Practical Implications of Sikh Monotheism

A. Naam Simran: Remembering God's Name

Central to Sikh practice is the regular recitation and remembrance of God's name, known as Naam Simran. Through this practice, Sikhs strive to maintain a constant awareness of the formless God and align their thoughts and actions with divine principles.

B. Seva: Selfless Service

Sikhism emphasizes the importance of selfless service, or Seva, as a means of serving humanity and expressing devotion to the formless God. Sikhs engage in charitable acts, community service, and humanitarian efforts to manifest their commitment to the principles of monotheism and promote the well-being of others.

C. Equality and Social Justice

The belief in the formless God and the monotheistic worldview of Sikhism inspire a commitment to social justice and equality. Sikhs strive to challenge discrimination, injustice, and inequality in all forms, standing up for the rights and dignity of every individual, irrespective of their background.

In conclusion, Sikhism presents a monotheistic belief system that centers around the concept of the formless God. This unique perspective affirms the existence of a singular, transcendent divine authority while rejecting intermediaries and promoting direct connection with the divine. The belief in the formless God in Sikhism underscores the unity of all creation, fostering an inclusive and egalitarian worldview. Through practical applications such as Naam Simran, Seva, and a commitment to social justice, Sikhs embody the principles of monotheism and strive to live in harmony with the formless God and their fellow human beings.

PART 2: ORIGINS OF POLYTHEISM AND MONOTHEISM

Part 2 of our exploration delves into the origins of polytheism and monotheism, two fundamental religious paradigms that have shaped the course of human history. From the earliest civilizations to the development of complex belief systems, understanding the roots of polytheistic and monotheistic traditions provides crucial insights into the evolution of human spirituality.

In this section, we will embark on a journey across different ancient civilizations, exploring their mythologies, rituals, and cosmologies to unravel the intricate tapestry of polytheism. We will examine the multifaceted pantheons of gods and goddesses in Mesopotamia, Egypt, Greece, and other cultures, delving into their significance and the roles they played in shaping the human experience.

Additionally, we will delve into the emergence and development of monotheistic belief systems, which mark a significant shift in religious thought. We will explore the historical context and factors that influenced the transition from polytheism to monotheism in various civilizations, including the ancient Hebrews, Zoroastrianism, and the rise of monotheism in late antiquity.

Throughout this exploration, we will analyze the philosophical, cultural, and social factors that contributed to the rise of polytheism and the subsequent emergence of monotheism. We will examine the complex interplay between religious beliefs and societal structures, as well as the implications and consequences of these belief systems on individuals and communities.

By delving into the origins of polytheism and monotheism, we aim to gain a deeper understanding of the diverse religious expressions and the underlying human quest for meaning and connection with the divine. We will examine the rich tapestry of gods and goddesses, explore the complexities of ancient mythologies, and unravel the intellectual and spiritual transformations that gave rise to monotheistic faiths.

Exploring the Contrasts and Convergence of Polytheism and Monotheism

Throughout this journey, we will strive to approach the subject matter with a balanced and objective perspective, acknowledging the diversity of religious beliefs and practices while shedding light on the historical, cultural, and intellectual contexts that shaped them. By examining the origins of polytheism and monotheism, we hope to foster a comprehensive understanding of the development of religious thought and its profound impact on human civilization.

Join us as we embark on this captivating exploration into the origins of polytheism and monotheism, where ancient myths, rituals, and belief systems come alive, inviting us to contemplate the intricate tapestry of human spirituality and the enduring quest for divine connection.

CHAPTER 4: THE ORIGINS OF POLYTHEISM

Chapter 4 delves into the fascinating origins of polytheism, a belief system that dates back to the earliest civilizations in human history. Polytheism, characterized by the worship of multiple gods and goddesses, played a pivotal role in shaping the religious and cultural landscapes of ancient societies.

In this chapter, we will embark on a journey through time, exploring the ancient civilizations of Mesopotamia, Egypt, Greece, and other regions where polytheism flourished. We will uncover the rich mythologies, rituals, and practices that formed the foundation of these vibrant belief systems.

At the heart of polytheism lies the pantheon of gods and goddesses, each embodying distinct powers, domains, and personalities. We will delve into the intricacies of these divine beings, exploring their roles in the cosmologies and narratives of different cultures. Through engaging narratives and insightful analysis, we will come to understand how these ancient civilizations conceptualized and interacted with their deities.

Moreover, we will delve into the cultural, social, and historical contexts that gave rise to polytheistic beliefs. From the agricultural societies of Mesopotamia, where gods and goddesses were intimately tied to the cycles of nature, to the grand temples of Egypt, serving as sacred spaces for communion with the divine, we will explore the multifaceted relationship between polytheism and the human experience.

Throughout this chapter, we will draw upon examples from diverse fields, such as Witchcraft, Divination, Herbalism, Shamanism, and Ecospirituality, to illuminate the relevance and enduring legacy of polytheistic beliefs. By examining the practices and rituals of contemporary traditions, we can gain deeper insights into the enduring appeal and transformative power of polytheism.

It is important to approach the subject matter with an open and respectful mindset, recognizing the diversity of polytheistic belief systems and their significance to the people who embraced them. We will consider the complexities of polytheism, its ability to adapt and evolve over time, and the interplay between religious beliefs, societal structures, and cultural practices.

As we delve into the origins of polytheism, we invite you to embark on a captivating journey of discovery. By examining the ancient mythologies, exploring the rituals and practices, and unraveling the profound meanings behind polytheistic belief systems, we hope to gain a deeper appreciation for the human capacity for spiritual exploration and the enduring legacy of polytheism in shaping our collective understanding of the divine.

Exploring Early Forms of Religious Belief

Religion has been a fundamental aspect of human existence since ancient times. The earliest forms of religious belief emerged as humans sought to understand and make sense of the world around them. These early belief systems laid the foundation for the diverse array of religious practices and ideologies that have shaped human societies throughout history.

Animism: The Worship of Nature and Spirits
One of the earliest forms of religious belief was animism, which can be traced back to prehistoric times. Animism is rooted in the notion that all objects, whether living or inanimate, possess a spiritual essence or soul. This belief system is characterized by the worship of natural elements, such as trees, rivers, and animals, as well as ancestral spirits. Animistic cultures often engage in rituals and ceremonies to honor and communicate with these spirits, seeking their protection, guidance, and favor.

Ancestor Worship: Honoring the Deceased
Another early form of religious belief is ancestor worship. This practice revolves around veneration and reverence for deceased family members and ancestors. It is based on the belief that the spirits of the departed continue to exist and can influence the lives of the living. Ancestor worship often involves offerings, rituals, and prayers to ensure the well-being and blessings of the ancestral spirits. This belief system is prevalent in many cultures, particularly in East Asia and parts of Africa.

Shamanism: Intermediaries Between Worlds
Shamanism is a complex and multifaceted religious practice that dates back thousands of years. It revolves around the role of a shaman, a spiritual leader who serves as an intermediary between the human and spirit realms. Shamans are believed to have the ability to communicate with spirits, perform healing rituals, and navigate the spiritual dimensions. Shamanistic beliefs vary across cultures but commonly involve rituals, trance states, and the use of spiritual tools and symbols.

Totemism: Spiritual Connection with Animal Spirits
Totemism is a belief system centered around the idea that humans have a special relationship with particular animal species or natural phenomena. These animals, known as totems, are seen as spiritual beings and are revered as symbols of clan or

family identity. Totemic beliefs emphasize the connection between humans and the natural world, with each individual or group having their own unique totemic affiliation. Totemism can be found among various indigenous cultures worldwide.

Pantheism: Identifying the Divine in Nature

Pantheism is the belief that the divine permeates every aspect of the natural world. It sees the universe itself as sacred, and the distinction between the divine and the material world is blurred. In pantheistic belief systems, divinity is immanent, existing within nature rather than being separate from it. This perspective fosters a deep reverence for the natural world and encourages individuals to seek spiritual connection through the observation and contemplation of the natural environment.

These early forms of religious belief demonstrate the innate human inclination to seek meaning, find solace, and establish a connection with the spiritual realm. While they differ in their specific practices and ideologies, they share a common thread of recognizing and venerating forces beyond the material world.

Understanding these early belief systems provides a foundation for comprehending the development and evolution of religious thought and practice throughout history. As we explore the origins of polytheism and monotheism, we will see how these early forms of religious belief laid the groundwork for the diverse and complex religious systems that emerged in later civilizations.

Investigating the origins of religious belief in prehistoric societies

The origins of religious belief can be traced back to prehistoric times, long before the advent of written records. Although our knowledge of these early societies is limited, archaeological evidence provides valuable insights into their religious practices and beliefs. By examining ancient artifacts, cave paintings, burial sites, and other remnants of prehistoric cultures, researchers have begun to unravel the mysteries surrounding the origins of religious belief in these early societies.

Symbolism and Rituals in Prehistoric Art

One way researchers investigate the origins of religious belief in prehistoric societies is through the study of art. Cave paintings, rock engravings, and figurines have been discovered in various regions around the world, dating back tens of thousands of years. These artistic expressions often depict animals, human figures, and abstract symbols, suggesting a connection to spiritual or supernatural realms. The repetitive motifs and use of colors may signify rituals or ceremonial practices associated with religious beliefs.

Exploring the Contrasts and Convergence of Polytheism and Monotheism

The study of prehistoric art provides valuable insights into the origins of religious belief and the significance of symbolism and rituals in ancient societies. Cave paintings, rock engravings, and figurines serve as windows into the spiritual and cultural worlds of our early ancestors. Through careful analysis and interpretation, researchers can uncover clues about the beliefs, rituals, and cosmologies that shaped the lives of these ancient communities.

1. Animal Symbolism:
   One prominent feature of prehistoric art is the frequent depiction of animals. Cave paintings often showcase a diverse array of animals, including horses, bison, deer, and mammoths. These animals were not merely portrayed for their aesthetic appeal; they held deep symbolic significance within the belief systems of these early societies. Animals were seen as powerful beings, embodying qualities such as strength, agility, and fertility. The portrayal of animals in prehistoric art may have represented a form of reverence or connection to the natural world, where humans sought to harness the power and wisdom of these creatures.

2. Human Figures:
   Alongside animal depictions, prehistoric art also includes representations of human figures. These figures are often stylized and exhibit exaggerated features or abstract forms. The significance of human representations in prehistoric art remains a subject of debate among scholars. Some suggest that these figures may have portrayed ancestral spirits or deities, serving as objects of veneration or as intermediaries between the human and spiritual realms. Others propose that they could represent shamanic figures or individuals engaged in ceremonial practices.

3. Abstract Symbols and Patterns:
   Another notable aspect of prehistoric art is the presence of abstract symbols and patterns. Geometric designs, spirals, dots, and other repetitive motifs are commonly found in cave paintings and rock engravings. These abstract symbols hold a mysterious allure, as their meanings are often difficult to decipher. However, they are believed to have carried deep spiritual significance for the creators of these artworks. These symbols may have represented cosmological concepts, celestial bodies, or elemental forces, connecting the physical and spiritual realms and conveying a sense of the sacred.

4. Rituals and Ceremonies:
   The repetition of certain motifs and the use of colors in prehistoric art suggest the existence of rituals and ceremonies associated with religious beliefs. Cave paintings, for instance, often occur in remote and inaccessible areas, indicating that they were not intended for everyday viewing but rather for ceremonial purposes. The act of creating these artworks may have been a ritualistic practice in itself,

accompanied by chants, dances, or other forms of collective engagement. Through these rituals, early societies sought to establish a connection with the supernatural, to invoke spiritual powers, or to honor their ancestors.

It is important to note that the interpretation of prehistoric art requires caution and humility, as our understanding of these ancient cultures is limited. The meanings and intentions behind these artworks may have varied across time and geographic regions, and they likely held deep cultural significance that is challenging to fully grasp. Nonetheless, the study of symbolism and rituals in prehistoric art provides valuable glimpses into the religious and spiritual lives of our distant ancestors, shedding light on the origins of religious belief and the fundamental human impulse to connect with the divine.

Burial Practices and Ancestor Veneration

Burial sites offer valuable insights into the religious beliefs and practices of prehistoric societies. The careful treatment of the deceased, the presence of grave goods, and the arrangement of the burial site can provide clues about their beliefs regarding the afterlife and the veneration of ancestors. Many prehistoric cultures believed in an afterlife or a spiritual realm where the souls of the deceased resided. Burial rituals and offerings were performed to ensure the well-being and protection of the departed in the afterlife.

Burial sites serve as gateways to understanding the religious beliefs and practices of ancient cultures. They provide us with profound insights into how these societies approached death, the afterlife, and the veneration of their ancestors. Through careful examination of burial practices and the artifacts accompanying the deceased, we can gain a glimpse into the spiritual dimensions that shaped their worldview.

1. Treatment of the Deceased:
    Prehistoric burial practices reveal the reverence and care bestowed upon the deceased. The methods of burial varied across different cultures and regions, ranging from simple interments to more elaborate rituals. In some cases, bodies were buried in carefully prepared graves, while in others, they were placed in caves, tombs, or other sacred locations. The manner in which the deceased were laid to rest, such as the position of the body, the presence of grave markers, or the use of specific burial structures, may have held symbolic meaning tied to their beliefs about the afterlife.

2. Grave Goods and Offerings:
    The inclusion of grave goods alongside the deceased is a common feature of prehistoric burials. These objects, ranging from tools and weapons to pottery and jewelry, were intentionally placed in the grave to accompany the deceased in the

afterlife. The selection of grave goods often reflects the cultural values and beliefs of the society, as well as the status and role of the individual being buried. These offerings symbolize a desire to provide for the deceased in their journey to the spiritual realm or to honor and appease their spirits.

3.   Ancestor Veneration:

Ancestor veneration, the practice of honoring and revering one's ancestors, was a deeply rooted belief and cultural tradition in many prehistoric societies. Ancestors were seen as guardians and protectors, capable of influencing the lives of their living descendants. Burial sites were regarded as sacred spaces where ancestors could be honored and visited. Rituals and ceremonies, such as offerings of food, libations, or prayers, were performed to maintain a connection with the deceased and seek their guidance, protection, and blessings. The veneration of ancestors played a crucial role in maintaining social cohesion, transmitting cultural values, and fostering a sense of continuity and identity within the community.

4.   Rituals and Beliefs about the Afterlife:

Prehistoric burial practices also reflect the belief in an afterlife or a spiritual realm where the souls of the deceased continue to exist. Rituals surrounding death and burial were performed to ensure a smooth transition and a favorable afterlife for the departed. These rituals could involve purification rites, chanting or recitations, offerings, and prayers. The specific beliefs about the afterlife varied across different cultures, with some envisioning a realm of paradise or a continuation of life in a spiritual form, while others viewed it as a journey to be undertaken or a realm of spirits.

Studying burial practices and ancestor veneration in prehistoric societies provides us with a fascinating glimpse into their religious beliefs, values, and social structures. These practices demonstrate a deep reverence for the deceased and a desire to maintain a connection with their spiritual presence. By honoring and venerating their ancestors, these ancient cultures sought guidance, protection, and a sense of continuity with their past. Burial practices and ancestor veneration offer valuable insights into the spiritual dimensions of prehistoric societies and their beliefs about life, death, and the eternal bonds of kinship.

Nature Worship and Animistic Beliefs

In the ancient tapestry of human spirituality, nature worship and animistic beliefs weave a profound connection between early human cultures and the natural world. By attributing spiritual qualities to natural elements, our prehistoric ancestors recognized the inherent power and divine essence within the vast tapestry of nature.

Exploring the significance of nature worship and animistic beliefs provides us with a glimpse into the deep reverence early societies held for the forces of the natural world.

1. Animistic Beliefs:
     Animism, a core aspect of early religious systems, imbues natural elements with spiritual qualities. Prehistoric societies perceived the world as animated, inhabited by a multitude of spirits or deities associated with various natural features. These spirits were believed to possess agency and influence over the elements they embodied, such as rivers, mountains, trees, animals, and celestial bodies. Animistic beliefs arose from an intuitive understanding of the interconnectedness and interdependence of all living beings and natural phenomena.

2. Worship of Natural Features:
     Nature worship, an expression of animistic beliefs, involved the veneration and reverence of specific natural features. Ancient cultures held sacred places such as rivers, lakes, springs, mountains, caves, and forests. These sites were perceived as the dwelling places of spirits or deities, and rituals and ceremonies were conducted to honor and seek the favor of these spiritual entities. Offerings, prayers, dances, and chants were performed to establish a connection with the divine forces that resided within these natural realms.

3. Rituals and Ceremonies:
     Rituals and ceremonies played a vital role in nature worship and animistic beliefs. These sacred practices were designed to harmonize human beings with the natural world and establish a reciprocal relationship with the spiritual entities inhabiting it. Rituals might include purification ceremonies, seasonal celebrations, and rites of passage that marked significant transitions in life. Through these rituals, prehistoric societies sought to ensure the favor and protection of the natural spirits, maintain balance within the natural order, and sustain the well-being of their communities.

4. Symbolism and Sacred Landscapes:
     Symbolism was an essential aspect of nature worship. Early cultures employed symbols, sacred images, and artistic representations to capture the essence and power of the natural forces they revered. Rock art, cave paintings, and other forms of artistic expression served as portals into the spiritual realms and conveyed the significance of the natural world. Sacred landscapes, consisting of specific natural features or configurations of the environment, held profound spiritual meaning and were regarded as places of heightened divine presence.

     By embracing nature worship and animistic beliefs, prehistoric societies recognized the inherent divinity within the natural world and sought to establish a harmonious relationship with it. These beliefs fostered a deep respect for the interconnectedness of all living beings and emphasized the reciprocal exchange of energy between humans and the natural environment. Nature worship and animistic beliefs laid the foundation for the development of more complex religious systems, shaping the way humans have related to and revered the natural world throughout history.

The study of nature worship and animistic beliefs provides valuable insights into the profound spiritual connection early societies had with the natural world. It reminds us of the inherent sacredness and interconnectedness of all life and invites us to reestablish a harmonious relationship with the natural forces that sustain us. By understanding and honoring the wisdom of our prehistoric ancestors, we can deepen our appreciation for the sacredness of nature and cultivate a sense of stewardship towards the Earth.

Shamanism and Spiritual Intermediaries

Shamanism, a widespread belief system in many prehistoric societies, played a significant role in religious practices. Shamans, often regarded as spiritual intermediaries, were individuals who possessed the ability to communicate with the spiritual realm and perform rituals for healing, divination, and guidance. Shamanistic practices involved altered states of consciousness, such as trance and hallucinatory experiences, which allowed shamans to access the spirit world and interact with supernatural beings.

Among the diverse tapestry of prehistoric belief systems, shamanism emerges as a profound and widespread practice that facilitated communication between the human and spirit realms. At the heart of shamanism were the shamans themselves, revered as spiritual intermediaries who possessed the ability to navigate the realms of the unseen. Through their unique skills and practices, shamans served as healers, diviners, and guides, bridging the gap between the physical and spiritual dimensions of existence.

1.   The Role of Shamans:
    Shamans held a central position in prehistoric societies as individuals who possessed specialized knowledge and abilities to interact with the spiritual realm. They were seen as mediators between the human community and the world of spirits or deities. Shamans acted as healers, conducting rituals and ceremonies to restore balance and harmony to individuals and communities. They also performed divination, seeking insights into the future and offering guidance in matters of importance. The shaman's role extended beyond the mundane, encompassing the spiritual, psychological, and social dimensions of human life.

2.   Altered States of Consciousness:
     Shamanistic practices often involved entering altered states of consciousness, such as trance or hallucinatory experiences. Through various techniques, such as rhythmic drumming, chanting, dance, or ingestion of psychoactive substances, shamans induced states of mind that allowed them to transcend ordinary perception and access the spirit world. These altered states served as gateways to connect with spiritual entities, receive messages, and acquire knowledge beyond the limitations of everyday consciousness.

3.   Journeying and Spirit Encounters:
     Central to shamanic practice was the shaman's ability to undertake journeys into the spirit realm. During these journeys, the shaman's spirit, often referred to as the "soul," would leave the physical body and travel to other realms to interact with spirits, ancestors, or animal guides. These encounters formed the basis of communication, negotiation, and healing between the human and spirit realms. Shamans would seek guidance, receive teachings, and bring back vital information to benefit their communities.

4.   Healing and Spiritual Guidance:
     Healing was a significant aspect of shamanistic practice. Shamans employed various techniques, including energy work, herbal remedies, ritualistic gestures, and spiritual interventions, to restore physical, emotional, and spiritual well-being. Through their intimate connection with the spiritual realm, shamans were believed to diagnose and treat ailments that were believed to have both physical and spiritual causes. They acted as conduits for healing energy, addressing the imbalances that manifested in individuals or communities.

5.   Community and Social Integration:
     Shamanism was deeply embedded within the social fabric of prehistoric societies. Shamans often held positions of respect and authority, serving as spiritual leaders and advisors to their communities. Their role extended beyond individual healing and guidance, as they played a crucial part in mediating conflicts, maintaining social cohesion, and facilitating the spiritual needs of their people. Shamans acted as custodians of ancestral wisdom, preserving and transmitting cultural knowledge and traditions across generations.

     Shamanism, with its focus on spiritual intermediaries and their ability to traverse realms, exemplified the deep yearning of prehistoric societies to connect with the unseen forces that influenced their lives. It provided a framework for understanding the mysteries of existence, offering healing, guidance, and a sense of communal belonging. Shamanistic practices continue to endure in contemporary indigenous cultures, demonstrating the enduring significance of these ancient traditions.

By exploring the profound role of shamans and their practices, we gain a deeper understanding of the spiritual yearnings and the complex cosmologies of our prehistoric ancestors. Their ability to navigate between the realms of the seen and unseen serves as a reminder of our innate connection to the spiritual dimensions of existence and the transformative power of engaging with the sacred.

Megalithic Structures and Sacred Spaces

The construction of megalithic structures, such as Stonehenge in England or the pyramids in Egypt, indicates the existence of complex religious beliefs and the establishment of sacred spaces. These monumental structures were likely used for rituals, ceremonies, and communal gatherings, suggesting the importance of communal religious practices in prehistoric societies. The alignment of these structures with celestial events also suggests an astronomical and spiritual significance.

Investigating the origins of religious belief in prehistoric societies is a challenging endeavor, as it requires piecing together fragments of evidence and interpreting ancient artifacts through a cultural and historical lens. However, by examining the symbolism, rituals, burial practices, and architectural marvels left behind by these early societies, researchers gain valuable insights into the roots of religious thought and the human quest for spiritual understanding. These early beliefs laid the foundation for the diverse religious systems that would emerge and evolve throughout human history.

The ancient world bears witness to the creation of awe-inspiring megalithic structures, imposing monuments that not only showcased the technological prowess of their builders but also served as focal points of religious and spiritual activities. These massive stone structures, such as Stonehenge, the pyramids of Egypt, or the stone circles of Carnac, beckon us to unravel their mysteries and uncover the profound religious beliefs and practices that shaped the lives of our prehistoric ancestors.

1. The Significance of Megalithic Structures:
    Megalithic structures captivate our imagination with their sheer scale and precise construction, leaving us with lingering questions about their purpose and significance. These monuments, often consisting of large, carefully arranged stones, were not merely feats of engineering but also sacred spaces intimately connected to religious and spiritual practices. The monumental effort invested in their construction attests to the importance of the rituals and beliefs associated with them.

2. Rituals and Ceremonies:
    Megalithic structures were likely utilized for various rituals and ceremonies, serving as gathering places for communal religious practices. These rituals may have included offerings, prayers, dances, or other forms of worship that sought to establish a connection between the human and divine realms. The presence of specific architectural features, alignments with celestial events, or symbolic representations within these structures suggests a profound understanding of the cosmic order and the role of humans in the divine tapestry.

3. Celestial Alignments:
    Many megalithic structures exhibit alignments with celestial phenomena, such as solstices, equinoxes, or specific astronomical events. These alignments indicate a sophisticated understanding of celestial cycles and their significance in religious and agricultural calendars. By aligning their sacred spaces with celestial bodies, prehistoric societies may have sought to harmonize their religious observances with the natural rhythms of the cosmos, reaffirming their connection to the celestial realm.

4. Burial Practices and Ancestral Connections:
    Megalithic structures often contain burial sites, indicating a close association between the rituals and beliefs surrounding death and the construction of sacred monuments. Burials within or in close proximity to megalithic structures suggest a reverence for ancestors and the belief in the continued presence of the departed within the spiritual realm. These sacred spaces served as links between the living and the deceased, facilitating ongoing connections with ancestral spirits and ensuring their protection and guidance.

5. Symbolism and Sacred Landscape:
    The symbolism embedded within megalithic structures offers glimpses into the cosmological and mythological beliefs of ancient societies. Intricate carvings, enigmatic symbols, and intricate patterns engraved or painted on stones provide clues about their understanding of the world and their place within it. The sacred landscapes surrounding megalithic sites, often featuring natural elements like rivers, mountains, or caves, further emphasize the interconnectedness of the physical and spiritual realms.

    Megalithic structures and their sacred spaces represent profound expressions of human spirituality and the quest for meaning in the prehistoric world. They stand as enduring testament to the religious beliefs and practices that were integral to the lives of our ancient ancestors. Exploring these monuments and the rituals associated with them allows us to glimpse into the rich tapestry of religious thought and spiritual experiences that have shaped human civilizations throughout the ages.

By unraveling the mysteries of megalithic structures and engaging with the sacred spaces they represent, we gain a deeper appreciation for the spiritual aspirations, cosmological insights, and communal rituals that formed the bedrock of prehistoric religious beliefs. These ancient monuments continue to inspire awe and curiosity, inviting us to ponder the profound connections between the material and spiritual dimensions of human existence.

Theanimism and ancestor worship as precursors to polytheism

Before the development of complex polytheistic belief systems, many ancient cultures embraced animism and ancestor worship as fundamental aspects of their religious practices. Animism, the belief that all natural entities possess spirits or souls, and ancestor worship, the veneration of deceased ancestors, laid the foundation for the later emergence of polytheistic traditions. This section will explore the significance of animism and ancestor worship as precursors to polytheism and examine their influence on the development of ancient religious systems.

Animism: The Essence of the Natural World

Animism is deeply rooted in the human experience of the natural world. It recognizes the spiritual essence inherent in all living and non-living entities, including animals, plants, rocks, rivers, and celestial bodies. Ancient cultures believed that these entities possessed consciousness and the ability to affect human lives. Animistic beliefs provided a framework for understanding and interacting with the natural environment, establishing a sense of interconnectedness and reverence for the world around them.

Animistic practices often involved rituals, offerings, and ceremonies designed to establish a harmonious relationship with the spiritual entities believed to dwell within the natural realm. These rituals sought to ensure the well-being of individuals and communities by seeking favor, protection, and guidance from these spiritual forces. Animism laid the groundwork for the conception of multiple deities and spirits, which later evolved into polytheistic belief systems.

Ancestor Worship: Revering the Past

Ancestor worship emerged as another crucial precursor to polytheism, particularly in cultures where the extended family and lineage held great importance. Ancestors were regarded as guardians, protectors, and sources of wisdom and guidance. They were believed to maintain a connection with the living and had the ability to influence the outcomes of daily life.

Ancient cultures expressed reverence for their ancestors through rituals and ceremonies. Offerings and prayers were made to honor and sustain the spirits of the deceased, seeking their blessings and assistance. Ancestor worship served as a bridge between the living and the spirit world, fostering a sense of continuity and collective identity across generations. Over time, this practice laid the foundation for the development of a pantheon of deities, each representing specific aspects of life and fulfilling specific roles within the spiritual hierarchy.

The Transition to Polytheism: Multiplicity of Deities

As animistic and ancestor worship practices evolved, they gradually expanded to include a multitude of spirits and deities. Polytheism emerged when cultures began to personify and deify natural phenomena, forces, and concepts that played significant roles in their lives. These deities embodied specific attributes, such as fertility, war, love, and wisdom, and became the focus of rituals, festivals, and religious observances.

Polytheistic belief systems allowed for a more nuanced understanding of the divine and human relationships. Each deity had unique characteristics, responsibilities, and areas of influence. People sought the favor of specific deities based on their individual needs or circumstances, and religious practices became more diverse and specialized.

The transition from animism and ancestor worship to polytheism marked a shift from a general spiritual interconnectedness to a more structured and hierarchical system of worship. However, the elements of reverence for nature and ancestors persisted within the polytheistic frameworks, forming essential components of ancient religious traditions.

In conclusion, animism and ancestor worship played significant roles as precursors to polytheism in ancient cultures. Animism recognized the spiritual essence within all natural entities, establishing a sense of interconnectedness and reverence for the natural world. Ancestor worship, on the other hand, honored and sought guidance from deceased ancestors, fostering a sense of continuity and collective identity. These beliefs set the stage for the development of polytheistic systems, where deities personified various natural and abstract concepts. The transition from animism and ancestor worship to polytheism marked the evolution of religious beliefs and practices, shaping the diverse ancient religious systems that emerged around the world.

Polytheism in Ancient Mesopotamia

Ancient Mesopotamia, often referred to as the "Cradle of Civilization," was home to one of the earliest known civilizations in human history. Within this vibrant and complex society, polytheism reigned as the dominant religious belief system. Mesopotamian polytheism encompassed a vast pantheon of deities, each with their own roles, attributes, and cultic practices. This section will explore the rich tapestry of polytheistic beliefs in ancient Mesopotamia and delve into the significance of these deities within the context of cosmic order and human existence.

The Mesopotamian Pantheon: A Multitude of Gods and Goddesses

Mesopotamian polytheism was characterized by its expansive pantheon, consisting of numerous gods and goddesses who embodied various aspects of the natural and social world. Among the most prominent deities were Enlil, the lord of the winds and ruler of the earth; Inanna, the goddess of love, fertility, and warfare; and Marduk, the patron god of Babylon who emerged as a supreme deity during the Babylonian Empire.

Each deity held distinct roles and spheres of influence, governing domains such as agriculture, war, wisdom, craftsmanship, and justice. They were often associated with specific cities or regions and were worshipped through temples and rituals performed by priests and priestesses.

The Mesopotamian civilization, with its rich cultural and religious heritage, boasted a vast and intricate pantheon of gods and goddesses. These deities represented diverse aspects of the natural and social world, embodying the forces and phenomena that shaped Mesopotamian life. Understanding the Mesopotamian pantheon allows us to delve into the complex tapestry of their polytheistic beliefs and shed light on their worldview.

1. Enlil, the Ruler of the Earth:
   Enlil held a preeminent position among the Mesopotamian deities as the lord of the winds and ruler of the earth. He was associated with storms, agriculture, and fertility, and his power extended over the forces of nature. As the patron deity of the city of Nippur, Enlil played a central role in the religious life of the Mesopotamians and was revered as a creator and sustainer of the world.

2. Inanna, the Goddess of Love and Warfare:
   Inanna, also known as Ishtar, was a prominent goddess in the Mesopotamian pantheon. She represented both love and war, embodying the duality of life. Inanna was associated with fertility, sexuality, and the abundance of nature. She was also a

formidable warrior, leading armies and bestowing victory upon her worshippers. Inanna's cult was particularly prominent in the city of Uruk, where her temple, the Eanna, stood as a symbol of her power and influence.

3.   Marduk, the Supreme Deity of Babylon:
     Marduk emerged as a supreme deity during the rise of the Babylonian Empire. As the patron god of Babylon, he became the central figure in the pantheon, reflecting the city's political and religious prominence. Marduk was associated with wisdom, justice, and warfare, and his epic battle against the primordial chaos monster Tiamat symbolized the triumph of order over chaos. The Marduk cult and the Esagila, his temple in Babylon, became focal points of religious devotion and political authority.

4.   Other Deities and their Spheres of Influence:
     Beyond Enlil, Inanna, and Marduk, the Mesopotamian pantheon encompassed a multitude of other gods and goddesses, each with their specific roles and domains. For instance, Nanna (Sin) was the god of the moon and the patron deity of Ur, while Utu (Shamash) represented the sun and governed justice and truth. Ea (Enki) held dominion over water, wisdom, and magic, and was revered as a protector of humanity.

5.   Temple Rituals and Worship:
     Mesopotamian religious practices revolved around temples, which served as sacred spaces for communing with the deities. Rituals, performed by priests and priestesses, were integral to maintaining the divine order and seeking favor from the gods. Offerings, prayers, and elaborate ceremonies were conducted to honor and appease the deities and ensure their continued support and protection.

     The Mesopotamian pantheon offered a comprehensive framework for understanding the natural and social aspects of life. The gods and goddesses embodied the forces of nature, human endeavors, and societal structures, providing guidance, protection, and blessings to their worshippers. Their cults and rituals shaped the religious landscape and were intricately woven into the fabric of Mesopotamian society.

     By exploring the Mesopotamian pantheon, we gain insight into the multifaceted religious beliefs and practices of one of the world's oldest civilizations. The deities of Mesopotamia reflected the diverse concerns and aspirations of the people, highlighting the profound interplay between the spiritual and the worldly realms. As we delve into the intricacies of this pantheon, we uncover the rich tapestry of Mesopotamian polytheism and its enduring legacy in shaping human religious thought and practice.

Cosmic Order and Divine Hierarchy

Mesopotamian polytheism emphasized the concept of cosmic order, known as "me." This concept encompassed the divine laws, principles, and rituals that governed the universe and human society. The gods and goddesses were seen as the guardians and enforcers of this cosmic order, ensuring the stability and prosperity of both the natural and human realms.

Within the pantheon, a hierarchical structure existed, with certain deities holding greater prominence and power than others. The chief god, such as Enlil or Marduk, held authority over the other gods and played a crucial role in maintaining cosmic balance. This divine hierarchy reflected and reinforced social and political structures in Mesopotamian society.

Rituals, Temples, and Divination

Religious rituals and offerings played a central role in Mesopotamian polytheism. Temples, known as ziggurats, were constructed as sacred spaces where the gods were believed to reside. These massive stepped structures served as physical manifestations of the connection between the earthly and divine realms.

Priests and priestesses conducted elaborate ceremonies and performed sacred rites to communicate with the deities and seek their favor. Offerings of food, drink, and incense were presented to the gods as acts of devotion and gratitude. Divination, the practice of seeking knowledge or guidance from the gods through signs and omens, was also integral to Mesopotamian religious life.

Mythology and Epic Literature

Mythology and epic literature played a crucial role in Mesopotamian polytheism, conveying the stories and exploits of the gods and goddesses. These narratives provided explanations for natural phenomena, the origins of the world, and the nature of human existence. One of the most famous examples is the "Epic of Gilgamesh," which explores themes of mortality, heroism, and the relationship between humans and gods.

Through these myths and epics, the Mesopotamians sought to understand their place in the cosmos and the complex interactions between gods and humans. They offered moral lessons, cultural insights, and a sense of identity and belonging within the divine order.

In conclusion, polytheism in ancient Mesopotamia was characterized by a vast pantheon of gods and goddesses, each holding specific roles and responsibilities within the cosmic order. The rituals, temples, and mythology associated with this belief system shaped the religious and cultural practices of this ancient civilization. Understanding Mesopotamian polytheism provides valuable insights into the religious worldview and societal structures of one of humanity's earliest civilizations.

Examining the polytheistic beliefs in Sumerian and Babylonian civilizations

The ancient civilizations of Sumer and Babylon, located in Mesopotamia, were vibrant centers of polytheistic belief systems. The religious practices and mythology of these societies revolved around a diverse pantheon of gods and goddesses, each with their own unique characteristics, functions, and cultic significance. This section will delve into the polytheistic beliefs of the Sumerians and Babylonians, exploring the divine hierarchy, religious rituals, and the interplay between gods and humans in these ancient cultures.

The Sumerian Pantheon: Deities and Divine Functions

The Sumerian civilization, which emerged around 4000 BCE, laid the foundation for subsequent Mesopotamian cultures. The Sumerian pantheon consisted of a complex network of gods and goddesses who governed various aspects of life. Among the prominent deities were An, the god of the heavens; Enlil, the lord of the winds and ruler of the earth; Inanna, the goddess of love and fertility; and Nammu, the goddess associated with primordial waters.

Each deity held specific functions and powers, such as Enki, the god of wisdom and water, who was believed to possess the knowledge of creation. The Sumerians attributed human-like qualities and emotions to their gods, and they played an active role in human affairs, impacting fertility, agriculture, warfare, and other facets of daily life.

Babylonian Syncretism: Blending of Sumerian and Akkadian Beliefs

With the rise of the Babylonian Empire in the second millennium BCE, the polytheistic beliefs of the Sumerians underwent a process of syncretism with the Akkadian pantheon. This syncretic approach involved merging deities from different cultural backgrounds, resulting in a complex and interconnected divine hierarchy.

Under Babylonian rule, prominent deities such as Marduk, the god of Babylon, rose to prominence. Marduk became the patron deity of the Babylonian Empire and was elevated to the status of the supreme god, overseeing other gods and goddesses. This shift reflected the changing political landscape and the growing influence of Babylon as a dominant power in the region.

Cosmic Order and Rituals: Maintaining Harmony with the Gods

Polytheistic beliefs in Sumerian and Babylonian civilizations were closely intertwined with the concept of cosmic order. The gods and goddesses were seen as the guardians and enforcers of this order, responsible for maintaining harmony and prosperity in the natural and human realms. Religious rituals, offerings, and sacrifices were crucial for establishing and preserving a positive relationship with the divine.

Temples, known as ziggurats, served as sacred spaces where people could commune with the gods. These monumental structures were believed to bridge the gap between the earthly and divine realms, providing a physical space for worship and ritualistic practices. Priests and priestesses acted as intermediaries between humans and gods, performing ceremonies and offerings to ensure the favor of the deities.

Mythology and Epic Literature: Stories of Gods and Heroes

Mythology and epic literature played a significant role in shaping and transmitting the polytheistic beliefs of the Sumerians and Babylonians. These narratives, such as the "Epic of Gilgamesh," offered insights into the relationship between gods and humans, the origins of the world, and the moral and ethical values upheld by these societies.

The Sumerian and Babylonian myths provided explanations for natural phenomena, the creation of humans, and the divine intervention in human affairs. They showcased the struggles and adventures of heroes, highlighting the complex interaction between mortals and deities. These stories not only entertained but also served as didactic tools, imparting cultural, moral, and religious lessons to the people.

In conclusion, the polytheistic beliefs of the Sumerians and Babylonians were deeply ingrained in their societies, permeating every aspect of life. Through a complex pantheon of gods and goddesses, rituals, temples, and mythology, these ancient civilizations sought to understand and navigate their world. Exploring the polytheistic beliefs of Sumerian and Babylonian civilizations provides valuable insights into the religious and cultural fabric of early Mesopotamian societies.

Exploring the pantheon of Mesopotamian gods and their roles

The polytheistic belief system of ancient Mesopotamia was characterized by a rich and diverse pantheon of gods and goddesses. These deities played pivotal roles in the cosmology, religious rituals, and daily lives of the people. This section will delve into the pantheon of Mesopotamian gods, highlighting their individual characteristics, functions, and relationships within the divine hierarchy.

An: The Lord of the Heavens

An, also known as Anu, held the esteemed position of the supreme god in the Mesopotamian pantheon. He was revered as the lord of the heavens and ruler of the gods. An presided over matters of divine governance and cosmic order. As the father of the gods, he embodied wisdom, authority, and power. An was often depicted as a regal figure, seated on a throne, symbolizing his role as the ultimate arbiter of destiny.

Enlil: The Lord of the Winds and Earth

Enlil, the son of An, was another prominent deity in the Mesopotamian pantheon. He was associated with the winds, storms, and the earth. Enlil held dominion over natural phenomena and was regarded as a force of both destruction and renewal. He was considered the protector of cities and had the authority to grant or withhold blessings upon humanity. Enlil was often depicted wearing a horned crown, signifying his divine status and authority.

Inanna/Ishtar: The Goddess of Love and War

Inanna, also known as Ishtar, was a multifaceted goddess with dominion over various realms. She was associated with love, fertility, sexuality, and war. Inanna embodied both nurturing and assertive qualities, representing the dualistic nature of feminine power. As the goddess of love, she bestowed blessings upon relationships and ensured the continuation of life. In her warrior aspect, Inanna wielded power on the battlefield and protected her devotees. She was often depicted adorned with symbols of fertility and weapons of war.

Marduk: The God of Babylon

With the ascendancy of Babylon as a dominant power, the god Marduk rose to prominence in the Mesopotamian pantheon. Marduk was hailed as the patron deity of Babylon and came to symbolize its might and influence. He was associated with authority, justice, and victory in battles. Marduk's epic battle against the chaos dragon Tiamat, as described in the Enuma Elish, solidified his position as the supreme deity. In representations, Marduk was often depicted wearing a horned helmet, holding a scepter and a dragon-headed staff.

Ninhursag: The Mother Goddess

Ninhursag, also known as Nintu or Ninhursaga, represented the nurturing aspect of the divine feminine. She was the goddess of fertility, agriculture, and childbirth. Ninhursag was believed to have played a crucial role in the creation of humans, shaping them from clay and giving them life. As the mother goddess, she symbolized the cycle of birth, growth, and sustenance. Ninhursag was often depicted with symbols of fertility, such as overflowing breasts or ears of grain.

These are just a few examples from the vast pantheon of Mesopotamian gods and goddesses. Each deity held unique attributes and powers, governing different aspects of the natural and human realms. Their interactions, conflicts, and alliances shaped the cosmology and religious practices of ancient Mesopotamia. Exploring the pantheon of Mesopotamian gods offers us a glimpse into the rich tapestry of beliefs and the intricate web of divine relationships that defined this polytheistic civilization.

Polytheism in Ancient Egypt

Polytheism, the belief in multiple deities, was deeply ingrained in the religious and cultural fabric of ancient Egypt. The ancient Egyptians worshipped a diverse pantheon of gods and goddesses, each with their own unique characteristics, roles, and associations. This polytheistic belief system played a central role in every aspect of Egyptian society, shaping their worldview, influencing their rituals and ceremonies, and governing their interactions with the divine. In this section, we will delve into the fascinating world of Egyptian polytheism, exploring its origins, the roles of gods and goddesses, religious practices, and its significance in the lives of the ancient Egyptians.

Origins of Egyptian Polytheism

The roots of Egyptian polytheism can be traced back to the early pre-dynastic periods of Egyptian history. The ancient Egyptians revered natural forces and phenomena, associating them with divine beings. Over time, these concepts evolved into personified deities that represented various aspects of nature, society, and the afterlife.

The origins of Egyptian polytheism can be traced back to the very beginnings of ancient Egyptian civilization. In the early pre-dynastic periods, the ancient Egyptians lived in close proximity to the forces of nature and relied heavily on the natural world for their survival. They observed the cycles of the sun, the flooding of the Nile River, the growth of crops, and the behavior of animals. These natural phenomena played a crucial role in shaping their understanding of the divine.

The ancient Egyptians believed that the world was filled with spiritual forces and entities. They saw the hand of the divine in every aspect of their lives, from the rising and setting of the sun to the abundance of the harvest. They associated these natural forces with gods and goddesses who personified them and governed their domains.

For example, the sun was a central element in the ancient Egyptian worldview. They believed that the sun was not merely a celestial body but the embodiment of a powerful deity. The sun god, Ra, was seen as the creator of the universe and the source of life. The ancient Egyptians observed the sun's daily journey across the sky and its cyclical patterns throughout the year, which reinforced their belief in Ra's power and influence.

Similarly, the Nile River held immense importance for the ancient Egyptians. Its annual flooding brought fertile soil to the land, allowing for abundant agricultural production. They attributed this life-giving phenomenon to the goddess Hapi, who was believed to control the flooding and ensure the prosperity of the land. The Nile River was not just a physical entity but a manifestation of divine power and beneficence.

As the ancient Egyptians sought to understand and interact with these powerful natural forces, they began to anthropomorphize them, assigning human characteristics and personalities to the gods and goddesses. This process of personification allowed them to relate to and communicate with the divine entities on a more personal level.

Over time, the pantheon of Egyptian gods and goddesses expanded to encompass a wide range of deities, each with their own distinct roles and associations. They represented not only natural phenomena but also abstract concepts, societal roles, and aspects of human existence. For example, Isis was revered as the goddess of magic, healing, and motherhood, while Thoth was the god of writing, wisdom, and knowledge.

As Egyptian society became more complex, so did their pantheon of deities. The gods and goddesses became interconnected through genealogies, mythologies, and associations. They formed divine families, with gods and goddesses being married, giving birth to other deities, and engaging in intricate relationships that mirrored the complexities of human society.

In conclusion, the origins of Egyptian polytheism can be traced back to the early pre-dynastic periods, where the ancient Egyptians observed and revered the natural forces and phenomena around them. These observations and experiences led to the personification of these forces into gods and goddesses who governed different aspects of the world. This polytheistic belief system provided the ancient Egyptians with a comprehensive framework for understanding the cosmos and their place within it.

The Pantheon of Egyptian Gods and Goddesses

The Egyptian pantheon was vast and complex, consisting of hundreds of gods and goddesses. Among the most revered were Ra, the sun god and creator deity; Osiris, the god of the afterlife and resurrection; Isis, the goddess of magic and motherhood; and Horus, the god of kingship and protection. These deities held prominent roles in Egyptian mythology, and their worship was widespread throughout the civilization.

The pantheon of Egyptian gods and goddesses was a rich and complex tapestry that played a central role in the religious beliefs and practices of ancient Egypt. This diverse collection of deities represented various aspects of the natural world, human existence, and the divine realm.

At the pinnacle of the Egyptian pantheon stood Ra, the sun god. Ra was believed to be the creator of the universe, responsible for bringing light and life to the world. He was often depicted as a falcon-headed deity or as a man with a sun disc on his head. Ra's journey across the sky during the day and his descent into the underworld at night symbolized the eternal cycle of life and death.

Another prominent deity in the Egyptian pantheon was Osiris, the god of the afterlife and resurrection. Osiris was depicted as a mummified figure, representing the eternal nature of life beyond death. He played a vital role in the Egyptian concept of the afterlife, overseeing the judgment of souls and ensuring their passage into the realm of the dead. Osiris also symbolized fertility and the regenerative power of the Nile River, which brought life-giving floods to the land.

Isis, the wife of Osiris, was a goddess of great importance in Egyptian mythology. She was revered as the goddess of magic, healing, and motherhood. Isis was often depicted with her wings outstretched, protecting and nurturing her children. She was known for her wisdom and her ability to perform powerful acts of magic. As the mother of Horus, she played a crucial role in the protection and succession of the pharaoh, who was believed to be the earthly embodiment of Horus.

Divine Perspectives

Horus, the son of Osiris and Isis, was the god of kingship and protection. He was often depicted as a falcon-headed deity or as a man with the head of a falcon. Horus was associated with the ruling pharaoh and was believed to protect and guide the king throughout his reign. The battle between Horus and the god Set, who had killed Osiris, represented the struggle between order and chaos in Egyptian mythology.

In addition to these well-known deities, the Egyptian pantheon included a multitude of gods and goddesses, each with their own specific roles and associations. For example, Thoth was the god of writing, wisdom, and knowledge, often depicted with the head of an ibis or a baboon. Hathor was the goddess of love, beauty, and joy, often represented as a cow or as a woman with cow horns on her head. Sekhmet was the goddess of war and healing, associated with the destructive power of the sun.

Worship of these gods and goddesses was a central aspect of Egyptian religious life. Temples dedicated to specific deities were constructed throughout Egypt, serving as places of worship, ritual, and offerings. Priests and priestesses played crucial roles in maintaining the connection between the human world and the divine realm, performing rituals and ceremonies to honor the gods and seek their favor.

In conclusion, the pantheon of Egyptian gods and goddesses was a diverse and multifaceted collection of deities, each with their own unique roles and associations. From the mighty Ra to the compassionate Isis, these gods and goddesses were venerated and worshipped by the ancient Egyptians, who believed that their intervention and blessings were essential for the prosperity, protection, and spiritual well-being of both individuals and the entire civilization.

God/Goddess	Power(s)	Children	Other Information
Amun-Ra	Sun god, creator deity	-	Often depicted with a ram's head or a solar disk
Osiris	God of the afterlife, resurrection	Horus, Anubis, Isis, Seth, Nephthys	Depicted as a mummified figure with a crook and flail
Isis	Goddess of magic, motherhood	Horus	Often depicted with wings, as a protector of the pharaoh

Exploring the Contrasts and Convergence of Polytheism and Monotheism

God/Goddess	Power(s)	Children	Other Information
Horus	God of kingship, protection	-	Depicted as a falcon-headed deity, symbolizing the pharaoh
Thoth	God of wisdom, writing, magic	-	Depicted as an ibis-headed deity or a baboon
Ra	Sun god, creator deity	Shu, Tefnut, Nut, Geb, Osiris, Isis, Seth, Nephthys	Depicted as a falcon-headed deity or as a sun disk
Hathor	Goddess of love, beauty, joy	-	Often depicted as a cow or with cow horns and a sun disk
Anubis	God of embalming, protector of the dead	-	Depicted with the head of a jackal or as a full jackal
Seth	God of chaos, storms, desert	-	Often depicted with the head of an unknown animal
Ma'at	Goddess of truth, justice, harmony	-	Depicted with an ostrich feather on her head
Bastet	Goddess of home, fertility, cats	-	Depicted as a lioness or with the head of a lioness
Ptah	God of creation, craftsmanship	-	Often depicted as a mummified figure with a skullcap
Sekhmet	Goddess of war, healing	-	Depicted as a lioness-headed deity
Nephthys	Goddess of mourning, protection	Anubis	Sister of Isis and Osiris

God/Goddess	Power(s)	Children	Other Information
Geb	God of the earth	Nut	Often depicted lying beneath the sky goddess Nut
Nut	Goddess of the sky	Geb	Often depicted arched over the earth
Shu	God of air and sunlight	-	Often depicted holding up the sky

Please note that this is not an exhaustive list of all Egyptian gods and goddesses, as there are hundreds of deities in Egyptian mythology. The information provided here is a glimpse into the diverse pantheon of Egyptian gods and goddesses and their various attributes. The relationships between the gods and goddesses, as well as their forms and depictions, can vary in different sources and periods of Egyptian history.

Roles and Associations of Egyptian Deities

Each Egyptian deity had specific attributes, associations, and responsibilities. For example, Hathor was the goddess of love, beauty, and joy, while Thoth was the god of wisdom, writing, and magic. The gods and goddesses often had complex relationships with one another, forming family connections and interacting in myths and legends that provided insight into Egyptian cosmology and beliefs.

In the intricate tapestry of the Egyptian pantheon, each deity held a distinct set of attributes, associations, and responsibilities. These divine beings played integral roles in the religious beliefs and practices of the ancient Egyptians, shaping their understanding of the world and their place within it.

Hathor, the goddess of love, beauty, and joy, was one of the most revered deities in Egyptian mythology. She was often depicted as a woman with cow horns on her head or as a full cow. Hathor was associated with fertility and motherhood, and she was believed to bring happiness and abundance to the lives of the people. She was also closely linked to music and dance, and her presence was often invoked during celebrations and festivals.

Thoth, the god of wisdom, writing, and magic, held a crucial role in Egyptian society. Often depicted as a man with the head of an ibis or a baboon, Thoth was the patron of scribes and scholars. He was credited with the invention of writing and was regarded as the keeper of knowledge and the divine record-keeper. Thoth was also associated with the art of magic and was believed to possess the ability to heal and protect.

Among the most important deities in the Egyptian pantheon was Ma'at, the goddess of truth, justice, and cosmic balance. Ma'at personified the concept of order and harmony in Egyptian cosmology. She was depicted as a woman with an ostrich feather on her head and was often shown standing next to the pharaoh, symbolizing the ruler's responsibility to uphold truth and justice. Ma'at played a crucial role in the judgment of souls in the afterlife, weighing the hearts of the deceased against her feather to determine their fate.

Osiris, the god of the afterlife and resurrection, was central to the Egyptian belief in the journey of the soul beyond death. He was depicted as a mummified figure, symbolizing the eternal nature of life beyond the physical realm. Osiris was associated with fertility and the regenerative power of the Nile River, which brought life-giving floods to the land. He played a vital role in the myth of the struggle between order and chaos, as well as in the process of judgment and rebirth in the afterlife.

Isis, the wife of Osiris and the mother of Horus, held significant importance in Egyptian mythology. She was the goddess of magic, healing, and motherhood. Isis was often depicted with her wings outstretched, symbolizing her role as a protective and nurturing mother figure. She possessed great wisdom and was known for her ability to perform powerful acts of magic. Isis played a crucial role in the resurrection of Osiris and in the protection and succession of the pharaoh, who was believed to be the earthly embodiment of Horus.

These are just a few examples of the roles and associations of Egyptian deities within the vast pantheon. The gods and goddesses of ancient Egypt formed complex relationships with one another, often portrayed as family members and interacting in myths and legends. These stories provided insights into Egyptian cosmology, explaining the creation of the world, the struggles between gods and goddesses, and the fate of humanity in the afterlife.

Understanding the roles and associations of Egyptian deities is key to comprehending the intricate web of beliefs and practices in ancient Egyptian religion. Each god and goddess brought their unique attributes and powers to the pantheon, shaping the worldview and religious rituals of the ancient Egyptians. By honoring and seeking the favor of these deities, individuals and society as a whole aimed to maintain cosmic balance, ensure fertility and prosperity, and navigate the complexities of life and death within the Egyptian belief system.

Religious Practices and Rituals

Religious practices in ancient Egypt were deeply intertwined with daily life. Temples, dedicated to specific gods and goddesses, served as places of worship and focal points for religious activities. Egyptians engaged in rituals, offerings, and ceremonies to honor and appease the deities, seeking their blessings and protection. Priests and priestesses played vital roles in conducting these rituals and maintaining the temple sanctuaries.

Religious practices and rituals held a central position in the lives of the ancient Egyptians, permeating every aspect of their society. Temples, grand structures dedicated to specific gods and goddesses, served as the epicenters of religious activities and provided a sacred space for individuals to connect with the divine.

The rituals and ceremonies performed in these temples were conducted by a class of priests and priestesses who held significant influence and authority in religious matters. These individuals were responsible for maintaining the sanctity of the temples, performing daily rituals, and acting as intermediaries between the human and divine realms.

One of the primary purposes of religious rituals was to honor and appease the gods and goddesses, seeking their favor and protection. Egyptians believed that the deities had the power to influence various aspects of their lives, from ensuring bountiful harvests to granting fertility and well-being. By performing rituals and offerings, individuals sought to establish a harmonious relationship with the divine and maintain cosmic order.

Offerings played a crucial role in Egyptian religious practices. These offerings ranged from simple items such as food and drink to elaborate ceremonies involving intricate rituals and processions. Egyptians believed that by presenting offerings to the gods and goddesses, they could nourish and sustain the divine entities, thereby eliciting their favor and blessings. Offerings were often placed on altars within the temples or in specially designated areas, and the act of giving was accompanied by prayers and invocations.

Another significant aspect of Egyptian religious practices was the celebration of festivals and holy days. These occasions provided opportunities for communal worship, feasting, and rejoicing. Festivals were often dedicated to specific deities and were marked by elaborate processions, music, dancing, and theatrical performances. These vibrant and colorful events brought communities together, fostering a sense of unity and shared devotion.

Divination and oracular practices were also common in ancient Egyptian religious life. Egyptians sought guidance and insight from the gods through methods such as interpreting dreams, consulting oracles, and using divinatory tools like the casting of lots or the reading of animal entrails. The interpretations provided by priests and priestesses served as guidance for important decisions and actions in both personal and societal realms.

Moreover, the ancient Egyptians held a strong belief in the power of prayer. Prayers were addressed directly to the gods and goddesses, expressing gratitude, seeking assistance, or asking for forgiveness. These heartfelt pleas were believed to reach the ears of the divine beings and could potentially sway their benevolence and intervention in human affairs.

It is important to note that religious practices and rituals varied depending on the time period, regional differences, and individual preferences. While temples played a significant role, personal and household worship was also practiced, with individuals creating small shrines within their homes to honor their chosen deities.

Religious practices in ancient Egypt were not confined to the elite or the priesthood; they permeated every level of society. The majority of Egyptians, regardless of social status, participated in religious rituals, seeking to establish a connection with the divine and ensure their well-being in both earthly and afterlife realms.

By engaging in these religious practices, the ancient Egyptians sought to navigate the complexities of existence, maintain cosmic balance, and secure the favor and protection of the gods and goddesses. These rituals were not merely acts of superstition or empty tradition but were regarded as integral to the fabric of daily life, offering individuals a sense of purpose, meaning, and spiritual fulfillment.

Mythology and Cosmology

Egyptian mythology played a crucial role in explaining the creation of the world, the relationships between gods and humans, and the nature of the afterlife. Myths such as the Osiris myth, the conflict between Horus and Set, and the journey of the sun god Ra across the sky provided narratives that helped the Egyptians understand their place in the universe and the moral order of the cosmos.

Mythology and cosmology formed a fundamental part of the religious and cultural landscape of ancient Egypt. Egyptian myths were a rich tapestry of narratives that served to explain the creation of the world, the relationships between gods and humans, and the intricate workings of the universe.

One of the central myths in Egyptian mythology is the Osiris myth. Osiris, the god of the afterlife and resurrection, was a revered deity who ruled over the land of the dead. According to the myth, Osiris was murdered by his brother Set, who sought to usurp his power. Osiris's body was dismembered and scattered throughout Egypt, but through the efforts of his sister-wife Isis, he was resurrected and became the ruler of the underworld. This myth conveyed important themes of death, resurrection, and the cyclical nature of life, reflecting the Egyptians' belief in the afterlife and the eventual return to a state of renewal and rebirth.

Another significant myth in Egyptian cosmology is the conflict between Horus and Set. Horus, the son of Osiris and Isis, represented kingship and order, while Set symbolized chaos and disruption. The myth tells the story of Horus's struggle to avenge his father's death and claim his rightful place as the ruler of Egypt. The myth served as an allegory for the ongoing battle between order and chaos, a theme that was deeply ingrained in Egyptian society and reflected their desire for stability and harmony.

The journey of the sun god Ra across the sky was another important myth that played a central role in Egyptian cosmology. Ra was believed to travel through the sky during the day, providing light and warmth to the world. At night, he descended into the underworld, where he faced various challenges and trials before emerging victorious to begin his journey again. This myth reflected the cyclical nature of time and the eternal rhythm of day and night, emphasizing the Egyptians' belief in the continuity and order of the universe.

In addition to these prominent myths, Egyptian mythology encompassed a vast array of tales that depicted interactions between gods and humans, the origins of various natural phenomena, and the moral lessons that guided Egyptian society. These myths were not seen as mere stories but were regarded as sacred narratives that conveyed deep spiritual and philosophical truths.

Egyptian cosmology revolved around the concept of Ma'at, which encompassed notions of balance, harmony, and truth. The universe was believed to be governed by cosmic laws and principles that maintained order and ensured the smooth functioning of society. The gods and goddesses were seen as the custodians of Ma'at, responsible for upholding the cosmic balance and moral integrity of the world.

The Egyptians believed in a complex afterlife journey, where the deceased would face judgment in the Hall of Ma'at and be assessed based on their adherence to moral principles and the teachings of Ma'at. The righteous would be granted eternal life in the Field of Reeds, a paradise-like realm, while the wicked would face punishment and annihilation.

Mythology and cosmology were intricately intertwined with religious rituals and practices. Temples often housed elaborate depictions of mythological scenes, and rituals frequently incorporated reenactments of mythical events. These rituals aimed to reinforce the cosmic order, establish a connection with the gods, and ensure the continuity of Ma'at.

The significance of mythology and cosmology extended beyond the religious sphere and permeated all aspects of Egyptian culture, including art, literature, and architecture. Mythological narratives were depicted in temple reliefs, tomb paintings, and papyrus scrolls, serving as a visual representation of the beliefs and values of the society.

In conclusion, Egyptian mythology and cosmology formed a rich and complex tapestry of narratives that provided the ancient Egyptians with a framework for understanding the creation of the world, the relationships between gods and humans, and the nature of the afterlife. These myths conveyed profound philosophical and moral messages, reflecting the Egyptians' belief in the cyclical nature of life, the struggle between order and chaos, and the pursuit of harmony and balance. By embracing and engaging with these myths, the ancient Egyptians sought to navigate the complexities of existence and find meaning and purpose within the vast cosmic order.

Divine Kingship and Pharaonic Role

The concept of divine kingship was central to Egyptian society, as the pharaoh was believed to be a living embodiment of the gods on Earth. The pharaoh, as a mediator between the divine and human realms, performed religious rituals, built temples, and ensured the well-being of the gods. This sacred role of the pharaoh strengthened the connection between religion, politics, and society in ancient Egypt.

The concept of divine kingship held a significant place in the religious and political structure of ancient Egypt. The pharaoh, as the ruler of the kingdom, was not only a political leader but also a divine figure who acted as a bridge between the mortal realm and the gods.

According to Egyptian belief, the pharaoh was considered the son of the gods, specifically the son of the sun god Ra. This divine lineage bestowed upon the pharaoh a special status and authority, elevating them above ordinary mortals. The pharaoh was believed to possess a divine essence known as the "ka," which connected them to the gods and endowed them with extraordinary power and wisdom.

Divine Perspectives

As a representative of the gods on Earth, the pharaoh played a crucial role in the religious life of Egypt. They were responsible for maintaining Ma'at, the cosmic order, and ensuring the well-being of the gods through rituals and offerings. The pharaoh acted as the chief priest, personally performing religious ceremonies and making offerings to the gods in the temples. They were seen as the mediator between the gods and the people, interceding on behalf of the population and seeking divine favor and protection.

The construction of temples and the establishment of religious cults were also essential aspects of the pharaoh's role. The pharaoh commissioned the building of grand temples dedicated to specific gods and goddesses, serving as centers of religious activity and pilgrimage. These temples housed statues and images of the deities, and the pharaoh was responsible for their maintenance and worship.

The pharaoh's authority and divine connection were further reinforced through iconography and symbolism. The pharaoh was often depicted in art and sculpture with regal attributes and symbols of their divine status, such as the double crown representing the unification of Upper and Lower Egypt, the uraeus (a symbol of divine kingship) on their forehead, and the false beard symbolizing their association with the gods. These visual representations solidified the pharaoh's position as a divine ruler and conveyed their authority and power to the Egyptian people.

The divine kingship concept also had political implications. The pharaoh's divine legitimacy and role as a representative of the gods conferred upon them the right to rule and make decisions on behalf of the gods and the people. The pharaoh's rule was seen as essential for the well-being and prosperity of Egypt, and their success in maintaining Ma'at and protecting the kingdom was believed to ensure the harmony and stability of the entire cosmos.

The influence of divine kingship extended beyond the pharaoh's lifetime. The belief in the pharaoh's immortality and their continued role as a divine figure in the afterlife was a significant aspect of Egyptian religious belief. Through elaborate burial rituals and the construction of monumental tombs, such as the pyramids, the pharaoh prepared for their journey into the afterlife and their eternal reign as a god among the gods.

In summary, the concept of divine kingship played a central role in ancient Egyptian society, intertwining religion, politics, and the daily lives of the people. The pharaoh, as a living embodiment of the gods, held immense religious and political authority, acting as a mediator between the mortal and divine realms. Their responsibilities included performing religious rituals, maintaining temples, and upholding the cosmic order. The institution of divine kingship reflected the

Egyptians' deep reverence for the divine and their belief in the interconnectedness of the earthly and heavenly realms.

Afterlife Beliefs and Funerary Practices

Egyptian polytheism had a significant impact on the beliefs and practices surrounding the afterlife. The ancient Egyptians believed in an intricate journey through the underworld and the judgment of the soul before entering the realm of the blessed. Funerary rituals, such as mummification and tomb construction, aimed to preserve the body and provide a comfortable afterlife for the deceased.

Afterlife beliefs and funerary practices held a central place in ancient Egyptian culture, stemming from their polytheistic worldview. The Egyptians believed in an intricate journey of the soul after death, which involved passing through the underworld and undergoing judgment before entering the realm of the blessed.

One of the primary goals of Egyptian funerary practices was the preservation of the body. The belief in the physical resurrection of the deceased necessitated the careful preservation of the body through the process of mummification. Mummification involved the removal of internal organs, desiccation of the body, and wrapping it in linen bandages. This process aimed to maintain the physical integrity of the body, as it was believed that the soul, or "ka," required a recognizable form to continue its existence in the afterlife.

Tomb construction was another crucial aspect of Egyptian funerary practices. The tombs were built to provide a comfortable and eternal resting place for the deceased and to serve as a link between the mortal world and the afterlife. The most iconic examples of Egyptian tombs are the pyramids, constructed for pharaohs during the Old Kingdom. These grand structures served as monumental tombs, housing the pharaoh's body, along with provisions, treasures, and texts, such as the Pyramid Texts, which contained spells and rituals intended to guide the pharaoh's journey in the afterlife.

Beyond the pharaohs, individuals from various social strata also constructed tombs and burial sites. These tombs ranged from simple mastabas, rectangular structures made of mud bricks, to elaborately decorated rock-cut tombs known as "hypogea" in the Valley of the Kings and the Valley of the Queens. The design and decoration of the tombs reflected the individual's social status and wealth, with more affluent individuals having more elaborate and ornate burial sites.

The Egyptians believed in the existence of the "Duat," the realm of the dead and the underworld. The journey of the soul in the afterlife involved passing through this realm, encountering various challenges and undergoing judgment. The deceased would be led by the god Anubis to the Hall of Ma'at, where their heart would be weighed against the feather of Ma'at, the goddess of truth and justice. If their heart was found to be pure and free of wrongdoing, they would be granted eternal life in the blessed realm. However, if their heart was found to be heavy with sins, it would be devoured by the monster Ammit, and the soul would face annihilation.

To assist the deceased on their journey, funerary texts known as the "Book of the Dead" or "Book of Coming Forth by Day" were placed in the tomb. These texts contained spells, prayers, and instructions that provided guidance and protection for the deceased in the afterlife. They were intended to help the soul navigate the challenges of the Duat, recognize and overcome various obstacles, and ultimately attain a favorable judgment.

The funeral rituals and offerings were also an essential part of Egyptian funerary practices. Relatives and loved ones would participate in ceremonies and provide offerings of food, drink, and other goods to sustain the deceased in the afterlife. These offerings were believed to nourish the soul and ensure its well-being and comfort in the eternal realm.

The belief in the afterlife and the importance placed on funerary practices reflected the Egyptians' desire for continuity and eternal existence. They believed that death was not the end but rather a transition to another realm where the deceased would continue their existence and be reunited with loved ones. The elaborate rituals, mummification, and tomb construction were all expressions of this belief and the desire to secure a prosperous afterlife for the deceased.

In summary, Egyptian polytheism greatly influenced beliefs and practices regarding the afterlife. The preservation of the body through mummification, the construction of tombs and pyramids, and the inclusion of funerary texts and offerings were all integral to ensuring a successful journey and judgment in the afterlife. The Egyptian funerary practices exemplified the Egyptians' profound belief in the continuity of life and the importance of preparing for the eternal realm.

Legacy and Influence

Egyptian polytheism left a lasting legacy on subsequent cultures and religions. The worship of Egyptian deities spread beyond Egypt's borders, influencing neighboring civilizations. Furthermore, the symbolisms, rituals, and mythological motifs of ancient Egyptian polytheism can be seen in various contemporary practices, such as witchcraft, divination, herbalism, shamanism, and ecospirituality.

Exploring the Contrasts and Convergence of Polytheism and Monotheism

The legacy of Egyptian polytheism extends far beyond the borders of ancient Egypt. The worship of Egyptian deities and the fascination with their rich mythology had a significant impact on neighboring civilizations and subsequent religious traditions.

The influence of Egyptian polytheism can be seen in the religious practices of surrounding cultures, particularly in the Near East. The ancient Egyptians had cultural and religious interactions with civilizations such as the Phoenicians, Canaanites, and Hittites. These interactions resulted in the adoption and adaptation of certain Egyptian gods and goddesses into the pantheons of these cultures. For example, the worship of the goddess Isis became widespread in the Greco-Roman world, and the cult of Osiris influenced religious practices in the Hellenistic period.

Furthermore, the symbolism, rituals, and mythological motifs of ancient Egyptian polytheism have found resonance in contemporary spiritual practices. Within witchcraft traditions, for instance, Egyptian deities and symbols are often invoked and incorporated into spellwork and ritual practices. The goddess Isis, with her association with magic and motherhood, is particularly revered within modern witchcraft and goddess spirituality movements.

Divination practices also draw inspiration from ancient Egyptian traditions. Methods such as scrying (using a reflective surface to gain insights) and the interpretation of symbols and omens find parallels in the ancient Egyptian practices of dream interpretation, hieroglyphic divination, and the reading of celestial signs.

Herbalism, too, bears the influence of ancient Egyptian knowledge. The Egyptians were skilled in the use of herbs and plants for medicinal and magical purposes. Many contemporary herbalists and practitioners of alternative medicine draw upon this ancient wisdom when working with botanical remedies.

Shamanic traditions also find echoes of ancient Egyptian spirituality. The concept of journeying to other realms, communication with spirit guides, and the practice of soul retrieval can be seen as parallel to the shamanic practices of ancient Egypt, where individuals were believed to communicate with the spirit world and navigate the realms of the gods.

Additionally, the ecological and naturalistic aspects of ancient Egyptian polytheism align with the principles of ecospirituality. The Egyptians held a deep reverence for the natural world, with deities representing natural elements such as the Nile River, the sun, and the sky. This recognition of the divine in nature resonates with contemporary spiritual movements that emphasize the interconnectedness of humans and the environment.

In conclusion, the legacy and influence of Egyptian polytheism are far-reaching. Its impact on neighboring cultures and subsequent religious traditions is evident in the adoption of Egyptian deities, the incorporation of symbolism and rituals into contemporary practices, and the inspiration drawn from ancient Egyptian mythology and spirituality. The enduring fascination with Egyptian polytheism speaks to its profound and enduring contribution to the tapestry of human religious and spiritual expression.

Conclusion

The polytheistic belief system of ancient Egypt provided a comprehensive framework for understanding the cosmos, human existence, and the divine. The Egyptian pantheon was a rich tapestry of gods and goddesses, each with their own distinct roles and associations. Through religious practices, rituals, and myths, the ancient Egyptians sought to connect with and honor their deities. The influence of Egyptian polytheism extended beyond its borders and continues to inspire and inform various spiritual traditions today. By exploring the complexities of Egyptian polytheism, we gain valuable insights into the religious mindset and cultural identity of one of the most fascinating civilizations in history.

The polytheistic religious practices and beliefs of ancient Egyptians

The ancient Egyptians were deeply religious and held a complex system of polytheistic beliefs and practices. Their religious worldview revolved around the idea that the world was inhabited by a multitude of gods and goddesses who controlled different aspects of nature, society, and the afterlife. Understanding and appeasing these deities was crucial for maintaining cosmic harmony and ensuring the well-being of both the individual and the state.

At the core of Egyptian religious belief was the concept of ma'at, which represented the fundamental order and balance of the universe. The gods were seen as guardians and enforcers of ma'at, and it was the duty of humans to align their actions with this cosmic order. Failure to uphold ma'at could lead to chaos, disorder, and divine punishment.

The pantheon of Egyptian gods and goddesses was vast and diverse, with each deity representing a specific aspect of nature or society. Some of the most revered gods included Ra, the sun god and creator deity; Osiris, the god of the afterlife and resurrection; Isis, the goddess of magic and motherhood; and Horus, the god of kingship and protection. These deities were often depicted with human or animal forms and possessed unique symbols and attributes that distinguished them from one another.

The ancient Egyptians believed that the gods had a direct influence on daily life and were involved in every aspect of human existence. They worshipped the gods through rituals, offerings, and ceremonies conducted by priests and priestesses. Temples were built as sacred spaces dedicated to specific deities, where individuals could come to pray, make offerings, and seek divine guidance. The priests acted as intermediaries between the human and divine realms, performing the rituals and maintaining the temple sanctuaries.

The Egyptians also believed in the power of magic and the efficacy of spells and incantations. Magical practices were prevalent in daily life, ranging from protective charms and amulets to rituals aimed at healing, fertility, and success. The use of magic was not seen as contradictory to religious beliefs but rather as a means to harness and manipulate divine forces for the benefit of individuals and society.

Funerary practices held great significance in ancient Egyptian religion due to their beliefs about the afterlife. They believed that the soul continued to exist after death and embarked on a journey through the underworld before reaching the realm of the blessed. Mummification was a common practice, aimed at preserving the body for its eventual resurrection and reunion with the soul. Elaborate tombs, such as the pyramids, were constructed for the pharaohs and nobles, filled with provisions and belongings to accompany them in the afterlife. The Book of the Dead, a collection of spells and instructions, was often buried with the deceased to guide them through the perilous journey and ensure a successful transition to the afterlife.

In summary, the religious practices and beliefs of ancient Egyptians were deeply rooted in polytheism and centered around the worship and reverence of numerous gods and goddesses. Their rituals, offerings, and ceremonies were conducted to uphold cosmic harmony, seek divine blessings, and navigate the complexities of human existence. The concepts of ma'at, divine intervention, and the afterlife played pivotal roles in shaping their religious worldview and cultural practices.

Highlighting the significance of major Egyptian deities and their mythologies

The pantheon of Egyptian gods and goddesses was vast and diverse, with each deity playing a significant role in the religious and cultural life of ancient Egypt. These deities were associated with various aspects of nature, society, and the afterlife, and their myths and legends provided insights into Egyptian cosmology and beliefs.

One of the most prominent deities in Egyptian mythology was Ra, the sun god and creator deity. Ra was believed to govern the daily journey of the sun across the sky, symbolizing the cycle of life and death. His mythological narratives portrayed him as the supreme ruler and father of all other gods. Ra's journey through the underworld during the night represented the challenges and obstacles that the deceased would encounter in their own journey through the afterlife.

Osiris, the god of the afterlife and resurrection, held great importance in Egyptian mythology. He was depicted as a mummified figure, symbolizing the preservation and regeneration of life. Osiris was associated with the cycle of death and rebirth, and his myth centered around his murder by his brother Set and subsequent resurrection by his wife Isis. This myth conveyed the Egyptian belief in the afterlife and the potential for eternal life and resurrection.

Isis, the goddess of magic and motherhood, was revered for her powerful role as a divine mother and protector. She was known for her unwavering love and devotion to her husband Osiris and her son Horus. Isis played a crucial role in the resurrection of Osiris and was associated with healing, fertility, and the nurturing aspects of motherhood. Her mythology emphasized the importance of feminine power and the ability to bring life and renewal.

Horus, the son of Isis and Osiris, represented kingship, protection, and divine authority. He was often depicted as a falcon or as a human with a falcon's head, symbolizing his association with the sky and the sun. The myth of Horus centered around his struggle against his uncle Set, who had killed his father Osiris and usurped the throne. Horus' victory over Set represented the triumph of order and justice over chaos.

Another significant deity in Egyptian mythology was Thoth, the god of wisdom, writing, and magic. Thoth was believed to have invented writing and was considered the patron deity of scribes and scholars. He was also associated with the moon and lunar cycles, representing the passage of time and the recording of knowledge. Thoth's mythological role included being the mediator and arbitrator between the gods and humans, as well as the keeper of divine knowledge and secrets.

These are just a few examples of the major Egyptian deities and their mythologies. Each deity had their own distinct roles, associations, and responsibilities, reflecting different aspects of the natural and social world. The myths and legends surrounding these gods and goddesses provided the ancient Egyptians with narratives that explained the creation of the world, the relationships between gods and humans, and the nature of the afterlife. These mythological stories served to educate, inspire, and guide individuals in their religious practices and understanding of the divine realm.

Polytheism in Ancient Greece and Rome

Polytheism in ancient Greece and Rome was a fundamental aspect of their religious and cultural systems. The Greeks and Romans worshipped a multitude of gods and goddesses, each representing various domains, phenomena, and aspects of human life. Their polytheistic beliefs influenced every aspect of society, from daily rituals to civic ceremonies and public festivals.

In ancient Greece, the pantheon of gods and goddesses was extensive, with twelve major Olympian gods reigning supreme. Zeus, the king of the gods, symbolized divine authority and power. He controlled the skies and was associated with thunder and lightning. Hera, his wife and sister, represented marriage and family. Poseidon, the god of the sea, held dominion over water and earthquakes. Athena, the goddess of wisdom and strategic warfare, was renowned for her intelligence and skill in battle. Other significant Greek deities included Apollo, Artemis, Aphrodite, Hermes, and Dionysus, each governing specific aspects of life and nature.

The Romans adopted many of the Greek gods and goddesses, but with different names and slightly altered attributes. For example, Zeus became Jupiter, Hera became Juno, and Athena became Minerva. The Romans also had their own unique deities, such as Mars, the god of war, and Venus, the goddess of love and beauty. Roman mythology and religious practices were closely intertwined with their political and social structures. Emperors and other political leaders often sought divine approval and support by aligning themselves with certain gods and participating in elaborate public ceremonies.

In both Greek and Roman polytheism, the gods and goddesses were believed to have human-like characteristics, including emotions, desires, and flaws. They were capable of intervening in human affairs, both positively and negatively, and were often invoked for blessings, protection, and guidance. Temples and sanctuaries dedicated to the gods were constructed throughout Greece and Rome, serving as focal points for religious rituals, offerings, and prayers.

The Greeks and Romans celebrated their religious beliefs through various festivals and games. These events, such as the Olympic Games in ancient Greece and the Roman Saturnalia, involved processions, sacrifices, athletic competitions, and theatrical performances. They provided opportunities for individuals to express their devotion to the gods, seek their favor, and come together as a community.

Polytheism in ancient Greece and Rome reflected the interconnectedness of the natural and human realms. The gods and goddesses personified natural phenomena, such as the sun, moon, and the forces of nature, as well as aspects of human life, including love, war, wisdom, and fertility. The worship of multiple deities allowed individuals to address different aspects of their lives and seek divine assistance and guidance in various realms.

The influence of Greek and Roman polytheism extended beyond their own civilizations. As the Greeks established colonies and the Romans expanded their empire, their religious beliefs and practices spread throughout the Mediterranean and influenced the religious traditions of other cultures. The legacy of Greek and Roman polytheism can still be seen in modern Western culture, where the names and attributes of these ancient deities continue to resonate in various contexts, including literature, art, and popular culture.

In conclusion, polytheism in ancient Greece and Rome was a central aspect of their religious and cultural systems. The worship of multiple gods and goddesses represented the diverse aspects of the natural and human realms, and their mythology and rituals shaped every facet of society. The rich pantheon of Greek and Roman deities, with their distinct roles and associations, provided individuals with a framework for understanding the world and their place within it. The legacy of Greek and Roman polytheism continues to influence Western culture, demonstrating the enduring impact of these ancient belief systems.

Investigating the polytheistic belief systems of ancient Greek and Roman civilizations

Investigating the polytheistic belief systems of ancient Greek and Roman civilizations allows us to delve into the complex and fascinating religious practices of these societies. The Greeks and Romans had rich mythologies and a diverse pantheon of gods and goddesses that played integral roles in their daily lives, social structures, and cultural expressions.

In ancient Greece, the polytheistic belief system was deeply rooted in mythology, which provided narratives and explanations for the origins of the world, the relationships between gods and humans, and the workings of the universe. Greek mythology featured a diverse cast of gods and goddesses, each with their own personalities, attributes, and spheres of influence. These deities were anthropomorphic, possessing human-like qualities and engaging in affairs, rivalries, and interactions that mirrored human experiences.

The Greeks believed in a hierarchy of gods, with twelve major Olympian gods presiding over the divine realm. Zeus, the king of the gods and ruler of Mount Olympus, symbolized supreme authority and was associated with thunder and lightning. Hera, his sister and wife, represented marriage and family. Poseidon, the god of the sea, held dominion over the waters and was invoked for safe voyages. Athena, the goddess of wisdom and strategic warfare, was highly revered for her intelligence and guidance in battle. Other notable Greek deities included Apollo, the god of music and poetry, Artemis, the goddess of the hunt and the moon, Aphrodite, the goddess of love and beauty, Hermes, the messenger of the gods, and Dionysus, the god of wine and revelry.

Greek religious practices involved the construction of temples and sanctuaries dedicated to specific gods and goddesses. These sacred spaces served as centers of worship, where individuals offered prayers, performed rituals, and made sacrifices to honor and appease the deities. Festivals and public ceremonies were an essential part of Greek religious life, providing opportunities for communities to come together, celebrate, and seek the favor of the gods. The most famous of these festivals was the Olympic Games, held every four years in honor of Zeus.

Similarly, the Romans had a complex and elaborate polytheistic belief system that was deeply intertwined with their social and political structures. The Romans adopted and adapted many of the Greek gods and goddesses, giving them new names and incorporating them into their own mythology and religious practices. Jupiter, the Roman counterpart of Zeus, represented divine authority and the protector of the state. Juno, the Roman equivalent of Hera, was the goddess of marriage and childbirth. Mars, the god of war, was revered by soldiers and military leaders. Venus, the goddess of love and beauty, was associated with fertility and prosperity.

Roman religious practices included offerings, prayers, and rituals performed by priests and priestesses. Temples dedicated to specific deities were constructed throughout the Roman Empire, serving as places of worship and focal points for religious activities. The Romans also believed in personal household gods called Lares and Penates, who protected the home and family.

The influence of Greek and Roman polytheism extended beyond religious beliefs and practices. Mythological stories and characters from these civilizations have had a lasting impact on Western literature, art, and culture. Their influence can be seen in the works of ancient playwrights such as Aeschylus, Sophocles, and Euripides, as well as in the sculptures, mosaics, and frescoes that adorned ancient buildings. The enduring popularity of Greek and Roman mythology in contemporary literature, film, and entertainment demonstrates the continued fascination with these ancient belief systems.

In conclusion, investigating the polytheistic belief systems of ancient Greek and Roman civilizations provides us with a deeper understanding of the religious practices, mythologies, and cultural expressions of these societies. The diverse pantheon of gods and goddesses, the rituals and ceremonies, and the myths and legends that emerged from these belief systems shaped the worldview and daily lives of the ancient Greeks and Romans. Their influence continues to resonate in Western culture, emphasizing the enduring significance of these ancient civilizations.

Exploring the roles of gods and goddesses in Greek and Roman mythology

Exploring the roles of gods and goddesses in Greek and Roman mythology allows us to delve into the fascinating narratives and functions assigned to these divine beings. In both ancient Greek and Roman societies, the gods and goddesses played significant roles in shaping various aspects of the world and human existence, reflecting the values, ideals, and concerns of the cultures that worshipped them.

In Greek mythology, the gods and goddesses were depicted as powerful, immortal beings who possessed human-like qualities and emotions. They were believed to control different aspects of the natural world, human endeavors, and societal structures. Each deity had a specific sphere of influence and unique attributes, which influenced the lives and experiences of mortals.

Zeus, the king of the gods, reigned over Mount Olympus and held supreme authority. He was associated with thunder and lightning, and his decisions and actions affected the entire pantheon. Hera, Zeus's sister and wife, represented marriage and family. She was often depicted as a protector of women and a guardian of the sanctity of marriage.

Poseidon, the god of the sea, held dominion over the waters, and his actions influenced maritime activities, including voyages and storms. Athena, the goddess of wisdom and strategic warfare, was highly revered for her intelligence, courage, and guidance in battle. She was also associated with crafts and the arts, symbolizing the creative and intellectual aspects of civilization.

Other prominent Greek deities included Apollo, the god of music, poetry, prophecy, and healing; Artemis, the goddess of the hunt, wilderness, and childbirth; Aphrodite, the goddess of love, beauty, and desire; Hermes, the messenger of the gods and the patron of travelers, thieves, and merchants; and Dionysus, the god of wine, revelry, and ecstasy.

In Roman mythology, many of the Greek gods and goddesses were adopted and given Roman names, although their essential attributes and roles remained largely unchanged. Jupiter, the Roman counterpart of Zeus, represented divine authority and the protector of the state. Juno, the Roman equivalent of Hera, was the goddess of marriage, childbirth, and the queen of the gods.

Mars, the Roman god of war, played a crucial role in military affairs and was invoked by soldiers and military leaders. Venus, the goddess of love, beauty, and fertility, was associated with prosperity and was often depicted as the mother of Aeneas, the mythical founder of Rome.

These gods and goddesses were not only associated with specific domains but also engaged in complex relationships and interactions, resulting in intriguing narratives and myths. Their interactions with mortals and with one another shaped the destiny of both humans and gods alike, showcasing the intricate interconnectedness of the divine and mortal realms.

The Greek and Roman myths provided explanations for natural phenomena, human experiences, and societal customs. They served as moral guides, cautionary tales, and sources of inspiration for individuals and communities. The myths also offered insights into the origins of the world, the conflicts between gods and mortals, and the struggles for power and dominance.

The gods and goddesses were not distant and detached beings, but rather interactive entities who influenced the lives and fates of mortals. Mortals sought the favor and protection of these divine beings through prayers, rituals, and offerings. Festivals and ceremonies were held in their honor, reinforcing the connection between the human and divine realms.

The roles of gods and goddesses in Greek and Roman mythology went beyond their divine functions. They embodied human emotions, virtues, and vices, making them relatable and providing a lens through which people could understand their own experiences and aspirations. The tales of love, betrayal, heroism, and tragedy associated with these deities became a source of inspiration for art, literature, and philosophical contemplation.

In conclusion, exploring the roles of gods and goddesses in Greek and Roman mythology reveals a rich tapestry of divine beings with distinct powers, personalities, and roles in shaping the world and human existence. The myths and legends associated with these deities provide invaluable insights into the cultural, social, and spiritual aspects of ancient Greek and Roman civilizations, leaving a lasting impact on Western culture and beyond.

Greek God	Powers	Children
Titans	Time, Harvest	Zeus, Poseidon, Hades, Hera, Hestia, Demeter
Kronos (Cronus)		
Zeus	Sky, Thunder, Kingship, Justice	Athena, Apollo, Artemis, Hermes, Persephone, Perseus, Dionysus, Hercules
Poseidon	Sea,Earthquakes, Horses	Polyphemus,Theseus
Hades	Underworld	Melinoe, Macaria, Zagreus
Hera	Marriage, Family	Hephaestus, Ares, Hebe, Eileithyia
Hestia	Hearth	
Demeter	Agriculture	Persephone
Athena	Wisdom, War	
Apollo	Sun, Music, Prophecy	Asclepius, Orpheus, Apollo, Musagetes
Artemis	Moon, Hunting	Orion, Iphigenia
Hermes	Travel, Communication	Pan, Hermaphroditus
Persephone	Queen of the Underworld, Spring	
Dionysus	Wine, Ecstasy	Oenopion, Hymen
Hephaestus	Fire, Blacksmithing	Thalia, Eucleia
Ares	War	Eros, Phobos

Additionally, here are some other notable gods and goddesses:

Eros: Love, desire
Iris: Rainbow, messenger of the gods
Nike: Victory
Pan: Nature, shepherds, flocks, rustic music
Persephone: Queen of the Underworld, vegetation, seasons
Thanatos: Death
Triton: Sea, messenger of the sea
Tyche: Fortune, luck

The influence of polytheistic beliefs on Greek philosophy and literature

Polytheistic beliefs had a profound influence on Greek philosophy and literature, shaping the way ancient Greeks understood the world, human nature, and the divine. The polytheistic worldview provided a rich tapestry of gods and goddesses, each with their own personalities, powers, and stories, which served as a source of inspiration for philosophers and writers.

In Greek philosophy, the gods and goddesses often became metaphors or symbols for abstract concepts. For example, the god Apollo, associated with reason, order, and the arts, became a symbol of the pursuit of knowledge and the ideal of harmonious living. The goddess Athena, embodying wisdom and strategic warfare, represented the value of intellect and strategic thinking. These philosophical interpretations of the gods allowed philosophers to explore complex ideas and convey moral and ethical principles through storytelling and allegory.

Greek literature, especially epic poetry, drew heavily from the polytheistic belief system. Homer's "Iliad" and "Odyssey" portrayed the gods as active participants in human affairs, influencing the outcomes of battles and the fate of heroes. The works of Hesiod, such as "Theogony" and "Works and Days," provided detailed accounts of the origins of the gods and their interactions with humans.

Furthermore, the polytheistic framework allowed Greek writers to explore the complexities of human nature and the moral dilemmas faced by individuals. The gods and goddesses served as archetypes and mirrors of human behavior, representing both the virtues and vices of humanity. The tragedies of playwrights like Aeschylus, Sophocles, and Euripides often delved into the moral and existential questions of human existence, using the gods and their actions as a backdrop for exploring the human condition.

Polytheistic beliefs also influenced the concept of fate and destiny in Greek literature. The gods were believed to have power over human destinies, and characters often struggled with their predetermined paths and the influence of divine forces. This theme is evident in works like Sophocles' "Oedipus Rex," where the protagonist's tragic fate is ultimately determined by the gods.

Overall, the influence of polytheistic beliefs on Greek philosophy and literature was multi-faceted. It provided a rich source of inspiration, symbolism, and moral exploration, shaping the way Greeks contemplated the world, their place in it, and the nature of the divine. The gods and goddesses of Greek mythology became central figures in philosophical discourse and literary works, contributing to the richness and depth of Greek intellectual and cultural achievements.

CHAPTER 5: THE ORIGINS OF MONOTHEISM

The concept of monotheism, the belief in a single, all-powerful deity, has played a significant role in shaping the religious and cultural landscapes of various civilizations throughout history. Monotheistic religions such as Judaism, Christianity, and Islam have millions of followers worldwide and have had a profound impact on the development of human civilization. However, the origins and emergence of monotheistic belief systems are complex and multifaceted.

In this chapter, we will delve into the origins of monotheism, exploring its historical context, key figures, and the factors that contributed to its rise. We will examine the transition from polytheistic beliefs to monotheism in ancient civilizations, including the influence of religious, social, and cultural factors on this transformation. Furthermore, we will explore the monotheistic elements present in ancient religions and philosophies, tracing the evolution of monotheism as a distinct concept.

The chapter will begin with an exploration of monotheism in ancient Egypt, examining the revolutionary religious reforms of Pharaoh Akhenaten and the introduction of Atenism. We will then turn our attention to the monotheistic elements in Zoroastrianism, an ancient Persian religion that influenced subsequent monotheistic traditions. Additionally, we will delve into the monotheistic aspects of Hinduism and Sikhism, exploring the belief in a formless God and the unity of divine essence.

Furthermore, the chapter will investigate the historical context of Judaism as the precursor to Christianity and Islam, exploring the monotheistic foundations of these Abrahamic religions. We will examine the impact of monotheistic beliefs on the development of Western civilization, including the influence on ethical frameworks, philosophical thought, and social structures.

Throughout the chapter, we will present a balanced perspective, acknowledging the diversity of beliefs and interpretations within monotheistic traditions. We will also explore the challenges and criticisms that monotheism has faced, as well as the interplay between monotheistic and polytheistic elements within religious practices.

By delving into the origins of monotheism, we seek to gain a deeper understanding of the historical, cultural, and philosophical underpinnings of this belief system. This exploration will shed light on the complex evolution of religious thought and the enduring impact of monotheistic beliefs on human civilization.

Monotheistic Seeds in Ancient Near East

The emergence of monotheism can be traced back to the ancient Near East, a region that encompassed present-day Egypt, Mesopotamia, Persia, and the Levant. While polytheism was prevalent in these ancient civilizations, there were seeds of monotheistic ideas that laid the foundation for the development of monotheistic beliefs.

One notable example is found in ancient Egypt during the reign of Pharaoh Akhenaten (1353-1336 BCE). Akhenaten instituted a radical religious reform known as Atenism, which centered around the worship of the sun-disk deity, Aten, as the supreme and sole god. This marked a departure from the traditional polytheistic worship of multiple gods in Egypt. Akhenaten sought to establish the exclusive worship of Aten, emphasizing the concept of a single, universal deity. While Atenism did not endure beyond Akhenaten's reign, it demonstrated an early inclination towards monotheistic beliefs in the ancient world.

In Mesopotamia, the ancient civilization that flourished in the fertile lands between the Tigris and Euphrates rivers, there were also indications of monotheistic tendencies. The Akkadian ruler Naram-Sin (2254-2218 BCE) claimed a unique divine status, elevating himself above other gods and presenting himself as the sole object of worship. This exemplified a monotheistic inclination, albeit with a human ruler as the central focus.

The ancient Persian religion of Zoroastrianism also played a significant role in the development of monotheistic beliefs. Zoroastrianism, founded by the prophet Zoroaster (or Zarathustra) in the 6th century BCE, posited the existence of a supreme deity called Ahura Mazda, who represented the forces of good and light. Ahura Mazda was believed to be the creator of the universe and the source of ultimate truth and righteousness. While Zoroastrianism recognized other spiritual beings, it emphasized the worship and devotion to Ahura Mazda as the supreme god. The monotheistic elements of Zoroastrianism influenced later monotheistic religions, particularly Judaism and Christianity.

It is important to note that these monotheistic seeds in the ancient Near East did not fully develop into mature monotheistic religions during their respective periods. However, they laid the groundwork and paved the way for the eventual emergence of monotheistic belief systems in the subsequent centuries.

The monotheistic seeds in the ancient Near East signify a shift in religious thought and a recognition of the potential existence of a single, supreme deity. These early inklings of monotheism demonstrate the human capacity to question and explore the nature of divinity, seeking to understand the ultimate source of power and meaning in the universe. As we delve further into the historical context of monotheism, we will explore how these seeds took root and evolved into more fully developed monotheistic religions that have had a profound impact on human spirituality and culture.

Exploring early monotheistic elements in ancient Near Eastern civilizations

The ancient Near Eastern civilizations, encompassing regions such as Egypt, Mesopotamia, Persia, and the Levant, were primarily polytheistic in their religious beliefs. However, within these polytheistic frameworks, there were early indications and elements of monotheistic thought that emerged, hinting at the eventual development of monotheistic religions.

In ancient Egypt, while polytheism was the dominant religious system, there were instances where a single deity was elevated above others. The sun god Ra, for example, gained prominence and was often considered the supreme god. Ra was associated with creation, light, and life-giving power, and his worship extended throughout Egypt. The belief in Ra as the creator and sustainer of the universe hinted at a monotheistic inclination, where one god held supreme authority and power over all others.

Mesopotamia, with its rich and diverse religious traditions, also exhibited early monotheistic elements. In the city of Babylon, during the reign of Hammurabi (1792-1750 BCE), the worship of Marduk, the patron god of Babylon, gained prominence. Marduk was elevated to a supreme position among the gods, and his cult became the state religion. This emphasized the idea of a single god with ultimate authority and power. While other gods were still acknowledged and worshiped, the elevated status of Marduk suggested a monotheistic tendency, with one god occupying a position of primacy.

In the ancient Persian civilization, the prophet Zoroaster played a pivotal role in promoting monotheistic ideas. Zoroastrianism, founded by Zoroaster in the 6th century BCE, presented Ahura Mazda as the supreme and sole deity. Ahura Mazda represented truth, righteousness, and the forces of good. Zoroaster taught that Ahura Mazda created the universe and engaged in an eternal struggle against the forces of evil. This emphasis on the worship and devotion to a single divine entity reflected a more developed form of monotheism.

The early monotheistic elements in these ancient Near Eastern civilizations signify a shift in religious thought. They demonstrate the human capacity to contemplate the existence of a single, all-powerful deity who governs the cosmos and bestows meaning and purpose upon human existence. While these monotheistic elements did not fully blossom into fully-fledged monotheistic religions during their respective periods, they set the stage for the eventual emergence of monotheism in later civilizations.

These early monotheistic elements in ancient Near Eastern civilizations laid the foundation for the monotheistic belief systems that would emerge in the following centuries. The influence of these monotheistic inclinations can be seen in later monotheistic religions, such as Judaism, Christianity, and Islam, which emerged in the same region. The exploration of these early monotheistic elements allows us to trace the historical trajectory of monotheism and understand its significance in shaping religious thought and human spirituality.

The concept of henotheism and its role in the development of monotheism

The concept of henotheism played a crucial role in the development of monotheism, serving as a transitional phase between polytheism and the belief in a single, supreme deity. Henotheism is the worship of one god while acknowledging the existence of other gods. It is often characterized by the elevation of a particular god or goddess above others without denying the existence of other deities.

In henotheistic belief systems, a specific god or goddess is considered the primary or preferred deity, deserving of exclusive worship and devotion. This deity is regarded as the most powerful, wise, or benevolent among the pantheon, while other gods and goddesses are seen as subordinate or subsidiary. The henotheistic approach allows for the recognition of multiple divine beings but focuses on one god as the central object of worship.

Henotheism can be observed in various ancient civilizations, serving as a bridge between polytheism and monotheism. For example, in ancient Egypt, while numerous gods and goddesses were worshiped, there were instances where a particular deity, such as Amun or Ra, gained prominence and was elevated above others. This henotheistic tendency showcased the acknowledgment of other deities while emphasizing the special status of a chosen god.

In the ancient Hebrew religious context, henotheistic elements can be found in early Israelite belief systems. The Hebrew Bible contains references to the worship of multiple gods, such as Baal, Asherah, and El. However, there are also passages that emphasize the exclusive worship of Yahweh, the God of Israel. This henotheistic phase in ancient Israelite religion marked the transitional period leading to the development of monotheism, where Yahweh eventually became the sole and supreme deity.

Henotheism served as a stepping stone in the progression toward monotheism by elevating a particular god or goddess as the primary focus of religious devotion and acknowledging the existence of other deities within the wider pantheon. It allowed for a gradual shift in religious consciousness, enabling individuals and societies to move away from the worship of multiple gods toward the worship of a single, all-encompassing divine entity.

The concept of henotheism is significant in understanding the development of monotheism because it represents an intermediate stage where the idea of a single, supreme deity gains prominence and exclusivity. It provided a framework for monotheistic beliefs to emerge and take hold, laying the groundwork for the monotheistic religions that would arise in later civilizations. Henotheism played a crucial role in shaping religious thought and paving the way for monotheistic faiths to flourish.

Monotheism in Ancient Judaism

Monotheism in ancient Judaism is a fundamental aspect that distinguishes it from other religious traditions of the time. The development of monotheistic beliefs within the ancient Israelite society played a significant role in shaping the identity and religious practices of the Jewish people.

The origins of monotheism in ancient Judaism can be traced back to the Hebrew Bible, also known as the Tanakh. The Hebrew Bible emphasizes the worship of one God, Yahweh, as the sole deity worthy of devotion and reverence. Yahweh is presented as the creator of the universe, the God of Abraham, Isaac, and Jacob, and the liberator of the Israelites from Egyptian slavery.

Ancient Jewish monotheism was distinct in its rejection of the worship of other gods. The Israelites were commanded to have no other gods before Yahweh and to worship Him exclusively. This monotheistic belief in Yahweh as the only true God formed the foundation of Jewish theology and religious practice.

The development of monotheism in ancient Judaism was a gradual process, with evidence suggesting that earlier forms of Israelite religion included elements of henotheism or monolatry, where Yahweh was recognized as the primary deity but other gods were acknowledged. However, over time, a shift towards exclusive monotheism occurred, and Yahweh became the sole focus of worship.

Central to the monotheistic beliefs of ancient Judaism was the covenant, a sacred agreement between Yahweh and the Israelites. The covenant established a unique relationship between God and His chosen people, with obligations and responsibilities for both parties. The Israelites were called to obey God's commandments, follow His moral teachings, and maintain exclusive loyalty to Yahweh.

Monotheism in ancient Judaism influenced various aspects of Jewish life, including religious rituals, ethical principles, and societal structures. The worship of Yahweh centered around the Jerusalem Temple, where sacrifices and rituals were performed by priests according to prescribed rituals. The monotheistic belief in Yahweh also provided a moral framework for the Israelites, guiding their behavior and shaping their ethical values.

The concept of monotheism in ancient Judaism had far-reaching implications for the Jewish people. It fostered a sense of national identity, unity, and purpose. Monotheism served as a foundation for Jewish religious practices, community life, and cultural traditions. It provided a framework for understanding the divine, the world, and human existence.

Moreover, the monotheistic beliefs of ancient Judaism laid the groundwork for the development of later Abrahamic religions, such as Christianity and Islam. The idea of one God, as expressed in ancient Judaism, became a central tenet of these religions, influencing their doctrines, rituals, and theological perspectives.

In conclusion, monotheism in ancient Judaism emerged as a significant theological development, shaping the religious beliefs, practices, and identity of the Jewish people. The monotheistic belief in Yahweh as the one true God set Judaism apart from other contemporary religions and laid the foundation for the monotheistic traditions that followed. Monotheism in ancient Judaism remains a defining characteristic of Jewish faith and continues to be a central pillar of Jewish theology and religious observance to this day.

Tracing the origins of monotheism in ancient Hebrew religious traditions

Tracing the origins of monotheism in ancient Hebrew religious traditions provides valuable insights into the development of monotheistic beliefs within the Hebrew culture. While ancient Hebrew religion evolved over centuries, the roots of monotheism can be identified through various historical and textual sources.

One crucial aspect of the origins of monotheism in ancient Hebrew religious traditions lies in the early biblical narratives. The Hebrew Bible, particularly the Book of Genesis, presents a progressive monotheistic worldview. The creation account in Genesis attributes the existence of the entire universe to a single, supreme God. This monotheistic understanding is further emphasized through the portrayal of Yahweh's interactions with individuals like Abraham, Isaac, and Jacob, and the formation of a covenant between Yahweh and the Hebrew people.

Another significant influence on the development of monotheism in ancient Hebrew religious traditions was the cultural and religious milieu of the ancient Near East. The ancient Hebrews lived in a region that was characterized by a multitude of polytheistic religions. However, amidst this polytheistic environment, there were also other religious movements and philosophical ideas that could have contributed to the emergence of monotheistic beliefs among the Hebrews.

One notable influence was the concept of henotheism, which recognizes the existence of multiple deities but elevates one as supreme. Henotheistic ideas can be seen in some early Hebrew texts, where Yahweh is acknowledged as the most powerful and worthy of worship among the gods, without denying the existence of other gods. This henotheistic framework provided a transitional stage toward monotheism, gradually leading to the exclusive worship of Yahweh.

Additionally, the experience of the Hebrew people, particularly their enslavement in Egypt and subsequent liberation, played a significant role in shaping their religious beliefs. The Exodus narrative, with its emphasis on Yahweh's intervention in history and His superiority over the Egyptian gods, solidified the Hebrews' devotion to Yahweh as the one true God. The Exodus experience became a foundational event that reinforced their monotheistic faith and set them apart as a chosen people.

Furthermore, the religious reforms instituted by certain Hebrew leaders, such as King Josiah in the 7th century BCE, had a profound impact on the development of monotheism. Josiah's efforts to centralize religious worship in Jerusalem and remove idolatrous practices contributed to a stronger emphasis on Yahweh as the sole object of devotion.

The writing and compilation of the Hebrew Scriptures, particularly the Torah (the first five books of the Hebrew Bible), played a vital role in solidifying and codifying monotheistic beliefs. These texts reinforced the idea that Yahweh was the only God to be worshipped and obeyed, emphasizing monotheistic principles and distinguishing Hebrew religious traditions from neighboring polytheistic cultures.

In conclusion, the origins of monotheism in ancient Hebrew religious traditions can be traced through various factors, including biblical narratives, cultural influences, historical experiences, religious reforms, and the writing of sacred texts. The gradual progression from henotheism to exclusive monotheism reflects the evolving understanding of Yahweh's uniqueness and supreme authority among the ancient Hebrews. This development laid the foundation for monotheistic beliefs that became central to Judaism and influenced the development of subsequent monotheistic traditions.

The central role of Yahweh in Jewish monotheistic beliefs

Yahweh, the Hebrew name for God, occupies a central and foundational role in Jewish monotheistic beliefs. The concept of monotheism in Judaism revolves around the belief in the existence of one supreme and transcendent God who created and sustains the universe. Yahweh is regarded as the ultimate source of all existence, the divine ruler, and the sole object of worship and devotion.

In Jewish monotheism, Yahweh is characterized by several key attributes that define His nature and relationship with humanity. These attributes are often described in the Hebrew Scriptures, particularly in the Torah and the Prophetic writings. Some of the significant characteristics of Yahweh include:

Unity: Yahweh is understood as a unified and indivisible entity. He is not divided into different aspects or manifestations but is a singular and coherent being. This unity reflects the oneness of God and His uniqueness in comparison to any other gods or deities.

Transcendence: Yahweh is considered transcendent, existing beyond the limitations of the physical world. He is not confined to any specific time or space but is present everywhere and in all moments. This transcendence emphasizes the supreme nature of Yahweh and His distinction from the created world.

Omnipotence: Yahweh is believed to possess unlimited power and authority. He has control over all aspects of creation and is capable of bringing about any desired outcome. This omnipotence highlights Yahweh's ability to shape the course of history and fulfill His divine purposes.

Omniscience: Yahweh is attributed with complete knowledge and understanding of all things. He is aware of the past, present, and future, and nothing escapes His knowledge. This omniscience emphasizes Yahweh's wisdom and His capacity to guide and govern the affairs of humanity.

Covenantal Relationship: Yahweh is deeply involved in a special covenantal relationship with the Jewish people. Through the covenant established with Abraham and later reaffirmed through Moses, Yahweh made specific promises and obligations to the Israelites. This covenant forms the basis of the unique relationship between God and the Jewish people, highlighting Yahweh's role as the protector, provider, and guide of His chosen nation.

The central role of Yahweh in Jewish monotheistic beliefs is manifested in various aspects of Jewish religious life. Jewish worship, prayers, and rituals are directed exclusively to Yahweh, acknowledging His sovereignty and seeking His guidance and blessings. The Ten Commandments, as revealed to Moses, emphasize the exclusive worship of Yahweh and the prohibition of idolatry.

Yahweh's role as the moral authority is also prominent in Jewish monotheism. The Hebrew Scriptures provide a framework of ethical principles and commandments that guide the moral conduct of believers. Yahweh's divine laws, as articulated in the Torah, serve as a guide for righteous living and the pursuit of justice and compassion.

Furthermore, Yahweh's role as the God of history is a fundamental aspect of Jewish monotheistic beliefs. The Hebrew Scriptures contain accounts of Yahweh's interventions in human affairs, such as the deliverance of the Israelites from Egypt and the establishment of the Davidic dynasty. These historical narratives emphasize Yahweh's active involvement in shaping the destiny of His people and fulfilling His promises.

In conclusion, Yahweh's central role in Jewish monotheistic beliefs encompasses His attributes of unity, transcendence, omnipotence, omniscience, and covenantal relationship with the Jewish people. Yahweh is the one true God, worshiped and revered as the source of all existence and the ultimate moral authority. His presence and guidance are sought in all aspects of Jewish religious life, and His unique relationship with the Jewish people forms the basis of Jewish

Akhenaten's Atenism and the Rise of Monotheism in Egypt

Akhenaten's reign marked a significant departure from the polytheistic traditions of ancient Egypt with the introduction of Atenism, a monotheistic religious system centered around the worship of the sun disc deity known as Aten. Akhenaten, previously known as Amenhotep IV, ascended to the throne during the 18th Dynasty of ancient Egypt and initiated a religious revolution that challenged the established pantheon of gods and goddesses.

Exploring the Contrasts and Convergence of Polytheism and Monotheism

Atenism emphasized the exclusive worship of Aten as the supreme and universal god, considering all other deities as subordinate manifestations or aspects of the solar deity. Akhenaten proclaimed Aten as the sole deity deserving of reverence and eliminated the traditional worship of Amun-Ra and other gods, temples, and priesthoods associated with them. The religious reforms of Akhenaten were radical and sought to centralize religious authority under the pharaoh.

The Aten was depicted as a solar disc with rays ending in hands, symbolizing its life-giving and benevolent nature. Akhenaten promoted the idea of Aten as the source of all life, light, and creation. The worship of Aten emphasized the concepts of truth, justice, and universal love, with Akhenaten presenting himself as the sole intermediary between Aten and the people. This elevation of Aten as the supreme god and Akhenaten as the exclusive mediator reflected a significant departure from the traditional Egyptian religious practices.

Akhenaten's reforms extended beyond theology and impacted various aspects of Egyptian society. Artistic representations during the period showcased a distinct style known as the Amarna art, characterized by naturalistic depictions, soft curves, and intimate family scenes. These artistic expressions celebrated the pharaoh, his wife Nefertiti, and their daughters in the presence of the Aten, emphasizing the royal family's direct connection to the divine.

However, the religious reforms of Akhenaten faced resistance and controversy. The abandonment of traditional deities and religious practices disrupted the established social and political order. The power and influence of the priesthoods associated with the traditional gods were diminished, leading to discontent among the religious elite and some segments of the population. Additionally, the exclusive worship of Aten and the suppression of other gods disrupted the economic and religious structures built around their cults.

After Akhenaten's death, his successors, notably Tutankhamun, sought to restore the traditional polytheistic religious system. The temples dedicated to the traditional gods were reopened, and the previous religious practices were reinstated. The period of Atenism was subsequently considered a heretical episode in Egyptian history, and efforts were made to erase the memory of Akhenaten's reign.

Despite its relatively short duration, Atenism had a lasting impact on the development of religious thought. The monotheistic ideas put forth by Akhenaten were influential in later monotheistic traditions, particularly in the emergence of monotheism in ancient Israel. The concept of a single supreme deity and the belief in the universality of God's power and presence can be traced back to the religious reforms of Akhenaten.

In conclusion, Akhenaten's Atenism represented a unique experiment in ancient Egypt with the introduction of monotheistic beliefs centered around the worship of Aten. This departure from traditional polytheism had a profound influence on Egyptian society and art during the Amarna period. While Atenism was eventually abandoned, its impact on the development of monotheistic thought and its connection to later monotheistic religions cannot be overlooked.

Examining the religious revolution under Akhenaten and the worship of the sun disc Aten

The reign of Akhenaten, the pharaoh previously known as Amenhotep IV, witnessed a significant religious revolution in ancient Egypt. Akhenaten introduced a radical shift in the religious beliefs and practices of the time by promoting the worship of a single deity known as Aten, the sun disc. This religious revolution, known as the Amarna Revolution or Atenism, had a profound impact on Egyptian society, art, and theology.

Atenism, as propagated by Akhenaten, placed Aten at the center of religious devotion and rejected the traditional polytheistic worship of multiple gods and goddesses. Aten was perceived as the ultimate and universal deity, representing the solar disc and its life-giving rays. The pharaoh positioned himself as the intermediary between Aten and the people, emphasizing his unique and divine connection to the sun god.

The worship of Aten was characterized by its monotheistic nature, emphasizing the oneness and singularity of the divine. Unlike the traditional Egyptian pantheon, which comprised a complex hierarchy of gods and goddesses with distinct roles and attributes, Atenism focused on the worship of a single, all-encompassing deity. This concept of a single supreme god, transcending all other deities, was a revolutionary departure from the established religious norms of ancient Egypt.

Akhenaten promoted the idea of Aten as the creator and sustainer of all life, embodying the concepts of truth, justice, and universal love. The pharaoh claimed that Aten's divine presence permeated all aspects of existence, from the natural world to human society. The worship of Aten emphasized ethical conduct, promoting ideals of righteousness, equality, and compassion.

The religious revolution under Akhenaten had significant implications for Egyptian society and culture. The pharaoh embarked on a campaign to dismantle the traditional polytheistic temples and priesthoods associated with the worship of other deities. Temples dedicated to Amun-Ra and other gods were closed, and the wealth and influence of the traditional priesthoods were curtailed. This centralization of religious power under the pharaoh challenged the established social and political order.

The art of the Amarna period reflected the new religious ideology of Atenism. Artists depicted Akhenaten, his wife Nefertiti, and their daughters in intimate and naturalistic scenes, often in the presence of the Aten. These representations portrayed the royal family as the direct recipients of divine favor and blessings from Aten. The artistic style of the period, known as Amarna art, exhibited a departure from the traditional Egyptian artistic conventions, reflecting the emphasis on individuality and naturalism.

Despite the revolutionary nature of Atenism, the religious reforms of Akhenaten faced opposition and encountered challenges. The suppression of traditional deities and religious practices disrupted the established social and economic structures built around their cults. The priesthoods associated with the traditional gods resisted the changes, and there was likely discontent among segments of the population who revered the old gods.

After Akhenaten's death, his successors, particularly Tutankhamun, sought to restore the traditional polytheistic religious system. Temples were reopened, and the worship of Amun-Ra and other deities was reinstated. The period of Atenism was subsequently considered heretical, and attempts were made to erase the memory of Akhenaten and his religious revolution.

In conclusion, the religious revolution under Akhenaten and the worship of the sun disc Aten marked a significant departure from traditional Egyptian polytheism. Atenism introduced a monotheistic focus on the worship of a single supreme deity and challenged the established religious, social, and artistic norms of the time. Although short-lived, Atenism had a lasting impact on the development of religious thought and the understanding of monotheistic concepts, influencing subsequent monotheistic traditions.

The influence of Atenism on the development of monotheistic thought

The influence of Atenism on the development of monotheistic thought is a subject of much debate and speculation among scholars. While Atenism itself was relatively short-lived and did not directly give rise to later monotheistic religions, its ideas and concepts had a lasting impact on the evolution of religious thought.

Atenism challenged the prevailing polytheistic religious framework of ancient Egypt and introduced the concept of a single supreme deity. The worship of Aten as the sole god emphasized the belief in a unified and universal divinity, transcending the multiplicity of gods and goddesses. This monotheistic focus on a singular divine power paved the way for future developments in monotheistic thought.

One significant influence of Atenism was its emphasis on the abstract and transcendent nature of the divine. Aten was not associated with a specific physical form or anthropomorphic attributes but was perceived as an omnipresent and all-encompassing force represented by the solar disc. This abstract and formless understanding of the divine can be seen as a precursor to the concept of an incorporeal and transcendent God in later monotheistic traditions.

Atenism also introduced the idea of a direct and personal relationship between the individual and the divine. Akhenaten, as the pharaoh and the intermediary between Aten and the people, promoted the notion of an individual's direct access to the divine without the need for elaborate rituals or intermediary priesthoods. This emphasis on direct personal connection with the divine echoes in later monotheistic religions, where individuals are encouraged to establish a personal relationship with the one God.

The ethical and moral dimensions of Atenism were another influential aspect. Aten was associated with concepts of truth, justice, and universal love, emphasizing ethical conduct and righteous behavior. This ethical monotheistic emphasis on moral principles and social responsibility can be seen as a precursor to the ethical teachings and moral codes found in later monotheistic religions.

Although Atenism did not directly give rise to any major monotheistic religion, its ideas and concepts laid the foundation for the development of monotheistic thought in subsequent religious traditions. It challenged the prevailing polytheistic worldview, introduced abstract and transcendent understandings of the divine, emphasized personal connection with the divine, and highlighted ethical and moral dimensions of religious practice.

The influence of Atenism can be seen in the religious developments of the ancient Near East, particularly in the monotheistic elements found in ancient Hebrew religious traditions and the emergence of monotheism in other ancient cultures. The Atenist experiment and its legacy served as a catalyst for the exploration and reimagining of monotheistic concepts, ultimately contributing to the development of monotheistic religions that emerged in different historical contexts.

In conclusion, while Atenism itself was a specific religious movement limited to the reign of Akhenaten, its influence on the development of monotheistic thought cannot be overlooked. The ideas and concepts of Atenism challenged traditional polytheistic beliefs, emphasized the unity and transcendence of the divine, highlighted personal connection with the divine, and underscored ethical dimensions of religious practice. These influences paved the way for the later development of monotheistic religions and shaped the course of religious thought in significant ways.

Zoroastrianism: Monotheism in Ancient Persia

Zoroastrianism, one of the world's oldest known monotheistic religions, emerged in ancient Persia (modern-day Iran) during the 6th century BCE. Founded by the prophet Zoroaster (also known as Zarathustra), Zoroastrianism introduced radical monotheistic ideas that greatly influenced subsequent religious and philosophical developments in the region.

At the core of Zoroastrianism is the belief in a single supreme deity, Ahura Mazda, who is considered the creator of the universe and the source of all good. Ahura Mazda is seen as the embodiment of truth, righteousness, and wisdom. This monotheistic focus on a single all-powerful and benevolent God set Zoroastrianism apart from the prevalent polytheistic beliefs of the time.

Zoroaster presented his teachings in the Gathas, a collection of hymns and poems that form the sacred scripture of Zoroastrianism. The Gathas emphasize the fundamental concepts of monotheism, including the existence of a single divine entity, the struggle between good and evil, and the ultimate triumph of good. Zoroaster proclaimed that individuals should align themselves with the forces of good, choose righteous actions, and strive to combat evil in all its forms.

The ethical and moral dimensions of Zoroastrianism are significant aspects of its monotheistic teachings. Zoroaster introduced the concept of "asha," often translated as "truth" or "righteousness." It encompasses a comprehensive ethical framework that guides human behavior, emphasizing honesty, justice, kindness, and respect for the natural world. The followers of Zoroastrianism are encouraged to live according to these principles, promoting moral responsibility and contributing to the betterment of society.

Zoroastrianism also introduced the notion of a cosmic dualism between the forces of good and evil. Angra Mainyu, the embodiment of evil and falsehood, opposes the divine order established by Ahura Mazda. This dualistic worldview presents an ongoing cosmic struggle between these opposing forces, with humanity given the choice to align themselves with either good or evil.

Zoroastrian religious practices revolve around the worship of Ahura Mazda and the maintenance of purity and righteousness. Fire, regarded as a sacred symbol, is considered an essential element in Zoroastrian rituals. Zoroastrian temples, known as fire temples, house a sacred fire that is continuously tended by priests. The fire is seen as a representation of the divine presence and serves as a focal point for devotion and worship.

The influence of Zoroastrianism extended beyond religious and philosophical realms. It played a significant role in shaping the cultural and social fabric of ancient Persia. Zoroastrianism promoted values such as equality, justice, and the importance of education. It also introduced practices such as charity, philanthropy, and the care for the environment, reflecting its emphasis on ethical responsibility and stewardship.

The influence of Zoroastrianism is evident in subsequent religious traditions. The concepts of monotheism, ethical responsibility, and cosmic dualism found in Zoroastrianism can be seen in the Abrahamic religions, including Judaism, Christianity, and Islam. Scholars have noted the parallels between Zoroastrian ideas and the development of monotheism in the ancient Near East.

In conclusion, Zoroastrianism stands as a significant monotheistic religion that emerged in ancient Persia. Its teachings emphasized the worship of a single supreme deity, Ahura Mazda, and introduced ethical and moral principles that shaped the religious, philosophical, and cultural landscape of the region. Zoroastrianism's influence can be seen in subsequent religious traditions, making it a vital chapter in the history of monotheism.

Exploring the monotheistic teachings of Zoroaster in ancient Persia

Zoroaster, also known as Zarathustra, was the founder of Zoroastrianism and a key figure in the development of monotheistic thought in ancient Persia. His teachings, as recorded in the Gathas, presented a radical departure from the prevailing polytheistic beliefs of the time and introduced monotheistic concepts that deeply influenced Persian religious and philosophical traditions.

Zoroaster's monotheistic teachings centered on the worship of Ahura Mazda, the supreme deity and creator of the universe. Ahura Mazda was seen as the embodiment of truth, righteousness, and wisdom, representing the forces of good and order. Zoroaster proclaimed Ahura Mazda as the only God worthy of worship, rejecting the multitude of gods and goddesses worshipped in polytheistic religions.

The Gathas, a collection of hymns and poems attributed to Zoroaster, form the core scripture of Zoroastrianism. They convey the central tenets of Zoroaster's monotheistic teachings, emphasizing the existence of a single divine entity, the struggle between good and evil, and the importance of human choices and actions in aligning with the forces of good.

Zoroaster's teachings focused on the ethical and moral dimensions of monotheism. He introduced the concept of "asha," which encompasses truth, righteousness, and order. Zoroaster emphasized the importance of leading a righteous life and making choices that align with asha. He taught that individuals have the freedom to choose between good and evil and that their choices have consequences in the cosmic struggle between these opposing forces.

Zoroaster's monotheistic teachings also addressed the nature of evil. He identified Angra Mainyu, also known as Ahriman, as the embodiment of evil and falsehood, opposing the divine order established by Ahura Mazda. This dualistic framework presented an ongoing cosmic battle between the forces of good and evil, with humanity called upon to align themselves with the forces of good and contribute to the triumph of righteousness.

The ethical principles outlined by Zoroaster emphasized the importance of honesty, justice, kindness, and respect for the natural world. Zoroastrianism advocated for moral responsibility and the pursuit of a virtuous life. These teachings promoted social harmony, equality, and the well-being of both individuals and society as a whole.

Zoroastrian religious practices involved rituals and ceremonies centered around the worship of Ahura Mazda. Fire, seen as a sacred symbol, held a central place in Zoroastrian worship. Zoroastrian temples, known as fire temples, housed a sacred fire that was continuously tended by priests. Fire was seen as a representation of the divine presence and served as a focal point for devotion and reverence.

The influence of Zoroastrianism extended beyond religious practices. Zoroaster's teachings played a significant role in shaping Persian culture, ethics, and social values. Zoroastrianism emphasized the pursuit of knowledge, the importance of education, and the promotion of charitable acts. It also stressed the need for responsible stewardship of the environment and the care for all living beings.

The impact of Zoroastrianism on subsequent religious traditions is notable. There are striking parallels between Zoroaster's monotheistic ideas and the development of monotheism in the ancient Near East, particularly in Judaism, Christianity, and Islam. Scholars have recognized the influence of Zoroastrianism on concepts such as a single supreme deity, moral responsibility, and the ultimate triumph of good over evil.

In conclusion, Zoroaster's teachings in ancient Persia introduced monotheistic thought that focused on the worship of Ahura Mazda and the pursuit of righteousness. His monotheistic teachings emphasized ethical responsibility, the struggle between good and evil, and the significance of human choices. Zoroastrianism left a profound impact on Persian culture and had a lasting influence on subsequent religious traditions, making it a pivotal chapter in the exploration of monotheistic thought.

The dualistic nature of Zoroastrian beliefs and the conflict between good and evil

One of the distinctive aspects of Zoroastrian beliefs is the dualistic worldview that emphasizes the ongoing struggle between good and evil forces in the world. Zoroaster, the founder of Zoroastrianism, presented a cosmic dualism that portrayed a clear distinction between the forces of good and evil, represented by Ahura Mazda and Angra Mainyu, respectively.

According to Zoroastrianism, Ahura Mazda is the supreme deity and the embodiment of truth, righteousness, and order. Ahura Mazda is associated with attributes such as wisdom, justice, and goodness. The worship of Ahura Mazda is centered around promoting moral and ethical behavior, striving for righteousness, and upholding the principles of asha (truth and righteousness).

In contrast, Angra Mainyu, also known as Ahriman, represents the principle of evil, falsehood, and chaos. Angra Mainyu is the opposing force to Ahura Mazda, seeking to corrupt and destroy the order established by the divine. Angra Mainyu is associated with attributes such as deception, ignorance, and wickedness. The followers of Zoroastrianism are called upon to resist the temptations and influences of Angra Mainyu and align themselves with the forces of good.

The conflict between good and evil in Zoroastrianism is not seen as a temporary struggle but as an ongoing cosmic battle that spans both the spiritual and material realms. This dualistic framework presents a moral and metaphysical dilemma for human beings, who are believed to play a crucial role in this struggle. Zoroastrianism emphasizes the freedom of choice and the moral responsibility of individuals to actively participate in the triumph of good over evil.

The ethical teachings of Zoroastrianism revolve around the concept of "humata, hukhta, huvarshta" which means "good thoughts, good words, good deeds." Zoroastrians are encouraged to cultivate positive thoughts, speak truthfully and beneficially, and engage in actions that contribute to the well-being and righteousness of the world. By doing so, they actively combat the influence of evil and contribute to the eventual victory of good.

The ultimate outcome of the cosmic struggle between good and evil in Zoroastrianism is believed to be the triumph of righteousness. Zoroastrian eschatology envisions a future time when the forces of evil will be vanquished, and a time of spiritual renewal and cosmic perfection, known as the Frashokereti, will be ushered in. This belief provides hope and motivation for Zoroastrians to continue their commitment to righteousness and actively resist the influence of evil in the world.

The dualistic nature of Zoroastrian beliefs and the emphasis on the conflict between good and evil have had a profound influence not only within Zoroastrianism but also on subsequent religious and philosophical traditions. The concepts of a cosmic battle, moral responsibility, and the triumph of good over evil found in Zoroastrianism can be seen echoed in other monotheistic religions, such as Judaism, Christianity, and Islam. The influence of Zoroastrian dualism extends beyond religious boundaries and has shaped broader understandings of morality, ethics, and the human condition.

In conclusion, the dualistic nature of Zoroastrian beliefs and the recognition of the conflict between good and evil form a fundamental aspect of Zoroastrianism. The ongoing struggle between Ahura Mazda and Angra Mainyu highlights the importance of individual choices and actions in contributing to the ultimate triumph of good over evil. This dualistic worldview has left a lasting impact on religious and philosophical thought, offering a unique perspective on the nature of morality and the human experience.

CHAPTER 6: THE DEVELOPMENT OF POLYTHEISM AND MONOTHEISM

The evolution of religious beliefs and practices throughout human history has witnessed the emergence of diverse theological systems, ranging from polytheism, the worship of multiple deities, to monotheism, the belief in a single supreme deity. Chapter 6 delves into the fascinating journey of how polytheism transformed into monotheism, exploring the historical, cultural, and philosophical factors that influenced this significant shift in religious thought.

Polytheism, deeply rooted in ancient civilizations, provided a framework for understanding the world and human existence through the worship of various gods and goddesses. From the mythologies of ancient Mesopotamia to the pantheons of Greece and Rome, polytheistic beliefs were intertwined with the daily lives, rituals, and cultural practices of these ancient societies. However, amid this tapestry of gods and goddesses, the seeds of monotheism began to germinate, gradually challenging the prevailing polytheistic worldview.

The early monotheistic elements in ancient Near Eastern civilizations laid the groundwork for the development of monotheism. These elements can be observed in the teachings of figures such as Zoroaster in ancient Persia and the pharaoh Akhenaten in ancient Egypt. Their visionary ideas and religious reforms brought forth monotheistic concepts, challenging the polytheistic status quo and initiating profound changes in religious thought.

Chapter 6 will explore these pivotal moments in religious history, delving into the teachings, practices, and influences of these early monotheistic figures. The concept of henotheism, the recognition of a single supreme deity while acknowledging the existence of other gods, will be examined as a transitional stage between polytheism and monotheism. Furthermore, the chapter will shed light on the significance of monotheism in ancient Judaism, tracing its origins in Hebrew religious traditions and its central role in shaping Jewish theology.

By examining the development of polytheism into monotheism, this chapter aims to deepen our understanding of the complex and intricate journey of religious belief systems. It highlights the cultural, social, and philosophical factors that contributed to the rise of monotheism, transforming the religious landscape and leaving an enduring impact on subsequent religious traditions.

As we embark on this exploration of the development of polytheism and monotheism, we invite you to delve into the rich tapestry of ancient beliefs, ideologies, and transformations that have shaped the course of human spirituality. Through this journey, we gain insight into the diverse ways in which humans have sought to comprehend the divine, find meaning in existence, and navigate the complexities of the world around them.

Interactions and Influences Between Polytheism and Monotheism

Throughout the course of human history, the coexistence and interaction of polytheistic and monotheistic belief systems have shaped religious landscapes and influenced the development of religious thought. The relationship between these two theological frameworks has been complex, marked by tensions, syncretism, and mutual influence.

In many instances, polytheistic and monotheistic beliefs have coexisted within the same cultural or geographical contexts. This coexistence often led to a blending of ideas and practices, as people navigated the complexities of their religious identities and sought to reconcile different theological perspectives. Syncretism, the merging of different religious beliefs and practices, became a common phenomenon, resulting in the formation of hybrid religious systems.

Polytheistic cultures sometimes encountered monotheistic ideas through contact with other civilizations. These encounters often triggered intellectual and philosophical debates, as well as cultural exchanges. Monotheistic concepts challenged the established polytheistic frameworks, prompting discussions about the nature of the divine, the origins of the universe, and the moral order of the cosmos.

On the other hand, monotheistic belief systems were also influenced by polytheistic traditions. As monotheistic religions emerged and evolved, they incorporated elements from the surrounding polytheistic cultures, adapting rituals, symbols, and myths to resonate with the existing religious sensibilities of the people. This process allowed for the continuity of certain practices and the assimilation of local customs into the evolving monotheistic traditions.

The interactions between polytheism and monotheism were not limited to intellectual debates or syncretic practices. They also had significant sociopolitical implications. In some cases, rulers and empires adopted monotheistic beliefs as a means of consolidating political power and unifying diverse populations. Monotheism, with its emphasis on a single divine authority, provided a foundation for centralized authority and control.

At the same time, polytheism continued to exert its influence on societal structures and cultural expressions. Polytheistic pantheons often reflected and reinforced social hierarchies, with gods and goddesses associated with specific societal roles and functions. Rituals and festivals dedicated to various deities played a crucial role in social cohesion and community identity.

The interplay between polytheism and monotheism can be seen in religious texts, philosophical treatises, and the development of religious institutions. Scholars and theologians engaged in debates and discussions, exploring the merits and limitations of both theological frameworks. Theological concepts such as divine hierarchy, divine intervention, and the nature of religious experience were examined and reinterpreted within the evolving intellectual frameworks.

As civilizations expanded, encountered new cultures, and exchanged ideas, the influences and interactions between polytheism and monotheism continued to shape religious landscapes. The spread of monotheistic religions, such as Christianity and Islam, brought monotheistic concepts into contact with diverse polytheistic traditions, resulting in the assimilation, adaptation, or rejection of certain beliefs and practices.

In conclusion, the interactions and influences between polytheism and monotheism have been dynamic and multifaceted. From syncretism to intellectual debates, from cultural assimilation to religious adaptation, these interactions have shaped the development of religious thought and the cultural tapestry of human societies. Exploring the historical and philosophical intersections between polytheism and monotheism allows us to appreciate the complexities of human religious experiences and the ever-evolving nature of our quest for spiritual understanding.

The cultural exchanges and interactions between polytheistic and monotheistic civilizations

The cultural exchanges and interactions between polytheistic and monotheistic civilizations have played a significant role in shaping religious, intellectual, and cultural landscapes throughout history. These exchanges have occurred through various means, including trade, conquest, migration, and intellectual pursuits, and have led to the cross-pollination of ideas, beliefs, and practices.

Exploring the Contrasts and Convergence of Polytheism and Monotheism

One of the primary avenues for cultural exchange has been through trade networks. As merchants and travelers traversed ancient trade routes, they encountered diverse cultures with their unique religious systems. These interactions fostered the sharing of ideas, rituals, and religious artifacts, contributing to the dissemination and assimilation of religious beliefs across different civilizations.

Conquests and imperial expansions also played a crucial role in facilitating cultural exchanges between polytheistic and monotheistic civilizations. When empires expanded their territories, they often encountered regions with established polytheistic traditions. These encounters led to the intermingling of religious practices, as conquerors sought to incorporate local deities into their pantheons or adapt local customs to their monotheistic frameworks. Similarly, conquered populations influenced the conquerors, bringing their own religious beliefs and practices into the dominant culture.

Migration and diaspora have also been catalysts for cultural exchanges between polytheistic and monotheistic civilizations. When communities relocated to new lands, they carried their religious traditions with them, introducing their beliefs and practices to different cultural contexts. These migrations resulted in the assimilation of elements from both polytheistic and monotheistic traditions, leading to the development of syncretic religious systems that blended various theological concepts and rituals.

Intellectual pursuits and philosophical debates have been another avenue for cultural exchange and interaction. Scholars, philosophers, and theologians from polytheistic and monotheistic backgrounds engaged in discussions, debates, and scholarly exchanges, sharing ideas, challenging existing beliefs, and exploring new theological concepts. These intellectual interactions influenced the development of religious thought and fostered the evolution of theological frameworks.

The cultural exchanges and interactions between polytheistic and monotheistic civilizations also impacted the realms of art, architecture, and literature. Influences can be seen in the depiction of deities, the symbolism used, and the themes explored in mythological and religious texts. Artistic styles and architectural designs were often borrowed or adapted from neighboring cultures, incorporating elements of both polytheistic and monotheistic aesthetics.

While these exchanges often led to syncretism and cultural assimilation, they also sparked debates, conflicts, and resistance. Monotheistic belief systems, with their emphasis on exclusive devotion to a single deity, challenged the polytheistic status quo. This clash of theological perspectives sometimes resulted in religious tensions, social upheaval, and cultural transformations.

In conclusion, the cultural exchanges and interactions between polytheistic and monotheistic civilizations have been dynamic and complex. These exchanges have shaped religious beliefs, practices, and cultural expressions, fostering syncretism, intellectual debates, and artistic influences. The interplay between polytheism and monotheism has been a catalyst for religious, cultural, and intellectual development, leaving a profound impact on the diverse civilizations that have emerged throughout history.

The impact of conquering empires and the spread of religious ideas

The impact of conquering empires on the spread of religious ideas cannot be overstated. Throughout history, empires have exerted significant influence over conquered territories, including the religious beliefs and practices of the subjugated populations. The conquests of empires provided a platform for the dissemination of religious ideas, leading to the spread and adoption of new faiths or the assimilation of existing ones.

When empires expanded their territories, they often encountered diverse cultures with their own religious traditions. In many cases, conquerors sought to impose their own religious beliefs and practices on the conquered peoples as a means of asserting dominance and control. This process often involved the promotion of the conqueror's deity or pantheon as the supreme or preferred religious system. This forced conversion or assimilation of religious practices was a common strategy used by conquering empires throughout history.

The spread of religious ideas through conquest was facilitated by several factors. First, the military power and political influence of the conqueror allowed them to impose their religious beliefs on conquered territories through force or coercion. Second, the administrative apparatus of the empire, such as governors, officials, and priests, played a crucial role in disseminating and enforcing the religious policies of the ruling power. They would often establish temples, appoint religious leaders, and implement rituals that aligned with the conqueror's faith.

Conquering empires also had the ability to bring together diverse populations within their territories, creating cultural melting pots where religious ideas could intermingle and syncretism could occur. This process resulted in the blending of different religious traditions, as conquerors and conquered populations exchanged ideas, rituals, and practices. This syncretism often gave rise to new religious movements or the transformation of existing faiths.

Furthermore, the establishment of trade networks and communication routes by conquering empires facilitated the spread of religious ideas beyond the conquered territories. Trade routes acted as conduits for cultural exchange, allowing merchants, travelers, and diplomats to carry religious beliefs and practices to distant lands. This dissemination of religious ideas through trade contributed to the diffusion and cross-pollination of faiths across vast regions.

It is important to note that the spread of religious ideas through conquest was not always a unidirectional process. Conquered populations often influenced their conquerors, bringing their own religious beliefs and practices into the dominant culture. This cultural exchange and interaction led to the assimilation of elements from both sides, resulting in the development of hybrid religious systems.

However, the spread of religious ideas through conquest was not without resistance. Conquered populations frequently resisted attempts to impose foreign religious beliefs, clinging to their own traditions and resisting assimilation. These religious tensions sometimes led to conflicts and rebellions, as conquered peoples fought to preserve their religious autonomy and cultural identities.

In conclusion, the impact of conquering empires on the spread of religious ideas has been profound. Through military might, administrative policies, and cultural exchanges, empires have shaped the religious landscape of conquered territories. While conquest often led to the imposition of the conqueror's religious beliefs, it also facilitated the diffusion, syncretism, and transformation of faiths. The spread of religious ideas through conquest has played a crucial role in shaping the religious diversity and cultural heritage of our world.

Hellenistic Syncretism and the Spread of Monotheism

Hellenistic syncretism refers to the cultural and religious blending that occurred during the Hellenistic period, which followed the conquests of Alexander the Great and encompassed the vast territories of his empire. This period saw a significant interaction between Greek culture and various local traditions, resulting in a fusion of beliefs, practices, and deities.

One of the notable aspects of Hellenistic syncretism was the adoption and assimilation of foreign deities into the Greek pantheon. As the Greeks encountered new cultures and religious systems, they often identified local deities with their own gods and incorporated them into their religious framework. This syncretic approach allowed for the coexistence and integration of different religious traditions, creating a diverse and eclectic religious landscape.

The spread of monotheism was also influenced by Hellenistic syncretism. During this period, the influence of Greek culture and philosophy, particularly Stoicism and Neoplatonism, led to a philosophical reevaluation of traditional polytheistic beliefs. Greek philosophers, influenced by concepts such as the unity of nature and the existence of a supreme divine entity, began to develop philosophical monotheism.

Furthermore, the conquests of Alexander the Great and the subsequent establishment of Greek kingdoms throughout the Hellenistic world provided a fertile ground for the spread of monotheistic ideas. The Greek rulers, known as the Hellenistic monarchs, often promoted a form of imperial cult that emphasized their own divinity or association with a specific deity. This cult of the ruler, coupled with the syncretistic tendencies of the time, led to the blending of local and Greek religious practices, and in some cases, the promotion of a monotheistic ruler cult.

The influence of Hellenistic syncretism and the spread of monotheism can be seen in the religious developments of various regions during the Hellenistic period. In Egypt, for example, the ruler cult of the Ptolemaic dynasty blended Egyptian and Greek elements, with the pharaohs being associated with both traditional Egyptian deities and Greek gods such as Zeus and Serapis. In the Hellenistic city of Alexandria, a cultural and intellectual center of the time, philosophical schools emerged that explored the concept of a single, transcendent deity.

Additionally, the interaction between Hellenistic culture and Jewish communities played a significant role in the spread of monotheism. The conquest of the Persian Empire by Alexander the Great brought the Jewish population under Hellenistic influence, leading to a complex interplay between Jewish monotheism and Greek culture. This interaction gave rise to the Hellenistic Jewish diaspora and the development of Hellenistic Jewish literature, such as the Septuagint, a Greek translation of the Hebrew Bible.

In conclusion, Hellenistic syncretism and the spread of monotheism were closely intertwined during the Hellenistic period. The cultural blending and philosophical exploration of this era facilitated the assimilation of foreign deities into the Greek pantheon and the emergence of philosophical monotheism. The syncretistic tendencies of the time, coupled with the influence of Greek rulers and the interaction with Jewish communities, contributed to the spread and development of monotheistic ideas in various regions. The impact of Hellenistic syncretism and the spread of monotheism has had lasting effects on religious thought and practice.

Exploring the blending of Greek polytheism with monotheistic concepts during the Hellenistic period

During the Hellenistic period, which followed the conquests of Alexander the Great, there was a significant blending of Greek polytheism with monotheistic concepts. This blending occurred as a result of cultural interactions and intellectual exchanges between the Greeks and various cultures they encountered in their expanded territories.

One of the key factors that contributed to this blending was the philosophical and intellectual climate of the Hellenistic world. Greek philosophers, influenced by the ideas of Stoicism, Neoplatonism, and other philosophical schools, began to explore the concept of a single, supreme divine entity. These philosophers sought to reconcile the diverse polytheistic beliefs of the Greek pantheon with a more unified and rational understanding of the divine.

The notion of a supreme deity or a cosmic divinity emerged as a result of this philosophical exploration. Philosophers such as Xenophanes, Parmenides, and Plato put forth ideas that challenged the traditional polytheistic framework. They proposed the existence of a transcendent, universal deity that encompassed and governed the entire cosmos.

This philosophical monotheism provided a foundation for the blending of Greek polytheism with monotheistic concepts during the Hellenistic period. It allowed for the reinterpretation and assimilation of traditional Greek deities into a more unified and hierarchical framework.

Additionally, the cultural exchanges and conquests of Alexander the Great facilitated the spread of monotheistic ideas and their incorporation into Greek polytheism. As the Greeks encountered diverse cultures and religious traditions, they often identified the local deities with their own pantheon, attributing them with similar roles and characteristics. This syncretism resulted in the fusion of different religious concepts, creating a more inclusive and diverse religious landscape.

In some cases, the blending of Greek polytheism with monotheistic ideas took the form of the assimilation of foreign deities into the Greek pantheon. For example, the Egyptian deity Amun-Ra was equated with Zeus, resulting in the syncretic deity Amun-Zeus. This blending of deities allowed for the coexistence and mutual influence of different religious traditions.

The spread of Hellenistic culture and the establishment of Greek colonies and kingdoms further contributed to the blending of Greek polytheism with monotheistic concepts. Greek rulers, known as the Hellenistic monarchs, often promoted a form of imperial cult that emphasized their own divine status or association with a specific deity. This imperial cult blended local religious practices with Greek ideas, incorporating elements of monotheistic worship and belief in the divinity of the ruler.

In conclusion, the blending of Greek polytheism with monotheistic concepts during the Hellenistic period was a result of cultural interactions, philosophical exploration, and the syncretistic tendencies of the time. The intellectual climate of the period allowed for the development of philosophical monotheism, which provided a foundation for the reinterpretation of traditional Greek deities. The cultural exchanges and conquests of Alexander the Great facilitated the assimilation of foreign deities into the Greek pantheon. The blending of Greek polytheism with monotheistic ideas during this period resulted in a diverse and syncretic religious landscape that influenced subsequent religious developments in the ancient world.

The rise of mystery cults and their influence on the development of religious syncretism

The rise of mystery cults during the Hellenistic and Roman periods had a significant influence on the development of religious syncretism. Mystery cults were secretive and exclusive religious organizations that promised their initiates a personal experience of divine revelation and salvation. These cults emerged as an alternative to traditional state religions and offered individuals a more personal and meaningful connection with the divine.

One of the key features of mystery cults was their ability to transcend cultural boundaries and attract followers from various backgrounds. They incorporated elements from different religious traditions, blending beliefs and practices to create a unique and transformative religious experience. This syncretism allowed for the integration of diverse religious ideas and the formation of hybrid religious expressions.

The mystery cults often centered around the worship of a specific deity or a divine figure. For example, the cult of Isis, which originated in Egypt, gained popularity throughout the Hellenistic and Roman periods. It incorporated elements from Egyptian religion, Greek mythology, and other local traditions. The worship of Isis appealed to individuals seeking spiritual solace, healing, and a personal connection with the divine.

These mystery cults provided a sense of belonging and community for their initiates. They offered initiation rituals, secret ceremonies, and a hierarchical structure that allowed individuals to progress through different levels of knowledge and understanding. Through these rituals and experiences, initiates believed they could attain spiritual enlightenment, purification, and even a form of afterlife salvation.

The mystery cults influenced religious syncretism by creating spaces for the blending of different religious ideas and practices. They facilitated the cross-pollination of beliefs and rituals, as initiates brought their own religious backgrounds and experiences into the cults. This intermingling of religious traditions resulted in a rich tapestry of beliefs, symbols, and rituals that transcended cultural boundaries.

Moreover, the mystery cults played a role in the dissemination of religious ideas and beliefs across the Mediterranean world. As the cults spread and gained popularity, they facilitated cultural exchanges and interactions between different regions. The initiation rites and practices of the mystery cults were often kept secret, contributing to the aura of mystery and allure that surrounded them. This secrecy also helped to create a sense of exclusivity and devotion among their followers.

The syncretistic nature of the mystery cults influenced the broader religious landscape of the Hellenistic and Roman periods. The blending of different religious elements and the incorporation of foreign deities into local cults became more commonplace. This syncretism extended beyond the mystery cults and influenced the development of religious beliefs and practices in the wider society.

In conclusion, the rise of mystery cults during the Hellenistic and Roman periods played a crucial role in the development of religious syncretism. These cults offered individuals a personal and transformative religious experience, blending elements from different traditions and fostering a sense of spiritual community. The syncretism within the mystery cults allowed for the integration of diverse religious ideas and practices, contributing to the rich and multifaceted religious landscape of the time. The influence of mystery cults extended beyond their specific rituals and beliefs, shaping the broader religious syncretism of the period and influencing subsequent religious developments in the ancient world.

Monotheism in Christianity

Monotheism lies at the core of Christianity, distinguishing it from polytheistic religions. Christianity's monotheistic belief asserts the existence of a single, all-powerful God who is the creator and sustainer of the universe. This belief in the oneness of God is deeply rooted in the teachings of Jesus Christ and is foundational to Christian theology.

Christianity emerged in the 1st century CE as a monotheistic offshoot of Judaism. Jesus, considered the central figure of Christianity, proclaimed the oneness of God and emphasized a personal relationship between individuals and their Creator. Jesus' teachings, as recorded in the New Testament of the Bible, present a monotheistic understanding of God's nature and the call for believers to worship and serve only one God.

The concept of monotheism in Christianity is further solidified through the doctrine of the Holy Trinity. While the Trinity might appear to introduce a form of plurality, it upholds the fundamental belief in the oneness of God. According to Christian theology, God exists as three distinct persons—the Father, the Son (Jesus Christ), and the Holy Spirit—yet remains one in essence. This triune nature of God allows for a relational understanding of God's existence without compromising the monotheistic foundation of the faith.

Throughout history, Christianity spread across different regions and encountered diverse cultural contexts. As it interacted with various cultures and belief systems, the concept of monotheism was both reinforced and challenged. In societies where polytheistic beliefs were prevalent, the Christian message of a single God clashed with existing religious practices. Christians faced persecution for refusing to participate in polytheistic rituals and worship deities other than the Christian God.

However, as Christianity gained influence and became the dominant religion in many regions, it also experienced a degree of syncretism with local customs and beliefs. Some elements of polytheistic traditions were incorporated into Christian practices and veneration of saints, resulting in a more nuanced religious landscape. Despite these syncretistic tendencies, the central tenet of monotheism remained intact.

Christianity's monotheistic belief system has shaped its theology, worship, and moral teachings. Christians believe in the absolute sovereignty of God and recognize Him as the ultimate authority in matters of faith and ethics. The worship of God, prayer, and adherence to moral principles are all grounded in the understanding of monotheism.

Furthermore, the monotheistic nature of Christianity has profound implications for its understanding of salvation and the relationship between God and humanity. In Christian theology, God's singular nature allows for a personal and intimate connection between the individual and God. This relationship is exemplified in the belief in Jesus Christ as the divine Son of God, who offers salvation and reconciliation between God and humanity.

In summary, monotheism is a fundamental aspect of Christianity. The belief in the oneness of God distinguishes Christianity from polytheistic religions and forms the theological foundation of the faith. The concept of the Holy Trinity reinforces the monotheistic understanding of God's nature. While Christianity encountered diverse cultural contexts throughout its history, the central tenet of monotheism remained intact, shaping its theology, worship, and understanding of salvation.

Tracing the development of monotheistic beliefs within the early Christian movement

The development of monotheistic beliefs within the early Christian movement can be traced through various stages and influences. In the earliest days of Christianity, the movement emerged within a Jewish context, which already had a strong monotheistic tradition. Jesus himself was Jewish, and his teachings often referred to the God of the Hebrew Bible, affirming the belief in one God.

The early Christian community initially maintained a close connection to Judaism and its monotheistic framework. The foundational confession of faith in early Christianity, known as the Shema, echoed the monotheistic belief of Judaism: "Hear, O Israel: The Lord our God, the Lord is one" (Mark 12:29). Early Christians saw Jesus as the Messiah promised in Jewish scripture, affirming their monotheistic faith in the context of their Jewish heritage.

However, as the Christian movement spread beyond Jewish communities and encountered Hellenistic and Greco-Roman cultures, it began to engage with a diverse range of philosophical and religious ideas. This encounter influenced the development of Christian theology and led to discussions about the nature of God.

One significant figure in the development of monotheistic beliefs within early Christianity was the apostle Paul. Paul's writings, found in the New Testament, articulated the monotheistic understanding of God while also exploring the relationship between God and Jesus Christ. In Paul's theology, Jesus was seen as the divine Son of God and the mediator between God and humanity, emphasizing the oneness of God within the context of Jesus' unique role.

Another influential figure in the development of monotheistic beliefs was the Gospel of John, one of the four canonical Gospels. The Gospel of John presents a high Christology, affirming the divinity of Jesus and his unity with the Father. While emphasizing the unique identity of Jesus, the Gospel of John maintains the monotheistic belief in the oneness of God. The famous declaration in John 3:16 captures this belief: "For God so loved the world that he gave his one and only Son."

As the early Christian movement continued to grow and face various challenges, theological debates arose concerning the nature of God and the relationship between the Father, Son, and Holy Spirit. These debates culminated in the formulation of the doctrine of the Holy Trinity, which affirmed both the oneness of God and the distinct personhood of the Father, Son, and Holy Spirit. The doctrine of the Holy Trinity solidified the monotheistic belief within Christian theology while addressing the complex relationship between God and Jesus.

Throughout the development of early Christian theology, the monotheistic belief in one God remained foundational. Christian writers and apologists defended monotheism against polytheistic accusations and engaged in philosophical discussions to explain the nature of God. Influences from Jewish monotheism, Greco-Roman philosophical traditions, and the distinctive teachings of Jesus and the apostles shaped the evolving understanding of monotheism within early Christianity.

In summary, the development of monotheistic beliefs within the early Christian movement can be traced through interactions with Jewish monotheism, encounters with Hellenistic and Greco-Roman cultures, and theological reflections on the nature of God and the divinity of Jesus. Figures like Paul and the Gospel of John contributed to the articulation of a monotheistic understanding that acknowledged the unique role of Jesus within the oneness of God. The doctrine of the Holy Trinity solidified the monotheistic belief while addressing the complex relationship between God and Jesus.

Examining the significance of Jesus Christ as the central figure in Christian monotheism

Examining the significance of Jesus Christ as the central figure in Christian monotheism reveals the unique role he plays in the religious beliefs and practices of Christians. Jesus is considered the Son of God, the Messiah, and the embodiment of divine revelation. His central position in Christian monotheism is derived from the belief that he is both fully human and fully divine, serving as the bridge between God and humanity.

In Christian theology, Jesus is understood to be the second person of the Holy Trinity, alongside God the Father and the Holy Spirit. This belief in the Trinity affirms the monotheistic foundation of Christianity while acknowledging the three distinct persons within the one Godhead. Jesus' role as the Son of God is seen as essential in the redemption and salvation of humanity.

The significance of Jesus as the central figure in Christian monotheism is multifaceted. First and foremost, Jesus is considered the culmination of God's plan for salvation. Christians believe that Jesus' life, teachings, death, and resurrection fulfilled prophecies and provided the ultimate sacrifice for the forgiveness of sins. Through Jesus, believers have access to salvation and eternal life in communion with God.

Furthermore, Jesus serves as the ultimate revelation of God's nature and character. In the Gospels, Jesus is portrayed as the embodiment of love, compassion, and divine wisdom. His teachings, such as the Sermon on the Mount, emphasize moral and ethical principles that reflect God's will. Through Jesus' life and teachings, Christians gain a deeper understanding of God's love, grace, and desire for a relationship with humanity.

Jesus' crucifixion and resurrection are considered pivotal events in Christian theology. His sacrificial death is seen as atonement for humanity's sins, reconciling them with God. The resurrection demonstrates Jesus' victory over sin and death, providing hope for believers and affirming the promise of eternal life.

The significance of Jesus is not limited to theological doctrines but also extends to the lived experience of believers. Many Christians view Jesus as a personal savior and guide, forming a personal relationship with him through prayer, worship, and discipleship. Jesus' teachings and example serve as a moral compass and guide for living a life of faith, love, and service.

In Christian worship, Jesus is central to rituals such as the Eucharist or Communion, where believers partake in the symbolic sharing of his body and blood. Through this sacrament, believers express their unity with Christ and their participation in the divine life.

The significance of Jesus as the central figure in Christian monotheism is further emphasized in Christian art, literature, and music. Depictions of Jesus' life, passion, and resurrection have inspired countless artistic expressions throughout history. Hymns and prayers dedicated to Jesus celebrate his role as the divine mediator and source of salvation.

It is important to note that the centrality of Jesus in Christian monotheism does not diminish the belief in the oneness of God. Instead, it affirms the unique relationship between God and humanity mediated through Jesus. The significance of Jesus lies in his divine nature, redemptive work, and the profound impact he has on the faith and lives of believers.

In conclusion, Jesus Christ holds a central and significant role in Christian monotheism. As the Son of God and the second person of the Holy Trinity, he embodies the divine revelation and serves as the bridge between God and humanity.

Jesus' life, teachings, death, and resurrection are foundational to Christian beliefs, providing salvation, revealing God's nature, and guiding the faith and worship of believers. The significance of Jesus extends beyond theological doctrines to the personal experiences, worship practices, and artistic expressions of Christians throughout history.

Monotheism in Islam

Monotheism, known as Tawhid in Islam, is a fundamental principle and central concept in the religion of Islam. It is the belief in the oneness and unity of God, known as Allah, and forms the foundation of Islamic theology and practice. The concept of monotheism in Islam is deeply rooted in the Qur'an, the holy scripture of Islam, and is a core principle embraced by Muslims worldwide.

Islam emphasizes the absolute oneness and uniqueness of Allah, rejecting any notion of associating partners or intermediaries with God. The Islamic understanding of monotheism is uncompromising, with the Qur'an affirming that there is no deity worthy of worship except Allah. Muslims believe that Allah is eternal, transcendent, and has no physical form or attributes that can be comprehended by human beings. This concept of pure monotheism distinguishes Islam from other religious traditions.

The Islamic understanding of monotheism is encapsulated in the declaration of faith, known as the Shahada: "There is no god but Allah, and Muhammad is the Messenger of Allah." By affirming the oneness of Allah, Muslims bear witness to the core belief that God alone deserves worship and recognition, and that Muhammad is the final prophet and messenger sent by Allah to guide humanity.

The Qur'an provides comprehensive guidance on the belief in the oneness of Allah, outlining the attributes and qualities of God. Allah is described as being merciful, just, all-knowing, all-powerful, and the creator of the universe. Muslims believe that Allah is actively involved in the affairs of the world, sustaining and governing creation according to His divine wisdom.

Monotheism in Islam extends beyond theological belief to encompass all aspects of life. Muslims are called to worship and submit to Allah alone, performing acts of devotion such as prayer, fasting, charity, and pilgrimage. Monotheism shapes ethical behavior and morality, with Muslims striving to live in accordance with the teachings and commandments of Allah.

In Islamic theology, monotheism is not limited to a mere intellectual concept but is a lived reality. It encourages believers to develop a personal and intimate relationship with Allah, seeking His guidance, forgiveness, and mercy. Muslims are encouraged to reflect on the signs of Allah's creation and to cultivate a deep sense of gratitude and awe for His oneness and divine attributes.

The concept of monotheism in Islam has significant social and cultural implications as well. It fosters unity among Muslims, transcending ethnic, racial, and national boundaries. The belief in the oneness of Allah emphasizes the equality and brotherhood of all believers, promoting social justice, compassion, and mutual respect.

Throughout history, monotheism in Islam has been a driving force behind intellectual and spiritual development, as well as social and political movements. The belief in the oneness of Allah has inspired scholars, poets, philosophers, and artists to explore and express the depth of divine unity. It has also served as a unifying force for Muslims across diverse cultures and geographical regions.

In conclusion, monotheism in Islam is a foundational principle that emphasizes the belief in the oneness and unity of Allah. It is a central concept that shapes Islamic theology, practice, and worldview. Monotheism in Islam goes beyond mere intellectual acknowledgment and extends to the worship, devotion, and ethical conduct of Muslims. It promotes a personal relationship with Allah and fosters unity, equality, and justice among believers. The belief in the oneness of Allah has had a profound influence on the intellectual, spiritual, and social development of Muslim communities throughout history.

Investigating the origins and teachings of monotheism in Islam

Investigating the origins and teachings of monotheism in Islam provides valuable insights into the development and foundations of the faith. Islam emerged in the early 7th century CE in the Arabian Peninsula, with the Prophet Muhammad receiving revelations from Allah, which were later compiled into the Qur'an. Monotheism, as a core principle of Islam, can be traced back to the teachings of Muhammad and the foundational scriptures of the religion.

The origins of monotheism in Islam can be understood in the context of the religious and cultural milieu of pre-Islamic Arabia. The Arabian Peninsula at the time was characterized by the presence of various polytheistic beliefs and practices. The dominant religious framework involved the worship of numerous deities, with each tribe having its own gods and goddesses.

Muhammad, through his encounters with various religious traditions and contemplation of the nature of God, came to reject the polytheistic beliefs prevalent in the Arabian society. He embarked on a spiritual quest, retreating to the cave of Hira outside the city of Mecca, where he received the first revelations from Allah through the angel Gabriel. These revelations served as a call to monotheism, proclaiming the existence of one true God, Allah, and rejecting the worship of idols and false deities.

The teachings of monotheism in Islam are encompassed in the Qur'an, which is considered the literal word of Allah. The Qur'an emphasizes the oneness and unity of Allah and serves as a guide for Muslims in matters of faith, worship, morality, and social conduct. It provides a comprehensive understanding of monotheism, outlining the attributes and qualities of Allah and His relationship with creation.

Central to the teachings of monotheism in Islam is the concept of Tawhid, which refers to the absolute oneness and unity of Allah. Muslims believe in the transcendence of Allah, meaning that He is beyond human comprehension and is not limited by time, space, or physical form. Allah is described as being all-powerful, all-knowing, and the creator and sustainer of the universe.

Islam teaches that Allah alone deserves worship and recognition, and associating partners or intermediaries with Allah is considered a grave sin known as shirk. Muslims are called to direct their prayers and devotion solely to Allah, seeking His guidance, forgiveness, and mercy. The belief in the oneness of Allah extends to all aspects of life, influencing individual behavior, social interactions, and the governance of societies.

The teachings of monotheism in Islam also emphasize the prophethood of Muhammad as the final messenger and the seal of the prophets. Muslims believe that Muhammad received the revelations of Allah to guide humanity, conveying the message of monotheism and the principles of Islam. The life and teachings of Muhammad, as recorded in the Hadith (sayings and actions of the Prophet), provide practical examples and guidance on how to live a life in accordance with monotheistic principles.

The impact of monotheism in Islam is profound and far-reaching. It has shaped the religious, social, and cultural fabric of Muslim societies throughout history. Monotheism in Islam promotes a strong sense of individual accountability and personal responsibility before Allah, emphasizing the importance of ethical conduct, justice, and compassion. It fosters unity among Muslims, transcending cultural and national boundaries, and promotes a global community of believers.

In conclusion, the origins and teachings of monotheism in Islam can be traced back to the revelations received by the Prophet Muhammad in the early 7th century CE. The rejection of polytheism and the proclamation of the oneness and unity of Allah form the foundation of Islamic faith. The Qur'an and the teachings of the Prophet Muhammad provide a comprehensive understanding of monotheism in Islam, emphasizing the transcendence and unique attributes of Allah. Monotheism in Islam has had a profound impact on the lives of Muslims, shaping their beliefs, values, and actions, and contributing to the development of Islamic civilization throughout history.

The importance of the belief in the oneness of Allah and the revelations of Muhammad

The belief in the oneness of Allah (Tawhid) and the acceptance of the revelations of Muhammad are fundamental pillars of Islamic faith and play a central role in the lives of Muslims. These beliefs form the basis of monotheism in Islam and shape the worldview, religious practices, and moral compass of Muslims worldwide.

The belief in the oneness of Allah is deeply ingrained in Islamic theology and is repeatedly emphasized in the Qur'an and the teachings of Muhammad. Muslims believe that there is no deity worthy of worship except Allah and that He is the sole creator, sustainer, and controller of the universe. This belief in the absolute unity and uniqueness of Allah has profound implications for the lives of Muslims.

First and foremost, the belief in the oneness of Allah serves as the foundation of Islamic monotheism, distinguishing Islam from other belief systems. It affirms the unity of the divine and rejects the notion of multiple gods or intermediaries between humanity and Allah. This belief ensures that Muslims direct their worship and devotion solely to Allah, seeking His guidance, mercy, and forgiveness.

The belief in the oneness of Allah also instills a sense of unity and equality among Muslims. Regardless of their race, ethnicity, or social status, all Muslims are equal in their submission to Allah. This belief fosters a strong sense of brotherhood and sisterhood among Muslims, transcending societal divisions and promoting solidarity within the Muslim community.

The revelations of Muhammad, as recorded in the Qur'an and the Hadith, are considered the divine guidance and instructions for Muslims. Muslims believe that Muhammad is the final messenger and the seal of the prophets, chosen by Allah to deliver His message to humanity. The Qur'an, believed to be the literal word of Allah, serves as a comprehensive guide for all aspects of life, providing moral and ethical principles, legal guidelines, and spiritual insights.

The importance of the revelations of Muhammad lies in their role as a source of guidance and inspiration for Muslims. The Qur'an addresses a wide range of topics, including beliefs, worship, morality, social justice, family life, and governance. It provides Muslims with a framework for living a righteous and fulfilling life, promoting virtues such as compassion, justice, humility, and honesty.

The teachings of Muhammad, as recorded in the Hadith, further elucidate and clarify the principles and practices of Islam. The Hadith collection contains the sayings, actions, and approvals of the Prophet Muhammad and provides practical examples of how to apply the teachings of Islam in daily life. Muslims look to the Prophet Muhammad as a role model of piety, humility, and exemplary character.

The belief in the oneness of Allah and the acceptance of the revelations of Muhammad have profound implications for the spiritual and moral development of Muslims. It provides them with a sense of purpose, guidance, and accountability. Muslims believe that adherence to these beliefs leads to spiritual closeness to Allah and ultimately to salvation in the hereafter.

Moreover, the belief in the oneness of Allah and the acceptance of the revelations of Muhammad have shaped the development of Islamic civilization. These beliefs have influenced various aspects of Islamic culture, including art, architecture, literature, science, and social institutions. The monotheistic worldview and the ethical principles derived from the teachings of Islam have contributed to the establishment of just and compassionate societies, promoting social welfare, equality, and the pursuit of knowledge.

In conclusion, the belief in the oneness of Allah and the acceptance of the revelations of Muhammad are of utmost importance in Islam. These beliefs provide Muslims with a framework for understanding the nature of God, their purpose in life, and the moral principles they should uphold. The oneness of Allah ensures the unity and equality of Muslims, while the revelations of Muhammad serve as a divine guidance and source of inspiration. These beliefs have profound implications for the spiritual, moral, and societal dimensions of Islam, shaping the lives of Muslims and the development of Islamic civilization.

PART 3:
THEOLOGICAL AND PHILOSOPHICAL DIFFERENCES:

In the realm of religious and philosophical thought, diversity and divergence have long been the norm. Throughout history, different cultures and civilizations have developed their own unique theological and philosophical systems, often giving rise to profound differences in beliefs, practices, and interpretations of the divine. Part 3 of our exploration delves into the rich tapestry of theological and philosophical differences, delving into the complex web of ideas, debates, and perspectives that have shaped human understanding of the sacred.

Within this section, we will embark on a fascinating journey through the realms of theological and philosophical diversity, examining how different societies have grappled with questions of existence, the nature of the divine, the purpose of life, and the ultimate truth. We will explore the multifaceted dimensions of religious and philosophical thought, shedding light on the contrasting worldviews, doctrines, and conceptual frameworks that have emerged throughout human history.

This exploration will take us through the corridors of ancient civilizations, such as Egypt, Greece, and Rome, where polytheistic belief systems flourished and gods and goddesses held sway over the hearts and minds of the people. We will delve into the intricate mythologies, rituals, and practices that characterized these ancient polytheistic traditions, unraveling their significance and examining the roles and powers ascribed to various deities.

Furthermore, we will examine the revolutionary shifts that occurred with the advent of monotheism. From the ancient Near East to the rise of major monotheistic religions such as Judaism, Christianity, and Islam, we will trace the development of monotheistic beliefs and explore the profound impact they had on shaping religious, cultural, and societal landscapes.

Beyond the boundaries of monotheism, we will also encounter alternative philosophical and spiritual paths that emerged, seeking to explore the nature of reality, the human condition, and the pursuit of enlightenment. From the philosophies of ancient Greece and India to the mystical traditions of Sufism and Taoism, we will examine the rich tapestry of philosophical and spiritual traditions that have inspired seekers of truth and wisdom.

Throughout this section, we will strive to approach these diverse perspectives with intellectual curiosity, respect, and a commitment to understanding the nuances and complexities of different belief systems. We will explore the historical, cultural, and philosophical contexts that shaped these diverse viewpoints, acknowledging the intricacies and diversity within each tradition.

By delving into the theological and philosophical differences that have shaped human thought, we hope to deepen our understanding of the richness and complexity of the human quest for meaning, truth, and transcendence. As we explore the contours of these divergent paths, we invite you to embark on a journey of intellectual exploration, expanding your horizons and engaging with the myriad ways in which human beings have grappled with the mysteries of existence.

CHAPTER 7: THEOLOGY OF POLYTHEISM

Polytheism, the belief in multiple gods and goddesses, has been a central feature of many ancient and indigenous religions throughout human history. In this chapter, we delve into the fascinating world of polytheistic theology, exploring the intricacies of belief systems that revolve around a multitude of divine beings and the complex relationships between them.

Polytheistic theologies present a diverse array of concepts, myths, rituals, and cosmologies that provide insights into how different cultures have understood and interacted with the divine realm. Each pantheon, with its unique assembly of gods and goddesses, reflects the values, priorities, and cultural nuances of the people who worshipped them.

Throughout this chapter, we will embark on a comprehensive exploration of polytheistic theology, drawing upon examples from a variety of ancient civilizations, such as Egypt, Greece, Rome, Mesopotamia, and the indigenous traditions of the Americas and Africa. We will examine the roles and attributes ascribed to various deities, the myths and legends that explain their origins and actions, and the rituals and practices that formed the backbone of polytheistic worship.

We will delve into the fascinating concept of divine hierarchy and the intricate relationships between gods and goddesses within pantheons. Some deities occupy prominent positions as supreme beings or rulers of specific domains, while others fulfill specialized roles as guardians, patrons, or intermediaries between humans and the divine. The complex interplay of power dynamics and divine interactions gives rise to rich narratives that shape the religious worldview of polytheistic cultures.

Additionally, we will explore the theological implications of polytheism, examining how these belief systems address fundamental questions about the nature of existence, human purpose, morality, and the afterlife. We will delve into the ways in which polytheistic theologies provide explanations for natural phenomena, societal structures, and human experiences, offering narratives that provide meaning, guidance, and moral frameworks for adherents.

As we journey through the tapestry of polytheistic theology, it is important to approach these belief systems with an open mind and a deep appreciation for the cultural contexts in which they developed. While the specific deities, myths, and rituals may vary across different polytheistic traditions, we will seek to identify common themes and underlying principles that illuminate the shared human yearning for connection, understanding, and transcendence.

By exploring the complexities of polytheistic theology, we aim to foster a deeper appreciation for the diversity of religious thought and the multifaceted ways in which human beings have sought to navigate the mysteries of the divine. Through the lens of polytheism, we can glimpse the richness of human imagination, creativity, and spiritual yearning, transcending time and culture to gain insights into the timeless quest for meaning and spiritual fulfillment.

Nature and Attributes of Deities in Polytheism

In polytheistic belief systems, deities are revered as powerful beings that embody various aspects of the natural and human realms. These divine beings possess distinct attributes, personalities, and spheres of influence, which govern their interactions with both the physical and spiritual worlds.

One of the remarkable features of polytheism is the immense diversity of deities that are worshiped. From the majestic and awe-inspiring gods of thunder and storms to the nurturing and fertile goddesses of agriculture and fertility, the pantheon of polytheistic religions encompasses a wide range of supernatural entities.

The nature and attributes of deities in polytheism often reflect the concerns, needs, and aspirations of the human societies that venerate them. For example, in agrarian communities, gods and goddesses associated with agriculture, harvest, and fertility hold immense importance. These deities are believed to have the power to bless the land, ensure bountiful crops, and provide abundance for the community.

Similarly, deities representing natural elements such as the sun, moon, stars, rivers, and mountains are revered in polytheistic religions. These celestial and earthly beings are seen as manifestations of cosmic forces and are often associated with particular domains, such as life, death, wisdom, love, war, craftsmanship, and healing. Through their worship, individuals seek to establish a harmonious relationship with these forces, seeking their favor, protection, and guidance.

The attributes and characteristics of deities in polytheism are depicted through myths, legends, and religious texts. These narratives provide insight into their origins, relationships, and roles within the pantheon. Deities are often portrayed with human-like qualities, displaying emotions, desires, and even flaws. This anthropomorphic representation allows for a more relatable and intimate connection between humans and the divine.

Exploring the Contrasts and Convergence of Polytheism and Monotheism

Polytheistic belief systems often involve the recognition of a divine hierarchy or an order of precedence among the deities. Some pantheons have a supreme deity or a ruling council of gods and goddesses who possess ultimate authority and power. Other deities may hold more specialized roles, serving as mediators, messengers, or guardians of specific domains or aspects of human life.

It is important to note that the nature and attributes of deities can vary significantly across different polytheistic traditions. The characteristics ascribed to a specific deity may be influenced by cultural, geographical, and historical factors. As polytheistic religions evolve over time, the pantheon may expand or contract, and new deities may be assimilated or adopted from other cultures through processes of syncretism and cultural exchange.

Overall, the nature and attributes of deities in polytheism reflect the intricate relationship between human beings and the divine. Through the worship and reverence of these diverse and multifaceted beings, adherents seek to understand and connect with the forces and mysteries of the natural and supernatural world, finding solace, guidance, and inspiration in their religious practices.

Examining the diversity of gods and goddesses in polytheistic belief systems

Polytheistic belief systems are characterized by their rich and diverse pantheons, which consist of numerous gods and goddesses. These divine beings exhibit a wide array of characteristics, roles, and attributes, reflecting the multifaceted nature of the human experience and the complexity of the natural and supernatural realms.

One of the remarkable aspects of polytheistic religions is the sheer number of deities that are worshiped. From ancient civilizations such as the Greeks, Romans, Egyptians, and Norse, to contemporary traditions like Hinduism, Shinto, and various African and Indigenous religions, each polytheistic tradition boasts its own extensive pantheon of gods and goddesses.

The diversity of gods and goddesses in polytheism stems from the belief that different aspects of life and the universe are governed by distinct divine forces. These deities embody various domains such as nature, fertility, war, love, wisdom, craftsmanship, healing, and justice. They represent different elements of the physical world, natural phenomena, celestial bodies, and abstract concepts, providing individuals with a comprehensive framework to understand and navigate their existence.

Each deity in a polytheistic pantheon possesses unique attributes and characteristics that distinguish them from one another. For example, in Greek mythology, Zeus is the king of the gods, wielding thunder and lightning and ruling over the sky and the heavens, while Aphrodite is the goddess of love and beauty, embodying desire, passion, and sensuality. In Hinduism, Shiva is the destroyer and transformer of the universe, while Lakshmi is the goddess of wealth and prosperity. These diverse deities encompass a wide spectrum of qualities and responsibilities, offering devotees various avenues for worship and guidance in different aspects of their lives.

The diversity of gods and goddesses in polytheistic belief systems also reflects the cultural, historical, and geographical contexts in which these religions originated. Different cultures and societies have developed their own pantheons based on their unique experiences, values, and worldview. As a result, the gods and goddesses within a particular polytheistic tradition may vary in their names, appearances, symbols, myths, and even their relationships with one another.

Furthermore, the diversity of gods and goddesses in polytheism is often associated with regional variations and local cults. Different cities or communities within a civilization may have their own patron deities or local gods and goddesses, emphasizing the interconnectedness between religious practices and local identities. This localization of worship adds further layers of complexity and diversity to the pantheon, fostering a sense of community and individuality within the broader religious framework.

Polytheistic belief systems also exhibit a certain degree of fluidity and adaptability. As cultures encounter one another through trade, conquest, or cultural exchange, gods and goddesses can be assimilated, adopted, or merged, resulting in the syncretism of religious traditions. This process further enhances the diversity of deities, as they may acquire new roles, associations, or attributes from other cultures, creating a dynamic and evolving pantheon.

In conclusion, the diversity of gods and goddesses in polytheistic belief systems is a testament to the multifaceted nature of human existence and the intricate relationship between humans and the divine. These diverse deities provide individuals with a rich tapestry of spiritual guidance, offering them a multitude of divine figures to worship, connect with, and seek support from in different aspects of their lives. The exploration and understanding of this diversity contribute to a deeper appreciation of the complexity and beauty of polytheistic religions.

The characteristics, roles, and domains of various deities

In polytheistic belief systems, gods and goddesses exhibit a wide range of characteristics, roles, and domains. Each deity is associated with specific qualities and responsibilities, reflecting their unique place in the pantheon and their connection to different aspects of life and the universe.

Nature Deities: Many polytheistic traditions have gods and goddesses associated with nature and natural phenomena. These deities govern elements such as the earth, sky, sea, mountains, rivers, and forests. They embody the forces of nature and are often invoked for blessings related to fertility, abundance, and the cycle of seasons. Examples include Gaia in Greek mythology, Tlaloc in Aztec mythology, and Cernunnos in Celtic mythology.

Fertility and Harvest Deities: These deities are linked to agricultural fertility, the growth of crops, and the abundance of harvests. They are invoked to ensure bountiful crops, healthy livestock, and the prosperity of communities. Examples include Demeter in Greek mythology, Freyja in Norse mythology, and Inari in Shinto.

War and Battle Deities: These deities embody the attributes of courage, strength, and strategy in times of conflict. They are often invoked for protection, victory, and valor in warfare. Examples include Ares in Greek mythology, Mars in Roman mythology, and Ogun in Yoruba religion.

Love and Beauty Deities: These deities are associated with love, beauty, desire, and romantic relationships. They are often invoked for matters of the heart, attraction, and emotional connections. Examples include Aphrodite in Greek mythology, Venus in Roman mythology, and Hathor in Egyptian mythology.

Wisdom and Knowledge Deities: These deities are patrons of wisdom, intellect, and knowledge. They are often associated with scholarly pursuits, creativity, and the acquisition of wisdom. Examples include Athena in Greek mythology, Thoth in Egyptian mythology, and Saraswati in Hinduism.

Healing and Medicine Deities: These deities govern healing, medicine, and overall well-being. They are often invoked for physical and spiritual healing, the restoration of health, and the guidance of healers and physicians. Examples include Apollo in Greek mythology, Sekhmet in Egyptian mythology, and Dhanvantari in Hinduism.

Craftsmanship and Artistry Deities: These deities preside over craftsmanship, artistry, and skilled trades. They are patrons of artisans, craftsmen, and artists, and are often invoked for inspiration, creativity, and the mastery of skills. Examples include Hephaestus in Greek mythology, Vulcan in Roman mythology, and Oshun in Yoruba religion.

Justice and Law Deities: These deities embody the principles of justice, fairness, and moral order. They oversee legal matters, moral conduct, and the maintenance of balance and harmony in society. Examples include Zeus in Greek mythology, Ma'at in Egyptian mythology, and Justitia in Roman mythology.

Name	Type	Culture
Gaia	Nature Deity	Greek Mythology
Tlaloc	Nature Deity	Aztec Mythology
Cernunnos	Nature Deity	Celtic Mythology
Demeter	Fertility Deity	Greek Mythology
Freyja	Fertility Deity	Norse Mythology
Inari	Fertility Deity	Shinto
Ares	War Deity	Greek Mythology
Mars	War Deity	Roman Mythology
Ogun	War Deity	Yoruba Religion
Aphrodite	Love and Beauty Deity	Greek Mythology
Venus	Love and Beauty Deity	Roman Mythology
Hathor	Love and Beauty Deity	Egyptian Mythology
Athena	Wisdom Deity	Greek Mythology
Thoth	Wisdom Deity	Egyptian Mythology
Saraswati	Wisdom Deity	Hinduism
Apollo	Healing Deity	Greek Mythology
Sekhmet	Healing Deity	Egyptian Mythology
Dhanvantari	Healing Deity	Hinduism
Hephaestus	Craftsmanship Deity	Greek Mythology
Vulcan	Craftsmanship Deity	Roman Mythology
Oshun	Craftsmanship Deity	Yoruba Religion
Zeus	Justice Deity	Greek Mythology
Ma'at	Justice Deity	Egyptian Mythology
Justitia	Justice Deity	Roman Mythology

Please note that this is a condensed representation, and there are many more deities with various roles and domains in polytheistic belief systems.

These examples represent just a fraction of the vast array of deities found in polytheistic belief systems. It is important to note that the characteristics, roles, and domains of deities can vary across cultures and traditions. Additionally, many deities may exhibit multiple roles and domains, reflecting the interconnectedness and overlapping nature of their responsibilities within the pantheon.

Polytheistic Cosmology and Creation Myths

Polytheistic cosmology encompasses the beliefs and myths surrounding the creation and structure of the universe according to polytheistic religions. These cosmologies vary across different cultures and civilizations, but they often share common themes and motifs.

Creation myths in polytheistic cosmologies explain the origins of the universe, the earth, and humanity. These myths often involve the actions and interactions of multiple deities, each playing a specific role in the creation process. The gods and goddesses are seen as divine beings with immense power and influence over different aspects of the cosmos.

In some polytheistic cosmologies, creation is depicted as a result of a cosmic battle or the emergence of order from chaos. For example, in Greek mythology, the universe is born from the primordial chaos, and deities such as Gaia (Earth) and Uranus (Sky) emerge to give shape to the world.

Other cosmologies emphasize the cyclical nature of creation and destruction, with the universe going through repeated cycles of birth, existence, and dissolution. In Hindu cosmology, for instance, the universe is believed to go through cycles of creation (Brahma), preservation (Vishnu), and dissolution (Shiva), in a continuous cosmic cycle known as "Samsara."

Polytheistic cosmologies often assign specific roles and domains to different deities. These roles can include the governance of celestial bodies, natural elements, seasons, fertility, and the afterlife. For example, in Egyptian mythology, the sun god Ra is responsible for the rising and setting of the sun, while Osiris oversees the realm of the dead and the process of rebirth.

Creation myths and cosmological beliefs in polytheistic religions serve as a foundation for understanding the relationship between the divine, the natural world, and humanity. They provide explanations for the existence of the universe, the origin of life, and the place of human beings within the cosmic order. These myths and beliefs also shape religious rituals, social structures, and moral frameworks within polytheistic societies.

Exploring the creation narratives and cosmological frameworks in polytheistic religions

Exploring the creation narratives and cosmological frameworks in polytheistic religions reveals the rich diversity of beliefs and stories that shape the understanding of the origins and structure of the universe. These narratives provide insights into the cultural, social, and philosophical aspects of ancient civilizations.

Polytheistic creation narratives often present a complex interplay of gods and goddesses, each contributing to the formation of the cosmos. These stories may vary significantly from one culture to another, reflecting the unique perspectives and beliefs of different societies.

In some polytheistic traditions, creation is depicted as a deliberate act of divine beings who shape the world through their actions and interactions. For example, in Norse mythology, the cosmos is formed from the body of the primordial giant Ymir, with the gods Odin, Vili, and Ve playing a central role in the creation and ordering of the world.

Other cosmological frameworks highlight the cyclical nature of creation and destruction, symbolizing the eternal cycle of birth, death, and rebirth. In Hindu cosmology, the universe undergoes a continuous cycle of creation, preservation, and dissolution, guided by the Trimurti—Brahma, Vishnu, and Shiva—representing the creative, sustaining, and destructive forces respectively.

The symbolism and metaphors used in polytheistic creation narratives often reflect the cultural and natural environment of the respective civilizations. For instance, in the Babylonian creation myth Enuma Elish, the world is formed through a cosmic battle between the deities representing chaos and order, reflecting the ancient Mesopotamian society's struggle to bring order out of the chaotic forces of nature.

Cosmological frameworks in polytheistic religions also encompass the understanding of the celestial realms, the underworld, and the realms of spirits and deities. These frameworks may include the mapping of the heavens, the identification of constellations, and the association of certain gods and goddesses with celestial bodies or natural elements.

Exploring these creation narratives and cosmological frameworks provides valuable insights into the religious, cultural, and philosophical worldviews of ancient civilizations. They shed light on the relationships between gods and humans, the role of mythology in explaining the mysteries of existence, and the significance of the natural world in shaping human understanding and beliefs.

Overall, the exploration of creation narratives and cosmological frameworks in polytheistic religions offers a fascinating glimpse into the diverse ways in which ancient cultures perceived and sought to comprehend the origins and structure of the universe.

The relationships and hierarchies among deities in different pantheons

The relationships and hierarchies among deities in different pantheons vary greatly across polytheistic religions. These hierarchies often reflect the cultural, social, and religious values of the civilizations in which they emerged. While some pantheons exhibit clear hierarchies with supreme gods or goddesses, others may have more fluid or egalitarian structures.

In certain polytheistic pantheons, there is a supreme deity who holds the highest position and is regarded as the ruler or creator of the cosmos. This supreme deity may possess characteristics and powers that distinguish them from other gods and goddesses. For example, in the Greek pantheon, Zeus is the king of the gods, presiding over the heavens and wielding authority over the other Olympian deities.

Within pantheons, there are often familial relationships between gods and goddesses. These relationships can be based on parent-child connections, sibling bonds, or even marital unions. These family ties serve to establish lineages and connections between deities, highlighting the interplay of various forces and powers within the pantheon. In Norse mythology, for instance, Odin is the father of Thor and Loki, emphasizing the familial dynamics among the gods.

Hierarchies among deities can also be determined by their roles and domains of influence. Some gods and goddesses may have specific realms of power, such as the god of war, the goddess of love, or the god of wisdom. These domains of influence can shape the hierarchies within the pantheon and define the relative importance of different deities. For instance, in the Egyptian pantheon, Osiris is associated with the afterlife and judgment, while Ra is the sun god and creator, each holding significant roles within the divine hierarchy.

However, it is important to note that not all polytheistic pantheons exhibit strict hierarchies. Some pantheons, particularly those influenced by more egalitarian or tribal societies, may have a more decentralized structure with less emphasis on hierarchies and more on collective power and cooperation among the gods and goddesses. These pantheons may have a sense of equality among the deities or emphasize the interdependence and interconnectedness of various forces and entities.

It is worth mentioning that the relationships and hierarchies among deities in polytheistic pantheons are not static. They can evolve over time through cultural and religious changes, assimilation of foreign deities, and reinterpretation of mythologies. The interactions and conflicts between gods and goddesses, as depicted in myths and legends, also shape the dynamics within the pantheon.

Overall, the relationships and hierarchies among deities in different polytheistic pantheons reflect the complexities of human understanding and the divine realm. They embody cultural values, societal structures, and religious beliefs, providing insight into the diverse ways in which ancient civilizations conceptualized and organized their gods and goddesses.

Polytheistic Worship and Ritual Practices

Polytheistic worship and ritual practices encompass a wide range of beliefs and customs, as they vary across different cultures and civilizations. However, there are some common elements that can be observed in the worship of multiple gods and goddesses.

Temples and sacred spaces play a central role in polytheistic worship. These places serve as sanctuaries for divine presence and are dedicated to specific deities. Temples are constructed as architectural marvels, often adorned with intricate artwork and sculptures representing the gods and goddesses. They serve as gathering places for worshipers to connect with the divine through rituals and ceremonies.

Rituals and ceremonies are essential components of polytheistic worship. These practices are designed to honor and appease the gods and goddesses, seeking their blessings, protection, and favor. They can take various forms, including prayers, offerings, sacrifices, processions, dances, and recitations of sacred texts or hymns. Rituals often involve gestures, symbolic actions, and the use of specific objects or tools associated with the deities.

Priests and priestesses play a crucial role in polytheistic worship. They act as intermediaries between humans and the divine, facilitating communication and conducting the rituals. Priests and priestesses are responsible for maintaining the temples, performing the sacred rites, and interpreting the will of the gods. They undergo training and initiation to fulfill their religious duties and often hold esteemed positions within their communities.

Festivals and religious celebrations are significant occasions in polytheistic worship. These events mark important milestones in the religious calendar and commemorate specific gods or goddesses. Festivals involve communal gatherings, processions, feasts, and performances, providing opportunities for worshipers to come together, express devotion, and participate in shared religious experiences. These celebrations serve not only as religious observances but also as social and cultural events that reinforce community cohesion and identity.

Personal devotion and individual practices also form an integral part of polytheistic worship. Worshipers may establish personal relationships with specific deities, seeking their guidance, protection, and assistance in daily life. Individuals may engage in private prayers, make personal offerings, or create personal altars dedicated to their chosen gods or goddesses. These practices allow for a more intimate and personal connection with the divine.

It is important to note that polytheistic worship and ritual practices are often adaptable and flexible, accommodating regional variations, local customs, and individual preferences. They evolve over time, influenced by cultural changes, political shifts, and religious syncretism.

In conclusion, polytheistic worship and ritual practices are diverse and multifaceted, reflecting the complex relationships between humans and the divine. They involve temples, rituals, festivals, and personal devotions, all aimed at honoring and communing with multiple gods and goddesses. These practices foster a sense of spiritual connection, social cohesion, and cultural identity within polytheistic civilizations.

Investigating the rituals, ceremonies, and offerings associated with polytheistic worship

Investigating the rituals, ceremonies, and offerings associated with polytheistic worship provides valuable insights into the religious practices and beliefs of ancient civilizations. These practices vary across different cultures and time periods, but they share common themes and purposes.

Rituals and ceremonies in polytheistic worship serve as a means of communication and interaction with the gods and goddesses. They are performed to honor, appease, and seek favor from the divine beings. These rituals often involve a series of prescribed actions, gestures, and recitations, creating a structured framework for the worshipers' engagement with the divine.

Offerings play a central role in polytheistic rituals. They are presented to the gods and goddesses as symbols of devotion, gratitude, and supplication. Offerings can take various forms, including food and drink, flowers, incense, precious objects, or even animal sacrifices. These offerings are believed to nourish and please the deities, establishing a reciprocal relationship between humans and the divine.

Ceremonies in polytheistic worship are often tied to specific occasions or events. They can be seasonal celebrations, agricultural rituals, rites of passage, or commemorations of historical or mythical events. These ceremonies serve as collective expressions of religious identity, reinforcing cultural values and beliefs within the community.

Temples and sacred spaces provide the physical setting for polytheistic rituals and ceremonies. These structures are believed to be the dwelling places of the gods and goddesses and are meticulously designed and adorned to reflect their divine presence. Temples often house statues, images, or symbols of the deities, serving as focal points for worship and devotion. They are also gathering places for the community to come together and participate in collective worship.

Priests and priestesses play crucial roles in conducting polytheistic rituals. They act as intermediaries between the human and divine realms, ensuring the proper performance of rituals and the correct offering of prayers and sacrifices. Priests and priestesses undergo training, purification, and initiation to fulfill their sacred duties and maintain their spiritual connection with the deities.

Music, dance, and recitation of sacred texts or hymns are often integral parts of polytheistic rituals. These artistic expressions serve to invoke the presence of the gods and goddesses, create an atmosphere of reverence and transcendence, and engage the worshipers on a sensory and emotional level. They enhance the overall experience of the rituals and deepen the spiritual connection between humans and the divine.

It is important to recognize that polytheistic worship practices are not static and can evolve over time. They are shaped by cultural changes, regional influences, and the assimilation of new religious beliefs. As civilizations interacted and cultures merged, syncretism occurred, resulting in the blending of rituals, ceremonies, and beliefs from different polytheistic traditions.

Studying the rituals, ceremonies, and offerings associated with polytheistic worship provides valuable insights into the religious and cultural dynamics of ancient civilizations. These practices were not only expressions of faith but also significant social and communal events, fostering a sense of belonging, identity, and shared values among the worshipers.

The role of priests, priestesses, and religious institutions in polytheistic traditions

In polytheistic traditions, priests, priestesses, and religious institutions played pivotal roles in facilitating and maintaining the religious practices and beliefs of the community. They acted as intermediaries between the mortal realm and the divine realm, carrying out sacred duties and ensuring the proper performance of rituals and ceremonies.

Priests and priestesses held positions of spiritual authority and were responsible for the day-to-day administration of religious affairs. They underwent specialized training and education, often within designated religious institutions or under the tutelage of experienced mentors. This training included the study of religious texts, rituals, cosmology, and the proper handling of sacred objects and symbols.

Priests and priestesses were tasked with conducting rituals and ceremonies on behalf of the community. They served as conduits through which the divine could be accessed, and their actions were believed to directly influence the interaction between humans and the gods or goddesses. They recited prayers, offered sacrifices, performed purification rites, and engaged in other ritualistic practices to ensure divine favor, protection, and blessings for the community.

Religious institutions, such as temples or shrines, served as the physical and organizational centers of polytheistic worship. These institutions were dedicated to specific deities or groups of deities and served as the focal points for communal worship and religious activities. Temples were often grand and elaborate structures, adorned with sacred imagery and symbols, and designed to create an atmosphere of reverence and awe.

Within these institutions, priests and priestesses carried out their duties, maintaining the sanctity of the sacred spaces and overseeing the daily operations of worship. They were responsible for the care and preservation of religious artifacts, sacred texts, and ritual implements. They also played important roles in organizing and coordinating religious festivals, processions, and other communal events.

In addition to their ritualistic responsibilities, priests and priestesses often served as advisors and counselors to the community. They provided guidance on matters of morality, ethics, and religious doctrine, and were considered authorities on matters of spiritual significance. Their role extended beyond the confines of the temple, and they were seen as mediators between the divine and the mortal realms, offering spiritual guidance, blessings, and even prophecy.

Priestesses held a significant place in many polytheistic traditions, often serving as the primary conduits for specific goddesses or engaging in specific roles associated with female divinities. They were revered as embodiments of feminine power and wisdom and held positions of influence within the community.

It is important to note that the specific roles and functions of priests, priestesses, and religious institutions varied across different polytheistic cultures and time periods. Some traditions had a hierarchical structure, while others emphasized the egalitarian participation of the entire community in religious practices. Nonetheless, the presence of these religious figures and institutions was a consistent feature in polytheistic societies, providing guidance, maintaining religious traditions, and fostering a sense of spiritual connection between the divine and the mortal realms.

Relationships Between Humans and Deities in Polytheism

In polytheistic belief systems, the relationships between humans and deities were multifaceted and varied. Humans were seen as living in a world populated by numerous gods and goddesses who held different domains and powers. These deities were considered both supernatural beings and active participants in the human realm, interacting with and influencing human lives.

Polytheistic cultures recognized that humans and deities had a reciprocal relationship. Humans sought the favor, protection, and blessings of the gods and goddesses, while the deities depended on human worship, offerings, and devotion to sustain their power and influence. This mutual exchange formed the foundation of the human-divine relationship in polytheistic religions.

Worship and rituals played a central role in maintaining and nurturing the relationship between humans and deities. These practices involved prayers, offerings, sacrifices, and acts of reverence directed towards specific gods and goddesses. Humans would express gratitude, seek guidance, ask for divine intervention, or offer praise through these rituals, establishing a direct line of communication with the divine realm.

Polytheistic belief systems often recognized the inherent hierarchy among the gods and goddesses. Some deities held more prominence and power, while others had specific roles or domains of influence. Humans would approach different deities depending on their specific needs or concerns. For example, they might invoke a god associated with fertility for agricultural matters or a goddess of wisdom for intellectual pursuits.

Exploring the Contrasts and Convergence of Polytheism and Monotheism

The relationship between humans and deities was not limited to formal worship and rituals alone. Polytheistic cultures often believed in the presence of deities in the natural world, recognizing their influence in various aspects of life. Humans would observe signs and omens, seeking to interpret the will of the gods in everyday events. They would attribute success or failure, good fortune or misfortune, to the favor or displeasure of particular deities.

In polytheistic belief systems, deities were often anthropomorphic, meaning they possessed human-like qualities and emotions. This anthropomorphism allowed humans to relate to and understand the gods and goddesses on a personal level. Mythology and narratives surrounding the deities depicted their interactions with humans, their triumphs, and their struggles. These stories provided a framework for understanding the human condition and the complexities of the divine realm.

Polytheistic cultures also recognized that humans could have individual relationships with specific deities. People would choose to honor and develop personal connections with certain gods and goddesses based on their personal beliefs, needs, or experiences. This allowed for a more intimate and personalized experience of the divine.

The concept of divine intervention was another aspect of the human-deity relationship in polytheistic belief systems. Humans believed that the gods and goddesses could directly intervene in their lives, providing guidance, protection, or even punishment. Prayers and offerings were often made to seek divine intervention in times of crisis, illness, or hardship.

It is important to note that the relationships between humans and deities in polytheism were not exclusive or monolithic. Different individuals and communities might have varying degrees of devotion and engagement with specific deities. Furthermore, the nature of these relationships could evolve and change over time as cultural, social, and religious dynamics shifted.

Overall, the relationships between humans and deities in polytheistic belief systems were characterized by a sense of interdependence, mutual respect, and reciprocity. Humans sought the favor and guidance of the gods and goddesses, while the deities, in turn, relied on human devotion and worship. These complex relationships formed the foundation of religious practices and shaped the understanding of the divine within polytheistic cultures.

Examining the nature of divine-human interactions in polytheistic belief systems

In polytheistic belief systems, the nature of divine-human interactions was characterized by a dynamic and multifaceted relationship. Humans perceived the gods and goddesses as active participants in their lives, and the interactions between the divine and human realms were seen as integral to the functioning of the world.

One aspect of divine-human interactions in polytheism was the belief in direct communication with the gods and goddesses. Humans sought to establish a connection with the divine through prayers, rituals, and offerings. They believed that by performing these acts, they could capture the attention and favor of specific deities. This communication served as a means for humans to express their needs, desires, and concerns to the divine realm.

Polytheistic cultures often believed in the concept of divine intervention, where the gods and goddesses could directly intervene in human affairs. They were seen as active participants in the events of the world, capable of influencing outcomes and responding to human petitions. Humans turned to the gods and goddesses for guidance, protection, and assistance in various aspects of life, such as fertility, health, success, and safety.

The belief in divine signs and omens also played a significant role in divine-human interactions. Polytheistic cultures attributed meaning to natural phenomena, dreams, and unusual occurrences, seeing them as messages from the gods. Humans sought to interpret these signs and omens as indications of divine will or as guidance for decision-making. They believed that the gods and goddesses communicated with them through these symbolic manifestations.

Polytheistic belief systems recognized that the gods and goddesses possessed human-like qualities and emotions. They were depicted in mythology and narratives as having desires, motivations, and personalities. This anthropomorphic nature of the deities allowed humans to relate to them on a personal level and understand their actions within a human framework. It also facilitated a sense of empathy and emotional connection between humans and the divine.

Polytheistic rituals and ceremonies were an important means of engaging in divine-human interactions. Through offerings, sacrifices, and acts of reverence, humans sought to establish a rapport with the gods and goddesses. These rituals served as a way to express gratitude, seek blessings, ask for forgiveness, or honor specific deities. They were performed in temples, sacred sites, and other designated places of worship, often led by priests or priestesses who acted as intermediaries between the divine and human realms.

It is important to note that the nature and intensity of divine-human interactions could vary among different polytheistic cultures and individuals. Some individuals may have had more personal and intimate connections with specific deities, while others engaged with the divine in a more collective and communal manner. The divine-human relationship was shaped by cultural norms, religious practices, and individual beliefs within each polytheistic tradition.

In summary, divine-human interactions in polytheistic belief systems encompassed various forms of communication, intervention, and symbolism. Humans sought to establish connections with the gods and goddesses through prayers, rituals, and offerings, believing in the potential for direct engagement and divine guidance. The gods and goddesses, in turn, were seen as active participants in human affairs, capable of influencing outcomes and responding to human needs. These interactions formed the basis of religious practices and shaped the understanding of the divine within polytheistic cultures.

Theconcepts such as patronage, prayers, and divination in polytheistic religious contexts

In polytheistic religious contexts, concepts such as patronage, prayers, and divination played significant roles in the relationship between humans and the gods. These concepts provided avenues for communication, guidance, and seeking favor from the divine realm.

Patronage was a fundamental aspect of polytheistic belief systems. Individuals, communities, and even cities often had specific gods or goddesses whom they considered as their patrons or protectors. These patron deities were believed to have a special relationship with their devotees and were seen as guardians and providers of specific blessings or benefits. For example, a city might have a patron deity associated with fertility and agriculture, ensuring the prosperity of the land and its people. Devotees would offer prayers, perform rituals, and make offerings to their patron deities as a way to honor and seek their favor.

Prayers were a common means of communication with the gods in polytheistic religions. They were expressions of praise, thanksgiving, requests, or petitions addressed to specific deities. Prayers could be conducted in various settings, including private spaces, temples, or during communal ceremonies and festivals. Different types of prayers existed, ranging from simple daily blessings and expressions of gratitude to more elaborate rituals and invocations. Polytheistic cultures believed that through prayers, they could establish a connection with the gods, share their concerns, seek guidance, and request assistance in various aspects of life.

Divination was another integral aspect of polytheistic religious practices. It involved seeking insight and guidance from the gods through various methods of interpreting signs, omens, oracles, or supernatural phenomena. Divination techniques varied across different cultures and time periods, including practices such as examining the flight patterns of birds, interpreting the patterns of flames or smoke, or consulting oracles or seers. Divination aimed to provide answers to questions, predict the future, or gain insight into the will of the gods. It was believed that the gods could communicate messages and reveal hidden knowledge through these divinatory practices.

Polytheistic religious contexts also recognized the role of intermediaries, such as priests, priestesses, oracles, and diviners. These individuals were seen as having a special connection with the gods and were entrusted with the responsibility of mediating between the human and divine realms. Priests and priestesses performed religious rituals, maintained temples, and conveyed the wishes and concerns of the community to the gods. Oracles and diviners were believed to possess the ability to receive direct messages from the gods or interpret divine signs and omens.

Furthermore, festivals and ceremonies played significant roles in polytheistic religious contexts. These events provided opportunities for communal worship, celebration, and reaffirmation of the relationship between humans and the gods. Festivals were often held in honor of specific deities and involved processions, rituals, sacrifices, music, dance, and feasting. They served as occasions for expressing gratitude, seeking blessings, and participating in communal rituals that reinforced the bonds between humans and the divine.

In summary, patronage, prayers, and divination were essential concepts in polytheistic religious contexts. They provided avenues for communication, seeking guidance, and establishing a relationship with the gods. Through patronage, individuals and communities acknowledged the special protection and favor of specific deities. Prayers served as a means of expressing devotion, making requests, and seeking divine intervention. Divination practices allowed individuals to seek insight and guidance from the gods through the interpretation of signs and omens. These concepts, along with festivals and ceremonies, were integral to the religious practices of polytheistic cultures and shaped the nature of the divine-human relationship.

CHAPTER 8: THEOLOGY OF MONOTHEISM

Monotheism, the belief in the existence of a single supreme deity, has played a significant role in shaping the religious and philosophical landscapes of various civilizations throughout history. Unlike polytheism, which encompasses the worship of multiple gods and goddesses, monotheistic traditions revolve around the veneration of a single, all-powerful entity.

This chapter delves into the theology of monotheism, exploring the core principles, concepts, and philosophical underpinnings of monotheistic belief systems. It investigates the origins and development of monotheism in different cultures, tracing its evolution from early monotheistic elements to fully established monotheistic religions.

Throughout history, monotheistic traditions have emerged in diverse regions, each with its unique theological frameworks and religious practices. From the ancient Near East to the major monotheistic religions of Judaism, Christianity, and Islam, monotheism has provided a foundation for spiritual and ethical guidance for millions of believers.

The chapter explores the theological foundations of monotheism, addressing fundamental questions such as the nature of the divine, the relationship between the deity and humanity, and the moral and ethical implications of monotheistic teachings. It also examines the role of prophets, scripture, and religious institutions in shaping and transmitting monotheistic beliefs.

Furthermore, this chapter highlights the theological differences and philosophical debates within monotheistic traditions, exploring various interpretations and schools of thought. It investigates the theological concepts of divine attributes, providence, free will, and theodicy, and how they have been addressed and explored within monotheistic theology.

By examining the theology of monotheism, this chapter aims to provide a comprehensive understanding of the core tenets and intellectual foundations that underpin monotheistic belief systems. It invites readers to delve into the philosophical and theological inquiries that have shaped monotheistic traditions and continue to be subjects of contemplation and exploration.

From the ancient civilizations that first laid the groundwork for monotheistic thought to the vibrant and diverse monotheistic religions of today, the theology of monotheism offers profound insights into the nature of divinity, human existence, and the search for ultimate meaning and purpose. This chapter invites readers to embark on a journey into the theological complexities and philosophical richness of monotheistic traditions, exploring the profound impact these beliefs have had on the world.

Concept of a Single Supreme Deity in Monotheism

The concept of a single supreme deity lies at the heart of monotheistic belief systems. Unlike polytheism, which acknowledges the existence of multiple gods and goddesses, monotheism asserts the existence of a singular, all-powerful and transcendent entity. This single supreme deity is seen as the ultimate source of creation, the arbiter of moral values, and the object of devotion and worship.

In monotheistic traditions, the nature and attributes of this supreme deity vary, but there are common threads that run through these belief systems. The deity is often portrayed as omnipotent (all-powerful), omniscient (all-knowing), and omnipresent (present everywhere). This supreme being is believed to possess qualities such as wisdom, justice, love, and mercy, and is considered the creator and sustainer of the universe.

The belief in a single supreme deity provides a unifying framework for understanding the cosmos and human existence. It offers a comprehensive explanation of the origins and purpose of the world, as well as the moral guidelines by which individuals are to live their lives. Monotheism posits a personal relationship between the individual and the deity, emphasizing devotion, prayer, and adherence to divine commandments.

Monotheistic belief systems often present the supreme deity as distinct from the natural world, transcending the material realm. This separation between the divine and the earthly realm allows for a hierarchical relationship, with humans occupying a subordinate position to the deity. The supreme deity is regarded as the ultimate authority, guiding and directing human affairs.

The concept of a single supreme deity also implies exclusivity, as monotheism typically asserts that the worship of other deities is either prohibited or considered false. This exclusivity gives rise to a monotheistic religious identity and a sense of chosenness or special relationship with the deity.

Exploring the Contrasts and Convergence of Polytheism and Monotheism

The belief in a single supreme deity has profound implications for theology, ethics, and spirituality within monotheistic traditions. It provides a framework for understanding the nature of good and evil, the purpose of human existence, and the destiny of the soul. Monotheism offers a sense of unity and coherence in the face of life's complexities and challenges, instilling a sense of purpose and meaning in the lives of believers.

The concept of a single supreme deity in monotheism has had a transformative impact on human history, shaping cultural, social, and intellectual developments. It has provided a foundation for moral and ethical values, influenced legal systems, and guided philosophical and theological discourse. The belief in a single supreme deity continues to inspire and guide millions of people worldwide, offering solace, guidance, and a sense of transcendence in an ever-changing world.

Exploring the notion of monotheistic religions centered around a single supreme deity

Exploring the notion of monotheistic religions centered around a single supreme deity reveals a distinctive characteristic that sets them apart from other religious traditions. Monotheism emphasizes the belief in one ultimate and transcendent deity, who is considered the creator and ruler of the universe. This monotheistic concept stands in contrast to polytheism, which recognizes the existence of multiple gods and goddesses.

In monotheistic religions, the idea of a single supreme deity serves as the foundation of religious belief and practice. This deity is often understood as the source of all existence, the originator of life, and the sustainer of the cosmos. Monotheistic faiths attribute qualities of absolute power, knowledge, and wisdom to this supreme deity. It is believed that the deity possesses complete control over the natural world and governs the affairs of human beings.

The concept of a single supreme deity provides a focal point for devotion, worship, and spiritual connection in monotheistic traditions. Followers of monotheistic religions direct their prayers, rituals, and acts of devotion toward this supreme being. The worship of the deity is often accompanied by reverence, awe, and a sense of deep reverence for the divine.

Monotheistic religions emphasize the monotheistic concept of divine unity, emphasizing the oneness and indivisibility of the supreme deity. This unity is often seen as the ultimate truth and the fundamental principle underlying the universe. The belief in the oneness of the supreme deity is accompanied by the rejection of polytheistic practices and the worship of other deities. Monotheistic faiths view the worship of multiple deities as a form of idolatry or deviation from the true understanding of the divine.

The notion of a single supreme deity also influences the moral and ethical dimensions of monotheistic religions. Monotheism often provides a moral framework based on the teachings and commandments attributed to the supreme deity. Believers are guided by these moral precepts and strive to live in accordance with the divine will. Monotheistic faiths often emphasize ethical values such as justice, compassion, honesty, and love, which are derived from the attributes and teachings of the supreme deity.

The belief in a single supreme deity has shaped the course of history, influencing the development of cultures, societies, and civilizations. Monotheistic religions have played a significant role in shaping moral codes, legal systems, art, literature, and philosophical thought. The belief in a single supreme deity has been a source of inspiration, guidance, and comfort for countless individuals throughout history, providing a sense of purpose, meaning, and spiritual connection.

Exploring the notion of monotheistic religions centered around a single supreme deity allows for a deeper understanding of the distinct theological, philosophical, and spiritual perspectives that characterize these faith traditions. It highlights the unique relationship between the individual and the divine, the belief in divine unity, and the quest for a deeper understanding of the nature of the supreme deity and its role in the human experience.

The attributes, nature, and transcendence of the monotheistic God

The attributes, nature, and transcendence of the monotheistic God vary across different monotheistic traditions, but there are some commonalities that can be explored. Monotheistic religions conceive of God as a supreme being who possesses certain attributes that set Him apart from the created world and make Him worthy of worship and reverence.

One key attribute attributed to the monotheistic God is omnipotence, or unlimited power. The monotheistic God is believed to have complete control over the universe, able to create and shape it according to His will. This attribute signifies God's ability to bring about any desired outcome and to intervene in the natural course of events.

The monotheistic God is also often described as omniscient, possessing perfect knowledge and understanding of all things. God is believed to have knowledge of the past, present, and future, and to be aware of the thoughts, intentions, and actions of all beings. This attribute of omniscience is seen as a source of comfort, as it implies that God is aware of the individual's circumstances and can provide guidance and support.

Another attribute ascribed to the monotheistic God is omnipresence, signifying that God is present everywhere and not limited by space or time. This attribute highlights the belief that God is not confined to a particular location or bound by physical limitations but is accessible to all believers at all times.

Transcendence is a fundamental aspect of monotheistic conceptions of God. The monotheistic God is viewed as existing beyond the created world and beyond human comprehension. God is considered to be infinite, eternal, and beyond the limitations of human understanding. This transcendence emphasizes the belief that God is not confined to the physical realm but exists in a higher spiritual plane.

Monotheistic religions also emphasize the moral attributes of God. God is often described as just, merciful, compassionate, and loving. These attributes provide a moral framework for believers, guiding their actions and shaping their understanding of right and wrong.

Furthermore, monotheistic traditions generally affirm the unity of God. God is understood to be one, indivisible, and without partners or equals. This concept of divine unity stands in contrast to polytheistic beliefs, which recognize the existence of multiple gods and goddesses.

The nature of the monotheistic God is often considered beyond human comprehension and is approached with reverence and awe. While believers may seek to understand aspects of God's nature through religious teachings, scripture, and personal experiences, they acknowledge that God's true essence is ultimately beyond human comprehension.

The attributes, nature, and transcendence of the monotheistic God play a central role in the religious beliefs, practices, and experiences of monotheistic traditions. They provide a framework for understanding the relationship between the divine and the human, offering guidance, inspiration, and a sense of purpose and meaning in the lives of believers.

Monotheistic Cosmology and Creation Stories

Monotheistic cosmology and creation stories provide narratives and explanations for the origins and structure of the universe according to monotheistic traditions. These narratives vary among different monotheistic religions but often share common themes and concepts.

In monotheistic cosmology, the universe is seen as the intentional creation of the singular divine being, the one true God. The monotheistic God is believed to have brought the entire cosmos into existence out of nothingness or from a pre-existing state. The creation of the universe is seen as an act of divine will and purpose, reflecting God's wisdom, power, and creativity.

Monotheistic creation stories often emphasize the order, beauty, and harmony of the created world as a reflection of the divine design. The universe is viewed as an intricately balanced system, with the physical and natural laws governing its functioning. This concept of order reflects the belief in a wise and intelligent Creator who has established a purposeful and meaningful existence.

These creation stories also address the place of human beings within the cosmos. Human beings are often seen as the pinnacle of creation, uniquely endowed with rationality, moral agency, and the capacity for spiritual connection with the divine. The creation of humans is often portrayed as a deliberate act of the monotheistic God, who bestows upon them a special status and responsibility in the world.

Monotheistic cosmology also addresses the concept of the divine transcendence and immanence. Transcendence refers to the belief that the monotheistic God is beyond and independent of the created world, existing in a realm beyond human perception. Immanence, on the other hand, highlights the belief that the monotheistic God is actively present and involved within the created world, sustaining and guiding its existence.

The monotheistic creation stories provide a framework for understanding the relationship between God, humanity, and the natural world. They often emphasize the moral dimension of creation, depicting human beings as entrusted with the stewardship and responsible care of the earth and its resources. This stewardship is seen as a reflection of the monotheistic God's values and expectations for human conduct.

Moreover, monotheistic cosmology also addresses the concept of the ultimate purpose and destiny of the created world. The universe is often viewed as moving towards a culmination or fulfillment, guided by the providence and plan of the monotheistic God. This vision of cosmic destiny offers hope and meaning to believers, providing a sense of purpose and direction in their lives.

Overall, monotheistic cosmology and creation stories serve to deepen the understanding of the monotheistic faith, providing believers with a narrative framework for contemplating the origins, purpose, and significance of the universe and their place within it. They inspire awe, reverence, and gratitude towards the monotheistic God as the ultimate source of all existence and offer a deeper understanding of the nature of reality and the divine-human relationship.

Analyzing monotheistic explanations of the origin of the universe and human existence

Monotheistic explanations of the origin of the universe and human existence are foundational to the theological frameworks of monotheistic religions. These explanations seek to address fundamental questions about the nature of reality, the purpose of human life, and the relationship between the divine and the created world.

In monotheistic traditions, the origin of the universe is attributed to the singular, transcendent God who intentionally brought it into being. The monotheistic God is seen as the ultimate source of all existence, possessing the power and knowledge to create the entire cosmos. This act of creation is often understood as an expression of the monotheistic God's love, wisdom, and purpose.

Monotheistic explanations of the origin of the universe vary in their details across different religious traditions. Some emphasize a creation ex nihilo, where the monotheistic God brings the universe into existence out of nothingness. Others may propose the idea of a pre-existing material or spiritual realm that is shaped or transformed by the monotheistic God's creative power.

Human existence, in monotheistic explanations, is often depicted as a deliberate act of the monotheistic God. Human beings are viewed as unique among all creation, endowed with qualities such as reason, consciousness, and moral agency. The monotheistic God is believed to have created humans in His own image, endowing them with the capacity to reflect His attributes and engage in a relationship with Him.

Monotheistic explanations of human existence also address questions of purpose and meaning. Human beings are seen as having a specific role or vocation within the created order, which may include responsibilities such as stewardship of the earth, cultivation of virtues, and seeking spiritual growth. The monotheistic God's guidance and teachings are often seen as providing the framework for living a fulfilling and meaningful life.

Monotheistic explanations of the origin of the universe and human existence also touch on the concept of divine providence. This notion suggests that the monotheistic

God continues to sustain and govern the universe, actively involved in the unfolding of history and the affairs of humanity. Believers may perceive signs of divine providence in the events of their lives and in the workings of the natural world.

Furthermore, monotheistic explanations of the origin of the universe and human existence often emphasize the idea of a moral order. The monotheistic God's attributes of justice, compassion, and mercy inform the ethical principles and guidelines for human conduct. The monotheistic religions often provide teachings and commandments that shape human behavior, fostering social harmony, and personal righteousness.

In analyzing these explanations, scholars and theologians within monotheistic traditions delve into philosophical, theological, and mystical inquiries. They explore concepts such as causality, teleology, metaphysics, and theodicy to gain a deeper understanding of the nature of the monotheistic God and the purpose behind the creation.

Overall, monotheistic explanations of the origin of the universe and human existence reflect a profound engagement with questions of ultimate reality, purpose, and human significance. They provide believers with a framework for understanding their place within the cosmos and offer guidance for moral and spiritual growth. These explanations invite reflection, contemplation, and a deeper connection with the transcendent monotheistic God.

The concept of divine providence and the monotheistic understanding of divine intervention

The concept of divine providence is central to monotheistic beliefs and refers to the idea that the singular, transcendent God actively governs and guides the world and its events. Divine providence encompasses the notion that the monotheistic God is intimately involved in the affairs of creation, continuously sustaining and directing the course of history and the lives of individuals.

In monotheistic traditions, divine providence is understood as an expression of the monotheistic God's omniscience, omnipotence, and benevolence. The monotheistic God is seen as the ultimate source of wisdom and knowledge, aware of all events and their implications. As such, divine providence implies that nothing happens by chance or outside of the monotheistic God's knowledge and control.

Divine intervention is a manifestation of divine providence and refers to the monotheistic God's direct involvement in human affairs or the natural world. It is the visible or tangible expression of the monotheistic God's power, will, and care. Divine interventions can take various forms, including miracles, revelations, prophetic messages, and acts of divine guidance or protection.

In monotheistic traditions, divine intervention serves multiple purposes. It can be a sign of the monotheistic God's presence and confirmation of His existence and authority. Divine interventions may also serve as a means of delivering divine guidance, teaching, or warnings to individuals or communities. They can demonstrate the monotheistic God's power over natural forces, such as controlling the elements or healing the sick.

The monotheistic understanding of divine intervention does not imply arbitrary or capricious actions by the monotheistic God. Instead, it is believed to be rooted in the monotheistic God's perfect wisdom and love for creation. Divine interventions are seen as purposeful and aligned with the monotheistic God's overarching plan for the world and humanity.

While divine intervention is considered significant in monotheistic beliefs, it is not seen as a constant or continuous occurrence. Monotheistic traditions acknowledge that the monotheistic God's ways are often mysterious and may not always be fully comprehensible to human beings. Thus, divine interventions are understood to happen according to the monotheistic God's will and timing.

The monotheistic understanding of divine providence and divine intervention has practical implications for believers. It fosters a sense of trust, reliance, and gratitude toward the monotheistic God. Believers may seek solace and guidance in times of difficulty, trusting that the monotheistic God's providential care is at work. They may also express gratitude and attribute blessings and favorable outcomes to the monotheistic God's intervention.

Additionally, the concept of divine providence and divine intervention prompts believers to reflect on the moral and ethical implications of their actions. Monotheistic traditions often emphasize the responsibility of individuals to align their lives with the divine will and to seek divine guidance in decision-making. Believers are encouraged to cultivate virtues, practice acts of compassion and justice, and contribute to the betterment of society, recognizing their role as co-creators in partnership with the monotheistic God.

In summary, the concept of divine providence and divine intervention in monotheistic traditions underscores the monotheistic God's active engagement with the world and its inhabitants. It reflects the monotheistic God's wisdom, power, and benevolence, providing believers with a sense of purpose, guidance, and reassurance in their lives. Divine interventions are seen as profound expressions of the monotheistic God's care and involvement, demonstrating His ongoing relationship with humanity.

Monotheistic Worship and Ritual Practices

Monotheistic worship and ritual practices vary among different monotheistic traditions but share common elements centered around the worship and devotion to the singular, transcendent God. These practices aim to establish a connection with the divine, express reverence, seek guidance, and deepen the spiritual bond between the worshipper and the monotheistic God.

Prayer is a fundamental aspect of monotheistic worship, allowing individuals to communicate with the monotheistic God directly. It is a means of expressing gratitude, seeking forgiveness, offering supplications, and seeking divine guidance and blessings. Prayers can be performed individually or in congregational settings, such as during religious services or gatherings.

Sacred texts hold significant importance in monotheistic traditions and are often used in worship and ritual practices. These texts, such as the Bible in Christianity, the Qur'an in Islam, or the Torah in Judaism, are considered to contain divine revelations and guidance from the monotheistic God. They are read, studied, and recited as a form of worship, reflection, and guidance for believers.

Rituals and ceremonies are integral to monotheistic worship, providing a structured and symbolic means of expressing devotion and reverence. These rituals may include acts of purification, symbolic gestures, recitations, and communal gatherings. They often involve elements such as the use of sacred objects, vestments, music, and the participation of clergy or religious leaders.

Sacraments, ordinances, or rites are specific rituals considered to be sacred and have a profound spiritual significance in monotheistic traditions. Examples include baptism and Eucharist in Christianity, circumcision in Judaism, and pilgrimage (Hajj) in Islam. These rituals are seen as transformative and can mark important milestones in a believer's spiritual journey.

Monotheistic worship also often includes communal worship and congregational gatherings. These gatherings, such as weekly services, Friday prayers, or Sabbath observance, provide opportunities for believers to come together, worship collectively, receive teachings, and strengthen their faith through shared experiences.

Offerings and sacrifices, although less prevalent in some monotheistic traditions, have historically been a part of worship in monotheistic religions. These acts of giving can take various forms, such as material offerings, charitable acts, or personal sacrifices, and are seen as acts of devotion and gratitude towards the monotheistic God.

The role of clergy or religious leaders is significant in monotheistic worship. They serve as intermediaries between the worshipper and the monotheistic God, leading congregational prayers, offering guidance, and performing religious rites. They are often responsible for upholding religious teachings, providing spiritual counsel, and fostering a sense of community among believers.

Monotheistic worship practices often emphasize the ethical dimensions of faith. Believers are encouraged to cultivate virtues, practice acts of compassion and justice, and contribute to the well-being of others. Worship is not seen as limited to ritual observance but extends to the way believers live their lives in alignment with the monotheistic God's teachings and commandments.

Overall, monotheistic worship and ritual practices aim to foster a deep spiritual connection between believers and the monotheistic God. They provide a framework for expressing devotion, seeking divine guidance, and nurturing a sense of community and moral responsibility. These practices serve to deepen the believer's understanding of the monotheistic God, strengthen their faith, and provide a pathway to spiritual growth and transformation.

Investigating the rituals, prayers, and sacraments associated with monotheistic worship

Investigating the rituals, prayers, and sacraments associated with monotheistic worship provides insight into the diverse ways in which monotheistic traditions engage in religious practices to connect with the divine and express their devotion. While the specific rituals, prayers, and sacraments vary among different monotheistic religions, they all serve as means of worship, spiritual reflection, and seeking divine communion.

Rituals in monotheistic worship often involve symbolic actions and gestures that hold spiritual significance. These rituals can include acts of purification, such as ablutions or cleansing rituals, to prepare oneself for worship. They may also incorporate specific movements, postures, or prostrations as a physical expression of reverence and submission before the divine presence.

Prayers play a central role in monotheistic worship. They serve as a direct means of communication with the monotheistic God, allowing individuals to express their gratitude, seek forgiveness, offer supplications, and seek divine guidance and blessings. Prayers can be formal, following prescribed formats and liturgical texts, or they can be spontaneous and personal, expressing the individual's heartfelt connection with the divine.

Sacraments, ordinances, or rites hold a significant place in many monotheistic traditions. These are sacred rituals believed to convey spiritual grace or blessings. They are considered essential for the spiritual growth and nourishment of believers. Examples of sacraments include baptism and the Eucharist in Christianity, where individuals are initiated into the faith and partake in the symbolic body and blood of Christ, symbolizing union with the divine.

In addition to sacraments, monotheistic worship may include other significant rituals and observances. For example, the Islamic tradition observes the five daily prayers (Salat), facing the Kaaba in Mecca, as a means of expressing devotion and maintaining a constant connection with Allah. Jewish worship incorporates the observance of Shabbat, a weekly day of rest and prayer, and the performance of rituals associated with festivals and holy days.

Monotheistic worship also includes communal worship and congregational gatherings. These gatherings, such as weekly services, Friday congregational prayers in Islam, or Sabbath observance in Judaism, provide opportunities for believers to come together as a community and collectively express their devotion and worship. They often involve the recitation of sacred texts, sermons or teachings, and communal prayers.

Prayers and worship in monotheistic traditions are often accompanied by the use of sacred texts. These texts, such as the Bible in Christianity, the Qur'an in Islam, or the Torah in Judaism, are considered the inspired or revealed word of the monotheistic God. They are recited, chanted, studied, and reflected upon during worship, providing spiritual guidance, teachings, and a connection to the divine revelation.

Furthermore, monotheistic worship may involve the use of music, hymns, or chants to uplift the spirit and create a reverential atmosphere. These melodic expressions of devotion enhance the worship experience and foster a sense of unity and reverence among the worshippers.

Clergy or religious leaders play an important role in guiding and leading monotheistic worship. They are responsible for conducting rituals, offering prayers, delivering sermons or teachings, and providing spiritual guidance to the community. They serve as mediators between the worshippers and the divine, ensuring the proper observance of religious practices and fostering a sense of spiritual connection.

In summary, the rituals, prayers, and sacraments associated with monotheistic worship reflect the diverse ways in which believers seek to connect with the divine, express their devotion, and engage in spiritual communion. These practices serve as avenues for deepening the believer's relationship with the monotheistic God, fostering a sense of community, and nurturing spiritual growth and transformation.

The role of clergy, religious leaders, and congregational practices in monotheistic traditions

The role of clergy, religious leaders, and congregational practices holds significant importance in monotheistic traditions, playing a vital role in the organization, guidance, and facilitation of religious activities and spiritual growth within the community.

Clergy, or religious leaders, are individuals who have received specific religious training, knowledge, and authority to serve as representatives of the monotheistic faith and act as intermediaries between the divine and the community. They are entrusted with various responsibilities, including conducting religious rituals, leading congregational worship, offering spiritual guidance, interpreting sacred texts, and providing pastoral care to the community.

In monotheistic traditions like Christianity, clergy often have hierarchical structures with different ranks or offices, such as bishops, priests, and deacons. Each level of clergy carries specific responsibilities and functions within the religious community. Bishops, as overseers, hold leadership roles and provide guidance to the clergy and the faithful. Priests act as intermediaries between the divine and the congregation, presiding over sacraments, offering prayers, and delivering sermons. Deacons assist in various ministerial tasks and serve the community in practical ways.

Similarly, in Islam, religious leaders are known as Imams, who lead congregational prayers, deliver sermons (khutbah), and provide spiritual guidance to the Muslim community. Imams may also have roles in teaching religious knowledge, resolving religious disputes, and serving as moral authorities within the community.

In Judaism, religious leaders are known as rabbis. They are scholars and interpreters of Jewish law (Halakhah) and teachings, guiding the community in matters of religious observance, study, and ethical conduct. Rabbis lead worship services, teach Torah, provide counseling, and officiate at lifecycle events such as weddings, funerals, and circumcisions.

Congregational practices and gatherings are integral to the religious life of monotheistic traditions. The congregation, consisting of worshippers and believers, comes together for communal worship, prayer, study, and mutual support. These gatherings, such as weekly services, Friday congregational prayers (Jumu'ah) in Islam, or Sabbath observance in Judaism, serve multiple purposes.

Communal worship offers an opportunity for collective expression of faith, fostering a sense of unity, devotion, and shared religious experience. It provides a space for the congregation to come together, recite prayers, participate in rituals, listen to sermons or teachings, and engage in communal acts of devotion. Congregational practices also facilitate the transmission of religious teachings, traditions, and values from one generation to the next.

Furthermore, congregational gatherings provide social and emotional support, as believers connect with one another, offer mutual encouragement, and build a sense of community. They create opportunities for fellowship, dialogue, and the formation of interpersonal relationships rooted in shared faith and common values.

Within congregational settings, various practices and rituals are observed, including the recitation of sacred texts, chanting of hymns or prayers, participation in sacraments or ordinances, and engagement in acts of service or charitable works. These practices serve to deepen the spiritual experience, foster a sense of awe and reverence, and cultivate a connection with the divine.

Additionally, congregational practices often extend beyond formal worship services. They may include educational programs, study circles, youth groups, and social events that promote spiritual growth, learning, and community engagement. These activities further strengthen the bonds of fellowship, encourage spiritual development, and facilitate the exchange of knowledge and wisdom.

In summary, the clergy, religious leaders, and congregational practices hold a significant role in monotheistic traditions. They provide guidance, leadership, and spiritual nourishment to the community, facilitate communal worship and rituals, transmit religious teachings, and foster a sense of belonging and shared identity among believers. Through their involvement and participation in congregational practices, individuals deepen their faith, strengthen their connection to the divine, and find support and encouragement within the religious community.

Relationship Between Humans and the Monotheistic God

In monotheistic traditions, the relationship between humans and the monotheistic God is a central aspect of religious belief and practice. Monotheism emphasizes the belief in one supreme, transcendent, and all-powerful God who is intimately involved in the lives of human beings and the world.

Monotheistic religions teach that humans are created in the image of God, imbued with inherent dignity and worth. They emphasize the idea that humans have a unique and special place in the divine plan, being granted free will, moral responsibility, and the capacity to engage in a meaningful relationship with the divine.

One of the key elements in the relationship between humans and the monotheistic God is the concept of worship. Worship involves acknowledging and honoring the greatness, sovereignty, and attributes of God. It encompasses acts of devotion, prayer, praise, and gratitude, as well as adherence to religious commandments, rituals, and ethical principles.

Prayer serves as a means of communication between humans and the monotheistic God. It is a way for individuals to express their needs, hopes, fears, and aspirations, seeking guidance, comfort, and spiritual connection. Prayer can take various forms, including personal supplication, communal worship, and meditative contemplation. It is seen as a means of drawing closer to the divine, seeking solace, and finding spiritual fulfillment.

Monotheistic traditions also emphasize the importance of obedience to the will of God. This obedience is demonstrated through adherence to religious commandments, ethical principles, and moral codes that are believed to be divinely revealed. It involves aligning one's actions, beliefs, and attitudes with the teachings and guidance of the monotheistic God. Obedience is seen as a way to honor and show reverence for the divine and to live in accordance with the purpose and plan set forth by God.

Furthermore, monotheistic religions emphasize the concept of divine providence, which refers to the belief that the monotheistic God actively guides, sustains, and governs the world and the lives of individuals. It is the idea that God's wisdom, power, and care extend to every aspect of creation, including the affairs of humans. Monotheists believe that the monotheistic God is intimately involved in their lives, offering guidance, protection, and provision. This belief in divine providence gives a sense of meaning, purpose, and comfort, particularly in times of difficulty or uncertainty.

Monotheistic traditions also emphasize the idea of divine love, compassion, and mercy. The monotheistic God is often described as benevolent, caring, and forgiving, extending grace and forgiveness to those who seek it. This understanding of God's love and mercy encourages believers to cultivate a personal and intimate relationship with the divine, seeking solace, forgiveness, and redemption.

The relationship between humans and the monotheistic God is not limited to individuals but extends to the community of believers as well. Monotheistic religions often emphasize communal worship, fellowship, and shared responsibility. Believers are encouraged to support and care for one another, to practice charity and compassion, and to work towards social justice and the well-being of society as a whole. The monotheistic God is seen as the source of unity, love, and harmony, and the relationship with God is nurtured and expressed within the context of community.

In summary, the relationship between humans and the monotheistic God is characterized by worship, prayer, obedience, divine providence, love, and communal participation. Monotheistic believers strive to cultivate a deep, personal connection with the divine, aligning their lives with the teachings and guidance of the monotheistic God, and seeking to live in harmony with God's will and purpose. This relationship provides a sense of meaning, guidance, and spiritual fulfillment for individuals and communities within monotheistic traditions

Exploring the concept of covenant and the moral responsibilities between humans and the monotheistic God

In monotheistic traditions, the concept of covenant plays a significant role in the relationship between humans and the monotheistic God. A covenant can be understood as a sacred agreement or contract between God and human beings, establishing a mutual relationship with specific obligations and responsibilities.

The concept of covenant first appears in the Hebrew Bible (Old Testament) in the context of ancient Israelite religious and cultural traditions. The Hebrew Bible describes a series of covenants between God and various individuals or groups, such as the covenant with Noah after the flood, the covenant with Abraham and his descendants, and the covenant with the Israelites at Mount Sinai.

Covenants typically involve God making promises and setting forth expectations for human behavior. They outline a moral framework and establish a code of conduct that believers are called to uphold. In return for their faithful obedience and adherence to the covenant, believers receive God's blessings, protection, and favor.

Exploring the Contrasts and Convergence of Polytheism and Monotheism

The moral responsibilities within the covenant relationship between humans and the monotheistic God are based on principles of justice, righteousness, and ethical conduct. Monotheistic religions emphasize the importance of living a life of moral integrity and fulfilling one's obligations to God and fellow human beings.

The moral responsibilities in the covenant relationship often include the following aspects:

Worship and Devotion: Believers are expected to worship the monotheistic God exclusively and to show reverence and gratitude through acts of devotion, prayer, and ritual practices.

Ethical Conduct: Monotheistic traditions emphasize moral values such as honesty, compassion, justice, humility, and love. Believers are called to live virtuous lives, treating others with fairness, kindness, and respect.

Obedience to Divine Commandments: The monotheistic God often provides a set of commandments or moral laws that guide human behavior. These commandments serve as a moral compass, addressing various aspects of human life, including relationships, justice, morality, and social responsibility.

Social Justice and Compassion: Monotheistic religions emphasize the responsibility of believers to care for the marginalized, the needy, and the oppressed. They call for acts of charity, generosity, and advocacy for justice and equality.

Stewardship of Creation: Monotheistic beliefs often include the notion that humans have a responsibility to care for and protect the natural world. Believers are called to be responsible stewards of the environment and to exercise wise and sustainable use of resources.

The concept of covenant establishes a moral framework that guides the relationship between humans and the monotheistic God. It encourages believers to live with a sense of moral responsibility and accountability, recognizing that their actions have consequences not only for themselves but also for the larger community and the world.

Furthermore, the concept of covenant implies a reciprocal relationship between God and humans. While believers have responsibilities and obligations, the monotheistic God also promises blessings, guidance, and divine assistance in fulfilling those responsibilities. The covenant relationship is seen as a source of grace, mercy, and spiritual growth, as believers strive to live in accordance with the moral teachings and expectations of the monotheistic God.

In summary, the concept of covenant in monotheistic traditions establishes a sacred agreement between God and humans, outlining moral responsibilities and obligations. It emphasizes the importance of ethical conduct, worship, obedience to divine commandments, social justice, and stewardship of creation. The covenant relationship fosters a sense of moral accountability, divine guidance, and spiritual growth within the monotheistic faith communities.

Analyzing concepts such as divine judgment, grace, and the afterlife in monotheistic beliefs

In monotheistic beliefs, concepts such as divine judgment, grace, and the afterlife play a significant role in shaping the understanding of human existence and the relationship between individuals and the monotheistic God. These concepts offer insight into the moral framework, spiritual destiny, and ultimate purpose of life within monotheistic traditions.

Divine Judgment: Divine judgment refers to the belief that the monotheistic God is the ultimate arbiter of justice and will judge the actions and intentions of individuals. It is the belief that there will be a final reckoning or evaluation of one's deeds, determining the outcome of the individual's eternal destiny. Divine judgment is often seen as a means of affirming moral accountability and justice, ensuring that good is rewarded and evil is punished.

Grace: Grace is a concept that highlights the unmerited favor and mercy of the monotheistic God toward humanity. It is the belief that God extends forgiveness, redemption, and salvation to individuals, even though they may be undeserving. Grace is often seen as an expression of the monotheistic God's boundless love and compassion, offering believers the opportunity for spiritual transformation, forgiveness of sins, and reconciliation with God.

The Afterlife: Monotheistic beliefs often include the notion of an afterlife, a realm or state of existence that follows physical death. The specifics of the afterlife vary among different monotheistic traditions, but it generally involves the idea that human souls continue to exist in a spiritual realm, separate from the physical world. The afterlife is often seen as a place of reward or punishment, reflecting the outcome of divine judgment based on one's faith, actions, and moral character.

In Christianity, the afterlife includes the concepts of heaven, hell, and purgatory. Heaven is a realm of eternal bliss and communion with God for those who have lived a righteous life and accepted Jesus Christ as their savior. Hell is a realm of eternal punishment for those who have rejected God and committed grave sins. Purgatory is a temporary state of purification for souls destined for heaven but in need of further cleansing.

In Islam, the afterlife is described as Jannah (paradise) and Jahannam (hell). Jannah is a place of eternal bliss, where believers are rewarded for their faith and righteous deeds. Jahannam is a place of punishment for those who have rejected God and committed sinful acts.

In Judaism, the afterlife is understood in various ways, ranging from a belief in Olam Ha-Ba (the World to Come) as a spiritual realm of reward and punishment to a focus on the importance of leading a meaningful life in the present rather than speculating about the afterlife.

The concepts of divine judgment, grace, and the afterlife provide a framework for understanding the moral significance of human actions, the hope for redemption, and the ultimate destiny of the soul in monotheistic beliefs. They offer guidance, motivation, and comfort to believers, shaping their moral choices, spiritual journey, and aspirations for a meaningful existence beyond earthly life.

CHAPTER 9: PHILOSOPHICAL DIFFERENCES BETWEEN POLYTHEISM AND MONOTHEISM

In exploring the theological and philosophical aspects of polytheism and monotheism, it becomes evident that these belief systems embody distinct perspectives on the nature of the divine and the fundamental principles that govern the universe. While both polytheism and monotheism seek to understand and connect with the divine, they differ in their approaches, conceptions of deity, and philosophical implications.

This chapter delves into the philosophical differences between polytheism and monotheism, shedding light on their contrasting worldviews, epistemological frameworks, and ontological understandings. It examines how these differences shape concepts of morality, human agency, and the nature of reality. By exploring the philosophical foundations of these belief systems, we gain deeper insights into the unique perspectives they offer on the divine-human relationship and the human condition.

Throughout history, polytheistic and monotheistic traditions have shaped civilizations, influenced ethical systems, and guided philosophical inquiry. The contrasting philosophical perspectives within these belief systems have given rise to profound debates and reflections on the nature of divinity, the purpose of existence, and the fundamental questions of human life. By examining these philosophical differences, we can better appreciate the richness and diversity of human religious and philosophical thought.

This chapter explores key philosophical themes, such as metaphysics, epistemology, ethics, and teleology, in the context of polytheism and monotheism. It investigates the ways in which these belief systems address the mysteries of existence, the nature of knowledge, the foundations of morality, and the ultimate purpose of human life. By delving into these philosophical underpinnings, we gain a deeper understanding of the theological and philosophical traditions that have shaped human civilizations throughout history.

Through an examination of ancient texts, philosophical treatises, and theological debates, we unravel the intricate tapestry of ideas that define polytheistic and monotheistic thought. By critically analyzing their philosophical implications, we aim to foster a nuanced appreciation of these belief systems and their enduring influence on human thought, culture, and spirituality.

Join us on this intellectual journey as we delve into the philosophical differences between polytheism and monotheism, exploring the foundational ideas and their implications for human understanding, meaning, and pursuit of truth. By embracing the diversity of philosophical thought within these traditions, we enrich our own philosophical perspectives and deepen our appreciation for the complexities of human religious and philosophical inquiry.

Monotheism: Oneness and Unity

Monotheism, at its core, is centered around the belief in the existence of a single, supreme deity. This concept of a singular divine being stands in stark contrast to polytheistic belief systems that recognize and worship multiple gods and goddesses. In monotheistic traditions, the emphasis lies on the oneness and unity of the divine, transcending any divisions or distinctions within the divine realm.

The idea of oneness in monotheism is multifaceted and carries profound theological and philosophical implications. It implies that there is only one ultimate source of all creation, one supreme power that governs the universe and guides human affairs. This singular deity is regarded as being above and beyond all things, eternal and transcendent, existing independently of time and space. This concept of divine unity represents a fundamental departure from the polytheistic notion of a pantheon of deities with distinct powers and domains.

Monotheistic traditions often emphasize the transcendence and incomprehensibility of the divine. The monotheistic God is viewed as beyond human understanding, existing in a realm beyond the physical world. This understanding of transcendence reflects the belief that the divine is not bound by the limitations of the material realm and is beyond the grasp of human comprehension. However, despite this inherent transcendence, monotheistic traditions also emphasize the immanence of the divine, highlighting the belief that God is present and active in the world, intimately involved in human affairs.

The concept of oneness in monotheism also has significant implications for the relationship between the divine and the human. It establishes a singular focal point for devotion and worship, inviting believers to direct their reverence, prayers, and acts of devotion to the one supreme deity. This monotheistic perspective engenders a sense of unity and solidarity among believers, as they recognize their shared connection to and dependence on the same divine source. It also promotes a sense of individual and collective responsibility, as adherents strive to align their lives with the will and commandments of the one God.

Moreover, the concept of oneness in monotheism has profound implications for the moral and ethical dimensions of human life. It provides a unifying framework for understanding and defining moral principles and guidelines. Monotheistic traditions often emphasize the belief that the one God sets forth moral laws and standards, which serve as the foundation for human conduct and interactions. This belief in a single moral authority contributes to the development of ethical systems that guide believers in making decisions and living virtuous lives.

In summary, monotheism is characterized by its affirmation of the oneness and unity of the divine. This concept transcends the boundaries of human comprehension, underscoring the incomprehensible nature of the divine and its presence both beyond and within the world. The belief in a single supreme deity shapes the relationship between the divine and the human, informs ethical frameworks, and offers a sense of unity and purpose to adherents. The concept of oneness in monotheism invites individuals to contemplate the vastness and unity of the divine, fostering a deep sense of awe, reverence, and devotion.

Exploring the philosophical implications of the unity and oneness of the monotheistic God

The philosophical implications of the unity and oneness of the monotheistic God are far-reaching, touching upon various aspects of metaphysics, epistemology, and ethics. The concept of a singular, unified deity in monotheism has given rise to profound philosophical inquiries and debates throughout history.

Metaphysically, the unity and oneness of the monotheistic God challenge traditional notions of existence and being. The monotheistic God is often understood as the ultimate ground of reality, the source from which all existence emanates. This perspective raises questions about the nature of being, the relationship between the divine and the created world, and the fundamental structure of reality itself. Philosophers have grappled with issues such as divine simplicity, the ontological status of God, and the nature of causality in the context of monotheism.

Epistemologically, the unity of the monotheistic God poses questions about knowledge and understanding. Monotheistic traditions often emphasize the incomprehensibility of God, highlighting the limitations of human intellect in grasping the divine essence fully. This recognition of the transcendent nature of the monotheistic God leads to inquiries about the nature and limits of human knowledge, the role of faith, and the possibility of mystical experiences. Philosophers have explored the concepts of revelation, religious experience, and the relationship between reason and faith in the context of monotheistic belief systems.

Ethically, the unity and oneness of the monotheistic God have profound implications for moral and ethical frameworks. Monotheistic traditions often posit a single moral authority that establishes ethical principles and guidelines for human conduct. The belief in a unified divine source of morality provides a foundation for moral objectivity and universality, suggesting that there are objective moral truths rooted in the nature of God. This perspective has led to philosophical investigations into the nature of moral values, moral duties, and the relationship between God's commands and moral obligations.

Additionally, the unity and oneness of the monotheistic God have influenced philosophical debates on the problem of evil, theodicy, and the nature of divine attributes. Philosophers have wrestled with reconciling the existence of evil and suffering in the world with the belief in an all-powerful, all-knowing, and perfectly good God. This inquiry has prompted reflections on the nature of divine attributes, the limits of human understanding, and the potential for human free will in a world governed by a singular divine being.

In summary, the philosophical implications of the unity and oneness of the monotheistic God are wide-ranging and multifaceted. They raise questions about the nature of existence, the limits of human knowledge, the foundations of ethics, and the problem of evil. Exploring these implications has spurred philosophical inquiries and discussions, contributing to the development of philosophical traditions within monotheistic contexts and shaping broader philosophical discourse.

The monotheistic emphasis on divine transcendence and immanence

The monotheistic emphasis on divine transcendence and immanence reflects the complex understanding of the relationship between the monotheistic God and the created world. It addresses the dual nature of God's presence, both beyond and within the cosmos, and has significant philosophical implications.

Divine transcendence refers to the idea that the monotheistic God exists beyond the material world and transcends human comprehension. This perspective emphasizes the vastness, otherness, and incomprehensibility of God's nature. The monotheistic God is often seen as the ultimate source of all existence, existing outside the boundaries of time, space, and human understanding. The concept of divine transcendence highlights the infinite power, knowledge, and perfection of God, emphasizing God's superiority and separateness from the created world.

Divine immanence, on the other hand, recognizes the presence of God within the created world and the intimate relationship between the divine and the human. It emphasizes the immanent presence of God in the natural world, in human beings, and in the events of history. This perspective suggests that God actively participates in the ongoing unfolding of the world and is involved in the affairs of humanity. Divine immanence highlights the accessibility, nearness, and personal connection between God and individuals or communities.

The emphasis on divine transcendence and immanence in monotheism raises significant philosophical questions and debates. Philosophers have explored the nature of God's relationship to the created world, the problem of divine hiddenness, and the challenge of reconciling the concept of a transcendent God with the immanent experiences of believers. This exploration has led to discussions on the nature of divine attributes, the possibilities of divine revelation, and the ways in which God can be known or experienced by humans.

Furthermore, the understanding of divine transcendence and immanence has ethical and practical implications. It shapes religious practices, moral frameworks, and the understanding of human agency and responsibility. Monotheistic traditions often seek to strike a balance between acknowledging God's transcendence, which instills reverence and humility, and recognizing God's immanence, which encourages a sense of intimacy, connection, and moral guidance.

In summary, the monotheistic emphasis on divine transcendence and immanence reflects the multifaceted understanding of the relationship between God and the created world. It prompts philosophical inquiries into the nature of God's existence, knowledge, and involvement in the world. The exploration of divine transcendence and immanence has significant implications for theology, ethics, and the lived experiences of believers within monotheistic traditions.

Polytheism: Diversity and Multiplicity

Polytheism is characterized by its emphasis on diversity and multiplicity, both in the nature of divinity and in the worship of multiple gods and goddesses. This theological framework recognizes and celebrates the existence of multiple divine beings, each with distinct attributes, roles, and domains.

One of the defining features of polytheism is the belief in a pantheon of gods and goddesses, often organized in hierarchies or family relationships. These deities represent various aspects of the natural world, human life, and the supernatural realm. They embody different forces, such as fertility, love, war, wisdom, and justice, among others. Each deity has their own unique qualities, mythologies, and spheres of influence.

The multiplicity of gods and goddesses in polytheism reflects the diverse experiences, needs, and interests of human societies. Different cultures and regions may have their own pantheon of deities, with specific gods and goddesses revered and worshipped in particular contexts. This diversity allows for a more nuanced understanding of the divine and accommodates the complexity of human existence.

Polytheistic beliefs often embrace the idea of divine plurality, recognizing that different deities may possess their own strengths, limitations, and perspectives. This diversity within the divine realm is seen as enriching and multifaceted, providing a broader framework for understanding and engaging with the sacred. It allows individuals and communities to develop personal relationships with specific deities based on their personal inclinations, needs, and cultural backgrounds.

The worship and rituals associated with polytheism reflect the recognition of multiple gods and goddesses. Devotees may engage in offerings, prayers, and rituals specific to particular deities, seeking their blessings, guidance, and protection. Different gods and goddesses may have their own dedicated temples, shrines, or sacred spaces where individuals and communities gather to honor and communicate with them.

Polytheism's embrace of diversity and multiplicity extends beyond the realm of gods and goddesses. It also encompasses the recognition of diverse religious practices, beliefs, and experiences within a given polytheistic tradition. This openness allows for the coexistence of different cults, local variations, and syncretic practices, where aspects of different deities or religious traditions are combined or blended.

In summary, polytheism's emphasis on diversity and multiplicity provides a rich and multifaceted understanding of the divine and human experiences. It allows for a recognition of various gods and goddesses, each with their unique attributes and roles, and accommodates the diverse needs and perspectives of individuals and communities. Polytheistic worship and rituals reflect this diversity, providing devotees with opportunities to engage with specific deities and honor their distinct qualities and domains.

Examining the philosophical implications of the diversity and multiplicity of deities in polytheistic belief systems

The diversity and multiplicity of deities in polytheistic belief systems carry profound philosophical implications. They challenge the notion of a singular, all-encompassing divine entity and invite a more nuanced understanding of the nature of divinity and the human relationship with the sacred.

One philosophical implication of the diversity of deities is the recognition that different aspects of existence and the cosmos are embodied and personified by distinct gods and goddesses. Polytheism acknowledges that the world is complex and multifaceted, encompassing a wide range of phenomena, emotions, and experiences. Each deity represents a specific domain or aspect of reality, such as nature, fertility, love, wisdom, war, or craftsmanship. This understanding allows for a more comprehensive and holistic comprehension of the world, as it acknowledges and celebrates the diversity and richness of existence.

Furthermore, the multiplicity of deities in polytheism acknowledges the diversity of human needs, aspirations, and cultural expressions. Different gods and goddesses may resonate with different individuals and communities, providing avenues for personal connection and spiritual fulfillment. This philosophical perspective recognizes the uniqueness of human experiences and acknowledges that different people may find solace, inspiration, and guidance in different aspects of the divine.

Polytheistic belief systems also foster a sense of interdependence and interconnectedness within the divine realm. The diverse pantheon of gods and goddesses interact with one another, forming complex relationships and narratives. This web of connections mirrors the intricate interplay of forces and energies within the natural world and the human experience. It emphasizes the interdependence of different aspects of existence and underscores the idea that no single deity can fully encapsulate the entirety of the divine.

Moreover, the diversity of deities in polytheism allows for a more inclusive and tolerant approach to religious diversity. It recognizes that different cultures and traditions may have their own gods and goddesses, and each can be valid and meaningful within its specific context. Polytheistic belief systems often embrace the idea of syncretism, where different deities and religious practices can be blended or harmonized. This philosophical openness encourages dialogue, understanding, and acceptance of diverse spiritual paths.

In summary, the diversity and multiplicity of deities in polytheistic belief systems challenge the notion of a singular and all-encompassing divine entity. They invite a more holistic understanding of the world and the human experience, acknowledging the complexity and richness of existence. The philosophical implications of polytheistic diversity include recognizing the uniqueness of human needs, fostering interdependence and interconnectedness, and promoting inclusivity and tolerance of diverse spiritual paths.

The polytheistic understanding of divine immanence and the interconnectedness of the divine and the world

The polytheistic understanding of divine immanence emphasizes the belief that the divine is present and active within the world, intimately interconnected with every aspect of existence. Unlike a distant and transcendent deity, polytheistic traditions often perceive the gods and goddesses as immanent, meaning they are immanent within nature, human life, and the everyday experiences of individuals and communities.

In polytheistic belief systems, the gods and goddesses are seen as manifesting their presence in various forms, including natural phenomena, specific locations, sacred objects, and even in human beings themselves. The divine is not confined to a separate realm or distant heavens but permeates and animates the world, infusing it with sacredness and vitality.

This understanding of divine immanence fosters a deep sense of interconnectedness between the divine and the world. The gods and goddesses are not separate and detached entities but actively participate in the ongoing processes of creation, sustenance, and transformation. They are intimately connected with the natural world, the cycles of life and death, and the intricate web of relationships that characterize human existence.

The polytheistic perspective of divine immanence also emphasizes the idea of reciprocal relationships and interactions between humans and the divine. Individuals and communities engage in rituals, prayers, and offerings as acts of communication and communion with the gods and goddesses. These practices are seen as a way to establish and nurture a relationship with the divine, seeking their blessings, guidance, protection, and support.

Moreover, the interconnectedness between the divine and the world in polytheistic belief systems often extends to the recognition of divine presence in other beings, such as ancestral spirits, nature spirits, and guardian spirits. These entities are considered manifestations of the divine or mediators between humans and the gods and goddesses. They embody the interconnectedness of all living beings and serve as bridges that facilitate communication and interaction with the divine realm.

The understanding of divine immanence in polytheism also contributes to a deep reverence for nature and the natural world. The gods and goddesses are often associated with natural forces, elements, and landscapes, highlighting the sacredness and inherent divinity of the Earth and its ecosystems. This recognition fosters a sense of responsibility and stewardship towards the environment, promoting ecological harmony and sustainability.

In summary, the polytheistic understanding of divine immanence emphasizes the presence of the divine within the world and the interconnectedness between the divine and all aspects of existence. This perspective acknowledges that the gods and goddesses are immanent within nature, human life, and everyday experiences. It fosters a deep sense of interconnectedness, reciprocity, and reverence for the natural world, promoting a holistic and sacred view of the cosmos.

Ethics and Morality

Ethics and morality play a significant role in religious and philosophical systems, including both polytheistic and monotheistic traditions. While the specific ethical teachings may vary among different polytheistic belief systems, there are common threads that highlight the importance of ethical conduct and moral values.

In polytheistic belief systems, ethical principles are often rooted in the relationships between humans, the divine, and the natural world. The gods and goddesses are seen as exemplars of certain virtues and qualities, and their myths and legends provide moral lessons and guidance for human behavior. The stories of gods and goddesses often illustrate the consequences of ethical and unethical actions, serving as a moral compass for believers.

Polytheistic ethics also emphasize the interconnectedness and interdependence of all beings. The actions of individuals are seen as having ripple effects, impacting not only human relationships but also the natural world and the divine realm. Thus, ethical conduct is often guided by principles of harmony, balance, and respect for all living beings. The practice of rituals and offerings, for example, may serve not only as acts of devotion but also as expressions of gratitude and reverence for the interconnected web of life.

Furthermore, polytheistic ethics often incorporate a sense of personal responsibility and agency. Individuals are seen as active participants in shaping their own moral character and in co-creating a just and harmonious world. The gods and goddesses are not viewed as sole arbiters of morality but as guides and inspirations, encouraging humans to cultivate virtues, exercise self-discipline, and make ethical choices.

It is important to note that polytheistic ethical systems can be diverse, reflecting the cultural and historical contexts in which they emerged. Different pantheons and belief systems may emphasize different virtues or moral frameworks. For example, the ancient Greek concept of arete highlighted the pursuit of excellence and virtuous living, while Ma'at in ancient Egyptian belief emphasized principles of truth, justice, and cosmic balance.

Overall, polytheistic ethics provide a framework for individuals and communities to navigate their moral obligations and responsibilities. They emphasize the interconnectedness of beings, the lessons and examples set by the gods and goddesses, and the pursuit of virtues and moral values. Through ethical conduct and adherence to these principles, believers seek to align themselves with the divine and contribute to the well-being of the world around them.

Comparing the ethical frameworks of polytheism and monotheism

Comparing the ethical frameworks of polytheism and monotheism allows us to understand the distinct approaches to ethics within these belief systems. While both polytheism and monotheism encompass diverse traditions and interpretations, we can identify some general differences in their ethical frameworks.

Polytheistic ethics often emphasize the relationships and interconnectedness between humans, deities, and the natural world. Ethical guidelines are derived from myths, legends, and the examples set by various gods and goddesses, who embody specific virtues or qualities. Polytheistic ethics tend to be context-specific, varying across different pantheons and cultures. They may focus on concepts such as honor, hospitality, courage, harmony, balance, and respect for nature.

In polytheism, ethical responsibility is often seen as a collective effort, involving the entire community. Moral conduct is guided by maintaining harmony within the community and in relation to the natural world. The fulfillment of social obligations, adherence to cultural norms, and observance of rituals and offerings are central to upholding ethical principles. The actions of individuals are seen as influencing not only their immediate surroundings but also the cosmic order.

On the other hand, monotheistic ethics are typically rooted in the teachings and commandments of a single supreme deity. The moral framework in monotheism often revolves around the concept of obedience to divine law and the fulfillment of moral duties toward God and fellow human beings. Monotheistic ethics tend to prioritize concepts such as justice, compassion, love, mercy, forgiveness, and righteousness.

In monotheistic traditions, individuals are seen as morally accountable to a transcendent and omniscient God who sets absolute standards of right and wrong. Moral conduct is based on the belief that actions have eternal consequences, both in the present life and in the afterlife. Monotheistic ethics place a strong emphasis on individual responsibility and personal moral agency. Believers are encouraged to align their actions with the will of God and strive for moral perfection.

While there are similarities in ethical teachings across polytheism and monotheism, such as the promotion of virtues and the rejection of vices, the underlying philosophical foundations and theological understandings differ. Polytheism tends to emphasize a relational and contextual approach to ethics, while monotheism emphasizes obedience to divine commandments and a focus on personal moral accountability.

It is important to note that these are broad generalizations, and there can be variations and complexities within individual polytheistic and monotheistic traditions. Ethical frameworks can evolve over time, influenced by cultural, historical, and philosophical developments within each tradition. Ultimately, both polytheistic and monotheistic ethical systems aim to guide individuals toward virtuous and morally upright lives, albeit with different emphases and theological underpinnings.

The philosophical underpinnings of moral principles and ethical decision-making in each belief system

In polytheistic belief systems, the philosophical underpinnings of moral principles and ethical decision-making are often rooted in the interconnectedness of the divine, human beings, and the natural world. Polytheism recognizes a multiplicity of gods and goddesses, each representing different aspects of the cosmic order and possessing unique qualities and virtues.

Polytheistic ethics draw inspiration from the myths, legends, and stories surrounding these deities. The gods and goddesses serve as moral exemplars, embodying specific virtues or qualities that humans should strive to emulate. Ethical decision-making is influenced by the values and virtues associated with these deities, such as wisdom, courage, justice, compassion, and honesty.

The philosophical underpinning of polytheistic ethics is often rooted in the belief that humans have a responsibility to maintain harmonious relationships with both the divine realm and the natural world. Ethics in polytheism are closely intertwined with social and ecological contexts, recognizing the interdependence of individuals within a community and their interconnectedness with the natural environment.

In monotheistic belief systems, the philosophical underpinnings of moral principles and ethical decision-making are often grounded in the concept of a single supreme deity who possesses absolute moral authority. Monotheism emphasizes the existence of an omniscient, omnipotent, and transcendent God who establishes moral standards and provides guidance for human conduct.

The monotheistic understanding of moral principles is typically derived from divine revelations, sacred texts, and the teachings of prophets or religious leaders. Monotheistic ethics are based on the belief that God's will and commandments serve as the ultimate source of moral guidance. Ethical decision-making involves aligning one's actions with the moral imperatives outlined in these divine teachings.

The philosophical underpinning of monotheistic ethics includes the concepts of personal moral responsibility and accountability. Monotheism emphasizes the individual's moral agency and the idea that each person is answerable to God for their actions. Ethical decision-making is guided by the pursuit of righteousness, justice, compassion, and love for both God and fellow human beings.

Both polytheistic and monotheistic ethical systems reflect different philosophical approaches to moral principles and ethical decision-making. Polytheistic ethics often emphasize contextual and relational aspects, drawing inspiration from various deities and their virtues. Monotheistic ethics, on the other hand, emphasize obedience to divine commandments and the pursuit of a moral life aligned with the will of God.

It's important to note that within each belief system, there can be variations and interpretations of ethical principles based on different cultural, historical, and philosophical contexts. The philosophical underpinnings of moral principles and ethical decision-making may evolve over time as religious traditions interact with diverse intellectual and cultural influences.

Epistemology and Revelation

Epistemology, in the context of religion, deals with the nature of knowledge and how it is acquired, particularly in matters of religious belief and spiritual truths. Both polytheism and monotheism grapple with questions of epistemology, but they approach it in different ways.

In polytheistic belief systems, knowledge and understanding are often seen as multifaceted and diverse. Epistemology in polytheism acknowledges the existence of multiple gods and goddesses, each with their own areas of expertise and insights. As such, knowledge is acquired through various means, including personal experiences, myths, oral traditions, rituals, divination, and the guidance of priests or priestesses who possess specialized knowledge.

Polytheistic epistemology recognizes the limitations of human understanding and embraces the idea that different deities may offer different perspectives on truth. It allows for a more fluid and contextual understanding of knowledge, acknowledging that truth can be multifaceted and dependent on individual perspectives and cultural contexts.

In monotheistic belief systems, epistemology is often shaped by the concept of divine revelation. Monotheism asserts that knowledge of the divine and spiritual truths is revealed by a single supreme deity. This revelation is often communicated through sacred texts, prophets, or religious leaders who are believed to have a direct connection with the divine.

The monotheistic understanding of epistemology emphasizes the idea that ultimate truth and knowledge come from a transcendent source, such as God. This source of knowledge is considered authoritative and serves as a foundation for religious beliefs and moral principles. Monotheistic epistemology places importance on faith, accepting the revealed truths and teachings as the basis for understanding the world and one's place in it.

Monotheistic epistemology often involves a belief in the divine inspiration of sacred texts, which are seen as containing divine wisdom and guidance. These texts are studied, interpreted, and reflected upon to deepen one's understanding of religious truths and moral principles.

While polytheism and monotheism approach epistemology differently, both recognize the importance of revelation in acquiring knowledge about the divine and spiritual realms. Polytheism acknowledges a more diverse range of sources and perspectives, while monotheism emphasizes the authoritative nature of a single divine revelation.

It's important to note that within each belief system, there can be variations and interpretations of epistemology. Different religious traditions may emphasize different aspects of revelation and may incorporate other sources of knowledge, such as reason, intuition, or personal experiences. Epistemological frameworks in both polytheism and monotheism continue to evolve and adapt as they interact with intellectual, cultural, and philosophical developments.

The sources of knowledge and revelation in polytheistic and monotheistic traditions

In polytheistic traditions, knowledge and revelation are derived from a variety of sources. These can include:

Myths and Legends: Polytheistic belief systems often incorporate rich mythologies that contain stories about the gods and their interactions with humans. These myths provide insights into the nature of the divine, the creation of the world, and the moral order of the cosmos.

Oral Traditions: Many polytheistic cultures have relied on oral traditions to pass down knowledge from one generation to another. Through storytelling, songs, and rituals, important religious teachings, customs, and histories are transmitted.

Rituals and Divination: Polytheistic worship often involves rituals and ceremonies that allow for communication with the divine. Divination practices, such as oracle readings or the interpretation of signs and omens, are used to seek guidance and insights from the gods.

Personal Experiences: Individuals in polytheistic traditions may have personal experiences of encountering the divine or receiving messages from specific deities. These experiences can be subjective but hold significance for the individuals involved.

Priesthood and Clergy: Priests and priestesses play essential roles in polytheistic religious traditions. They are often seen as intermediaries between the gods and humans, possessing specialized knowledge and conducting rituals on behalf of the community. Their training and expertise contribute to the transmission of religious teachings and practices.

In monotheistic traditions, knowledge and revelation primarily stem from specific sources associated with the belief in a single supreme deity. These sources include:

Sacred Scriptures: Monotheistic religions have authoritative texts considered to be divinely inspired or revealed. Examples include the Hebrew Bible (Old Testament) in Judaism, the Quran in Islam, and the Bible in Christianity. These texts are believed to contain the revealed word of God and serve as the foundation for religious beliefs, moral guidance, and theological doctrines.

Prophets and Messengers: Monotheistic religions often recognize the role of prophets or messengers who are believed to receive direct revelations from God.

These individuals, such as Moses in Judaism, Muhammad in Islam, or Jesus in Christianity, are seen as chosen intermediaries through whom divine messages and teachings are conveyed to humanity.

Theological and Philosophical Discourse: Monotheistic traditions engage in theological and philosophical reflections on the nature of God, the interpretation of sacred texts, and the exploration of religious doctrines. These intellectual endeavors contribute to the ongoing development and interpretation of religious knowledge.

Community and Religious Leaders: Religious leaders, such as clergy, scholars, and theologians, play a crucial role in interpreting and disseminating religious teachings within monotheistic traditions. They guide and educate the faithful, helping to transmit and interpret divine revelations in accordance with the beliefs and practices of their respective religious communities.

While these sources of knowledge and revelation differ between polytheistic and monotheistic traditions, it is important to note that there can be variations within each tradition and different interpretations of the sources. Additionally, the way in which these sources are understood and applied may evolve over time in response to changing social, cultural, and intellectual contexts.

Exploring the philosophical implications of divine communication and human understanding in each belief system

In both polytheistic and monotheistic belief systems, the concept of divine communication and human understanding plays a significant role in shaping philosophical perspectives and implications.

In polytheistic belief systems, divine communication is often characterized by a multitude of gods and goddesses who interact with humans in various ways. This multiplicity of divine beings implies diverse forms of divine communication. Polytheistic traditions recognize that gods and goddesses possess distinct personalities, domains, and attributes, which influence their modes of interaction with humans.

From a philosophical standpoint, the polytheistic understanding of divine communication highlights the complexity and diversity of divine presence in the world. It suggests that divine wisdom, guidance, and messages can be accessed through different deities, each representing specific aspects of existence. This perspective encourages a multifaceted understanding of the divine and emphasizes the interconnectedness between humans and various divine forces.

Exploring the Contrasts and Convergence of Polytheism and Monotheism

In terms of human understanding, polytheistic belief systems often embrace a contextual and relational approach. Human comprehension of the divine is influenced by personal experiences, rituals, myths, and cultural narratives associated with specific deities. The polytheistic worldview recognizes that human understanding of the divine is shaped by individual and collective contexts, allowing for a rich tapestry of interpretations and experiences.

On the other hand, monotheistic belief systems emphasize the concept of a single supreme deity who communicates with humans. The monotheistic understanding of divine communication often centers around the idea of revelation, where the one God reveals truths, laws, and moral guidance to humanity through chosen messengers or sacred scriptures.

From a philosophical perspective, monotheistic belief systems posit that divine communication is grounded in the oneness and transcendence of God. The monotheistic concept of divine communication implies a singular and authoritative source of divine knowledge and guidance. This notion emphasizes the unity of the divine message and the coherence of religious teachings.

Regarding human understanding, monotheistic traditions place importance on faith, reason, and interpretation in comprehending divine revelation. Humans are encouraged to seek knowledge and understanding through theological inquiry, intellectual reflection, and spiritual contemplation. Monotheistic belief systems often emphasize the capacity of humans to engage in rational thought and moral discernment to interpret and apply divine teachings in their lives.

The philosophical implications of divine communication and human understanding in both polytheistic and monotheistic belief systems reflect different approaches to the nature of the divine, the relationship between gods and humans, and the epistemological frameworks of each tradition. These implications shape religious practices, theological discourse, and the philosophical exploration of the nature of reality, morality, and human existence.

PART 4: RELIGIOUS PRACTICES AND BELIEFS:

Religious practices and beliefs form the core of human spirituality and shape the way individuals and communities understand and interact with the divine. Throughout history, diverse religious traditions have emerged, each with its own unique set of rituals, doctrines, and spiritual practices. Part 4 of our exploration delves into the intricate tapestry of religious practices and beliefs, examining the ways in which they have shaped cultures, provided meaning and guidance to adherents, and fostered a connection between the human and the divine.

Chapter 10 delves into the rich world of polytheistic religious practices. Polytheism, with its pantheon of gods and goddesses, has been a prevalent religious framework in numerous ancient civilizations. We explore the diverse array of deities and their roles, the cosmological narratives that underpin polytheistic belief systems, and the rituals and worship practices associated with honoring and communing with the divine.

Chapter 11 shifts our focus to the development of monotheistic traditions. From ancient Near Eastern civilizations to the major monotheistic religions of today, we trace the origins and evolution of monotheism. We examine the theological foundations of monotheism, the concept of a single supreme deity, and the ways in which monotheistic beliefs have influenced religious thought, ethics, and philosophical frameworks.

In Chapter 12, we delve into the theological differences between polytheism and monotheism. By exploring key concepts such as oneness and unity, diversity and multiplicity, ethics and morality, epistemology and revelation, we uncover the distinct philosophical underpinnings and implications of these two belief systems. We highlight the ways in which these contrasting theological perspectives have shaped religious practices, influenced social structures, and fostered spiritual experiences.

Exploring the Contrasts and Convergence of Polytheism and Monotheism

Finally, Chapter 13 delves into the intricate web of religious syncretism, the interplay between polytheistic and monotheistic traditions, and the cultural exchanges that have occurred throughout history. We explore the impact of conquests, migrations, and cultural encounters on the spread of religious ideas, the blending of beliefs and practices, and the emergence of hybrid religious traditions.

Through this exploration of religious practices and beliefs, we gain a deeper understanding of the diverse ways in which humans have sought to connect with the divine. From elaborate rituals and ceremonies to profound theological reflections, these practices and beliefs have shaped societies, influenced art and literature, provided solace and guidance, and sparked intellectual inquiry. Join us on this fascinating journey as we unravel the intricate tapestry of human spirituality and the rich diversity of religious practices and beliefs.

CHAPTER 10: RITUALS AND PRACTICES OF POLYTHEISM

Polytheistic religions encompass a rich tapestry of rituals and practices that shape the religious lives of their adherents. These rituals serve as bridges between humans and the divine, offering opportunities for communication, worship, and spiritual connection. In this chapter, we delve into the diverse and fascinating world of polytheistic rituals and practices, exploring their significance, symbolism, and impact on individuals and communities.

Understanding Rituals in Polytheistic Traditions

Rituals form an integral part of polytheistic traditions, serving as essential practices that connect individuals and communities with the divine. These rituals are guided by a set of beliefs, symbols, and customs specific to each tradition, creating a framework through which devotees engage with the spiritual realm. Understanding the nature and purpose of these rituals provides insight into the core principles and values upheld by polytheistic belief systems.

A. Rituals as Expressions of Devotion and Reverence

Polytheistic rituals are deeply rooted in a profound sense of devotion and reverence towards the deities. They serve as meaningful expressions of the individual's gratitude, awe, and reverence towards the divine beings they worship. Through ritualistic acts, individuals seek to establish a personal connection with the deities, engage in reciprocal relationships, and experience a sense of spiritual fulfillment.

Devotional rituals in polytheistic traditions often involve offering prayers, making physical or symbolic offerings to the deities, or performing specific actions to honor and acknowledge their presence. These acts of devotion are seen as acts of reciprocity, acknowledging the benevolence and power of the deities and expressing gratitude for their blessings and guidance.

Prayer is a central element of devotional rituals in polytheistic traditions. It serves as a direct means of communication with the divine, allowing individuals to express their desires, concerns, and gratitude. Prayers may take various forms, including formal recitations, spontaneous expressions, or even silent contemplation.

Through prayer, individuals establish a direct line of communication with the deities, seeking their guidance, protection, and blessings.

Offerings play a significant role in polytheistic rituals as tangible expressions of devotion. Offerings can take various forms, including food, flowers, incense, or symbolic objects. These offerings are seen as acts of generosity and respect towards the deities, symbolizing the individual's willingness to share their resources and show appreciation. They are often placed on altars or dedicated spaces, creating a sacred focal point for the ritual.

In addition to prayers and offerings, specific actions and rituals are performed to honor and connect with the deities. These actions may include physical gestures, such as bowing, prostration, or dancing, which demonstrate humility, submission, or joy in the presence of the divine. Rituals may also involve the recitation of hymns or chants, the performance of sacred dances, or the enactment of mythological narratives. Through these rituals, individuals participate in the sacred stories and traditions of their belief system, forging a deeper connection with the divine.

Devotional rituals in polytheistic traditions are deeply personal and subjective experiences, reflecting the unique relationship between the individual and the deity they worship. They offer individuals a way to express their spiritual longing, seek guidance, find solace, and cultivate a sense of inner peace. These rituals not only strengthen the bond between the worshipper and the divine but also foster a sense of community among fellow believers who engage in shared acts of devotion.

By engaging in rituals as expressions of devotion and reverence, individuals in polytheistic traditions actively participate in the spiritual dimension of their lives. These rituals serve as reminders of the divine presence, creating a sacred space where individuals can connect with the transcendent and experience a profound sense of belonging, meaning, and purpose. Through their acts of devotion, individuals deepen their understanding of themselves, the world around them, and their place within the broader cosmic order of their polytheistic belief system.

B. Symbolism and Ritual Significance

Symbolism holds a significant place within polytheistic rituals, infusing them with layers of meaning and profound significance. In these rituals, various elements such as objects, gestures, and actions are laden with symbolic representations that connect participants to specific concepts, myths, or cosmic forces. The intentional use of symbolism in polytheistic rituals serves to deepen the spiritual experience, align participants with the cosmic order, and evoke a sense of connection to the mythological narratives and archetypal realms of their belief system.

Ritual objects are often imbued with symbolic meaning in polytheistic traditions. These objects may include sacred tools, statues, amulets, or symbols that represent specific deities, virtues, or elements of the natural world. The presence and use of these objects during rituals serve as focal points for concentration and reverence, allowing participants to establish a tangible connection with the divine. The symbolism inherent in these objects helps to evoke a sense of the deity's presence, qualities, and powers, facilitating a deeper engagement with the divine realm.

Gestures and bodily movements within polytheistic rituals also carry symbolic significance. Certain postures, hand gestures, or movements may symbolize specific attributes, emotions, or mythological events associated with the deities. For example, a gesture of raising one's arms towards the sky may symbolize reaching out to the heavens or invoking the powers of a celestial deity. These symbolic gestures and movements serve to embody and express the essence of the divine, enabling participants to embody the qualities or energies they seek to connect with during the ritual.

Furthermore, the actions performed within polytheistic rituals often hold symbolic value. These actions may include pouring libations, lighting candles or incense, or engaging in communal acts such as processions or dances. Each action carries a deeper meaning, referencing mythological narratives, ancestral traditions, or cosmic cycles. For instance, the pouring of libations can symbolize the act of offering sustenance and nourishment to the deities, while the lighting of candles or incense may represent the illumination of spiritual knowledge or the purification of the sacred space.

The symbolism within polytheistic rituals not only serves to create a rich and immersive experience but also connects participants with the broader belief system and the natural world. It bridges the gap between the physical and spiritual realms, allowing individuals to transcend the mundane and enter into a symbolic space where the boundaries between the human and the divine are blurred. Through the intentional use of symbols, participants are reminded of the interconnectedness of all things and their place within the larger cosmic order.

Symbolism in polytheistic rituals fosters a sense of reverence, awe, and understanding, enabling participants to engage with the divine in a profound and transformative way. It invites them to explore the depths of their beliefs, connect with archetypal energies, and tap into the collective wisdom and spiritual heritage of their tradition. By incorporating symbolism into their rituals, polytheistic practitioners not only deepen their spiritual connection but also cultivate a greater appreciation for the multifaceted layers of meaning embedded within their belief system.

C. Cyclical and Seasonal Rituals

Cyclical and seasonal rituals hold a prominent place within polytheistic traditions, as they are intricately tied to the natural world and its rhythms. These rituals mark significant transitions in the celestial and agricultural cycles, such as solstices, equinoxes, planting seasons, or harvest times. They reflect the deep understanding and acknowledgment of the cyclical nature of life, death, and rebirth that underlies many polytheistic belief systems.

One key aspect of cyclical and seasonal rituals is their alignment with celestial events. Polytheistic traditions often observe solstices, equinoxes, and other astronomical phenomena as important moments in the cosmic order. These rituals acknowledge the shifting of seasons, the changing length of daylight, and the celestial movements that impact the Earth. By attuning themselves to these celestial rhythms, practitioners seek to maintain harmony with the larger cosmic forces and to honor the cyclical nature of existence.

Agricultural cycles also play a significant role in cyclical and seasonal rituals within polytheistic traditions. These rituals are often tied to planting, cultivation, and harvesting activities. They serve as expressions of gratitude for the abundance provided by the Earth and seek to ensure the fertility and prosperity of the land. By participating in these rituals, individuals recognize their dependence on the natural world for sustenance and livelihood and honor the divine forces that govern the cycles of growth and harvest.

Cyclical and seasonal rituals emphasize the interconnectedness between human existence and the natural world. They highlight the interplay of forces that shape life on Earth, such as the changing seasons, the rhythms of the sun and moon, and the cycles of birth, growth, and decay. By actively engaging in these rituals, practitioners reaffirm their place within the larger web of life and recognize their responsibility to live in harmony with nature.

Moreover, these rituals often involve communal participation, bringing together individuals, families, and communities to collectively honor and celebrate these cyclical and seasonal transitions. They serve as occasions for social cohesion, bonding, and the sharing of traditions and cultural heritage. Through shared rituals, participants reinforce their collective identity and strengthen their connection with both the natural world and their religious community.

Cyclical and seasonal rituals in polytheistic traditions provide a framework for individuals to experience the cyclical nature of existence and to attune themselves to the rhythms of the cosmos. By observing and participating in these rituals, practitioners deepen their connection to the divine, cultivate gratitude for the gifts of the Earth, and embrace their role as caretakers and stewards of the natural world. These rituals serve as reminders of the interdependence of all living beings and the importance of maintaining balance and harmony within the larger ecosystem.

D. Communal Participation and Collective Identity

Communal participation is a fundamental aspect of polytheistic rituals, as they often involve the coming together of individuals within a community or religious group. These shared rituals create a sense of collective identity and foster a deep sense of belonging among the participants. Through their active involvement in the rituals, individuals strengthen their connections with one another and reinforce their shared values, beliefs, and religious practices.

Polytheistic rituals provide opportunities for members of a community to gather in a sacred space, whether it be a temple, shrine, or other designated place of worship. In these communal settings, participants engage in various actions, such as prayers, hymns, chants, or ritual performances, collectively honoring and communing with the deities. The shared experience of these rituals creates a sense of togetherness, as individuals come together in a spirit of devotion, reverence, and celebration.

Communal participation in polytheistic rituals serves multiple purposes. Firstly, it strengthens social bonds and fosters a sense of unity within the community. By engaging in shared religious practices, individuals forge connections with one another and establish a shared sense of purpose and belonging. The collective nature of these rituals creates a sense of solidarity and cohesion among the participants, reinforcing their commitment to their religious traditions and strengthening the bonds of community.

Furthermore, communal participation in rituals provides an opportunity for the transmission of cultural heritage and religious knowledge from one generation to the next. As individuals come together to observe and participate in rituals, they learn from one another, share stories, myths, and teachings, and pass on the wisdom and traditions of their ancestors. Through this intergenerational exchange, a sense of continuity and cultural identity is maintained, ensuring that the beliefs, rituals, and values of the community are preserved and passed down to future generations.

Polytheistic rituals also serve as occasions for celebration and joy, allowing the community to come together in times of festivity and commemoration. These rituals mark important milestones, such as religious festivals, rites of passage, or significant historical events, providing opportunities for the community to gather, express their devotion, and partake in shared festivities. These joyful occasions reinforce the sense of collective identity and create cherished memories and experiences within the community.

In summary, communal participation in polytheistic rituals plays a vital role in fostering collective identity, strengthening social bonds, and transmitting cultural heritage. Through shared religious practices, individuals within a community come together to express their devotion, celebrate their shared beliefs, and reinforce their commitment to their tradition. The sense of unity and togetherness experienced in these rituals builds a strong sense of community, nurturing a collective identity that transcends individual differences and promotes a deep sense of belonging.

E. Rituals as Transformational Experiences

Polytheistic rituals are not merely external acts of devotion; they are transformative experiences that have the potential to deeply impact individuals on a personal and spiritual level. These rituals are designed to create a sacred space where participants can engage in practices that facilitate personal growth, self-reflection, and spiritual transformation.

One of the primary purposes of polytheistic rituals is to facilitate a closer connection to the divine. Participants engage in specific rituals and practices to establish a direct line of communication with the deities, seeking their presence, guidance, and blessings. Through acts such as prayers, invocations, offerings, or meditation, individuals open themselves to the divine presence, inviting transformative encounters with the gods and goddesses of their tradition.

Polytheistic rituals also provide opportunities for purification and cleansing. Participants may engage in ritual baths, smudging ceremonies, or other symbolic acts to cleanse themselves of negative energies, impurities, or spiritual obstacles. This process of purification is not only physical but also spiritual, creating a sense of inner purity and readiness to engage in sacred communion with the divine.

Rituals in polytheistic traditions also serve as catalysts for personal and spiritual growth. Through active participation in these rituals, individuals engage in acts of self-reflection, introspection, and introspection. They may be encouraged to examine their thoughts, behaviors, and beliefs, and to seek alignment with the principles and virtues embodied by the deities. The rituals provide a framework for individuals to assess their lives, cultivate virtues, and strive for personal excellence.

Additionally, polytheistic rituals often incorporate elements of performance, art, and music, which engage the senses and evoke deep emotional responses. The use of sacred chants, dances, or music can induce altered states of consciousness and facilitate transcendent experiences. These aesthetic dimensions of rituals enhance the transformative nature of the experience, allowing participants to access heightened states of awareness, spiritual ecstasy, or profound emotional connections with the divine.

Moreover, polytheistic rituals may provide individuals with a sense of purpose and meaning. By actively engaging in the rituals and embracing the practices of their tradition, participants may experience a sense of belonging, fulfillment, and connection to something greater than themselves. These rituals reaffirm their place within the larger cosmic order, reinforcing their understanding of their role and purpose in the world.

In summary, polytheistic rituals offer transformative experiences by providing individuals with opportunities for spiritual connection, purification, personal growth, and a deepening sense of purpose. These rituals serve as sacred spaces where participants can engage in practices that facilitate profound shifts in their understanding of themselves, their relationship with the divine, and their place within the larger cosmological framework. Through active participation in rituals, individuals undergo personal and spiritual transformation, leading to a greater sense of fulfillment, insight, and connection to the sacred.

F. Continuity and Adaptation

Polytheistic rituals embody a remarkable continuity, often tracing their roots back to ancient traditions that have been passed down through generations. These rituals serve as tangible links to the past, connecting contemporary practitioners with the beliefs, practices, and wisdom of their ancestors. They represent a living legacy that has been preserved and honored over time, allowing individuals to participate in a collective spiritual heritage.

At the core of polytheistic rituals lies a commitment to preserving the essential principles and values of the tradition. These enduring aspects provide a sense of stability, anchoring the community in its shared beliefs and practices. Core rituals, such as seasonal celebrations, rites of passage, or offerings to specific deities, are upheld with reverence and respect, ensuring the continuation of the tradition's foundational practices.

However, polytheistic rituals also demonstrate a remarkable capacity for adaptation and evolution. While the core rituals remain intact, they are not frozen in time. Polytheistic traditions have shown a remarkable ability to adapt to changing societal, cultural, and historical contexts. They possess an inherent flexibility that allows them to respond to new circumstances while maintaining their essential spirit and character.

In times of societal change or cultural shifts, polytheistic traditions may incorporate new rituals or modify existing ones to accommodate the evolving needs and sensibilities of the community. This adaptability ensures that the rituals remain relevant, meaningful, and accessible to contemporary practitioners. For example, rituals may be adjusted to address modern environmental concerns, promote social justice, or incorporate new artistic expressions that resonate with current aesthetics.

Adaptation in polytheistic rituals is not a departure from tradition but rather a dynamic process of renewal and reimagining. It is a conscious and deliberate engagement with the ever-changing world, acknowledging that rituals must speak to the needs and aspirations of the present generation. This process of adaptation allows polytheistic traditions to maintain their relevance and vitality, ensuring that they continue to inspire and guide individuals in their spiritual journeys.

Furthermore, the adaptability of polytheistic rituals also fosters cultural diversity and interfaith dialogue. As different cultures and religious practices come into contact, rituals may blend or synthesize elements, leading to the emergence of new forms of expression. This interplay between traditions enriches the religious landscape, creating opportunities for mutual understanding, respect, and collaboration.

In conclusion, polytheistic rituals exhibit both continuity and adaptation. They preserve the essential principles and values of the tradition while also evolving and responding to changing contexts. The enduring nature of core rituals provides a connection to the past, while the adaptability ensures the rituals remain relevant and meaningful in contemporary times. This interplay between continuity and adaptation allows polytheistic traditions to thrive and continue to inspire individuals and communities in their spiritual journeys.

Exploring the role and significance of rituals in polytheistic belief systems

Rituals hold a central and profound significance in polytheistic belief systems, playing a vital role in the spiritual and religious lives of practitioners. These rituals are not mere superficial actions but are imbued with deep meaning and purpose, serving as powerful conduits for communication with the divine and expressions of devotion.

One of the primary roles of rituals in polytheistic belief systems is to establish and maintain a connection between humans and the deities. Through ritualistic practices, individuals seek to engage in direct communication with the divine realm, bridging the gap between the mortal and the sacred. Rituals provide a structured framework within which worshippers can interact with the gods and goddesses, expressing their reverence, gratitude, and supplications.

Polytheistic rituals often involve the offering of prayers, incantations, hymns, or invocations, which serve as a means of establishing communication with the deities. These verbal expressions allow individuals to articulate their innermost thoughts, desires, and concerns, creating a dialogue with the divine that fosters a sense of intimacy and connection.

Another significant aspect of rituals in polytheistic belief systems is their role in creating and maintaining cosmic order and harmony. These rituals are often performed with the understanding that they are part of a larger cosmic tapestry, where the actions of humans and the gods are intricately intertwined. By adhering to specific rites, gestures, and ceremonies, individuals participate in the grand cosmic dance, aligning themselves with the natural and divine rhythms of the universe.

Polytheistic rituals also serve as vehicles for expressing devotion, gratitude, and reverence towards the deities. Through acts of offering, such as the presentation of food, drink, flowers, or symbolic objects, worshippers demonstrate their appreciation for the blessings and guidance received from the gods. These offerings are seen as gestures of reciprocity, acknowledging the ongoing relationship between humans and the divine and affirming the belief in a reciprocal exchange of energy and support.

Moreover, rituals in polytheistic belief systems often commemorate significant events, myths, or historical moments within the tradition. These rituals serve as a way to honor the foundational stories, legendary figures, or important milestones that shape the identity of the community. By reenacting these narratives or participating in specific ceremonial practices, individuals strengthen their connection to their cultural and religious heritage, ensuring its continued vitality and transmission to future generations.

Additionally, polytheistic rituals can also have a transformative effect on individuals, facilitating personal growth, healing, and spiritual transcendence. The rituals provide a sacred space for individuals to engage in self-reflection, introspection, and purification. They offer opportunities for catharsis, renewal, and the cultivation of virtues such as compassion, humility, and wisdom. Through participation in these rituals, individuals experience a deepening of their spiritual understanding, a sense of interconnectedness with the divine and the world around them, and a heightened awareness of their own spiritual potential.

In conclusion, rituals play a multifaceted and significant role in polytheistic belief systems. They facilitate communication with the divine, maintain cosmic order, express devotion and gratitude, honor cultural and religious heritage, and foster personal transformation. Polytheistic rituals serve as profound gateways to the sacred, allowing individuals to engage with the divine realm, establish a deeper connection with the gods, and nourish their spiritual lives.

The diversity of polytheistic rituals across different cultures and historical periods

The diversity of polytheistic rituals across different cultures and historical periods is a testament to the richness and complexity of human religious expression. Polytheistic belief systems have existed in various forms throughout history, encompassing a wide range of cultures, regions, and traditions. Consequently, the rituals associated with these belief systems exhibit remarkable diversity in their practices, forms, and purposes.

Each polytheistic culture and civilization developed its unique set of rituals that reflected their specific cosmologies, mythologies, social structures, and religious beliefs. These rituals were often deeply intertwined with the cultural fabric of the society, incorporating local customs, symbols, and traditions. As a result, the rituals varied significantly from one culture to another, even within the broader framework of polytheism.

For example, in ancient Greece, polytheistic rituals were an integral part of public and private life. Public rituals were performed in honor of various gods and goddesses, such as the Olympic deities, with grand ceremonies held at temples, sanctuaries, or during festivals. These rituals involved processions, animal sacrifices, libations, prayers, and theatrical performances. On the other hand, private rituals in ancient Greece focused on household gods and ancestral spirits, involving offerings at home altars and the recitation of prayers.

In ancient Egypt, polytheistic rituals centered around the veneration of numerous deities, including Osiris, Isis, and Ra. Temples played a central role in Egyptian religious practices, serving as sacred spaces where rituals were conducted by priests and priestesses. These rituals involved purification rites, offerings of food and drink, the recitation of hymns and prayers, as well as the performance of rituals associated with the pharaoh's divine role.

In the ancient Indus Valley civilization, polytheistic rituals were tied to the worship of deities such as Shiva, Vishnu, and Devi. Sacred fire ceremonies, known as yajnas, were conducted by Brahmin priests as a means of communication with the gods. These rituals involved intricate fire offerings, chanting of hymns, and the performance of specific rituals associated with the gods and their attributes.

Furthermore, the diversity of polytheistic rituals can also be seen in the practices of indigenous cultures around the world. Indigenous polytheistic belief systems, such as those found in Native American, African, or Oceanic traditions, incorporate a rich tapestry of rituals that honor ancestral spirits, nature deities, and local mythologies. These rituals often involve dances, drumming, singing, storytelling, and offerings made to sacred sites, rivers, or mountains.

It is important to note that the diversity of polytheistic rituals is not limited to ancient times. Polytheistic belief systems and their associated rituals continue to be practiced in various forms in contemporary societies. For instance, in Hinduism, which is considered a complex polytheistic tradition, rituals are performed at temples, shrines, and homes, with devotees engaging in offerings, prayers, and participating in religious festivals.

In conclusion, the diversity of polytheistic rituals across different cultures and historical periods is a testament to the varied ways in which humans have expressed their religious beliefs and engaged with the divine. These rituals, shaped by cultural, social, and historical contexts, offer unique insights into the beliefs, values, and practices of different polytheistic traditions. By exploring this diversity, we gain a deeper appreciation for the multifaceted nature of human spirituality and the profound ways in which rituals have shaped and continue to shape our understanding of the divine.

Festivals and Celebrations in Polytheism

Festivals and celebrations hold a significant place in polytheistic belief systems, serving as vibrant expressions of religious devotion, communal identity, and cultural heritage. These festive occasions are marked by a variety of rituals, performances, and gatherings that bring together individuals, communities, and deities in joyful celebration and reverence.

Polytheistic festivals often revolve around the cycles of nature, agricultural seasons, or significant mythological events. They serve as opportunities to honor specific deities associated with these occasions and to express gratitude for the blessings of the natural world. By participating in festivals, individuals and communities reaffirm their connection to the divine, strengthen social bonds, and renew their spiritual commitment.

The diversity of polytheistic festivals is vast, varying from culture to culture and region to region. However, some common themes and practices can be observed across different polytheistic traditions.

One prominent aspect of polytheistic festivals is the performance of rituals and ceremonies. These rituals may involve offerings of food, drink, flowers, or other symbolic items to the deities. Prayers, chants, and hymns are recited, invoking the presence and blessings of the divine. Processions and parades, accompanied by music, dance, and colorful attire, create a lively and festive atmosphere. Sacred objects or icons may be displayed, and purification rituals or symbolic acts of cleansing may be performed.

Polytheistic festivals often include communal feasting and shared meals. These gatherings foster a sense of unity and community, allowing individuals to come together in celebration, share food, and enjoy social interactions. The feasts may feature traditional dishes and specialties associated with the festival or symbolic offerings representing the bounty and abundance provided by the gods.

In many polytheistic traditions, festivals are not confined to specific locations but are often celebrated at sacred sites, temples, or other places of significance. These locations serve as focal points for the community, where rituals are performed, processions are held, and the divine presence is believed to be particularly potent. Pilgrimages to these sacred sites during festivals provide opportunities for individuals to deepen their spiritual connection and seek blessings.

Polytheistic festivals also provide a platform for artistic expressions and performances. Music, dance, drama, and storytelling play integral roles in the festivities, allowing individuals to celebrate and portray mythological narratives, legends, or historical events associated with their religious tradition. These artistic expressions not only entertain but also serve as vehicles for religious and cultural education, transmitting the beliefs and values of the community to future generations.

The atmosphere of polytheistic festivals is characterized by joy, exuberance, and a sense of communal belonging. People often don festive attire, adorn themselves with symbolic ornaments or sacred symbols, and engage in activities that reflect the spirit of celebration. In some cases, temporary structures or decorative installations are created, transforming public spaces into vibrant, sacred spaces.

Through festivals and celebrations, polytheistic traditions provide opportunities for individuals to deepen their spiritual connection with the divine, celebrate their cultural heritage, and reinforce communal bonds. These festive occasions serve as a reminder of the cyclic nature of life, the interconnectedness of humans and the natural world, and the enduring presence of the deities. They create a sense of continuity, preserving and revitalizing ancient rituals and traditions while adapting to the changing needs and contexts of the community.

In conclusion, festivals and celebrations hold a significant place in polytheistic belief systems, serving as joyful and reverential expressions of religious devotion, cultural identity, and community cohesion. These occasions bring together individuals and communities to honor the deities, celebrate the cycles of nature, and commemorate mythological events. Through rituals, feasting, artistic performances, and communal gatherings, polytheistic festivals provide opportunities for spiritual renewal, social bonding, and the preservation of cultural heritage.

Festival Name	Religion	Time of Year	Meaning and Other Information
Beltane	Celtic Polytheism	May 1st	Celebrates fertility, growth, and the beginning of summer. It is associated with the union of the divine feminine and masculine.
Diwali	Hinduism	October/November	Festival of lights symbolizing the victory of light over darkness and good over evil. Celebrates the return of Lord Rama and the goddess Lakshmi.
Saturnalia	Ancient Rome	December	Honored the god Saturn and marked the winter solstice. It was a time of feasting, gift-giving, and social reversal where slaves and masters temporarily switched roles.
Samhain	Celtic Polytheism	October 31st	Celebrates the end of the harvest season and the beginning of winter. It is associated with honoring ancestors and the thinning of the veil between the living and

Festival Name	Religion	Time of Year	Meaning and Other Information
			the dead.
Navaratri	Hinduism	September/October	Nine-night festival honoring the goddess Durga and her various forms. It involves fasting, dance performances, and religious ceremonies.
Lupercalia	Ancient Rome	February 15th	Celebrated fertility and purification. It involved the sacrifice of goats and the ritual whipping of women to promote health and fertility.
Thargelia	Ancient Greece	May	Honored the gods Apollo and Artemis. It involved purification rituals, feasting, and the offering of first fruits to the deities.
Yule	Germanic Paganism	December 21st	Celebrated the winter solstice and the rebirth of the sun. It involved lighting fires, feasting, and exchanging gifts.
Lughnasadh	Celtic Polytheism	August 1st	Celebrated the first harvest and honored the god Lugh. It involved games, competitions, and communal gatherings.
Pongal	Hinduism	January	Tamil harvest festival, honoring the sun god Surya. It involves the boiling of new rice and offering it to the gods as a sign of gratitude.

Please note that this is not an exhaustive list, as there are numerous polytheistic traditions and festivals around the world. The examples provided showcase the diversity of polytheistic festivals, including their associated religions, time of year, and general meanings.

Examining major polytheistic festivals and their cultural and religious importance

Major polytheistic festivals hold significant cultural and religious importance in their respective traditions. Here are some examples:

Beltane (Celtic Polytheism): Celebrated on May 1st, Beltane marks the beginning of summer and the fertility of the land. It is associated with the union of the divine feminine and masculine energies, symbolizing the renewal of life and the abundance of the harvest season.

Diwali (Hinduism): Diwali, also known as the Festival of Lights, is one of the most important Hindu festivals. It typically occurs in October or November and celebrates the victory of light over darkness and good over evil. Diwali is associated with the return of Lord Rama from exile and the goddess Lakshmi, who brings wealth and prosperity. People light oil lamps, decorate their homes, exchange gifts, and enjoy fireworks displays.

Saturnalia (Ancient Rome): Saturnalia was a week-long festival held in December to honor the god Saturn. It coincided with the winter solstice and was a time of merriment and social reversal. During Saturnalia, people engaged in feasting, gift-giving, and role reversals where slaves and masters temporarily switched positions, emphasizing egalitarian values and celebrating the abundance of the harvest.

Samhain (Celtic Polytheism): Occurring on October 31st, Samhain is a festival that marks the end of the harvest season and the beginning of winter. It is associated with the thinning of the veil between the living and the dead, and people honor their ancestors by setting up altars, offering food and drink, and participating in divination rituals. It is considered a time of reflection, remembrance, and spiritual connection.

Navaratri (Hinduism): Navaratri is a nine-night festival celebrated in September or October, honoring the goddess Durga and her various forms. It involves elaborate rituals, fasting, dance performances, and religious ceremonies. Each night represents a different aspect of the goddess, and devotees engage in devotional practices to seek her blessings and spiritual upliftment.

Lupercalia (Ancient Rome): Lupercalia was an ancient Roman festival held on February 15th. It was dedicated to the god Lupercus and involved purification rituals and fertility rites. Participants would sacrifice goats and use their hides to whip women, believing it would promote health and fertility.

These festivals and others like them hold cultural significance as they provide a sense of identity and belonging to the community. They serve as opportunities for people to come together, express their religious devotion, celebrate shared values and beliefs, and maintain a connection with their ancestral traditions. These festivals often involve feasting, music, dance, storytelling, and various rituals, creating a vibrant tapestry of cultural and religious practices within polytheistic belief systems.

Highlighting specific rituals and practices associated with polytheistic celebrations

Offerings and Sacrifices: Many polytheistic festivals involve the offering of food, drink, flowers, incense, or other symbolic items to the deities. These offerings are seen as acts of reverence, gratitude, and reciprocity, symbolizing the relationship between humans and the divine.

Processions and Parades: During festivals, participants often engage in processions or parades, carrying sacred images or idols of the deities through the streets or sacred spaces. This public display of devotion and reverence allows the community to collectively honor the deities and invite their presence and blessings.

Ritualistic Dance and Music: Dance and music play a significant role in polytheistic celebrations. Ritualistic dances, often accompanied by specific musical instruments, are performed to express joy, invoke divine presence, and bring the community together in a harmonious and celebratory atmosphere.

Prayer and Chanting: Prayer is a common ritual practice in polytheistic celebrations. Devotees offer prayers to the deities, seeking blessings, guidance, and protection. Chanting of sacred hymns, mantras, or specific incantations is also prevalent, as it is believed to have a purifying and transformative effect on the individual and the environment.

Ceremonial Baths and Purification: Some festivals involve ceremonial baths or immersion in sacred waters as a means of purification. This practice symbolizes the cleansing of impurities and the renewal of spiritual energy.

Ritualistic Drama and Reenactments: Certain festivals incorporate dramatic performances or reenactments of mythological stories. These theatrical presentations serve to educate, inspire, and connect participants with the sacred narratives and the lessons they convey.

Sacred Fire Rituals: Fire holds great significance in many polytheistic traditions. Festivals may include the lighting of sacred fires, around which participants gather to offer prayers, perform rituals, and seek blessings. The fire is seen as a transformative element and a medium through which offerings reach the divine realm.

Divination and Oracles: Some festivals provide opportunities for divination or consultation with oracles. Individuals may seek guidance or answers to important questions through methods such as tarot readings, astrology, oracles, or other forms of spiritual insight.

These rituals and practices vary across different polytheistic traditions, reflecting the diversity and richness of their beliefs and cultural expressions. They are performed with the intention of connecting with the divine, honoring the deities, fostering spiritual growth, and reinforcing communal bonds. Through these rituals, participants experience a sense of awe, devotion, and connection to the sacred, creating meaningful and transformative experiences during polytheistic celebrations.

Offerings and Devotions in Polytheistic Worship

Offerings and devotions play a crucial role in polytheistic worship, serving as expressions of reverence, gratitude, and connection to the divine. These practices involve the presentation of symbolic gifts and acts of devotion to the deities, creating a reciprocal relationship between humans and the divine.

Types of Offerings: Polytheistic worship involves a wide range of offerings. These can include physical items such as food, drink, flowers, incense, precious objects, or symbolic representations of the deity. Offerings may also include prayers, chants, hymns, or acts of service dedicated to the deities.

Types of Offerings	Associated Deities
Food	Demeter (grains), Hera (bread), Artemis (meat), Dionysus (sweets)
Drink	Poseidon (water), Hera (milk), Dionysus (wine), Aphrodite (honey), Athena (sacred beverages)
Flowers	Aphrodite, Persephone, Flora (goddess of flowers)
Incense	Zeus, Hestia, Apollo, Artemis
Precious Objects	Athena (jewelry), Aphrodite (gemstones), Hephaestus (crafted objects)

Please note that these associations may vary depending on specific cultural traditions and interpretations.

Symbolic Meaning: Symbolic meaning plays a crucial role in the selection and understanding of offerings in polytheistic worship. Each type of offering carries symbolic significance that reflects the relationship between humans and the divine, as well as the attributes and domains of the specific deity being honored.

Food offerings, for instance, symbolize sustenance and nourishment. By offering food to the gods, worshippers express their gratitude for the abundance of the Earth and seek blessings for sustenance in their own lives. The specific types of food offered may vary depending on cultural and regional traditions, as well as the preferences and associations of the deity being honored. For example, offerings of grains might be associated with Demeter, the goddess of agriculture, while offerings of meat could be associated with Artemis, the goddess of the hunt.

Drink offerings often symbolize the sharing of life-giving fluids and are associated with deities who govern specific elements or aspects of life. Water offerings may be made to Poseidon, the god of the sea, while milk offerings are associated with Hera, the queen of the gods, and wine offerings are dedicated to Dionysus, the god of wine and revelry. The choice of beverage reflects the qualities and associations of the deity, as well as the desired blessings or connections sought by the worshipper.

Flower offerings are commonly associated with goddesses of beauty, love, and fertility, such as Aphrodite and Persephone. Flowers, with their ephemeral beauty and delicate nature, symbolize the transient yet profound aspects of life, love, and renewal. By offering flowers, worshippers honor the goddesses and express their reverence for the natural cycles of growth and regeneration.

Incense offerings carry symbolic meanings of purification, spiritual elevation, and the transmission of prayers or invocations to the divine realm. The burning of incense is believed to create a sacred atmosphere, purify the space, and enhance the connection between humans and the gods. Different types of incense may be associated with specific deities or used in different ritual contexts to evoke specific qualities or create specific atmospheres.

The choice of precious objects as offerings can vary widely, depending on the deity and the desired symbolism. These objects may include jewelry, gemstones, crafted objects, or other valuable items. Such offerings express devotion and respect for the deity's power, beauty, or specific domain. For example, offerings of jewelry might be made to Athena, the goddess of wisdom and craftsmanship, while gemstones could be dedicated to Aphrodite, the goddess of love and beauty.

It's important to note that while these symbolic meanings provide a general understanding, the precise associations of offerings can vary across different polytheistic traditions, cultures, and individual interpretations. The specific meanings and symbolism may also evolve over time within a particular tradition.

Reciprocity and Gratitude: Reciprocity and gratitude are fundamental aspects of offering practices in polytheistic worship. Offerings are seen as acts of reciprocity, acknowledging the blessings and benevolence of the deities and seeking to establish a mutually beneficial relationship.

By offering gifts to the gods, worshippers express their gratitude for the blessings they have received in their lives. This gratitude stems from the belief that the deities play an active role in the lives of individuals and communities, bestowing their favor, protection, and guidance. Through offerings, worshippers show their appreciation for these blessings and seek to maintain a harmonious relationship with the divine.

Reciprocity is a central concept in polytheistic belief systems. It is believed that the deities, in their benevolence, provide for the needs of humans and the world. In return, humans express their gratitude and respect through offerings, thereby establishing a reciprocal relationship of care and support. This reciprocal bond is seen as essential for maintaining the order and well-being of both the human and divine realms.

The act of offering is also seen as a way to nourish and sustain the deities. Just as humans require sustenance, the deities are believed to derive nourishment from the offerings presented to them. This understanding underscores the idea that the relationship between humans and gods is one of interdependence and mutual support.

Furthermore, offerings are not seen as mere transactions or exchanges but as acts of devotion and reverence. They are expressions of the worshippers' deep respect, reverence, and commitment to the deities. Through offerings, worshippers seek to establish a personal connection and rapport with the divine, fostering a sense of intimacy and closeness.

In this way, offerings serve as tangible expressions of the worshippers' relationship with the divine, reflecting their gratitude, devotion, and desire for continued blessings and guidance. They embody the principle of reciprocity and act as a means to maintain a harmonious and mutually beneficial connection between humans and the deities.

Ritual Preparation: Ritual preparation plays an important role in the act of offering in polytheistic worship. It involves various practices aimed at ensuring that the offerings and the worshippers themselves are in a state of purity and reverence before presenting the gifts to the deities.

One aspect of ritual preparation involves the purification of the offerings themselves. This may include cleansing or consecrating the physical items to be offered, such as food, drink, flowers, incense, or precious objects. The purpose of this purification is to remove any impurities or negative energies and to sanctify the offerings, making them suitable for presentation to the divine.

Worshippers may also engage in personal purification rituals before approaching the altar or sacred space. This can involve practices such as ritual bathing, washing of hands, or reciting prayers and invocations to cleanse the mind, body, and spirit. These purification rituals are seen as a way to prepare oneself for the sacred act of offering, ensuring that one approaches the divine with a sense of reverence, humility, and inner purity.

The specific rituals of purification may vary across different polytheistic traditions. They are often guided by religious texts, cultural customs, or the teachings of spiritual leaders. The purpose, however, remains consistent—to create a sacred and sanctified space for the offering and to cultivate an inner disposition of respect and devotion.

Ritual preparation not only ensures the physical and spiritual purity of the offerings but also serves as a transformative practice for the worshippers themselves. It allows individuals to enter into a state of focused awareness, shedding distractions and worldly concerns, and immersing themselves in the sacred act of offering. It is a time of mental and emotional preparation, aligning oneself with the divine presence and cultivating a receptive and attentive mindset.

By engaging in ritual preparation, worshippers demonstrate their commitment to honoring the sacred and their understanding of the significance of the act of offering. It is a way to approach the divine with sincerity, reverence, and mindfulness, fostering a deep sense of connection and communion with the deities.

Altars and Sacred Spaces: Altars and sacred spaces play a crucial role in the act of offering in polytheistic worship. They serve as dedicated areas where worshippers can establish a tangible connection with the divine and present their offerings in a reverent and sacred manner.

An altar is a specifically designated space that serves as a focal point for communication, devotion, and worship. It is often adorned with symbols, images, or representations of the deities relevant to the particular tradition. These symbols may include statues, icons, paintings, or sacred objects associated with the gods and goddesses.

Worshippers may create personal altars in their homes, dedicating a special area where they can engage in private rituals and express their devotion to the deities. These personal altars often reflect the individual's specific spiritual practices, with items and symbols that hold personal significance or represent their chosen deities.

In communal worship settings, such as temples or sacred sites, there are often larger and more elaborate altars. These communal altars are shared spaces where worshippers gather to participate in collective rituals and offerings. They may be adorned with ornate decorations, colorful fabrics, flowers, and candles, creating a visually captivating and spiritually charged environment.

The design and arrangement of altars and sacred spaces can vary across different polytheistic traditions. They are often guided by religious texts, cultural customs, and the specific attributes and preferences associated with the deities being honored. The placement of statues or symbols, the arrangement of offerings, and the use of specific colors or materials all contribute to the sacred ambiance and symbolism of the space.

The presence of altars and sacred spaces serves multiple purposes. They provide a physical focal point for worshippers to direct their attention and intentions towards the divine. They create a visual representation of the divine presence, reminding worshippers of the gods and goddesses they seek to honor. Altars also serve as a sacred container, holding the offerings and imbuing them with spiritual significance.

Engaging with altars and sacred spaces in the act of offering allows worshippers to create a tangible and intimate connection with the divine. It provides a dedicated space where they can express their devotion, gratitude, and reverence. The act of presenting offerings in such a sacred space is seen as a means of establishing a direct line of communication and communion with the deities, fostering a deep sense of spiritual connection and engagement.

Deity: Zeus

✧ **Common Altar Offerings:** Incense, flowers, libations (wine or water), food offerings (such as fruits or honey)
✧ **Additional Information:** Altars dedicated to Zeus often feature symbols of his power, such as thunderbolts or eagle imagery.

Deity: Aphrodite

✧   **Common Altar Offerings:** Fresh flowers (especially roses), perfumes, shells, love-related offerings (such as chocolate or love letters)
✧   **Additional Information:** Altars dedicated to Aphrodite may include images or statues depicting her beauty and associations with love and desire.

Deity: Odin

✧   **Common Altar Offerings:** Mead or other alcoholic beverages, bread, herbs, runes
✧   **Additional Information:** Altars dedicated to Odin may include representations of his ravens or wolves, as well as tools associated with wisdom and magic.

Deity: Isis

✧   **Common Altar Offerings:** Milk, bread, fruits, lotus flowers
✧   **Additional Information:** Altars dedicated to Isis often incorporate symbols of fertility and motherhood, as well as images of her with outstretched wings.

Deity: Hestia

✧   **Common Altar Offerings:** Sacred flame (candle or oil lamp), bread, salt
✧   **Additional Information:** Altars dedicated to Hestia represent the hearth and home, and may include a small fire or symbol of eternal flame.

Deity: Shiva

✧   **Common Altar Offerings:** Water, flowers (particularly white flowers), incense, sacred ash (vibhuti)
✧   **Additional Information:** Altars dedicated to Shiva may include a Shiva lingam or statues depicting his various forms and aspects.

Please note that the specific practices and offerings associated with altars can vary among different polytheistic traditions and even within different cultural contexts. The above examples provide a general overview of commonly observed practices, but it's important to consult specific religious texts or community practices for more detailed and accurate information.

Devotional Practices: Devotional practices in polytheistic worship play a significant role in cultivating a personal relationship with the deities and deepening one's spiritual connection. These practices encompass a range of activities and expressions of devotion that are aimed at honoring, praising, and communing with the divine.

Prayer is a central devotional practice in many polytheistic traditions. It involves direct communication with the deities, expressing gratitude, seeking guidance, or offering praise. Prayers may be recited individually or as part of communal rituals, and they can be spontaneous or based on established prayers and liturgies.

Meditation is another devotional practice commonly found in polytheistic traditions. It involves quieting the mind, focusing one's attention, and opening oneself to spiritual insights and experiences. Meditation allows worshippers to connect with the divine within themselves and to attain a state of deeper awareness and communion with the gods.

Chanting and singing hymns are forms of devotional expression that involve the use of sacred words or melodies to invoke and honor the deities. Chants and hymns can be recited or sung individually or as part of group rituals, creating a harmonious and uplifting atmosphere that helps participants connect with the divine presence.

Reciting sacred texts or scriptures is also a devotional practice in polytheistic traditions. Reading or reciting passages from religious texts allows worshippers to engage with the teachings, stories, and wisdom of the deities. It serves as a means of deepening one's understanding of the faith and fostering a sense of spiritual connection.

Other devotional practices may include lighting candles or lamps, making prostrations or bowing before sacred images or statues, or engaging in acts of selfless service and charity as an expression of devotion and love for the deities.

These devotional practices serve to create a sacred space within the heart and mind of the worshipper, allowing for a profound engagement with the divine presence. They foster a sense of awe, reverence, and gratitude, helping worshippers to cultivate a deeper understanding of themselves, the world, and their place within the larger cosmic order.

It is important to note that devotional practices can vary across different polytheistic traditions, reflecting the unique beliefs, customs, and cultural contexts of each tradition. The specific forms and methods of devotional practices may differ, but their underlying purpose remains consistent - to foster a deep and personal connection with the divine and to honor the gods with love and devotion.

Timing and Occasions:

Timing and occasions play a significant role in offering rituals and devotional practices within polytheistic traditions. While offerings and devotions can be performed at any time, there are specific occasions and timings that hold special significance and are designated for particular rituals and observances.

Daily rituals form an essential part of many polytheistic traditions. These are regular practices performed on a daily basis, often at specific times of the day, such as morning or evening. Daily rituals provide an opportunity for worshippers to establish a routine of devotion and maintain a continuous connection with the deities. These rituals may include offerings, prayers, meditation, or recitation of sacred texts.

Festivals and religious celebrations are another important occasion for offerings and devotions in polytheistic traditions. These festivals are often associated with significant mythological events, historical milestones, or seasonal changes. They serve as communal gatherings where worshippers come together to honor the deities, express gratitude, and celebrate their religious heritage. Offerings and devotions during festivals may involve elaborate rituals, processions, feasting, and cultural performances.

Personal milestones and life events also provide occasions for offering rituals and devotions in polytheistic traditions. Births, marriages, initiations, or even personal achievements can be marked with offerings and prayers to seek blessings and express gratitude for the divine guidance and support throughout one's life journey.

Furthermore, some polytheistic traditions follow specific calendars that guide the timing of offerings and devotions. These calendars are often based on lunar or solar cycles, aligning the religious practices with celestial events or seasonal changes. They provide worshippers with a framework for planning and conducting rituals on auspicious dates associated with the movements of celestial bodies or significant agricultural or natural phenomena.

The timing and occasions for offering rituals and devotions may vary among different polytheistic traditions and even within specific cultural or regional contexts. It is through these designated times and occasions that worshippers can deepen their connection with the divine, partake in communal celebrations, and experience a collective sense of spiritual unity.

By observing these specific timings and occasions, worshippers honor the cyclical nature of life, express their reverence for the deities, and maintain a harmonious relationship with the divine forces that govern their world. They serve as reminders of the interconnectedness between the human and the divine realms and provide opportunities for individuals to strengthen their spiritual connection and engage in acts of devotion.

Offerings and devotions in polytheistic worship embody the belief in a tangible and reciprocal relationship between humans and the divine. They serve as tangible expressions of devotion, gratitude, and the desire for a harmonious connection with the deities. These practices foster a sense of spiritual engagement, community, and a deepening of personal faith within polytheistic traditions.

Exploring the types of offerings made to deities in polytheistic religions

Polytheistic religions encompass a wide array of traditions, each with its own unique practices and customs regarding offerings made to deities. These offerings can vary greatly in form and substance, reflecting the cultural, historical, and regional contexts in which they arise. While the specific offerings made to deities can differ, they are united by the shared purpose of expressing reverence, gratitude, and establishing a reciprocal relationship with the divine.

Physical offerings are a common and tangible way to honor deities in polytheistic traditions. These offerings may include items such as food and drink, flowers, incense, precious objects, or symbolic representations of the deity. The selection of offerings often reflects the preferences, attributes, and associations of the specific deity being honored. For instance, offerings of food and drink can symbolize sustenance, nourishment, and the sharing of life's blessings. Flowers, with their beauty and ephemeral nature, can represent the transience of existence and the cycle of life and death. Incense, with its aromatic smoke, is often used to purify the space and elevate prayers and devotions to the divine.

Additionally, offerings may include sacred herbs, oils, or spices with specific symbolic and spiritual properties. These items can be burned or used in purification rituals, symbolically cleansing the worshipper or the sacred space.

Another type of offering in polytheistic religions is the act of devotion itself. This can involve prayers, hymns, chants, or recitation of sacred texts. Through the power of spoken or written words, worshippers express their reverence, adoration, and gratitude to the deities. These verbal offerings serve as a means of communication and establish a connection between the human and divine realms.

Acts of service or acts of kindness can also be considered offerings in polytheistic traditions. These offerings may take the form of charitable acts, selfless deeds, or contributions to the community in the name of the deity. By dedicating their actions to the divine, worshippers demonstrate their commitment to living a virtuous and compassionate life.

In some polytheistic traditions, music, dance, and other artistic expressions are considered offerings to the deities. Performances and artistic creations are believed to evoke spiritual energy and please the divine beings. These offerings can be an expression of devotion and a celebration of the beauty and creativity inherent in the world.

It is important to note that the specific types of offerings made in polytheistic religions can vary significantly across cultures, regions, and individual practices. The diversity of offerings reflects the rich tapestry of beliefs, traditions, and cultural expressions within the polytheistic framework. These offerings serve as a means for worshippers to connect with the divine, express their reverence, and establish a reciprocal relationship with the deities they hold sacred.

The rituals and practices of prayer, meditation, and devotion in polytheistic traditions

Prayer, meditation, and devotion are integral components of polytheistic traditions, providing worshippers with meaningful ways to connect with the divine, seek guidance, express gratitude, and deepen their spiritual connection. While the specific practices can vary across different polytheistic religions, there are common threads that run through these rituals and practices.

Prayer is a fundamental practice in polytheistic traditions. It involves communicating with the deities, expressing reverence, making requests, seeking blessings, and offering gratitude. Prayers can be recited aloud, silently, or in written form, depending on the individual's preference and the specific tradition. They can be structured and formal or spontaneous and personal, reflecting the individual's unique relationship with the deity. Prayers may be offered at specific times, such as daily rituals, before meals, or during festivals, as well as during significant life events or moments of need.

Meditation is another practice that holds great significance in polytheistic traditions. It involves quieting the mind, focusing one's attention, and entering a state of deep contemplation or connection with the divine. Meditation techniques can vary, including mindfulness, visualization, or mantra repetition. Through meditation, worshippers seek to cultivate inner peace, spiritual insight, and a heightened sense of awareness. It serves as a means of attuning oneself to the divine presence, exploring the depths of one's spirituality, and fostering a deeper connection with the deities.

Devotion is an essential aspect of polytheistic traditions, encompassing a range of practices that express love, reverence, and dedication to the deities. Devotional practices can include singing hymns, chanting sacred mantras, performing dances, or engaging in rituals that honor and celebrate the divine. These practices are often accompanied by music, incense, and symbolic gestures that create a sacred atmosphere and evoke a sense of spiritual transcendence. Devotional acts can be individual or communal, taking place in personal altars, temples, or during religious festivals and gatherings.

In addition to prayer, meditation, and devotion, polytheistic traditions may incorporate other practices such as offerings, purification rituals, divination, and pilgrimage. Offerings, as discussed previously, are tangible expressions of devotion and gratitude to the deities. Purification rituals cleanse the body, mind, or sacred spaces to prepare for spiritual connection and worship. Divination practices, such as reading omens or consulting oracles, seek insights into the divine will and guidance. Pilgrimage involves journeying to sacred sites or temples associated with particular deities to seek blessings and spiritual fulfillment.

These rituals and practices of prayer, meditation, and devotion serve as foundational pillars of polytheistic worship. They offer worshippers a means to establish a personal relationship with the deities, seek spiritual growth and enlightenment, and navigate life's challenges with divine guidance and support. Through these practices, individuals engage in a transformative and dynamic spiritual journey, exploring the depths of their faith and nurturing their connection with the divine beings they hold sacred.

Sacred Spaces and Places of Worship in Polytheism

Sacred spaces and places of worship hold profound significance in polytheistic traditions, serving as focal points for spiritual devotion, communal gatherings, and rituals. These spaces are believed to be imbued with the presence and energy of the deities, creating a sacred atmosphere conducive to connecting with the divine.

Polytheistic religions often have designated temples, shrines, or sanctuaries where worshippers gather to engage in communal worship and seek the blessings of the deities. These places of worship are adorned with symbols, images, and representations of the deities, reflecting their attributes, mythology, and cultural context. They are meticulously designed to create a sense of awe, reverence, and transcendence, with architecture and decor that evoke a sacred ambiance.

Temples are typically constructed with careful attention to sacred geometry, alignment with celestial bodies, and the use of specific materials and colors associated with the deities. The layout of the temple may include different chambers or areas dedicated to different gods and goddesses, each with its own altar and sacred objects. Worshipers may offer prayers, make offerings, and perform rituals in front of these altars, seeking the direct presence and blessings of the deities they represent.

Shrines are smaller, more personal spaces within homes or other locations, where individuals or families create altars and dedicate them to specific deities. These private shrines serve as intimate spaces for personal devotion, reflection, and connection with the divine. They often include images or statues of the deity, along with offerings, candles, incense, and other sacred objects.

In addition to formal temples and shrines, polytheistic traditions may also consider certain natural sites as sacred, such as mountains, rivers, forests, or caves. These natural landscapes are seen as dwelling places or manifestations of the divine, offering a direct connection to the spiritual realm. Pilgrimages to these sacred sites are common, with worshippers undertaking journeys to seek spiritual rejuvenation, receive blessings, and deepen their connection to the deities and the natural world.

The rituals and practices performed in these sacred spaces vary across polytheistic traditions. They may include offerings of food, drink, flowers, incense, or precious objects, as well as prayers, chanting, singing of hymns, and ceremonial dances. The timing of worship and the frequency of rituals may also differ, with some traditions having daily or weekly practices, while others may emphasize specific festivals or seasonal celebrations.

Overall, sacred spaces and places of worship in polytheistic traditions serve as tangible embodiments of the divine presence and provide a sanctuary for spiritual connection, reflection, and communal worship. They are spaces where worshippers can transcend the mundane world and enter into a realm of sacred encounter, seeking guidance, solace, and a deeper understanding of themselves and the deities they revere.

Investigating the significance of temples, shrines, and natural landscapes in polytheistic worship

Temples, shrines, and natural landscapes hold profound significance in polytheistic worship, serving as physical and symbolic manifestations of the divine presence. These sacred spaces play a vital role in facilitating religious rituals, fostering a sense of community, and providing a tangible connection between worshippers and the deities they venerate.

Temples: Temples are dedicated structures specifically designed for worship and communal gatherings. They are often grand architectural marvels, meticulously constructed with intricate details and sacred symbolism. Temples serve as the abode of the deities, providing a dedicated space where worshippers can offer prayers, make offerings, and participate in rituals. The layout of the temple may reflect the cosmology of the belief system, with different chambers or areas dedicated to specific gods or goddesses. Temples act as centers of religious life, hosting festivals, ceremonies, and other important religious events that bring the community together.

Shrines: Shrines are smaller, more intimate spaces that can be found in homes, gardens, or public places. They are personal altars or sacred niches dedicated to specific deities or ancestral spirits. Shrines provide a focal point for individual or familial devotion, allowing worshippers to establish a direct connection with the divine in their daily lives. They are adorned with images, statues, or symbols of the deities, along with offerings and other sacred objects. Shrines serve as a reminder of the presence of the divine and provide a space for personal contemplation, prayer, and meditation.

Natural Landscapes: In polytheistic traditions, certain natural landscapes are revered as sacred, believed to be inhabited by deities or imbued with divine energy. These natural sites can include mountains, rivers, forests, caves, or sacred groves. Worshippers may visit these sites as part of pilgrimage or spiritual retreat, seeking solace, inspiration, and a direct connection with the divine in the beauty and grandeur of nature. Natural landscapes are seen as places where the boundaries between the human and divine realms are blurred, offering an opportunity for worshippers to experience a profound sense of awe, reverence, and spiritual transformation.

The significance of temples, shrines, and natural landscapes in polytheistic worship lies in their ability to create a sacred space where the divine and human realms intersect. These spaces serve as meeting points between worshippers and the deities, providing a physical environment conducive to spiritual communion, ritual practices, and the expression of devotion. They symbolize the sacred geography of the belief system and provide a tangible focal point for religious activities. Moreover, these sacred spaces foster a sense of belonging and community among worshippers, providing a shared ground for collective religious experiences, celebrations, and rites of passage.

In summary, temples, shrines, and natural landscapes hold deep religious and cultural significance in polytheistic worship. They serve as physical manifestations of the divine, facilitating rituals, fostering community, and providing worshippers with tangible connections to the deities they revere. These sacred spaces are revered as places of encounter, transformation, and spiritual nourishment, where the human and divine realms intersect in a profound and meaningful way.

Deity	Type	Still Used Today?
Amaterasu	Shrine	Yes
Zeus	Temple	No
Mount Olympus	Natural Landscape	Yes
Hathor	Temple	No
Stonehenge	Natural Landscape	Yes
Quetzalcoatl	Temple	No
Delphi	Temple	No
Ganges River	Natural Landscape	Yes
Lakshmi	Shrine	Yes
Mecca	Shrine	Yes

Note: The information provided in the graph is a general representation and may vary in specific cultural or historical contexts.

Examining pilgrimage traditions and the concept of sacred sites in polytheistic belief systems

Pilgrimage traditions and the concept of sacred sites hold significant importance in polytheistic belief systems. These traditions involve journeys to specific locations that are considered sacred or spiritually significant. Pilgrimages are undertaken by devotees seeking a deeper connection with the divine, spiritual purification, or the fulfillment of vows and prayers.

Sacred sites in polytheistic religions can take various forms, including temples, shrines, natural landscapes, mountains, rivers, or specific geographical locations. These sites are believed to possess a unique spiritual energy or presence of the deity or deities associated with them. They serve as focal points for worship, devotion, and communal gatherings, drawing believers from far and wide to experience the divine in a tangible and transformative way.

Pilgrimage routes and rituals associated with sacred sites are often steeped in tradition and symbolism. The journey itself is considered sacred and is seen as an opportunity for personal growth, self-discovery, and spiritual transformation.

Divine Perspectives

Pilgrims may undertake arduous physical or mental challenges, engage in prayer, meditation, or chanting, and participate in rituals and ceremonies specific to the sacred site they visit.

The act of pilgrimage fosters a sense of community and unity among the participants, as they embark on a shared spiritual quest. It strengthens the bonds between individuals, communities, and the divine, reinforcing the collective identity and devotion to the polytheistic tradition. Pilgrimage sites may also serve as centers of cultural and artistic expression, with architectural marvels, sculptures, and artworks depicting the myths and legends associated with the deities.

In some polytheistic traditions, certain pilgrimage sites continue to be actively visited and maintained, attracting pilgrims from around the world. These sites become hubs of religious activity, hosting festivals, rituals, and other religious gatherings throughout the year. The devotion and reverence displayed by pilgrims contribute to the vibrancy and continuity of the polytheistic belief system.

Overall, pilgrimage traditions and the concept of sacred sites in polytheistic belief systems provide a tangible and transformative way for believers to connect with the divine, deepen their spiritual practice, and experience the power and presence of the deities in the physical world. They serve as reminders of the rich cultural, historical, and spiritual heritage of polytheistic traditions and continue to inspire and guide generations of worshippers.

acred Site	Pilgrimage Rituals
Mount Olympus (Greece)	Hike to the summit of the mountain, believed to be the dwelling place of the gods. Offer prayers and offerings to various deities at their respective

sacred sites along the trail.

Angkor Wat (Cambodia)	Walk around the temple complex, exploring its intricate carvings and sacred spaces. Offer incense, flowers, and food to the deities depicted

in the temple.

Mount Sinai (Egypt)	Climb the mountain to reach the summit where Moses is believed to have received the Ten Commandments.

Exploring the Contrasts and Convergence of Polytheism and Monotheism

Engage in prayer, meditation, and reflection.

Chichen Itza (Mexico)	Visit the ancient Mayan city and the Temple of Kukulkan. Participate in ceremonies and rituals during the equinoxes to witness the shadow play

that creates the illusion of a descending serpent.

Uluru (Ayers Rock) (Australia)	Walk around the massive rock formation, acknowledging its sacredness. Observe traditional ceremonies performed by the Anangu people, the

traditional custodians of the land.

Machu Picchu (Peru)	Trek along the Inca Trail to reach the ancient citadel. Offer prayers and gratitude to the

mountain spirits and the Sun God.

Sacred Site	Pilgrimage Rituals
Stonehenge (United Kingdom)	Attend summer and winter solstice celebrations at Stonehenge, aligning with the sun's position.

Participate in druidic rituals and ceremonies.

Varanasi (India)	Take a sacred bath in the Ganges River to cleanse oneself of sins. Offer prayers and perform rituals along the riverbank. Visit important temples and

attend evening Aarti ceremonies.

Delphi (Greece)	Visit the Temple of Apollo, the oracle of Delphi. Seek guidance from the oracle and participate in

Divine Perspectives

rituals honoring Apollo.

Sedona (United States)	Explore the energy vortexes and red rock formations in Sedona. Engage in meditation, healing ceremonies

and connect with the spiritual energy of the place.

Mount Kailash (Tibet)	Circumambulate Mount Kailash in Tibet, considered sacred by Hindus, Buddhists, and Jains. This challenging pilgrimage is believed to cleanse

one's sins and grant spiritual enlightenment.

Mecca (Saudi Arabia)	Muslims perform the Hajj pilgrimage to Mecca following specific rituals, including the Tawaf,

Sai, and standing on the plains of Arafat.

Sacred Site	Pilgrimage Rituals
Jerusalem (Israel)	Visit the Western Wall (Wailing Wall) and offer prayers. Walk along the Via Dolorosa, following the footsteps of Jesus. Enter the Church of the Holy Sepulchre, the site of Jesus' crucifixion and

resurrection.

Amritsar (India)	Visit the Golden Temple (Harmandir Sahib) in Amritsar, the holiest shrine of Sikhism. Take part in the langar (community kitchen) where all are welcome to share a meal regardless of caste or

creed.

Mount Olympus (Greece)	Trek to the summit of Mount Olympus in Greece, considered the home of the gods in Greek mythology.

Exploring the Contrasts and Convergence of Polytheism and Monotheism

resurrection.

Pay homage to Zeus, the king of the gods, and

other Olympian deities.

Sacred Site	Pilgrimage Rituals
Chichen Itza (Mexico)	Visit the ancient Mayan city of Chichen Itza in Mexico. Attend the spring and autumn equinoxes to witness the serpent-shaped shadow descending the

steps of the El Castillo pyramid.

Uluru (Ayers Rock) (Australia)	Journey to Uluru in Australia, a sacred site for Aboriginal Australians. Participate in ceremonies,

storytelling, and walks led by Indigenous guides.

Eleusis (Greece)	Take part in the Eleusinian Mysteries, ancient initiation rites in Greece honoring Demeter and

Persephone. The exact rituals remain a mystery.

Sacred Site	Pilgrimage Rituals
Varanasi (India)	Bathe in the sacred Ganges River, perform rituals at the ghats (steps leading to the river), and

participate in evening aarti (prayer ceremony).

Delphi (Greece)	Visit the ancient site of Delphi in Greece and consult the Oracle of Delphi for prophetic advice.

Take part in rituals dedicated to Apollo and Zeus.

Stonehenge (United Kingdom)	Witness the summer solstice sunrise at Stonehenge in England. Join in druidic ceremonies and

celebrations honoring the solstice.

Mount Kailash (Tibet)	Undertake the Kailash Mansarovar Yatra, a pilgrimage in Tibet that circumambulates Mount Kailash, a sacred mountain in Hindu, Buddhist,

and Jain traditions.

Tikal (Guatemala)	Explore the ancient Mayan city of Tikal in Guatemala. Climb the pyramids, witness Mayan

rituals, and experience the mystical ambiance.

Mount Sinai (Egypt)	Ascend Mount Sinai in Egypt and reach the summit where Moses received the Ten Commandments.

Participate in prayers and reflections.

Mecca and Medina (Saudi Arabia)	Perform the Hajj pilgrimage to Mecca in Saudi Arabia, the holiest site in Islam. Visit the Kaaba and participate in the various rituals

associated with the Hajj.

Sacred Site	Pilgrimage Rituals
Santiago de Compostela (Spain)	Walk the Camino de Santiago, a famous pilgrimage route in Spain. Reach the Santiago de Compostela Cathedral and pay homage to the relics of Saint

James the Apostle.

Amritsar (India)	Visit the Golden Temple in Amritsar, India, and participate in the rituals of Sikhism, including the community kitchen (langar) and the washing

of the temple floors (seva).

Lourdes (France)	Make a pilgrimage to Lourdes in France, a site associated with the apparitions of the Virgin Mary. Attend Mass, bathe in the holy waters, and

participate in processions and prayers.

Uluru (Australia)	Journey to Uluru, also known as Ayers Rock, in Australia, a sacred site for the Indigenous Anangu people. Respect the spiritual significance

of the rock and learn about its cultural heritage.

Mount Olympus (Greece)	Hike to the summit of Mount Olympus in Greece, believed to be the dwelling place of the ancient Greek gods. Pay tribute to the gods and absorb

the majestic beauty of the mountain.

Mount Fuji (Japan)	Climb Mount Fuji in Japan, a sacred mountain revered in Shinto beliefs. Offer prayers at the shrines along the ascent and witness the sunrise

from the summit.

Angkor Wat (Cambodia)	Visit Angkor Wat in Cambodia, a magnificent temple complex dedicated to Hindu and Buddhist deities. Engage in meditation and contemplation

amidst the ancient ruins.

Sacred Site	Pilgrimage Rituals
Stonehenge (England)	Visit Stonehenge in England and participate in solstice and equinox celebrations, which include rituals, ceremonies, and gatherings to honor the

cycles of the sun and the changing seasons.

Bodh Gaya
(India)

Travel to Bodh Gaya in India, the site where Siddhartha Gautama, the Buddha, attained enlightenment. Meditate under the Bodhi tree and pay homage to the historical and spiritual

significance of the place.

Mecca
(Saudi Arabia)

Undertake the Hajj pilgrimage to Mecca, Saudi Arabia, as a Muslim. Perform the Tawaf, circling the Kaaba seven times, and participate in other prescribed rituals to demonstrate devotion and seek spiritual

purification.

Chichen Itza
(Mexico)

Journey to Chichen Itza in Mexico, a Mayan archaeological site. Observe the equinox phenomenon at the El Castillo pyramid, where shadows create a

visual effect resembling a serpent descending.

Delphi
(Greece)

Visit Delphi in Greece, an ancient sanctuary dedicated to the god Apollo. Consult the oracle at the Temple of Apollo and participate in rituals and

games held in honor of the god.

Rishikesh
(India)

Travel to Rishikesh in India, situated on the banks of the Ganges River. Engage in yoga, meditation, and participate in Ganga Aarti, a sacred ritual of offering prayers to the river, seeking blessings,

and witnessing the divine presence.

Machu Picchu

Trek to Machu Picchu in Peru, an ancient Incan

and witnessing the divine presence.

(Peru)

citadel. Connect with the spiritual energy of the site, participate in rituals, and pay homage to the

Please note these are not all of the pilgrimages as there are may others that transcend different religions and regions.

CHAPTER 11: RITUALS AND PRACTICES OF MONOTHEISM

Rituals and practices are integral components of religious traditions, providing a framework for believers to express their devotion, establish a connection with the divine, and cultivate a deeper spiritual understanding. In the context of monotheism, which centers around the belief in a single, all-encompassing God, rituals play a vital role in fostering a sense of reverence, worship, and communal identity.

This chapter delves into the rituals and practices observed within monotheistic traditions, exploring their significance, symbolism, and the ways in which they facilitate spiritual experiences for believers. From daily acts of worship to elaborate ceremonies and sacraments, the rituals of monotheism reflect the deep-rooted relationship between humans and the divine, guiding adherents in their quest for spiritual fulfillment and moral guidance.

Throughout this chapter, we will examine the diverse array of rituals and practices observed within monotheistic traditions, considering their historical, cultural, and theological contexts. We will explore the role of prayer, the observance of holy days and festivals, the significance of sacraments, and the function of sacred spaces and places of worship. Additionally, we will delve into the rituals associated with rites of passage, such as birth, marriage, and death, and how these rituals shape the religious and communal fabric of monotheistic communities.

By delving into the rituals and practices of monotheism, we seek to deepen our understanding of the rich tapestry of monotheistic religious expression and its transformative impact on the lives of believers. Through these rituals, believers engage in a sacred dialogue with the divine, fostering spiritual growth, communal cohesion, and a profound connection to their faith tradition.

Join us as we explore the multifaceted rituals and practices that form the heart and soul of monotheistic worship, illuminating the profound ways in which these rituals shape and sustain religious communities and provide a framework for believers to engage with the divine presence in their lives.

Key Rituals in Monotheistic Religions

Monotheistic religions, with their belief in a single, supreme deity, encompass a wide range of rituals and practices that serve to strengthen the bond between humans and the divine. These rituals form an integral part of religious observance, providing believers with opportunities for worship, spiritual connection, and the expression of devotion. While the specific rituals may vary across different monotheistic traditions, there are several key rituals that are commonly observed.

Prayer: Prayer is a fundamental practice in monotheistic religions, allowing believers to communicate with and seek guidance from the divine. Whether through individual or communal prayer, believers express their reverence, gratitude, and supplication to God. Prayer can take various forms, including recitation of sacred texts, spoken or silent contemplation, and physical gestures such as bowing or prostration.

Worship Services: Monotheistic religions often have structured worship services where believers gather in congregations to collectively worship and honor God. These services typically include elements such as hymns, readings from sacred texts, sermons or teachings, and communal prayers. They provide a space for communal reflection, inspiration, and the reaffirmation of faith.

Holy Days and Festivals: Monotheistic religions have designated holy days and festivals that commemorate important events in religious history or celebrate key aspects of faith. These occasions may include the commemoration of significant prophets or religious figures, the observation of historical events, or the celebration of divine attributes. Holy days and festivals often involve special rituals, such as fasting, feasting, specific prayers, or acts of charity.

Sacraments and Rituals of Initiation: Monotheistic religions often have sacraments or rituals of initiation that mark important milestones in the religious journey of individuals. Examples include baptism or christening, which symbolize spiritual rebirth and initiation into the faith, and confirmation, which signifies a deeper commitment to the religious community. These rituals often involve the use of water, anointing with oil, and the recitation of specific prayers or blessings.

Rites of Passage: Monotheistic religions also have rituals associated with significant life events, such as birth, marriage, and death. These rituals vary across different traditions but often involve prayers, blessings, and the involvement of religious leaders. They serve to invoke divine blessings, offer support and guidance during important life transitions, and provide a framework for understanding the sacred dimensions of these moments.

Pilgrimage: Pilgrimage is an important practice in monotheistic religions, where believers undertake a journey to a sacred site or shrine. The act of pilgrimage is seen as a means of deepening one's spiritual connection, seeking divine blessings, and engaging in acts of devotion. Pilgrimage sites may be associated with historical events, the lives of prophets or religious figures, or sites believed to be imbued with special spiritual power.

These key rituals in monotheistic religions provide believers with a means to engage in meaningful spiritual experiences, cultivate a sense of community, and foster a deeper connection with the divine. They offer opportunities for individuals to express their faith, seek spiritual guidance, and align their lives with the teachings and principles of their religious tradition. Through these rituals, believers find solace, inspiration, and a sense of purpose in their relationship with the one true God.

The central rituals and practices in monotheistic traditions

The central rituals and practices in monotheistic traditions revolve around worship, devotion, and spiritual connection with the one supreme deity. These rituals serve as vehicles for expressing faith, seeking divine guidance, and fostering a deeper relationship with God. While the specific rituals may vary among different monotheistic religions, there are some common elements that can be found across these traditions.

Prayer: Prayer is a foundational practice in monotheistic religions. It is a means for believers to communicate directly with God, expressing their thoughts, feelings, gratitude, and supplications. Prayers can be offered individually or in congregational settings, and they may be recited aloud or performed silently. Prayer serves as a way to seek solace, guidance, and a sense of connection with the divine.

Worship Services: Monotheistic religions often have structured worship services where believers come together to collectively express their devotion and reverence for God. These services typically include elements such as communal prayers, readings from sacred texts, hymns or chants, and sermons or teachings by religious leaders. Worship services provide a space for communal reflection, spiritual upliftment, and the reaffirmation of faith.

Sacred Scriptures: Monotheistic religions have sacred scriptures that serve as a guide for religious beliefs, moral principles, and spiritual practices. These scriptures, such as the Bible in Christianity, the Quran in Islam, and the Torah in Judaism, are revered as the word of God and hold central importance in the religious lives of believers. The study, recitation, and contemplation of these scriptures are integral to monotheistic rituals and practices.

Rituals of Initiation: Monotheistic religions often have rituals of initiation that mark the entry of individuals into the faith community. These rituals, such as baptism, circumcision, or confirmation, signify a formal acceptance of the religion's teachings and values. They may involve symbolic acts, blessings, prayers, and the involvement of religious leaders. Initiation rituals serve as a way to publicly express commitment to the faith and become a part of the religious community.

Commemorative Observances: Monotheistic traditions have special days or occasions that commemorate significant events in religious history or celebrate key aspects of faith. Examples include Christmas and Easter in Christianity, Eid al-Fitr and Eid al-Adha in Islam, and Passover and Yom Kippur in Judaism. These observances often involve specific rituals, such as fasting, feasting, prayers, or acts of charity, and provide an opportunity for believers to reflect on the core principles and teachings of their religion.

Personal and Family Devotions: In addition to communal rituals, monotheistic religions emphasize personal and family devotions. These practices involve individuals engaging in private prayers, meditation, reading of sacred texts, and acts of service. Personal and family devotions allow for a more intimate connection with God, fostering a sense of spirituality and deepening one's understanding of the religious teachings.

The central rituals and practices in monotheistic traditions are designed to cultivate a sense of reverence, foster spiritual growth, and promote a deep relationship with the one supreme deity. Through these rituals, believers express their faith, seek divine guidance, and strive to align their lives with the teachings and commandments of their religious tradition. They provide a framework for individuals to engage in acts of worship, devotion, and spiritual reflection, ultimately nurturing a sense of purpose, meaning, and connection with the divine.

Exploring the role of prayer, worship, and sacraments in monotheistic worship

Prayer, worship, and sacraments play significant roles in monotheistic worship, serving as key means of connecting with the divine and expressing devotion to the one supreme deity. Each of these practices holds its own unique significance and contributes to the spiritual life of believers in monotheistic traditions.

Prayer: Prayer is a fundamental practice in monotheistic worship, serving as a direct line of communication between individuals and God. Through prayer, believers express their thoughts, emotions, gratitude, and supplications to the divine. It is a means of seeking solace, guidance, and a deeper connection with God. Prayer can take various forms, including personal prayers offered in solitude, communal prayers in congregational settings, and formalized prayers with prescribed texts. It is seen as an act of submission, humility, and acknowledgment of God's presence and authority.

Worship: Worship in monotheistic traditions encompasses a wide range of practices aimed at honoring and glorifying God. It often includes acts of reverence, adoration, and praise. Worship services provide a structured and communal setting for believers to come together to express their devotion and reverence for God. These services may involve recitation of sacred texts, communal prayers, hymns or chants, sermons or teachings, and the performance of rituals or sacraments. Worship is seen as an act of acknowledging God's greatness, offering gratitude, and seeking spiritual connection and transformation.

Sacraments: Sacraments, also known as ordinances or rituals, are sacred practices that hold deep religious significance in monotheistic traditions. They are considered tangible means of receiving and conveying divine grace or blessings. The specific sacraments and their rituals vary among different monotheistic religions. For example, in Christianity, sacraments such as baptism, the Eucharist (or Holy

Communion), and confirmation are regarded as essential acts of faith and are believed to bestow spiritual blessings and signify one's relationship with God. In Islam, practices like prayer (salat), fasting (sawm), pilgrimage (hajj), and giving alms (zakat) are considered as acts of worship and devotion that draw believers closer to God. Sacraments are often administered by religious leaders and are seen as transformative experiences that deepen spiritual connections and affirm one's faith.

These practices of prayer, worship, and sacraments in monotheistic worship serve multiple purposes. They foster a sense of awe, reverence, and humility before the divine. They provide a means of expressing gratitude, seeking guidance, and finding solace in times of need. They also serve as acts of obedience and devotion, aligning believers with the teachings and commandments of their respective religious traditions. Moreover, these practices create a communal bond among believers, fostering a shared spiritual experience and a sense of unity in worship.

Through prayer, worship, and sacraments, believers in monotheistic traditions strive to deepen their spiritual connection with the one supreme deity. These practices offer avenues for personal transformation, spiritual growth, and the cultivation of a profound sense of faith, meaning, and purpose. They are considered sacred acts that bridge the gap between the human and the divine, allowing individuals to engage in a direct and intimate relationship with God.

Sacred Texts and Liturgical Practices in Monotheism

Sacred texts and liturgical practices hold immense significance in monotheistic traditions, serving as foundational sources of religious teachings, guidance, and rituals. These texts and practices play a central role in shaping the beliefs, values, and practices of believers, and they provide a framework for worship and spiritual engagement.

Sacred Texts: Monotheistic religions have sacred texts that are considered divinely inspired or revealed, containing the teachings, narratives, and laws that guide believers' lives. These texts are revered as the word of God and serve as authoritative sources of religious knowledge and moral guidance. Examples of sacred texts in monotheistic traditions include the Bible in Christianity, the Quran in Islam, and the Torah in Judaism. These texts are studied, interpreted, and revered as the embodiment of divine wisdom and guidance, offering insights into the nature of God, moral principles, and the path to salvation or enlightenment. They often contain narratives of creation, historical accounts, ethical teachings, and spiritual guidance, and they provide a foundation for understanding the nature of the divine-human relationship.

Exploring the Contrasts and Convergence of Polytheism and Monotheism

Liturgical Practices: Liturgical practices refer to the prescribed rituals, ceremonies, and worship services that are performed in monotheistic traditions. These practices are often based on the teachings and guidelines found in sacred texts and are intended to create a structured and meaningful worship experience. Liturgical practices may include prayers, hymns, readings from sacred texts, sermons or teachings by religious leaders, rituals for sacraments or ordinances, and observances of holy days or festivals. These practices are designed to engage believers in acts of devotion, reverence, and communal worship. They provide a structured framework for expressing faith, cultivating a sense of spirituality, and fostering a deeper connection with the divine.

The study and interpretation of sacred texts, along with the observance of liturgical practices, are central to the religious lives of monotheistic believers. Sacred texts are often studied individually or in group settings, and their teachings are explored and discussed to gain deeper understanding and application in daily life. Liturgical practices are performed in both personal and communal settings, providing opportunities for believers to engage in acts of worship, express their faith, and reaffirm their commitment to the divine.

The relationship between sacred texts and liturgical practices is intertwined. Sacred texts serve as a foundation for liturgical practices, guiding believers in the proper ways to worship, offer prayers, and engage in religious rituals. Liturgical practices, in turn, help believers to internalize the teachings and messages of sacred texts, bringing them to life through meaningful acts of devotion and worship.

Overall, sacred texts and liturgical practices hold a significant place in monotheistic traditions, serving as sources of spiritual guidance, moral teachings, and rituals of worship. They provide a framework for believers to deepen their understanding of the divine, strengthen their faith, and actively engage in a relationship with the one supreme deity.

Type of Sacred Text	Religion	First Known Date of Writing	Region
Bible	Christianity	13th - 2nd century BCE	Ancient Near East, primarily Israel
Quran	Islam	7th century CE	Arabian Peninsula, primarily Mecca and Medina
Torah	Judaism	5th - 4th century BCE	Ancient Near East, primarily Israel
Vedas	Hinduism	2nd millennium BCE	Indian subcontinent,

Type of Sacred Text	Religion	First Known Date of Writing	Region
			primarily India
Tripitaka	Buddhism	1st century BCE - 3rd century CE	Indian subcontinent, primarily India
Guru Granth Sahib	Sikhism	16th - 17th century CE	Indian subcontinent, primarily Punjab region
Avesta	Zoroastrianism	6th - 4th century BCE	Ancient Persia, primarily present-day Iran
Tao Te Ching	Taoism	4th century BCE	Ancient China
Book of Mormon	Mormonism	19th century CE	United States

Please note that the dates provided are approximate and represent the earliest known written records associated with these texts. The actual origins and oral traditions of these religious texts may predate their written forms.

Examining the significance of sacred texts and their role in monotheistic rituals

Sacred texts hold great significance in monotheistic traditions, serving as authoritative sources of religious teachings, guidance, and inspiration. These texts are considered sacred and are revered as the word of God or as divinely inspired revelations. They play a central role in shaping the beliefs, practices, and rituals of monotheistic worship.

One of the primary functions of sacred texts is to convey the religious doctrines, moral teachings, and ethical principles of monotheistic faiths. They provide a framework for understanding the nature of God, the purpose of human existence, and the guidelines for leading a virtuous life. Sacred texts often contain narratives, parables, commandments, and ethical teachings that serve as a moral compass for adherents.

In monotheistic rituals, sacred texts are frequently recited, chanted, or read aloud as part of worship services or personal devotions. These readings are often accompanied by specific liturgical practices, such as the use of specific prayers, hymns, or rituals that highlight the significance of the text being read. The act of reading or listening to the sacred text is seen as a means of connecting with the divine and seeking spiritual guidance.

Sacred texts also serve as a source of spiritual inspiration and comfort. They offer believers a source of solace, wisdom, and hope during times of challenge or personal reflection. The stories, teachings, and poetry within these texts can provide guidance for navigating life's complexities, offering insights into the nature of God, the human condition, and the pursuit of spiritual growth.

Furthermore, sacred texts often form the foundation for religious scholarship and theological inquiry. They serve as the basis for religious study, interpretation, and the development of religious doctrines and traditions. Scholars, clergy, and devotees engage in deep analysis and interpretation of these texts to understand their meaning and relevance in contemporary contexts.

The significance of sacred texts in monotheistic rituals extends beyond their textual content. They are considered vessels of divine presence and are treated with reverence and respect. Rituals associated with sacred texts may involve rituals of purification, elaborate displays or processions, and specific rules and customs for handling and preserving the texts.

Overall, sacred texts hold a central and revered place in monotheistic rituals. They are considered repositories of divine wisdom, guides for moral and ethical living, sources of spiritual inspiration, and foundations for religious practice and understanding. The rituals and practices associated with these texts reflect the deep reverence and belief in their divine origin and importance in monotheistic worship.

The liturgical practices and the importance of scripture readings, hymns, and sermons

Liturgical practices in monotheistic traditions encompass a range of rituals and activities that are performed as part of formal worship services or religious gatherings. These practices often revolve around the importance of scripture readings, hymns, and sermons, which hold significant roles in the worship experience.

Scripture readings are a fundamental element of liturgical practices in monotheistic worship. Selected passages from the sacred texts are read aloud, often by clergy or designated individuals, and listened to attentively by the congregation. The readings serve multiple purposes, including conveying religious teachings, sharing stories of faith, and providing spiritual guidance. They offer a direct connection to the divine revelations contained within the sacred texts and invite believers to reflect on their significance in their personal lives.

Hymns play a vital role in enhancing the worship experience in monotheistic traditions. These songs of praise, adoration, and thanksgiving are often sung collectively by the congregation. Hymns serve as a form of worship, allowing individuals to express their devotion, gratitude, and reverence towards the divine. They create a sense of unity and shared spirituality within the worship community, fostering a collective experience of transcendence and spiritual upliftment.

Sermons, or religious speeches delivered by clergy or spiritual leaders, are another significant aspect of liturgical practices. During sermons, preachers interpret and explain the teachings found in the sacred texts, offering insights, reflections, and practical applications for everyday life. Sermons serve as a means of educating, inspiring, and motivating the worship community. They provide guidance on moral and ethical issues, encourage spiritual growth, and address the religious needs and concerns of the congregation.

The importance of scripture readings, hymns, and sermons lies in their ability to deepen the worship experience and facilitate a deeper connection with the divine. Scripture readings bring the sacred texts to life, allowing believers to engage directly with the wisdom and teachings contained within them. Hymns provide a means of emotional expression and communal worship, fostering a sense of joy, awe, and spiritual upliftment. Sermons offer an opportunity for spiritual guidance, intellectual stimulation, and reflection on the religious teachings and their relevance to everyday life.

These liturgical practices not only serve as a means of communication with the divine but also contribute to the formation of religious identity, communal bonding, and spiritual growth. They create a sacred space where individuals can connect with their faith, deepen their understanding of religious teachings, and find solace, inspiration, and guidance.

In summary, liturgical practices in monotheistic traditions emphasize the importance of scripture readings, hymns, and sermons as integral elements of worship. These practices enhance the worship experience, provide spiritual nourishment, and foster a sense of communal devotion, allowing believers to engage with their faith, deepen their understanding, and cultivate a personal connection with the divine.

Observances and Festivals in Monotheism

Observances and festivals hold a significant place in monotheistic religions, providing opportunities for believers to commemorate important religious events, express their faith, and strengthen their spiritual connection with the divine. These occasions are marked by rituals, prayers, communal gatherings, and various forms of celebration.

Observances in monotheistic traditions include regular practices that are integral to the religious life of believers. For example, in Islam, Muslims observe the five daily prayers, which are performed at specific times throughout the day as a way to maintain a continuous connection with God. Similarly, in Judaism, the observance of Shabbat, a day of rest and spiritual reflection, is of utmost importance. Christians may engage in observances such as weekly worship services, participation in the Eucharist, and the observance of religious seasons such as Advent and Lent.

Festivals, on the other hand, are joyous occasions that commemorate significant events in religious history or celebrate important religious concepts. These festivals often involve a combination of rituals, prayers, communal gatherings, feasting, and acts of charity. They serve as a time for believers to reflect on their faith, renew their commitment to religious principles, and come together as a community.

In Islam, the festival of Eid al-Fitr marks the end of Ramadan, the month of fasting. It is a time of celebration, gratitude, and charitable giving. The Hajj pilgrimage, which is one of the Five Pillars of Islam, is another significant festival that brings Muslims from around the world together to perform religious rites in Mecca.

In Christianity, Christmas commemorates the birth of Jesus Christ, and Easter celebrates his resurrection. These festivals are marked by special church services, rituals, and celebrations that vary across different Christian denominations and cultural contexts.

In Judaism, Passover (Pesach) commemorates the liberation of the Israelites from slavery in Egypt. It is a time for family gatherings, the retelling of the Exodus story, and the observance of specific rituals and dietary practices.

These observances and festivals not only serve as occasions for religious expression but also play a crucial role in strengthening communal bonds, fostering a sense of identity, and passing down religious traditions from one generation to the next. They provide opportunities for believers to deepen their understanding of their faith, engage in acts of devotion, and experience a collective sense of belonging and shared spirituality.

In summary, observances and festivals in monotheistic religions are important markers in the religious calendar, providing occasions for believers to engage in rituals, prayers, and communal gatherings. These observances and festivals serve as a means of expressing faith, deepening spiritual connections, and fostering a sense of community and religious identity.

Observances and Festivals	Religion	Time of Year	Additional Information
Ramadan	Islam	Month of Ramadan (lunar calendar)	A month of fasting and spiritual reflection
Eid al-Fitr	Islam	After Ramadan	Celebration marking the end of Ramadan
Hajj	Islam	Dhu al-Hijjah (Islamic month)	Pilgrimage to Mecca
Shabbat	Judaism	Every Friday at sundown to Saturday at sundown	A day of rest and spiritual reflection
Passover (Pesach)	Judaism	Spring	Commemorates the liberation of the Israelites from slavery in Egypt
Yom Kippur	Judaism	Tishrei (Jewish month)	Day of Atonement and fasting
Rosh Hashanah	Judaism	Tishrei (Jewish month)	Jewish New Year
Christmas	Christianity	December 25	Commemorates the birth of Jesus Christ
Faster	Christianity	Spring	Commemorates the resurrection of Jesus Christ
Good Friday	Christianity	Friday before Easter Sunday	Commemorates the crucifixion of Jesus Christ
Lent	Christianity	40 days leading up to Easter	A period of reflection, fasting, and repentance
Advent	Christianity	Four Sundays before Christmas	Preparation for the birth of Jesus Christ

Please note that the specific dates of some festivals may vary depending on the lunar or Hebrew calendar. Additionally, there are many more observances and festivals within each religion, and the information provided here is a brief overview.

Investigating major monotheistic observances and their religious and cultural significance

Ramadan (Islam): Ramadan is the holiest month for Muslims. It involves fasting from dawn to sunset as a means of self-discipline, spiritual reflection, and increased devotion. Muslims abstain from food, drink, smoking, and other physical needs during daylight hours. The observance of Ramadan commemorates the revelation of the Quran to the Prophet Muhammad and emphasizes the values of compassion, self-control, and gratitude.

Exploring the Contrasts and Convergence of Polytheism and Monotheism

Eid al-Fitr (Islam): Eid al-Fitr is a joyous celebration that marks the end of Ramadan. It is a time of feasting, charitable acts, and communal prayers. Muslims gather for special prayers, exchange gifts, and visit family and friends. The festival serves as a time of unity, gratitude, and celebration of the spiritual growth achieved during Ramadan.

Hajj (Islam): Hajj is an annual pilgrimage to Mecca in Saudi Arabia and is one of the Five Pillars of Islam. It is a significant event for Muslims, symbolizing unity and equality before God. Millions of Muslims from around the world come together to perform a series of rituals over several days, including circling the Kaaba, walking between the hills of Safa and Marwa, and standing on the plains of Arafat. Hajj provides a profound spiritual experience and fosters a sense of communal devotion and connection.

Shabbat (Judaism): Shabbat is the Jewish day of rest and is observed from Friday evening to Saturday evening. It is a time to cease work and engage in prayer, family gatherings, and festive meals. Shabbat commemorates the seventh day of creation when God rested, and it is considered a gift from God to be enjoyed and celebrated. The observance of Shabbat provides a dedicated time for spiritual reflection, renewal, and connection with family and community.

Passover (Pesach) (Judaism): Passover is an eight-day festival that commemorates the liberation of the Israelites from slavery in Egypt as described in the Book of Exodus. The festival includes special meals (Seder) where the story of the Exodus is retold, the consumption of unleavened bread (matzah), and the prohibition of leavened products. Passover is a time of remembrance, gratitude, and the celebration of freedom and deliverance.

Christmas (Christianity): Christmas is a major Christian festival that celebrates the birth of Jesus Christ. It is observed on December 25th by many Christian denominations. Christmas includes various traditions such as attending church services, exchanging gifts, decorating trees, and sharing meals with family and friends. The festival is a time to commemorate the coming of Jesus into the world and to reflect on themes of hope, peace, and love.

Easter (Christianity): Easter is the most important festival in Christianity. It commemorates the resurrection of Jesus Christ from the dead, as described in the New Testament. The observance includes a period of preparation called Lent, which is marked by fasting, repentance, and spiritual reflection. Easter Sunday is a joyous celebration with church services, feasts, and the sharing of Easter eggs, symbolizing new life. Easter is a time of renewal, redemption, and the affirmation of faith in the resurrection.

These observances hold great religious and cultural significance within their respective monotheistic traditions. They provide opportunities for spiritual growth, community bonding, and the expression of faith through rituals, prayers, and festive gatherings.

Observance	Religion	Time of Year	Additional Information
Ramadan	Islam	Lunar month	Month of fasting and increased devotion
Eid al-Fitr	Islam	End of Ramadan	Celebration marking the end of fasting
Hajj	Islam	Islamic month	Pilgrimage to Mecca, symbolizing unity and equality
Shabbat	Judaism	Weekly (Friday sunset to Saturday sunset)	Day of rest, prayer, and community connection
Passover (Pesach)	Judaism	Spring	Commemoration of the Exodus from Egypt
Christmas	Christianity	December 25th	Celebration of the birth of Jesus Christ
Easter	Christianity	Spring	Commemoration of the resurrection of Jesus Christ

Please note that specific dates for some observances may vary based on the lunar or Hebrew calendars.

Exploring the rituals and practices associated with monotheistic festivals and holy days

Ramadan (Islam):

Rituals: Observing daily fasting from dawn to sunset, reciting special prayers (Taraweeh), reading the entire Quran, engaging in acts of charity (Zakat), and seeking spiritual purification.

Practices: Muslims refrain from eating, drinking, smoking, and engaging in sexual activities during daylight hours. They also focus on self-reflection, increased prayer, recitation of the Quran, and strengthening their relationship with Allah.

Eid al-Fitr (Islam):

Rituals: Attending special congregational prayers, giving to charity (Zakat al-Fitr), visiting family and friends, exchanging gifts, and feasting on special meals.

Practices: Muslims start the day with communal prayers at the mosque or in open spaces. They wear new clothes, offer greetings of "Eid Mubarak," and share meals and festive treats with loved ones. It is a time of joy, gratitude, and unity within the Muslim community.

Hajj (Islam):

Rituals: Pilgrims perform a series of rituals at specific locations in Mecca and its surroundings, including circumambulation of the Kaaba, running between the hills of Safa and Marwa, standing at the plain of Arafat, and stoning symbolic pillars representing Satan.

Practices: Muslims from around the world converge on Mecca to participate in the Hajj pilgrimage. They follow specific rituals that commemorate the life of Prophet Ibrahim and his family, seek forgiveness, and purify their souls. The Hajj represents the unity and equality of all Muslims.

Shabbat (Judaism):

Rituals: Lighting candles to usher in Shabbat, reciting blessings, attending synagogue services, partaking in festive meals, engaging in study and discussion of Jewish texts, and refraining from work and electronic devices.

Practices: Starting at sunset on Friday until nightfall on Saturday, Jewish individuals and families come together to honor and observe the day of rest. They gather for prayers, share a festive meal (Shabbat dinner), sing traditional songs, and spend quality time with family and friends.

Passover (Pesach) (Judaism):

Rituals: Conducting a ceremonial meal called the Seder, retelling the story of the Exodus, consuming symbolic foods, reading from the Haggadah, refraining from eating leavened bread (chametz), and observing dietary restrictions.

Practices: Jews gather for the Seder, a special meal that follows a prescribed order of storytelling, blessings, and symbolic actions. They recount the liberation of the Israelites from slavery in Egypt and reflect on the themes of freedom, redemption, and gratitude. Throughout the holiday, they abstain from eating bread products and consume matzah (unleavened bread) instead.

Christmas (Christianity):

Rituals: Attending special church services, such as Midnight Mass, participating in nativity plays or pageants, exchanging gifts, decorating homes and churches with festive decorations, and feasting on special meals.

Practices: Christians celebrate the birth of Jesus Christ, believed to be the Son of God. They gather for worship services, sing carols, read biblical accounts of the nativity, and reflect on the significance of Jesus' birth as a symbol of hope and salvation. Families come together to share meals, exchange gifts, and extend goodwill to others.

Easter (Christianity):

Rituals: Participating in special church services, including the Vigil service, engaging in fasting and abstinence during Lent, observing the Stations of the Cross, decorating eggs, and engaging in acts of charity.

Practices: Easter commemorates the resurrection of Jesus Christ. Christians attend church services, which include the proclamation of the resurrection, hymns of joy, and the sharing of the Eucharist. They reflect on the themes of sacrifice, redemption, and renewal. The holiday also involves the joyful tradition of egg decoration and hunting, symbolizing new life.

These rituals and practices play a significant role in deepening religious observance, fostering a sense of community, and reinforcing the religious and cultural significance of these monotheistic festivals and holy days.

Festival/Holy Day	Religion	Time of Year	Rituals	Practices
Ramadan	Islam	Lunar month	Fasting, Taraweeh prayers, Quran reading, charity (Zakat)	Daily fasting, self-reflection, increased prayer, recitation of Quran, acts of charity
Eid al-Fitr	Islam	Lunar month	Congregational prayers, charity (Zakat al-Fitr), visiting, feasting	Prayers, greetings, visiting family/friends, exchanging gifts, festive meals
Hajj	Islam	Dhu al-	Circumambulation,	Pilgrimage to Mecca,

Festival/Holy Day	Religion	Time of Year	Rituals	Practices
		Hijjah	running between hills, standing at Arafat	following prescribed rituals, seeking forgiveness, unity of Muslim community
Shabbat	Judaism	Weekly	Lighting candles, synagogue attendance, festive meals, rest	Prayers, blessings, family time, study, refraining from work and electronic devices
Passover (Pesach)	Judaism	Nissan	Seder meal, retelling Exodus story, dietary restrictions	Seder meal, storytelling, reflection on freedom and gratitude, abstaining from leavened bread
Christmas	Christianity	December	Church services, nativity plays, gift exchange, festive meals	Worship, carols, nativity reflection, family time, gift-giving
Easter	Christianity	Spring	Church services, fasting, Stations of the Cross, egg decoration	Church services, celebration of resurrection, reflection on sacrifice and renewal, egg decoration

Note: The exact timing of some festivals may vary based on the lunar or Hebrew calendar.

This graph provides a summary of the major monotheistic observances, their respective religions, the time of year they are celebrated, the rituals associated with each festival, and the corresponding practices observed by individuals and communities.

The importance of communal worship, congregational prayer, and religious gatherings in monotheism

Community and communal practices play a significant role in monotheistic traditions, fostering a sense of belonging, unity, and shared worship among believers. These practices vary among different monotheistic religions, but they often serve to strengthen the bonds within the community and deepen the collective experience of faith.

Congregational Prayer: In many monotheistic religions, congregational prayer is a central communal practice. Believers gather in designated places of worship, such as mosques, synagogues, or churches, to engage in collective prayer. This shared act of worship not only fosters a sense of unity but also allows individuals to draw strength and support from the community.

Religious Gatherings and Celebrations: Monotheistic traditions often have specific gatherings and celebrations that bring the community together. These can include religious holidays, festivals, or special occasions that are marked by communal rituals, prayers, and festivities. Examples include Eid al-Fitr and Eid al-Adha in Islam, Passover and Hanukkah in Judaism, and Christmas and Easter in Christianity.

Community Service and Charity: Many monotheistic traditions emphasize the importance of serving others and practicing charity. Community service initiatives, such as volunteering at soup kitchens, organizing food drives, or engaging in humanitarian projects, are common expressions of communal practices. These acts of service not only benefit those in need but also strengthen the bonds within the community through shared acts of compassion and giving.

Religious Education and Study Groups: Monotheistic traditions often encourage the pursuit of religious education and the study of sacred texts. Community members may come together in study groups, religious classes, or Sunday schools to deepen their knowledge of their faith and engage in discussions about religious teachings and practices. This shared learning experience fosters intellectual growth and provides an opportunity for individuals to connect and learn from one another.

Support Networks and Fellowship: Monotheistic communities often provide support networks and fellowship opportunities for their members. This can include mentorship programs, support groups, or social gatherings where individuals can find guidance, solace, and companionship. These communal practices create a sense of belonging and provide a space for individuals to share their joys, sorrows, and spiritual journeys.

Religious Leadership and Guidance: Monotheistic traditions have religious leaders, such as priests, imams, rabbis, or clergy, who provide spiritual guidance, lead communal rituals, and play a central role in the community. These leaders offer pastoral care, counsel individuals, and guide the community in matters of faith and practice.

Community and communal practices in monotheistic traditions contribute to the development of a shared identity, a sense of mutual support, and a deepening of religious commitment. They provide believers with a space to connect with one another, engage in collective worship, serve others, and grow spiritually within the context of a supportive and nurturing community.

Exploring the role of clergy and religious leaders in guiding and facilitating monotheistic practices

The role of clergy and religious leaders is pivotal in guiding and facilitating monotheistic practices within their respective communities. They are entrusted with the responsibility of providing spiritual guidance, leading religious rituals, interpreting sacred texts, and serving as moral exemplars. Here are some key aspects of their role:

Spiritual Leadership: Clergy and religious leaders serve as spiritual guides for their community members, offering wisdom, advice, and support in matters of faith and spirituality. They provide insights into religious teachings, help individuals deepen their understanding of religious principles, and offer guidance on how to navigate moral and ethical dilemmas.

Ritual Facilitation: Clergy and religious leaders are responsible for leading and facilitating religious rituals and ceremonies. They play a central role in conducting worship services, administering sacraments, and leading congregational prayers. Their presence and active participation in these rituals help create a sense of reverence, unity, and order within the community.

Teaching and Education: Religious leaders often engage in teaching and educational activities to foster religious knowledge and understanding within their community. They may deliver sermons, give lectures, lead study groups, or provide religious instruction to children and adults. Their role is to educate and inspire individuals to live in accordance with the teachings of their faith.

Pastoral Care: Clergy and religious leaders offer pastoral care and support to community members during times of joy, sorrow, and crisis. They provide counseling, comfort, and guidance to individuals and families, helping them navigate life's challenges, spiritual growth, and personal development. They are often seen as trusted confidants and sources of moral and emotional support.

Interfaith Dialogue and Outreach: Religious leaders may engage in interfaith dialogue and outreach efforts to promote understanding, tolerance, and cooperation among different religious communities. They may participate in interfaith gatherings, dialogue sessions, and collaborative projects aimed at fostering harmony, respect, and cooperation between different religious groups.

Moral and Ethical Guidance: Clergy and religious leaders are responsible for articulating and upholding the moral and ethical principles of their faith. They provide ethical guidance to community members, helping them navigate ethical dilemmas and make decisions in accordance with religious teachings. Their role includes promoting compassion, justice, and social responsibility within the community and society at large.

Symbolic Representation: Clergy and religious leaders often serve as symbolic representations of the religious tradition they represent. Their attire, rituals, and presence convey the sacredness and authority associated with their role. They embody the values, teachings, and traditions of the faith community, providing a visible and tangible connection to the divine.

The role of clergy and religious leaders is vital in nurturing and sustaining monotheistic practices within their communities. They serve as spiritual guides, ritual facilitators, educators, counselors, and moral exemplars. Their presence and leadership create a sense of continuity, unity, and guidance, ensuring the preservation and transmission of religious traditions from one generation to another.

CHAPTER 12: BELIEFS AND TRADITIONS OF POLYTHEISM AND MONOTHEISM

In the vast tapestry of human religious expression, polytheism and monotheism stand as two prominent and contrasting belief systems. Polytheism embraces the belief in multiple deities, each with their distinct characteristics, powers, and domains, while monotheism revolves around the worship and devotion to a single, supreme deity. These two approaches to the divine have shaped the religious and cultural landscapes of civilizations throughout history and continue to influence the beliefs and practices of contemporary communities.

This chapter delves into the rich and diverse world of polytheism and monotheism, exploring their foundational principles, rituals, and traditions. Through an examination of various examples from Witchcraft, Divination, Herbalism, Shamanism, and Ecospirituality, we will uncover the multifaceted nature of these belief systems and their profound impact on human spirituality.

The chapter begins by delving into the core tenets and philosophical underpinnings of polytheism. We will explore how the belief in multiple deities allows for a nuanced understanding of the divine and the interconnectedness of various aspects of existence. Drawing from ancient mythologies and contemporary practices, we will unravel the ways in which polytheistic traditions honor and interact with their pantheon of gods and goddesses.

Moving on to monotheism, we will delve into the concept of a single, all-encompassing deity and its implications for religious belief and practice. We will examine the Abrahamic religions of Judaism, Christianity, and Islam, exploring their shared monotheistic foundation while acknowledging the unique interpretations and rituals within each tradition.

Throughout the chapter, we will highlight the rituals and practices that shape the worship and devotion in polytheistic and monotheistic traditions. From elaborate ceremonies and seasonal celebrations to personal rituals and acts of devotion, we will explore how these practices serve as pathways to the divine, facilitating spiritual connection, personal growth, and community cohesion.

In addition to examining the similarities and differences between polytheism and monotheism, we will also explore the ways in which these belief systems have evolved and adapted over time. We will delve into the influence of cultural, historical, and social factors on the development and transformation of religious practices, and how these changes have shaped contemporary expressions of polytheism and monotheism.

Throughout this chapter, we encourage critical thinking and reflection on the diverse array of beliefs and practices within polytheism and monotheism. By engaging with the examples, problems, and exercises provided, students will deepen their understanding of these belief systems and develop a nuanced appreciation for the complexities of human spirituality.

As we embark on this exploration of polytheism and monotheism, let us embrace an open mind and a spirit of inquiry. By delving into the beliefs and traditions of these systems, we can gain insights into the human quest for meaning, the diversity of religious expression, and the enduring power of the divine in our lives.

Core Beliefs of Polytheism

Polytheism is a religious worldview that embraces the belief in multiple deities or gods and goddesses. While the specific beliefs and practices may vary across different polytheistic traditions, there are several core beliefs that underpin this belief system.

Multiple Deities: Polytheism recognizes and reveres the existence of multiple gods and goddesses. These deities are often associated with specific domains, such as love, wisdom, fertility, war, or nature. Each deity possesses unique qualities, powers, and characteristics, and is often honored and worshipped through rituals, prayers, and offerings.

Immanence of the Divine: Polytheistic belief systems emphasize the immanence of the divine. Unlike some monotheistic traditions that view the divine as separate and transcendent, polytheism sees the gods and goddesses as active participants in the world, interacting with humans and influencing various aspects of life. This immanence fosters a sense of connection and relationship between humans and the divine.

Sacred Cosmology: Polytheistic belief systems often incorporate a sacred cosmology that provides a framework for understanding the universe and the relationship between the divine and the natural world. These cosmologies may include concepts such as sacred realms, divine hierarchies, and mythologies that explain the creation of the world and the interactions between gods, humans, and other beings.

Personal Relationships: Polytheism emphasizes personal relationships with deities. Individuals may develop personal connections and devotion to specific gods and goddesses based on their needs, interests, or spiritual inclinations. This personalized approach allows for a more intimate and individualized experience of the divine.

Ritual and Worship: Rituals and worship play a central role in polytheistic practices. These rituals serve as a means to honor and communicate with the gods and goddesses. Offerings, prayers, and sacred ceremonies are performed to establish a connection, seek guidance, express gratitude, or seek assistance from the divine.

Harmony with Nature: Many polytheistic belief systems recognize the interconnectedness of humans, gods, and the natural world. Nature is often seen as sacred and divine, and polytheistic traditions may incorporate ecological principles and practices that promote a harmonious relationship with the environment.

It is important to note that the above points provide a general overview of core beliefs in polytheism, and specific beliefs and practices can vary significantly between different polytheistic traditions. To provide a more comprehensive and detailed analysis, further research into specific polytheistic traditions, such as ancient Greek mythology, Norse paganism, or Hinduism, would be necessary.

I hope this brief overview gives you a starting point for developing a more detailed section on the core beliefs of polytheism in your desired academic writing style.

Examining the fundamental beliefs and concepts in polytheistic religions

Examining the fundamental beliefs and concepts in polytheistic religions provides valuable insights into the diverse and intricate worldviews embraced by these belief systems. While each polytheistic tradition is unique in its own right, there are several fundamental beliefs and concepts that are commonly found across many polytheistic religions.

Multiple Deities: Polytheistic religions revolve around the belief in and worship of multiple deities or gods and goddesses. These deities are often associated with specific aspects of life, such as love, war, wisdom, fertility, or natural phenomena. They possess distinct personalities, powers, and roles within the divine realm and are often revered as both powerful and fallible beings.

Cosmic Order and Interconnectedness: Polytheistic religions often emphasize the interconnectedness and harmony of the universe. They believe in a divine cosmic order that governs the interactions between gods, humans, and the natural world. This order is maintained through rituals, offerings, and adherence to ethical principles that ensure balance and harmony in the universe.

Mythology and Sacred Stories: Mythology plays a significant role in polytheistic religions, serving as a source of divine narratives and teachings. Myths explain the creation of the world, the origin of gods and humans, and the relationships and interactions between them. These sacred stories provide a framework for understanding the nature of the divine, human existence, and the moral and ethical principles guiding human behavior.

Personal Relationships with Deities: Polytheistic religions often emphasize the potential for personal relationships between individuals and deities. Followers may develop personal connections with specific deities, forging a bond through devotion, prayer, and offerings. These relationships can provide guidance, protection, and support, and are often nurtured through acts of worship and ritual practices.

Rituals and Offerings: Rituals and offerings are integral components of polytheistic religions. They serve as means of communication and interaction with the divine. Rituals can range from elaborate ceremonies performed in temples to simple acts of devotion and prayer conducted in personal spaces. Offerings, such as food, drink, incense, or precious objects, are made to the deities as expressions of gratitude, respect, and reverence.

Sacred Spaces and Temples: Polytheistic religions often designate specific spaces as sacred, where the divine presence is believed to be more accessible. Temples and shrines are constructed as physical embodiments of the sacred, serving as places of worship, ritual, and community gathering. These spaces are adorned with symbols, images, and representations of the deities, creating a focal point for spiritual connection and devotion.

Cyclical Time and Seasonal Festivals: Many polytheistic religions recognize the cyclical nature of time and celebrate seasonal festivals and rituals. These festivals mark important transitions, such as solstices, equinoxes, or harvest seasons, and are aimed at aligning human life with the rhythms of the natural world. They celebrate the cyclical processes of birth, death, and rebirth, reinforcing the connection between humans and the larger cosmic order.

Ethics and Virtues: Polytheistic religions often emphasize ethical principles and virtues that guide human behavior. These principles vary across different traditions but commonly include concepts such as justice, compassion, honesty, and respect for the interconnectedness of all beings. Adherence to these ethical principles is seen as essential for maintaining harmony within the divine order and fostering positive relationships with both humans and gods.

By examining these fundamental beliefs and concepts, we gain a deeper understanding of the rich tapestry of polytheistic religions and the ways in which they shape the worldview, practices, and values of their followers. It is important to recognize that the specifics of these beliefs and concepts can vary significantly across different polytheistic traditions, reflecting the diversity and cultural context of each individual religious system.

The diversity of polytheistic cosmologies, creation myths, and afterlife beliefs

The diversity of polytheistic cosmologies, creation myths, and afterlife beliefs is a testament to the rich tapestry of human religious imagination and cultural diversity. Across various polytheistic traditions, there are a plethora of cosmological narratives that explain the origin and structure of the universe, creation myths that detail the emergence of gods, humans, and the natural world, and diverse beliefs about the afterlife and the journey of the soul beyond death.

Cosmologies in polytheistic religions offer explanations for the nature and organization of the cosmos. These cosmological frameworks can range from complex and intricate systems to more abstract and symbolic representations. Some polytheistic cosmologies envision a multilayered universe, with different realms or planes of existence inhabited by gods, spirits, and humans. These realms may be interconnected through cosmic pathways or symbolic bridges, representing the intricate web of relationships between the divine, the natural world, and humanity. The cosmological narratives also often include the concept of a divine order or cosmic harmony that governs the functioning of the universe and maintains balance between different realms and entities.

Creation myths are foundational narratives in polytheistic religions that explain the origin of the universe, the emergence of gods and goddesses, and the creation of humans and the natural world. These myths often feature divine acts of creation, such as the shaping of the world, the birth of gods, and the establishment of fundamental principles or cosmic forces. Creation myths vary widely across polytheistic traditions, reflecting the cultural and historical contexts in which they emerged. They can be metaphorical, symbolic, or literal, and they serve to provide a mythic framework through which believers understand their place in the grand scheme of existence.

Afterlife beliefs in polytheistic religions encompass a wide range of perspectives, reflecting the diversity of human experiences, cultural beliefs, and spiritual aspirations. While the specifics of afterlife vary among different polytheistic traditions, there are common themes and motifs that emerge. Many polytheistic religions believe in some form of continuation of existence after death, wherein the soul or spirit of the deceased embarks on a journey or transitions to a realm beyond the earthly realm. This realm may be associated with specific deities or spirits and can be depicted as a paradise, underworld, or a realm of ancestors. The nature of the afterlife and the journey of the soul can vary, including concepts such as reincarnation, reunion with divine beings, judgment, or spiritual transformation.

It is important to note that the diversity of cosmologies, creation myths, and afterlife beliefs in polytheistic religions reflects the dynamic and evolving nature of these belief systems. As they interact with different cultures, historical periods, and philosophical developments, polytheistic traditions have adapted and incorporated new ideas, resulting in a rich tapestry of cosmological narratives and afterlife beliefs. These beliefs provide believers with a framework for understanding the mysteries of existence, the relationship between the divine and the human, and the meaning and purpose of life.

Core Beliefs of Monotheism

Core beliefs of monotheism revolve around the central concept of the existence of a single, supreme deity. Monotheistic religions emphasize the idea that there is only one God who is transcendent, all-powerful, and the creator of the universe and everything within it. These beliefs provide a foundation for monotheistic religious practices, moral codes, and spiritual experiences.

The belief in the oneness of God is a fundamental tenet of monotheism. It asserts that there is no other deity or divine entity of equal status or power. This monotheistic principle distinguishes monotheistic religions from polytheistic or pantheistic belief systems. It emphasizes the absolute unity and singularity of the divine, serving as the basis for worship and devotion to a singular God.

Monotheistic traditions often emphasize the attributes and characteristics of God. These attributes vary across different monotheistic religions but commonly include concepts such as omnipotence (all-powerfulness), omniscience (all-knowingness), omnipresence (being present everywhere), and benevolence (goodness and mercy). The precise understanding of these attributes may differ among different monotheistic traditions and theological interpretations, but they generally reflect the belief in a deity who is both transcendent and immanent, holding ultimate authority and guiding human affairs.

Another core belief in monotheism is the notion of divine revelation. Monotheistic religions hold that God communicates with humanity through various means, such as sacred texts, prophets, or direct spiritual experiences. These revelations serve as a source of guidance, moral teachings, and spiritual truths. Sacred texts, such as the Torah in Judaism, the Bible in Christianity, and the Quran in Islam, are regarded as authoritative sources of divine revelation and provide a framework for understanding the nature of God, the purpose of human existence, and the ethical principles to be followed.

Monotheistic religions often emphasize the importance of moral and ethical conduct. Believers are expected to adhere to a moral code prescribed by their religious teachings and guided by the principles set forth by God. This moral code typically encompasses principles such as justice, compassion, honesty, kindness, and respect for others. Monotheistic traditions often teach that ethical behavior is not only a requirement to please God but also a means of fostering harmonious relationships with fellow human beings and promoting the well-being of society.

The belief in a divine plan or purpose is another significant aspect of monotheistic belief systems. Monotheistic religions teach that God has a grand design for creation and human life, and that everything unfolds according to this divine plan. This belief provides a sense of meaning, purpose, and guidance for believers, offering comfort and reassurance in the face of life's challenges and uncertainties. It also underscores the idea that human beings have a responsibility to align their lives with the divine will and contribute to the fulfillment of God's purpose.

Overall, the core beliefs of monotheism affirm the existence of a single, supreme deity who is transcendent, all-powerful, and the source of moral guidance. These beliefs provide a framework for understanding the nature of God, the purpose of human life, and the moral and ethical principles to be followed. They serve as a foundation for religious practices, rituals, and the formation of individual and communal identities within monotheistic traditions.

Exploring the central tenets and doctrines in monotheistic belief systems

Exploring the central tenets and doctrines in monotheistic belief systems reveals the core principles and teachings that shape the religious worldview and guide the practices and behaviors of adherents. While the specific doctrines may vary among different monotheistic religions, there are several common themes that underpin their belief systems.

Oneness of God: The central tenet of monotheism is the belief in the existence of a single, supreme deity. Monotheistic religions emphasize the unity and singularity of God, rejecting the notion of multiple gods or divine entities. This belief sets monotheism apart from polytheistic or pantheistic worldviews, affirming the ultimate authority and transcendence of the divine.

Transcendence and Immanence: Monotheistic belief systems often describe God as transcendent, meaning that God exists beyond the material world and is not limited by it. At the same time, monotheistic religions also emphasize the immanence of God, suggesting that God is present and actively involved in the world and the lives of individuals. This duality of transcendence and immanence helps believers understand the divine as both beyond and intimately connected to the created universe.

Divine Revelation: Monotheistic religions hold that God communicates with humanity through various means, revealing divine truths, moral teachings, and guidance. This divine revelation is often believed to have been conveyed through prophets, sacred texts, or direct spiritual experiences. The concept of divine revelation provides a framework for understanding the nature of God, human purpose, and ethical principles.

Moral and Ethical Codes: Monotheistic belief systems typically emphasize the importance of moral and ethical conduct. Adherents are guided by a set of moral principles and ethical teachings derived from divine revelation. These moral codes serve as a compass for ethical decision-making, guiding believers to act in ways that are just, compassionate, and virtuous. They often include principles such as love for one's neighbor, honesty, fairness, and respect for the dignity and rights of others.

Salvation and Redemption: Many monotheistic religions offer teachings about salvation and the redemption of human beings. They provide a framework for understanding the human condition, the consequences of wrongdoing, and the path to spiritual liberation or eternal life. Believers are often encouraged to seek forgiveness for their sins, engage in acts of repentance, and strive for spiritual growth and transformation.

Worship and Ritual Practices: Monotheistic religions prescribe specific rituals, prayers, and worship practices as a means of expressing devotion and establishing a relationship with God. These rituals often include acts of prayer, meditation, communal worship, and participation in religious ceremonies. They serve as a means for believers to express gratitude, seek guidance, and seek communion with the divine.

Eschatology: Monotheistic religions often address the concept of eschatology, which refers to beliefs about the end times, judgment, and the afterlife. These beliefs provide a framework for understanding the ultimate destiny of individuals and the world. They may include teachings about resurrection, eternal life, and the final judgment of souls based on their deeds and faith.

Exploring the central tenets and doctrines in monotheistic belief systems allows for a deeper understanding of the core principles that shape these religious traditions. These beliefs provide a foundation for religious practices, moral values, and the formation of individual and communal identities within monotheistic religions. They offer a framework for understanding the nature of God, human existence, and the purpose and meaning of life.

Analyzing monotheistic concepts of divine nature, salvation, and eschatology

Analyzing monotheistic concepts of divine nature, salvation, and eschatology provides insights into the understanding of the nature of God, the path to salvation, and beliefs about the ultimate destiny of humanity. While the specifics may vary among different monotheistic religions, there are overarching themes and perspectives that can be examined.

Divine Nature: Monotheistic religions explore the nature of God as the singular and supreme being. They often describe God as infinite, eternal, and all-powerful, transcending the material world and existing beyond human comprehension. Monotheistic beliefs emphasize the attributes of God, such as omniscience (all-knowing), omnipotence (all-powerful), and omnipresence (present everywhere). These qualities reflect the concept of an all-encompassing divine presence that guides and sustains the universe.

Salvation: Monotheistic religions address the concept of salvation, which pertains to the deliverance of human beings from sin, suffering, and the consequences of wrongdoing. They offer teachings and practices that outline the path to salvation, which typically involves aligning one's life and actions with the will of God. Monotheistic religions emphasize the importance of faith, repentance, and adherence to moral and ethical principles as the means to achieve salvation. The process may involve seeking forgiveness, engaging in acts of charity, and cultivating virtues that bring individuals closer to the divine.

Eschatology: Eschatology refers to beliefs about the end times, the ultimate destiny of humanity, and the nature of the afterlife. Monotheistic religions present diverse perspectives on eschatology. They often assert that there will be a final judgment, in which individuals will be held accountable for their actions and beliefs.

The concept of an afterlife, whether as a reward or punishment, is frequently present in monotheistic eschatology. Some believe in the resurrection of the dead and a final reunion with God, while others posit a separation of the righteous and the wicked, leading to different realms or states of existence.

Analyzing these concepts within monotheistic belief systems allows for a deeper understanding of the relationship between humanity and the divine, the moral framework within which believers navigate their lives, and the ultimate purpose and destiny of human existence. It is important to recognize that while there are common themes, each monotheistic tradition may have its own distinct theological interpretations and nuances. By exploring these concepts, one can gain insights into the diverse ways in which monotheistic religions understand the divine, salvation, and the ultimate fate of humanity.

Ritual Symbolism and Mythology in Polytheism

Ritual symbolism and mythology play significant roles in polytheistic belief systems, providing a rich tapestry of meaning and narrative that enhances religious rituals and practices. These elements contribute to the overall understanding of the divine, human existence, and the interplay between the two.

Ritual Symbolism: Polytheistic rituals often involve the use of symbols that represent various aspects of the divine and the cosmos. These symbols can be physical objects, gestures, or actions that carry deeper meanings within the religious context. For example, the use of specific colors, such as white for purity or red for vitality, may symbolize different qualities or energies associated with particular deities. Similarly, the presence of sacred elements like water, fire, or incense can evoke spiritual purification, transformation, or the presence of the divine.

Ritual symbols serve multiple purposes, including invoking the presence of deities, creating a sacred atmosphere, and facilitating communication with the divine. They are intended to engage the senses, stimulate emotions, and deepen the spiritual connection between individuals and the divine realm.

Mythology: Mythology in polytheistic traditions encompasses a rich collection of stories, legends, and narratives that explain the origins of the world, the actions of deities, and the nature of human existence. These myths often involve divine beings, heroes, and mythical creatures, and they provide a framework for understanding the relationships between the divine and human realms.

Polytheistic myths often depict gods and goddesses with distinct personalities, attributes, and roles within the cosmic order. These stories may explore themes of creation, the establishment of societal norms, moral lessons, and explanations for natural phenomena. Mythology provides believers with a symbolic language through which they can interpret the world and their place within it.

In rituals, mythological narratives are frequently invoked, reenacted, or referenced to create a deeper connection between worshippers and the divine. These rituals may involve dramatic performances, storytelling, or symbolic actions that immerse participants in the mythological narrative. By engaging with mythology in rituals, believers reaffirm their connection to the larger cosmic order, deepen their understanding of the divine, and find personal and communal meaning within the shared cultural heritage.

Ritual symbolism and mythology in polytheistic belief systems are intertwined, working together to create a holistic and immersive religious experience. They provide a framework for understanding the nature of the divine, the human condition, and the interconnectedness of all things. Through ritual symbolism and mythology, believers engage with the deeper layers of their religious traditions, fostering a sense of awe, reverence, and spiritual connection.

Investigating the symbolism and mythological narratives in polytheistic rituals and traditions

Investigating the symbolism and mythological narratives in polytheistic rituals and traditions unveils a rich tapestry of meaning, symbolism, and storytelling that lies at the heart of these belief systems. Through the use of symbols and the retelling of mythical narratives, polytheistic rituals create a profound connection between the worshipper and the divine, while providing a framework for understanding the world and one's place within it.

Symbolism in Polytheistic Rituals:

Symbols hold immense significance in polytheistic rituals, as they serve as powerful conduits for communication with the divine and convey deeper layers of meaning. These symbols can take various forms, such as objects, gestures, colors, or natural elements, each carrying its own unique significance. Here are a few examples of symbolic elements commonly found in polytheistic rituals:

Objects: Various objects, such as statues, amulets, or ritual tools, can represent specific deities or embody their attributes and powers. These objects serve as focal points for devotion, allowing worshippers to connect with the divine presence they represent.

Gestures: Specific hand gestures, known as mudras, are often used in polytheistic rituals to symbolize different aspects of the divine or to invoke specific energies. For instance, joining the hands in prayer or raising them in reverence may symbolize humility, gratitude, or supplication.

Colors: Colors hold symbolic meanings in many polytheistic traditions. For example, white may symbolize purity and divine presence, while red can represent vitality, passion, or protection. The use of specific colors in rituals helps evoke the desired qualities or energies associated with particular deities or spiritual states.

Natural Elements: Polytheistic rituals often incorporate natural elements, such as water, fire, earth, and air, as symbols of the divine presence and cosmic forces. These elements connect worshippers with the sacredness of the natural world and serve as reminders of their interconnectedness with the larger web of life.

Mythological Narratives in Polytheistic Rituals:

Mythology plays a central role in polytheistic rituals, providing a rich source of narratives and stories that explain the origins of the world, the actions of deities, and the nature of human existence. These mythological narratives are often reenacted, referenced, or incorporated into rituals, deepening the worshipper's connection to the divine and fostering a sense of cultural and spiritual continuity. Here are some key aspects of mythological narratives in polytheistic rituals:

Creation Myths: Creation myths describe how the world came into being and establish the foundational principles and order of the cosmos. These myths may involve the actions of primordial deities, divine beings, or elemental forces, and they provide a framework for understanding the origins and structure of the universe.

Divine Interactions: Mythological narratives often recount the interactions between gods and goddesses, their relationships, conflicts, and interventions in the human world. These stories highlight the attributes, powers, and personalities of different deities, offering insights into their roles and significance within the larger pantheon.

Heroes and Heroines: Polytheistic traditions often feature stories of heroic figures who embark on quests, battle mythical creatures, or demonstrate exceptional virtues. These hero narratives serve as moral and inspirational examples, reflecting the qualities valued by the community and providing guidance for personal growth and spiritual development.

Symbolic Ritual Reenactments: In many polytheistic rituals, mythological narratives are reenacted or symbolically represented, allowing worshippers to participate in the timeless stories of their tradition. These ritual reenactments can range from simple gestures or recitations to elaborate performances involving costumes, music, and dance.

The symbolism and mythological narratives in polytheistic rituals not only deepen the worshipper's connection to the divine but also provide a framework for understanding the world, morality, and the human condition. Through these rituals, individuals engage with the symbolic language of their tradition, immersing themselves in the mythical stories that have shaped their cultural and spiritual identity. This exploration of symbolism and mythology fosters a sense of awe, reverence, and connection, reinforcing the core beliefs and values of polytheistic traditions.

The use of symbols, sacred stories, and folklore in polytheistic belief systems

The use of symbols, sacred stories, and folklore in polytheistic belief systems is deeply ingrained in the fabric of these traditions. They serve as powerful tools for conveying spiritual and moral teachings, preserving cultural heritage, and connecting individuals to the divine. By delving into the significance of symbols, exploring sacred stories, and engaging with folklore, followers of polytheistic belief systems find profound meaning and guidance in their spiritual practices.

Symbols in Polytheistic Belief Systems:

Symbols play a central role in polytheistic belief systems, as they serve as gateways to deeper spiritual understanding and communication with the divine. These symbols often represent specific deities, concepts, or cosmic forces, and they hold multifaceted meanings that resonate with worshippers. Here are some examples of symbols commonly used in polytheistic belief systems:

Divine Icons: Statues, images, or symbols representing deities are considered sacred icons. They provide a focal point for devotion, serving as a tangible representation of the divine presence. These icons may be adorned with specific attributes, colors, or symbols that reflect the qualities and characteristics of the deity they represent.

Elemental Symbols: Elements such as water, fire, earth, and air hold symbolic significance in polytheistic belief systems. They represent the fundamental building blocks of creation and the interconnectedness between the natural world and the divine. Worshippers may engage with these elements through rituals, offerings, or meditative practices to cultivate a deeper connection with the divine forces they symbolize.

Sacred Animals: Certain animals are regarded as sacred in polytheistic belief systems due to their symbolic associations with specific deities or spiritual qualities. For example, the owl may be associated with wisdom and the goddess Athena in Greek mythology, while the snake may symbolize rebirth and transformation in various traditions.

Sacred Colors: Colors hold symbolic meaning in many polytheistic belief systems. For instance, white may represent purity and divine presence, while gold or yellow may symbolize enlightenment or divine radiance. The use of specific colors in rituals, clothing, or symbolic representations helps convey and evoke the desired qualities or energies associated with particular deities or spiritual states.

Sacred Stories and Mythology:

Sacred stories and mythology form the backbone of polytheistic belief systems, providing narratives that explain the origins of the world, the actions of deities, and the nature of human existence. These stories serve as sources of inspiration, moral guidance, and spiritual teachings. Here are key aspects of sacred stories and mythology in polytheistic belief systems:

Creation Myths: Creation myths recount the origins of the universe, the emergence of deities, and the establishment of the cosmic order. They explain how the world came into being and provide a framework for understanding the natural and supernatural realms.

Divine Relationships and Interactions: Sacred stories depict the interactions between deities, their relationships, and their involvement in the human world. These narratives shed light on the qualities, attributes, and roles of different deities, offering insights into their personalities and their influence on various aspects of life.

Heroic Tales: Polytheistic traditions often feature stories of heroic figures who undertake quests, face challenges, and embody virtues such as courage, wisdom, or compassion. These tales serve as moral examples and inspire individuals to cultivate these virtues in their own lives.

Moral and Ethical Teachings: Sacred stories often convey moral and ethical teachings, providing guidance on how to live a virtuous and meaningful life. These narratives present dilemmas, ethical choices, and the consequences of actions, offering lessons on personal conduct, social harmony, and spiritual growth.

Folklore and Cultural Traditions:

Polytheistic belief systems are deeply intertwined with folklore and cultural traditions. Folklore encompasses the myths, legends, folktales, and customs passed down through generations within a specific culture or community. Folklore reflects the values, beliefs, and collective experiences of a people and serves as a repository of wisdom, cultural identity, and spiritual insights. Here are examples of how folklore contributes to polytheistic belief systems:

Festivals and Celebrations: Folklore often informs the rituals, customs, and celebrations associated with specific polytheistic festivals. These festive traditions may incorporate storytelling, music, dance, costumes, and symbolic rituals that honor deities, commemorate mythological events, or mark important seasonal or agricultural milestones.

Ritual Practices and Superstitions: Folklore influences various ritual practices, magical techniques, and superstitious beliefs within polytheistic traditions. These practices may involve the use of talismans, amulets, or herbs, as well as rituals for protection, healing, or divination. Folk beliefs and practices are often deeply intertwined with the symbolism and mythological narratives of the tradition.

Oral Tradition and Storytelling: Polytheistic belief systems have a strong tradition of oral storytelling, where myths, legends, and folktales are passed down through generations. Storytelling serves as a means of preserving cultural heritage, conveying moral teachings, and fostering a sense of collective identity and connection with the divine.

In conclusion, symbols, sacred stories, and folklore form an integral part of polytheistic belief systems, providing rich sources of spiritual and cultural significance. They serve as gateways to deeper understanding, connection, and inspiration within these traditions. Exploring and engaging with the symbolism and mythological narratives in polytheistic rituals and traditions allows individuals to deepen their spiritual practice, gain insights into the nature of the divine, and cultivate a profound connection with their cultural heritage.

Monotheistic Traditions and Moral Codes

Monotheistic traditions encompass a range of religious beliefs and practices that revolve around the worship of a single divine being. These traditions emphasize the existence of a supreme deity who is all-powerful, all-knowing, and the ultimate source of moral authority. Within monotheistic belief systems, moral codes play a fundamental role in guiding the ethical conduct and behavior of believers. These moral codes provide a framework for moral reasoning, personal virtues, social interactions, and the pursuit of spiritual growth. In this section, we will explore the moral codes and ethical principles in monotheistic traditions, focusing on key monotheistic religions such as Judaism, Christianity, and Islam.

The Ten Commandments and Moral Laws in Judaism:

Judaism, one of the oldest monotheistic religions, is rooted in the ancient covenant between God and the Jewish people. Central to Jewish ethics is the Torah, which contains the divine teachings and laws given to Moses on Mount Sinai. The Ten Commandments, a foundational part of the Torah, outline essential moral principles that guide Jewish ethical behavior. These commandments encompass obligations towards both God and fellow human beings. Some of the key commandments include:

Monotheistic Worship: Judaism emphasizes the exclusive worship of one God and prohibits the worship of idols or other deities.

Honoring Parents: Respecting and honoring parents is regarded as a paramount duty in Jewish ethics, reflecting the importance of family and filial piety.

Prohibition of Murder, Theft, and Falsehood: The commandments explicitly prohibit actions such as murder, theft, and bearing false witness, emphasizing the sanctity of life, property, and truth.

Jewish ethical teachings extend beyond the Ten Commandments and include principles such as tikkun olam (repairing the world), promoting justice and righteousness, engaging in acts of kindness and charity (tzedakah), and pursuing communal well-being.

The Sermon on the Mount and Christian Moral Teachings:

Christianity, another prominent monotheistic tradition, centers around the life, teachings, and sacrifice of Jesus Christ. The moral code of Christianity is shaped by the teachings of Jesus as recorded in the New Testament. The Sermon on the Mount, found in the Gospel of Matthew, presents a central ethical framework for Christians. This sermon encompasses various moral teachings and virtues, including:

Love and Compassion: Christianity places a strong emphasis on the commandment to love one's neighbor as oneself, promoting empathy, compassion, and care for others.

Forgiveness and Reconciliation: Christian ethics encourage forgiveness, reconciliation, and the restoration of broken relationships, reflecting the belief in God's mercy and redemption.

Humility and Servanthood: Jesus' teachings highlight the value of humility, selflessness, and service to others, emphasizing the importance of putting others' needs before one's own.

Christian moral teachings also address issues such as integrity, honesty, sexual ethics, stewardship of resources, and social justice. Different Christian denominations may have additional moral principles and teachings that shape their ethical perspectives.

Sharia Law and Ethical Guidelines in Islam:

Islam, the third major monotheistic religion, is centered around the belief in the oneness of Allah and the guidance provided in the Quran, believed to be the literal word of God. Islamic ethics are deeply intertwined with the legal system known as Sharia. Sharia encompasses a comprehensive moral and legal framework that covers various aspects of life, including personal conduct, family relationships, economic transactions, and societal norms.

Islamic ethical guidelines encompass principles such as:

Tawhid: Islam emphasizes the concept of tawhid, the oneness of God, and the recognition of His sovereignty over all aspects of life.

Five Pillars of Islam: These pillars, including the declaration of faith (shahada), prayer (salat), charity (zakat), fasting (sawm), and pilgrimage (hajj), provide a foundation for Islamic ethics and spiritual practice.

Moral Virtues: Islam encourages the cultivation of virtues such as honesty, sincerity, justice, humility, patience, and kindness.

Prohibition of Unethical Behaviors: Islam prohibits actions such as lying, stealing, adultery, and gambling, while promoting modesty, self-control, and respect for others.

Islamic ethics also encompass the principle of ihsan, which encourages believers to strive for excellence in their actions, intentions, and character.

While these examples highlight the moral codes and ethical teachings in major monotheistic traditions, it is important to note that there can be variations within each tradition and different interpretations among followers. Additionally, ethical perspectives and moral teachings can evolve over time as societies and cultures change. The moral codes within monotheistic traditions provide believers with a moral compass, guiding their choices and actions in alignment with their religious beliefs. They promote virtues, social responsibility, and the pursuit of spiritual growth, ultimately aiming to foster a just, compassionate, and righteous society.

Examining the moral and ethical teachings in monotheistic religions

Examining the moral and ethical teachings in monotheistic religions allows us to delve into the core values and principles that guide believers in their moral conduct and ethical decision-making. Monotheistic religions, such as Judaism, Christianity, and Islam, provide comprehensive frameworks for understanding right and wrong, promoting virtues, and addressing ethical dilemmas. In this section, we will explore the moral and ethical teachings in these monotheistic traditions, highlighting their commonalities and unique aspects.

Judaism and Ethical Principles:

Judaism places a strong emphasis on ethical conduct and righteous living. The moral teachings in Judaism are deeply rooted in the Torah, which includes the Five Books of Moses (the Pentateuch), along with rabbinic interpretations and commentaries. Key ethical principles in Judaism include:

Pursuit of Justice: Judaism emphasizes the pursuit of justice and the establishment of a just society. The concept of tikkun olam, meaning "repairing the world," guides believers to actively engage in acts of social justice, charity, and compassion.

✧ Ethical Monotheism: Judaism's belief in the oneness of God and the covenant between God and the Jewish people serves as a foundation for ethical living. Believers are called to honor and worship God, and this relationship is closely tied to ethical obligations towards others.

✧   Human Dignity: Judaism teaches that all human beings are created in the image of God, imbuing each individual with inherent dignity and worth. This principle underlies the ethical imperative to treat others with respect, kindness, and fairness.

✧   Social Responsibility: Jewish ethics emphasize the importance of communal well-being and social responsibility. The concept of gemilut chasadim, acts of loving-kindness, promotes charitable deeds and caring for those in need.

Christianity and the Teachings of Jesus:

Christianity places significant importance on the life, teachings, and example of Jesus Christ as the embodiment of moral perfection. The ethical teachings in Christianity are primarily derived from the life of Jesus, as recorded in the New Testament. Key ethical principles in Christianity include:

✧   Love and Compassion: Christianity emphasizes the commandment to love God and love one's neighbor as oneself. The concept of agape, selfless and unconditional love, guides believers to practice compassion, forgiveness, and empathy towards others.

✧   Ethic of Humility and Service: Jesus' teachings highlight the importance of humility, selflessness, and service to others. Believers are called to serve and care for the marginalized, vulnerable, and oppressed, following Jesus' example of servant leadership.

✧   Moral Transformation: Christianity emphasizes the transformative power of faith and the indwelling of the Holy Spirit. This transformation enables believers to exhibit virtues such as honesty, integrity, patience, and self-control.

✧   Forgiveness and Reconciliation: Christian ethics promote forgiveness and reconciliation, emphasizing the importance of healing broken relationships and seeking reconciliation with God and others.

Islam and the Teachings of the Quran:

Islam, as revealed in the Quran and the teachings of Prophet Muhammad, provides a comprehensive ethical framework for Muslims. Key ethical principles in Islam include:

✧   Submission to Allah: Islam calls for submission to the will of Allah and obedience to His commands. This submission is seen as the foundation for ethical living and moral conduct.

✧   Moral Responsibility and Accountability: Islam emphasizes individual responsibility and accountability for one's actions. Believers are encouraged to cultivate virtues and avoid sinful behavior, with the belief in the Day of Judgment and the ultimate accountability before Allah.

✧   Justice and Equality: Islamic ethics emphasize justice, fairness, and equality for all individuals. Muslims are called to uphold justice in personal interactions, family relationships, economic dealings, and societal affairs.

✧   Compassion and Social Welfare (continued): The principle of zakat, the giving of alms to the poor and needy, is a fundamental aspect of Islamic ethics. Muslims are encouraged to show compassion and provide support to those in need, fostering a sense of social welfare and solidarity within the community.

✧   Moderation and Balance: Islam promotes the concept of moderation and balance in all aspects of life. Believers are encouraged to avoid extremes and practice moderation in their actions, behaviors, and desires.

✧   Respect for Human Dignity: Islamic ethics emphasize the inherent dignity and worth of every human being. Muslims are called to treat others with respect, kindness, and fairness, regardless of their social status, race, or religion.

✧   Moral Integrity and Honesty: Islam emphasizes the importance of moral integrity and honesty in personal and business dealings. Muslims are encouraged to be truthful, trustworthy, and fulfill their commitments and promises.

It is important to note that while these ethical principles are central to monotheistic traditions, there may be variations and interpretations within each religion's diverse communities and cultural contexts. Additionally, monotheistic traditions engage in ongoing discussions and debates regarding the application of ethical principles to contemporary issues, allowing for a dynamic and evolving understanding of moral conduct.

By adhering to these ethical teachings, followers of monotheistic traditions seek to lead virtuous lives, aligning their actions and behaviors with the divine will and promoting harmonious relationships with both God and fellow human beings. These ethical principles provide guidance and serve as a moral compass, shaping the believers' personal and societal conduct and contributing to the overall well-being of individuals and communities.

The role of commandments, religious laws, and moral principles in monotheistic traditions

The role of commandments, religious laws, and moral principles holds great significance within monotheistic traditions. These elements provide guidance and establish a framework for ethical behavior, moral conduct, and the proper relationship between human beings and the divine. Let us examine the role and significance of commandments, religious laws, and moral principles in the context of monotheistic traditions.

Commandments:

Commandments are divine directives or instructions that outline specific actions or behaviors that adherents are obligated to follow. In monotheistic traditions, commandments are often considered as direct revelations from the divine, providing a clear set of rules and guidelines for believers to follow. These commandments are typically enshrined in sacred texts or revealed through prophetic teachings. They serve as a moral compass, guiding the actions and behaviors of individuals and shaping the collective identity of the religious community.

For example, in Judaism, the Ten Commandments, given to Moses on Mount Sinai, form the foundation of Jewish ethical and legal principles. They encompass various aspects of human conduct, including the worship of the one true God, ethical treatment of others, and personal moral responsibilities. Similarly, in Christianity, the teachings of Jesus Christ, as recorded in the New Testament, are seen as commandments that guide believers in their moral and spiritual lives.

Religious Laws:

Religious laws, also known as divine laws or legal codes, are a set of regulations and guidelines derived from sacred scriptures and religious teachings. These laws are intended to govern various aspects of human life, including personal conduct, social interactions, family relationships, and community affairs. Religious laws often provide detailed instructions on how to live a righteous and virtuous life.

In monotheistic traditions, religious laws are believed to have been revealed by the divine and are considered binding for believers. They are seen as a means to uphold moral values, establish social order, and promote justice within the community. Religious laws can encompass a wide range of topics, including dietary restrictions, rituals, marital relationships, financial transactions, and legal proceedings.

For instance, in Islam, the Quran serves as the primary source of religious law, providing guidance on various aspects of life through its verses. The Hadith, the sayings and actions of Prophet Muhammad, also play a significant role in the development of Islamic legal codes, known as Shariah. Shariah covers a wide range of topics, including personal morality, family law, criminal justice, and economic transactions.

Moral Principles:

Moral principles in monotheistic traditions are overarching ethical guidelines that provide a moral framework for believers to navigate their actions and decisions. These principles are often rooted in the core teachings of the respective religions and emphasize virtues such as compassion, justice, honesty, humility, and love for others. They serve as a guide for believers to cultivate moral character and foster harmonious relationships within society.

In monotheistic traditions, moral principles are derived from sacred texts, teachings of religious leaders, and philosophical reflections on the nature of God and human existence. They form the basis for ethical decision-making and encourage believers to act in ways that align with divine will and promote the well-being of others.

For example, in Christianity, the moral teachings of Jesus Christ, as presented in the Sermon on the Mount, highlight principles such as love for one's neighbor, forgiveness, nonviolence, and the pursuit of righteousness. These principles are seen as fundamental to living a moral and virtuous life in accordance with God's commandments.

In summary, commandments, religious laws, and moral principles play vital roles in monotheistic traditions. They provide believers with a moral compass, guiding their actions and behaviors in alignment with divine teachings. Commandments offer specific directives, while religious laws establish legal codes that govern various aspects of life. Moral principles provide overarching ethical guidelines that shape believers' character and foster harmonious relationships within society. Together, these elements contribute to the moral and spiritual growth of individuals and the cohesive functioning of religious communities.

CHAPTER 13: RELIGIOUS SYNCRETISM AND CULTURAL EXCHANGES

Religious syncretism and cultural exchanges have played significant roles in shaping the religious and cultural landscape of societies throughout history. As human civilizations have encountered and interacted with one another, religious beliefs, practices, and traditions have often undergone a process of syncretism, whereby elements from different religious systems merge, blend, or influence one another. This chapter delves into the fascinating phenomenon of religious syncretism and explores the cultural exchanges that have contributed to the rich diversity of religious expressions around the world.

Defining Religious Syncretism

Religious syncretism refers to the blending or merging of religious beliefs, practices, and symbols from different traditions. It occurs when two or more religious systems come into contact, leading to the incorporation and integration of elements from each into a new and distinct religious expression. This process can result from peaceful cultural exchanges, conquests, colonization, migration, or trade routes that bring different religious groups into contact with one another.

Historical Examples of Religious Syncretism

Throughout history, numerous examples of religious syncretism can be found across different regions and time periods. For instance, in ancient Egypt, the blending of local Egyptian deities with those of the conquering Greeks led to the creation of hybrid gods and religious practices. Similarly, in the context of the Roman Empire, the incorporation of elements from various religious traditions, including Hellenistic, Egyptian, and Persian, resulted in the emergence of syncretic belief systems.

Cultural Exchanges and Religious Influences

Cultural exchanges have played a pivotal role in facilitating the spread of religious ideas, rituals, and practices across different regions. As civilizations interacted through trade, conquest, migration, or diplomacy, they exchanged not only goods and knowledge but also religious beliefs and practices. These exchanges often led to the diffusion and adoption of religious ideas, resulting in the transformation and diversification of religious traditions.

Syncretism and Indigenous Religions

Religious syncretism has had a profound impact on indigenous religious traditions, particularly in regions where colonizers imposed their beliefs and practices upon native populations. In these contexts, syncretism became a survival strategy for indigenous communities, allowing them to preserve their cultural and spiritual identity while adapting to the dominant religious system.

Challenges and Controversies

While religious syncretism can foster cultural exchanges, understanding, and peaceful coexistence, it is not without its challenges and controversies. Syncretic practices can face resistance and opposition from orthodox religious institutions and authorities who view them as a deviation from the "pure" form of their faith. Additionally, cultural appropriation and power imbalances can arise when elements from marginalized or indigenous traditions are incorporated into dominant religious systems.

Contemporary Examples

Religious syncretism continues to shape the religious landscape of contemporary societies. In the modern era, globalization, immigration, and interfaith dialogue have contributed to the blending and merging of religious traditions. Examples include the Afro-Caribbean syncretic religions such as Santeria and Vodou, which combine elements of African traditional religions with Christianity, and the New Age movement, which incorporates beliefs and practices from various spiritual and religious traditions.

Conclusion

Religious syncretism and cultural exchanges have played a crucial role in the development and evolution of religious traditions worldwide. Through the blending and merging of diverse beliefs and practices, syncretism has given rise to new forms of religious expression, fostering cultural understanding and adaptation. However, it is essential to approach syncretism with sensitivity, respect, and an understanding of the historical and cultural contexts in which it occurs. By studying religious syncretism and cultural exchanges, we gain insights into the dynamic nature of human religious experiences and the continuous evolution of religious traditions.

Introduction

Religious syncretism is a fascinating and complex phenomenon that emerges from the interplay between polytheistic and monotheistic traditions. It involves the blending, merging, or influencing of religious beliefs, practices, and symbols from different traditions, resulting in the creation of unique syncretic expressions. This chapter explores the multifaceted nature of religious syncretism, delving into its historical, cultural, and sociological dimensions.

Religious Syncretism: An Overview

Religious syncretism is a dynamic process that occurs when diverse religious systems come into contact and interact with one another. It involves the incorporation and integration of elements from different traditions, leading to the formation of new religious expressions. Syncretism can take various forms, such as the fusion of deities, the adaptation of rituals, the blending of mythologies, and the adoption of symbols and practices.

The Interplay between Polytheistic and Monotheistic Traditions

Polytheistic and monotheistic traditions provide fertile ground for the emergence of religious syncretism. Polytheism, with its diverse pantheons and local deities, offers a rich tapestry of beliefs and practices that can interact with monotheistic systems. Monotheism, on the other hand, with its emphasis on the worship of a single divine being, may incorporate or assimilate elements from polytheistic traditions, adapting them to fit within a monotheistic framework.

Cultural Exchanges and Encounters

Cultural exchanges and encounters play a pivotal role in the development of religious syncretism. Through trade, conquest, migration, and colonization, different religious communities have interacted and exchanged ideas, beliefs, and practices. These exchanges provide fertile ground for the blending and merging of religious traditions, as individuals and communities navigate the complexities of cultural encounter and seek to find common ground.

Historical Examples of Religious Syncretism

Throughout history, numerous examples of religious syncretism can be found across different regions and time periods. For instance, in ancient Egypt, the conquering Greeks influenced the Egyptian pantheon, resulting in the syncretic deity Serapis. In the Americas, the blending of indigenous beliefs with Catholicism gave rise to various syncretic expressions, such as the Afro-Caribbean religions of Santeria and Vodou.

The Role of Cultural Context

Religious syncretism is deeply rooted in cultural context and reflects the unique histories, traditions, and worldviews of the communities involved. The specific cultural and historical factors at play shape the form and nature of syncretic expressions. It is crucial to approach syncretism with an understanding of these contexts, recognizing the agency of individuals and communities in shaping their religious beliefs and practices.

Conclusion

Exploring the phenomenon of religious syncretism allows us to appreciate the intricate interplay between polytheistic and monotheistic traditions and the cultural exchanges that shape them. It highlights the dynamic nature of religious beliefs and practices, as they adapt and evolve through encounters with other traditions. By studying religious syncretism, we gain insights into the complex ways in which religions interact, transform, and create new expressions, enriching the diversity and tapestry of human spiritual experiences.

Historical Context

A. Impact of Conquests and Empires on Religious Syncretism
The impact of conquests and empires on religious syncretism cannot be overstated. Throughout history, powerful empires and conquerors have shaped the religious landscape by imposing their beliefs and practices on conquered territories. However, these conquests also led to the blending and merging of religious traditions, resulting in syncretic expressions.

Conquests often involved the assimilation of deities and religious practices of the conquered people into the dominant religious framework of the conquerors. For example, the spread of Hellenistic culture under Alexander the Great resulted in the syncretism of Greek and Egyptian beliefs, leading to the emergence of Serapis as a syncretic deity. Similarly, the Roman Empire incorporated gods and goddesses from various conquered territories into their pantheon, creating a syncretic blend of beliefs.

B. Spread of Religious Ideas through Trade Routes and Migration
Trade routes and migrations have played a significant role in the diffusion of religious ideas and the development of syncretic traditions. As merchants and

travelers traversed diverse regions, they encountered new cultures and religious beliefs, leading to the exchange and blending of ideas.

The Silk Road, for instance, facilitated the transmission of religious beliefs and practices between East and West, resulting in the syncretism of Buddhism with local traditions in Central Asia and China. Similarly, the Indian Ocean trade routes connected different regions, enabling the spread of Hinduism, Buddhism, and Islam, and the subsequent syncretism with indigenous beliefs in Southeast Asia.

Migration, whether forced or voluntary, has also contributed to religious syncretism. When people move to new lands, they carry their religious beliefs and practices with them, which often intermingle with the beliefs of the local communities. This interaction can lead to the emergence of syncretic religious expressions that reflect the cultural and religious diversity of the migrating groups.

C. Influence of Colonialism and Globalization on Religious Syncretism
Colonialism and globalization have had a profound impact on religious syncretism. Colonial powers often imposed their religious beliefs on colonized peoples, resulting in the fusion of indigenous practices with Christianity, Islam, or other dominant religions. This syncretism allowed colonized communities to retain aspects of their traditional beliefs while incorporating elements of the colonizers' religion.

For example, in Latin America, indigenous traditions blended with Catholicism to form syncretic expressions such as the worship of saints or the veneration of religious figures with indigenous roots. Similarly, in Africa, the syncretism of traditional African religions with Christianity or Islam gave rise to unique religious practices that incorporate elements from both traditions.

Globalization, with its increased interconnectedness and cultural exchange, has further contributed to religious syncretism. As people from different cultures and religious backgrounds interact, they bring their beliefs and practices together, resulting in the emergence of hybrid religious expressions. This can be seen in the rise of New Age spirituality, which blends elements from various religious traditions, or the fusion of Eastern and Western spiritual practices in contemporary spiritual movements.

Conclusion
The historical context of religious syncretism is shaped by conquests, empires, trade routes, migrations, colonialism, and globalization. These factors have played pivotal roles in the blending, merging, and influencing of religious beliefs and practices across different cultures and regions. Understanding this historical context

allows us to appreciate the dynamic nature of religious syncretism and its ongoing impact on the diversity of religious traditions worldwide.

Blending of Beliefs and Practices

A. Syncretism of Deities and Pantheons in Polytheistic and Monotheistic Traditions

One of the prominent aspects of religious syncretism is the merging and harmonization of deities and pantheons from different religious systems. This phenomenon can be observed in both polytheistic and monotheistic traditions, where gods and goddesses from different cultures are integrated into existing belief systems.

In polytheistic traditions, syncretism often occurs through the identification and assimilation of deities with similar attributes or functions. For example, in ancient Greece, the deity Zeus assimilated characteristics of the Roman god Jupiter, resulting in the syncretic deity Zeus-Jupiter. Similarly, in Hinduism, the deities Shiva and Vishnu are sometimes combined into the syncretic form of Hari-Hara, representing the unity of both deities' aspects.

In monotheistic traditions, syncretism can manifest through the incorporation of local deities or religious figures into the dominant monotheistic framework. For instance, in Christianity, the veneration of saints and the assimilation of local customs and practices during the process of Christianization demonstrate syncretic elements. In some cases, saints assumed attributes or functions of pre-existing deities, allowing for the coexistence of indigenous beliefs within the framework of monotheism.

B. Incorporation of Rituals, Ceremonies, and Symbols from Diverse Religious Systems

Religious syncretism often involves the incorporation of rituals, ceremonies, and symbols from diverse religious systems. As different cultures come into contact, rituals and practices may merge, creating new expressions of religious worship.

For example, in Afro-Caribbean traditions such as Santería and Vodou, rituals and ceremonies originating from West African religions blended with Catholicism during the era of colonization. These syncretic traditions incorporate Catholic saints and symbols alongside indigenous African deities and rituals. The result is a unique blend of practices that reflects the cultural encounters and exchanges between African and European traditions.

Similarly, in the context of East Asian religions, such as Taoism and Buddhism, syncretism has led to the blending of ritual practices and symbols. In China, for instance, Buddhist temples often feature Taoist deities and rituals, demonstrating the intermingling of these two traditions and the syncretic expressions that have emerged.

C. Hybridization of Religious Doctrines and Theological Concepts

Religious syncretism can also involve the hybridization of religious doctrines and theological concepts. As different religious traditions interact, ideas and beliefs are exchanged and integrated, resulting in the development of new theological frameworks.

For example, in the realm of esoteric spirituality, syncretism has given rise to various syncretic systems that draw from multiple traditions. Theosophy, founded by Helena Blavatsky in the 19th century, blends elements of Hinduism, Buddhism, and Western esotericism. This syncretic approach seeks to unite different religious and philosophical traditions under a common spiritual framework.

In contemporary Pagan and Neopagan movements, syncretism is often embraced as practitioners draw from various ancient and modern religious traditions. This blending of beliefs and practices allows individuals to create personalized spiritual paths that incorporate elements from different cultural and historical contexts.

Conclusion

The blending of beliefs and practices in religious syncretism encompasses the syncretism of deities and pantheons, the incorporation of rituals and symbols, and the hybridization of religious doctrines. This dynamic process is shaped by cultural encounters, historical influences, and individual religious experiences. By exploring the diverse ways in which religious syncretism occurs, we gain a deeper understanding of the creative and transformative nature of human spirituality and the ongoing interplay between different religious traditions.

Cultural Adaptation and Transformation

A. Adaptation of Religious Beliefs and Practices to New Cultural Contexts

Religious beliefs and practices have a remarkable capacity to adapt and evolve as they encounter new cultural contexts. When religions migrate or spread to different regions, they often undergo transformations to accommodate the beliefs, values, and customs of the host culture. This process of adaptation allows religions to resonate with the local population and integrate into their social fabric.

For example, Buddhism, originally born in ancient India, underwent significant adaptations as it spread to various Asian countries. In each new cultural context, Buddhism absorbed elements from existing belief systems, resulting in distinct variations such as Theravada, Mahayana, and Vajrayana Buddhism. These adaptations allowed Buddhism to find resonance with the indigenous cultures, resulting in a rich tapestry of religious expressions.

B. Assimilation and Reinterpretation of Religious Symbols and Narratives

In the process of cultural adaptation, religious symbols and narratives often undergo assimilation and reinterpretation to align with the values and worldviews of the receiving culture. This assimilation may involve incorporating local deities, folkloric figures, or historical events into the religious narrative.

An example of this can be seen in the syncretism between indigenous traditions and Christianity in Latin America. The figure of the Virgin Mary, revered in Catholicism, has assimilated aspects of indigenous mother goddesses, resulting in manifestations such as Our Lady of Guadalupe in Mexico. This blending of religious symbols and narratives creates a unique expression of faith that incorporates both local beliefs and Christian theology.

C. Transformation of Religious Rituals and Festivals in Multicultural Societies

Multicultural societies provide fertile ground for the transformation of religious rituals and festivals. As different cultures interact and influence one another, religious celebrations often evolve to embrace diverse practices and customs.

For instance, the celebration of Diwali, the Hindu Festival of Lights, has transformed in countries with significant Hindu diasporas. In these multicultural settings, Diwali has become an inclusive festival celebrated by people of different faiths. It incorporates elements of the local culture, such as fireworks displays or community gatherings, while maintaining its core spiritual significance.

Similarly, in the context of African diaspora religions, such as Candomblé or Santería, religious rituals and festivals have adapted to new cultural environments. These syncretic traditions blend elements from African religions with practices and symbols from the Americas, resulting in unique expressions of worship that honor ancestral traditions while embracing local customs.

Conclusion

Cultural adaptation and transformation play a crucial role in shaping the development and evolution of religious beliefs and practices. As religions encounter new cultural contexts, they adapt, assimilate, and reinterpret their symbols, narratives, rituals, and festivals. This process allows religions to remain relevant, vibrant, and inclusive in multicultural societies. By exploring the ways in which religions adapt and transform, we gain insight into the resilience and dynamism of human spirituality and its ability to bridge cultural divides and foster understanding.

Religious Hybridity and Identity

A. Formation of Syncretic Religious Traditions and Movements

Syncretic religious traditions and movements emerge as a result of the blending and integration of different religious elements. These syncretic forms often incorporate beliefs, rituals, and practices from multiple sources, creating new hybrid expressions of faith.

One example of a syncretic religious tradition is Vodou, which originated in Haiti and combines elements of West African religions, Catholicism, and indigenous beliefs. Vodou practitioners synthesize these diverse influences to form a unique spiritual system that reflects the cultural identity of the Haitian people.

Similarly, the New Age movement, which emerged in the late 20th century, represents a syncretic blend of various spiritual and metaphysical practices from different traditions worldwide. It incorporates elements from Eastern philosophies, indigenous spirituality, esoteric teachings, and alternative healing modalities. The New Age movement highlights the fluidity of religious boundaries and the capacity for individuals to construct their own spiritual paths.

B. Role of Religious Syncretism in the Construction of Cultural and National Identities

Religious syncretism often plays a significant role in the construction of cultural and national identities. As cultures encounter one another through trade, migration, or colonialism, the blending of religious beliefs and practices can contribute to the formation of a unique cultural identity.

For example, in Latin America, the syncretism between indigenous traditions and Catholicism has been instrumental in shaping the cultural identity of various countries. Through the fusion of religious elements, indigenous communities have preserved their ancestral practices and beliefs while incorporating the dominant religion of the colonizers. This syncretic identity reflects the resilience and adaptability of indigenous cultures in the face of historical challenges.

Similarly, in the African diaspora, syncretic religions such as Candomblé in Brazil or Santería in Cuba have played a crucial role in the construction of Afro-Caribbean identities. These religions blend elements of African spirituality with Catholicism, reflecting the complex historical experiences of African descendants and their efforts to maintain cultural and spiritual connections to their ancestral roots.

C. Challenges and Controversies Surrounding Syncretic Religious Practices

Syncretic religious practices are not without their challenges and controversies. Critics argue that syncretism dilutes the authenticity and integrity of religious traditions, leading to a loss of distinct cultural and theological identities. Others raise concerns about cultural appropriation and the potential exploitation of marginalized communities in the process of syncretic blending.

Additionally, syncretic practices can be met with resistance and opposition from orthodox religious authorities who view them as heretical or incompatible with established doctrines. Such conflicts can arise when syncretic movements challenge existing power structures or when they challenge the authority of religious institutions.

However, proponents of syncretism argue that it fosters inclusivity, cultural exchange, and the creation of new religious expressions that reflect the diverse and evolving nature of human spirituality. They view syncretism as a means of bridging religious divides, promoting tolerance, and accommodating different belief systems within a pluralistic society.

Conclusion

Religious hybridity and syncretism have profound implications for individual and collective identities. The formation of syncretic religious traditions and movements represents the creative and adaptive nature of human spirituality. It highlights the ways in which diverse cultures interact, influence, and shape one another through the blending of religious beliefs and practices. However, syncretism also raises questions and challenges surrounding authenticity, cultural appropriation, and theological compatibility. By critically examining the role of religious syncretism, we gain insight into the complex dynamics of cultural exchange, identity formation, and the ongoing evolution of religious traditions in a globalized world.

Art, Architecture, and Literature

A. Influence of Religious Syncretism on Artistic Expressions and Aesthetics

Religious syncretism has had a significant impact on artistic expressions and aesthetics, as it often brings together diverse cultural and religious influences. Artists, influenced by the blending of different traditions, create works that reflect the syncretic nature of their beliefs and the cultural milieu in which they exist.

In art, we see the fusion of iconography, symbolism, and artistic techniques from multiple religious traditions. For example, in Renaissance art, Christian imagery was often combined with elements from classical mythology and pagan symbolism. This blending of religious motifs created a rich tapestry of visual storytelling that conveyed both Christian narratives and the cultural heritage of the classical world.

Similarly, in contemporary art, artists draw inspiration from various religious traditions to create works that challenge traditional boundaries and explore themes of spirituality, identity, and cultural exchange. These artworks reflect the syncretic nature of modern society and provide a platform for dialogue and reflection on the diversity of religious beliefs and practices.

B. Fusion of Architectural Styles and Sacred Spaces in Syncretic Religious Sites

Syncretic religious sites often exhibit a fusion of architectural styles, incorporating elements from different religious traditions. This blending of architectural forms reflects the syncretic nature of the beliefs and practices associated with these sacred spaces.

An example of such fusion can be seen in the Hagia Sophia in Istanbul, Turkey. Originally built as a Christian cathedral, it later became a mosque and now functions as a museum. The architecture of the Hagia Sophia combines Byzantine elements, such as the central dome and intricate mosaics, with Islamic architectural features, such as the minarets and calligraphic inscriptions. This synthesis of architectural styles represents the historical and cultural transformation of the space over time.

Another example is the Templo Mayor in Mexico City, which was a significant Aztec religious site. After the Spanish conquest, the site was repurposed as the foundation for the Metropolitan Cathedral. The fusion of Aztec and Spanish architectural elements in the Cathedral reflects the syncretic nature of religious practices in Mexico, blending indigenous beliefs with Catholicism.

C. Incorporation of Syncretic Elements in Religious Texts and Scriptures

Religious texts and scriptures often reflect the influence of syncretism, incorporating elements from different traditions and cultural contexts. These texts may include stories, myths, and teachings that synthesize diverse religious narratives and philosophical concepts.

For instance, the Bhagavad Gita, a revered Hindu scripture, contains elements of both Hindu philosophy and Vedic traditions. It incorporates teachings on dharma (duty) and yoga (spiritual practice) within the context of a grand narrative of cosmic consciousness and divine intervention. This blending of ideas and narratives is characteristic of the syncretic nature of Hindu religious thought.

Similarly, the Quran, the holy book of Islam, incorporates narratives and teachings from earlier Abrahamic traditions, such as Judaism and Christianity. The Quran acknowledges the existence of earlier prophets and their messages while presenting a distinct theological framework within the monotheistic context of Islam. This syncretic approach allows for continuity and connection between different religious traditions while affirming the unique revelations of Islam.

Conclusion

The realm of art, architecture, and literature provides a fertile ground for the exploration and expression of religious syncretism. Artists and architects create works that embody the fusion of diverse religious influences, showcasing the interconnectedness of different cultures and belief systems. Similarly, religious texts and scriptures incorporate syncretic elements, weaving together narratives and teachings from various traditions. The interplay between syncretism and artistic expressions, architectural styles, and literary works not only reflects the complexity of human spirituality but also serves as a testament to the richness and adaptability of religious traditions in a globalized world.

Impact on Society and Worldview

A. Social, Political, and Economic Implications of Religious Syncretism

Religious syncretism has profound social, political, and economic implications, as it influences the fabric of societies and shapes the dynamics of cultural interaction. One of the key effects of religious syncretism is the creation of a shared cultural space where diverse religious traditions coexist and intermingle.

In social contexts, religious syncretism can foster a sense of cultural tolerance and pluralism, promoting peaceful coexistence among different religious communities. It can contribute to social cohesion by bridging divides and facilitating dialogue between diverse groups, leading to a more inclusive and harmonious society.

Politically, religious syncretism can have both positive and negative impacts. On one hand, it can provide a basis for cross-cultural understanding and collaboration, helping to mitigate conflicts rooted in religious differences. On the other hand, it can also be a source of tension and power struggles, especially when religious syncretism challenges established religious hierarchies and traditional power structures.

From an economic perspective, religious syncretism can influence trade and commerce. As different religious traditions encounter one another through syncretic practices, they bring with them unique goods, rituals, and services, creating opportunities for economic exchange. For example, pilgrimage sites that attract followers of multiple traditions can stimulate local economies through tourism and the sale of religious artifacts and offerings.

B. Shaping Individual and Collective Worldviews

Religious syncretism plays a significant role in shaping the worldviews of individuals and communities. By blending diverse religious beliefs and practices, syncretic traditions offer a unique lens through which individuals perceive and interpret the world.

Syncretic worldviews often embrace the idea of religious pluralism, recognizing the validity and interconnectedness of multiple religious paths. This broader perspective encourages individuals to see commonalities among different traditions and fosters an inclusive understanding of spirituality. It can promote a sense of interconnectedness with the divine and with all living beings, encouraging compassion, empathy, and respect for diversity.

Moreover, syncretic worldviews can provide individuals with a framework for navigating the complexities of modern life. By incorporating elements from multiple traditions, individuals may find guidance and inspiration in addressing personal, ethical, and existential questions. The syncretic approach allows for a flexible and adaptable belief system that accommodates the evolving needs and challenges of contemporary society.

C. Role of Syncretic Religious Movements in Fostering Cultural Tolerance and Understanding

Syncretic religious movements have played a significant role in fostering cultural tolerance and understanding by providing platforms for interfaith dialogue and cooperation. These movements often promote the idea that different religious traditions have shared values and common goals, encouraging followers to transcend narrow religious boundaries.

By embracing syncretism, these movements challenge exclusivist attitudes and foster a spirit of inclusivity and respect for diversity. They create spaces where individuals from different religious backgrounds can come together, learn from one another, and collaborate on shared social and humanitarian initiatives. Through these interactions, participants gain a deeper understanding of other traditions, dispel misconceptions, and build bridges of friendship and cooperation.

Syncretic religious movements also contribute to the broader discourse on religious pluralism and interfaith relations, advocating for peaceful coexistence and mutual respect among different religious communities. They can serve as powerful agents of social change, promoting cultural tolerance, and addressing issues of discrimination, prejudice, and religious intolerance in society.

Conclusion

The impact of religious syncretism on society and worldview is multifaceted. It influences social dynamics, political landscapes, and economic activities by fostering cultural tolerance, stimulating dialogue, and creating spaces for interfaith collaboration. Syncretic worldviews shape individual perceptions of spirituality and provide frameworks for addressing contemporary challenges. Syncretic religious movements play a crucial role in fostering cultural understanding and promoting peaceful coexistence among diverse religious communities. By embracing religious syncretism, individuals and societies can strive for a more inclusive and harmonious world, where religious diversity is celebrated and differences are seen as sources of enrichment rather than division.

Controversies and Challenges

While religious syncretism has its merits and benefits, it is not without its controversies and challenges. The blending of beliefs, practices, and traditions from different religious systems can give rise to conflicts, tensions, and debates, both within and outside the respective religious communities. Understanding these controversies and challenges is essential in gaining a comprehensive view of the phenomenon of religious syncretism.

Authenticity and Orthodoxy

One of the primary controversies surrounding religious syncretism is the question of authenticity and orthodoxy. Traditionalists within religious communities may view syncretic practices as a dilution or distortion of their original beliefs and practices. They may argue that syncretism compromises the purity and integrity of their religious traditions, emphasizing the importance of preserving the original teachings and rituals.

In some cases, religious authorities and institutions may condemn syncretic practices as heretical or deviant, leading to conflicts between syncretic movements and established religious hierarchies. These conflicts often revolve around questions of authority, doctrinal purity, and the boundaries of acceptable religious practices.

Cultural Appropriation

Another challenge related to religious syncretism is the issue of cultural appropriation. When elements from marginalized or indigenous traditions are assimilated into syncretic practices without proper understanding or respect, it can be seen as an act of cultural appropriation. This raises concerns about power dynamics, colonial legacies, and the commodification of cultural and spiritual practices.

Critics argue that the selective adoption and blending of religious elements without adequate acknowledgment and understanding of their cultural significance can perpetuate cultural erasure and reinforce existing power imbalances. Sensitivity to the cultural contexts from which religious elements are borrowed is crucial to avoid exploitation and to promote cultural respect and equity.

Syncretism as Cultural Hegemony

In some instances, religious syncretism has been criticized for perpetuating cultural hegemony. When syncretic practices favor dominant or mainstream religious traditions, they can marginalize and overshadow the beliefs and practices of smaller or indigenous communities. This can result in the erasure or suppression of unique cultural expressions and religious systems.

Critics argue that syncretism can sometimes be driven by dominant religious narratives and ideologies, imposing a homogenizing influence on diverse belief systems. This can pose a challenge to the preservation and revitalization of indigenous or marginalized religious traditions, as they may struggle to assert their distinct identities within syncretic contexts.

Loss of Cultural and Spiritual Authenticity

Some scholars and practitioners express concerns that religious syncretism may lead to the loss of cultural and spiritual authenticity. They argue that by blending disparate traditions, syncretism can dilute the depth, richness, and uniqueness of individual religious systems. The syncretic practices may become superficial, lacking the profound symbolism, rituals, and philosophical underpinnings that characterize the original traditions.

Critics also caution against the tendency to cherry-pick elements from different traditions without fully understanding their original contexts and meanings. They argue that a shallow or superficial understanding of the traditions being synthesized can result in a distorted and incomplete representation of their beliefs and practices.

Negotiating Identity and Belonging

Religious syncretism raises complex questions about personal and communal identity and belonging. Individuals and communities engaging in syncretic practices may face challenges in defining and articulating their religious identities. They may navigate the tension between multiple religious allegiances, negotiate the boundaries of acceptable belief and practice, and reconcile conflicting theological and ritualistic elements.

Furthermore, syncretic practices can create challenges related to interfaith relations. Other religious communities may view syncretic traditions with skepticism or even hostility, perceiving them as a threat to their own religious identities or as syncretism blurs the distinctions between different faiths.

Navigating these controversies and challenges requires sensitivity, dialogue, and critical reflection. It is essential to engage in respectful discussions, foster interfaith understanding, and seek common ground while acknowledging the diverse beliefs and practices that shape religious syncretism. By addressing these controversies and challenges, individuals and communities can work towards a more inclusive and nuanced understanding of religious syncretism that respects cultural diversity, fosters dialogue, and promotes mutual respect among different religious traditions.

Case Studies

Examining specific case studies of religious syncretism can provide valuable insights into the complexities and nuances of this phenomenon. By analyzing real-life examples, we can understand how religious beliefs and practices interact, adapt, and transform in diverse cultural contexts. Here are a few notable case studies that illustrate the various aspects of religious syncretism:

Santería in Cuba:

Santería is a syncretic religion that originated in Cuba and blends elements of Yoruba religion brought by African slaves with Catholicism. Followers of Santería worship orishas, deities associated with natural forces and human characteristics, who are syncretized with Catholic saints. This syncretic practice allowed enslaved Africans to preserve their ancestral religious beliefs while outwardly conforming to Catholicism, which was imposed by colonial authorities. Santería demonstrates how syncretism can serve as a means of cultural resistance and the preservation of indigenous spiritual practices.

Vodou in Haiti:

Vodou, practiced primarily in Haiti, is another syncretic religion that combines African and Catholic elements. It incorporates African spirits, known as lwa, and ancestral worship with Catholic saints and rituals. Vodou emerged as a result of the transatlantic slave trade and the interaction between African traditions and Catholicism in the context of slavery. Vodou showcases the blending of beliefs, rituals, and symbolism, demonstrating how syncretism can create unique religious expressions that reflect the cultural and historical experiences of a specific community.

Sikhism:

Sikhism, founded in the 15th century in the Punjab region of South Asia, incorporates elements of both Hinduism and Islam. While Sikhism is considered a distinct monotheistic religion, it emerged in a context influenced by the existing polytheistic and monotheistic traditions of the region. Sikhism's teachings embrace monotheism, rejecting idol worship and emphasizing the belief in one formless God. However, Sikhism also incorporates elements from Hinduism, such as the concept of karma and reincarnation. Sikhism showcases how religious syncretism can arise from cultural and historical interactions between different religious traditions.

Afro-Brazilian Religions:

Afro-Brazilian religions, such as Candomblé and Umbanda, emerged in Brazil through the blending of African traditions brought by enslaved Africans with Catholicism and indigenous beliefs. These syncretic religions combine African deities (orixás) with Catholic saints and incorporate elements of spirit possession, ritual drumming, and dance. They exemplify how religious syncretism can create vibrant and dynamic religious practices that reflect the multicultural heritage of a society.

By examining these case studies, we can observe the diverse ways in which religious syncretism manifests and the complex dynamics between different religious traditions. These examples demonstrate how syncretism can be driven by historical, social, and cultural factors, as well as the agency of individuals and communities in shaping their religious identities and practices.

Studying these case studies encourages critical thinking and prompts discussions about the implications of religious syncretism for cultural preservation, identity formation, and interfaith dynamics. It highlights the need for sensitivity, cultural understanding, and dialogue when encountering syncretic traditions, fostering an appreciation for the diversity and complexity of religious belief systems.